Martin Winstone is a writer and teacher.
He also undertakes educational work for
the Holocaust Educational Trust.

THE

Holocaust Sites
of Europe

An Historical Guide

MARTIN WINSTONE

I.B.TAURIS

LONDON · NEW YORK

Published in 2010 by I.B.Tauris & Co Ltd
6 Salem Road, London W2 4BU
175 Fifth Avenue, New York NY 10010
www.ibtauris.com

Distributed in the United States and Canada Exclusively by Palgrave Macmillan
175 Fifth Avenue, New York NY 10010

ISBN: 978 1 84885 290 7 (HB)
      978 1 84885 291 4 (PB)

A full CIP record for this book is available from the British Library
A full CIP record is available from the Library of Congress

Library of Congress Catalog Card Number: available

Printed and bound in India by Thomson Press India Ltd

CONTENTS

MAPS

FOREWORD

Martin Winstone has done a service to all those interested in the Holocaust, and to the increasing number of people, from many lands and often from great distances, who make the journey to the sites of the wartime murder and incarceration of Jews and other victims of Nazi racial policy. This book is both a history and a travel guide, combining a wealth of historical detail with the practical information needed by the visitor.

The essence of good travel book is that it can be enjoyed by one's own fireside, without ever leaving one's home or city. This book triumphantly achieves this aim. There are many places in its pages that, much as I should like to see them, I know that I will not be able to visit. Martin Winstone lets me fulfil my wishes without leaving my house. His descriptions, while always tailored to the facts and practicalities, are graphic and rich in detail. In this book is a description of the nature of the Nazi concentration camp system, explaining the different types and nature of the camps, and the part played by cities and ghettos in the process of destruction. Martin Winstone is not content to describe, he also guides his readers into a deeper understanding of what the Holocaust was. As he writes: 'The Holocaust was not only about the grisly mechanics of mass murder but also about the attempted destruction of both individuals and an entire civilisation that had flourished in Europe for centuries.' This is often forgotten.

Also forgotten – or badly neglected – is the Nazi euthanasia programme embarked upon before the start of the mass murder of Jews, and the fate of the Sinti and Roma: Martin Winstone gives these aspects of the war against civilians their proper place. Country by country, as the maps in this book show, he leads the reader to the sites that can be visited, describes them in detail, provides a considered historical background, and enables both the visitor and the armchair traveller to gain a clear insight into the spread, nature and range of the atrocities that ended more than six decades ago, but whose shadow, impact and legacy are with us to this day.

SIR MARTIN GILBERT

FOREWORD

M

ACKNOWLEDGEMENTS

I would like to thank all at I.B.Tauris who have contributed to bringing this book to life, especially Lester Crook for his consistently enthusiastic support. Liz Friend-Smith and Jayne Ansell have wisely overseen the editorial process whilst Rohini Krishnan and her team have ensured its smooth production.

My greatest debt of gratitude is to Sir Martin Gilbert, not only for his generous foreword and excellent maps, but also for sharing his unrivalled knowledge and for the encouragement, advice and hospitality which he and his wife Esther have provided since this project's inception. Without their support from the very beginning, my task would have been much more difficult.

Especial thanks are also due to Mike Tregenza in Lublin for giving so freely of his expertise, time and friendship. Mike's son-in-law Mariusz Drozd proved an expert driver whilst their respective wives Basia and Bożena Gadzała, along with Darek Gadzała and Dorota, were unstinting in their hospitality.

Of the great many other people who provided help and advice along the way, I would particularly like to thank Gabi Hadar and Sharon May of Yad Vashem, Benton Arnovitz of the United States Holocaust Memorial Museum, Professor David Cesarani, Alex Maws of the Holocaust Educational Trust, Kay Andrews, Zhenia Ivanova, Marina Bergmann, Eva Cyhlarova, Rachel Kostanian of the Vilna Gaon Jewish State Museum, the staff of the Vienna Jewish Cemetery, Caroline Evans, the staff of the Bełżec Memorial Museum, Teresa and Giza Gdula, and the two Romans of the Rava-Ruska militia.

At a more personal level, an immense debt is owed to the late Daniel and Jona Weiser and Naava Piatka for sharing so freely of their memories not to say their love and kindness. Thanks too to all other members of the extended Utin family. I naturally wish to thank my parents for their constant love and encouragement. Finally, and most importantly, I want to thank Elizabeth Burns for far more than the photographs which grace these pages. She has been, in a very real sense, the inspiration for this book and it would never have been completed without her love and support. It is, therefore, dedicated to her and to those who came before her.

INTRODUCTION

The Holocaust – the murder of approximately 6 million Jews by Nazi Germany and its collaborators in the Second World War – is the greatest crime in recorded history, committed on a human and geographical scale which far surpasses that of the other acts of genocide which all too frequently punctuated the twentieth century. Thousands of locations across Europe were associated with the tragedy but, with a few well-known exceptions, most languished in obscurity after the war, their names known only to survivors, perpetrators and a small number of historians. Certainly, few people beyond these groups would have considered visiting such sites. This situation has changed dramatically in the recent past and millions of people each year now travel to the former camps, ghettos and other murder sites.

The reasons for this development are varied. In part, it is a simple question of practicality. The majority of the most significant sites were for over four decades located behind the Iron Curtain which served as a practical and psychological barrier to travel. However, the change also reflects our greater awareness of the Holocaust. Extensive research, assisted by the opening of previously closed archives, means that historians now know far more than they did 30 or even 20 years ago. The Holocaust has become a staple of popular culture whilst, in most democracies, it is given a central role in the school curriculum. In this latter context, travel to relevant sites is increasingly seen as a key tool. For others, motives may be more personal. Whereas the associations were perhaps too close and painful for an older generation, many younger Jews are often eager to visit these sites not just to mourn but also to remember the vibrant communities in which their ancestors lived for centuries. This is most vividly expressed in the annual March of the Living which brings thousands of Jewish teenagers from around the world to Poland where they undertake educational activities and walk from Auschwitz to Birkenau on Yom HaShoah (Israel's Holocaust Memorial Day, on the 27th of Nisan). And then there are the great many people with no personal connection who nevertheless wish to honour the victims and to understand more about their fate.

It would be fatuous to pretend that by visiting these sites one can ever truly comprehend the awfulness of what occurred there. One of the distinguishing features of the Holocaust, after all, is the fact that it seems so unimaginable. Even so, as it recedes from living memory, the number of survivors (and perpetrators) diminishing with every passing year, such locations are becoming the principal physical reminders of what happened. Whilst the testimonies of survivors and the works of historians will and should always be pre-eminent, exploring for oneself the vast ruins of Birkenau or being shocked by the small area needed to kill close to 1 million people at Treblinka can bring another dimension to one's understanding.

TYPES OF SITE

The Holocaust is popularly associated with a relatively small number of places (chiefly in Poland and Germany) but it was, in reality, perpetrated in virtually every country occupied by or allied to the Third Reich. Indeed, a complete guide to Holocaust sites would fill an encyclopaedia, so this book is sadly but inevitably selective; apologies are offered for the many omissions. Yet even though the locations chosen form only a fraction of the many places associated with the Holocaust, they do serve to demonstrate the continental scale of what happened.

It is not only geographical diversity that characterises the sites associated with the Holocaust. There has understandably been the greatest focus on the gas chambers as the ultimate symbol of the industrialised killing machine created by the Nazis, but this can obscure the fact that the Germans and their allies killed Jews, and certain other groups, wherever and in whatever way they could. This means that the term 'Holocaust sites' can be applied to a wide variety of locations, the major categories of which are set out below.

Camps

The Nazi camps are synonymous in the public mind with the Holocaust and were indeed responsible for the deaths of the majority of victims. However, the common use of the term 'concentration camp' to describe all such institutions is rather misleading as the system encompassed a range of different types of camp, each with different functions and roles.

Strictly speaking, concentration camps were places of imprisonment and punishment primarily for opponents of the regime; although many people died in them as a result of ill-treatment, murder was not their principal function. The first were established within weeks of Hitler becoming chancellor and their earliest inmates were political prisoners such as socialists and trade unionists, later joined by so-called 'asocials' such as homosexuals, beggars and certain categories of criminal. In the first years of Nazism, their role was punishment and 're-education', the aim being to break the will of prisoners through hard labour and harsh discipline, including hours spent on the roll-call square (*Appellplatz*). However, the character of the camps changed in the late 1930s, becoming more similar to Stalin's Gulag. Instead of being forced to undertake back-breaking but often pointless work, prisoners were increasingly used as a source of slave labour for enterprises which had contracts with or were owned by the SS. New, larger camps were constructed, often near quarries. Following the outbreak of war, camps were also established in the occupied territories, most famously Auschwitz I in Poland. In the later stages of the war, the economic role of the camps became even more significant following the decision to exploit prisoners in armaments production. In particular, camps such as Mittelbau-Dora were created where prisoners were forced to dig vast tunnel complexes to house relocated weapons factories.

Appalling though the concentration camps were, Jews formed only a minority of their inmates until the last year of the war. Jews sent to camps in the early years were interned for their political beliefs rather than their race (although, even at this stage, they received the worst treatment). Larger numbers were arrested in the later 1930s, especially after the *Kristallnacht* pogrom of 1938, with most being released after promising to leave the Reich. Whilst gas chambers were constructed during the war at some camps, they were used for the murder of weakened inmates rather than systematic extermination. It was only from 1944 that most concentration camps assumed a central role in the genocide, chiefly as a result of the advance of the Red Army. Hundreds of thousands of surviving Jews and other prisoners in the USSR and Poland were forced westward in death marches towards the ever diminishing number of camps still in German hands. The consequently horrific level of over-crowding resulted in the deaths of tens of thousands from starvation, disease and SS brutality. It was these scenes which greeted the Allied liberators of camps such as Bergen-Belsen and Buchenwald, ensuring the central association of these names with the Holocaust in the English-speaking world.

However, the majority of Jews were murdered in even more appalling locations further east: the extermination camps. It is often said that there were six of these killing centres, all located in Poland, but the reality is again more complex. Four such camps were created in late 1941 and early 1942: Chełmno, where victims were murdered in gas vans (vehicles whose exhaust was redirected to their rear compartments), and the three *Aktion Reinhard* camps (Bełżec, Sobibór and Treblinka), which had fixed gas chambers fed by large carbon monoxide engines. All four existed purely for the purpose of murder, chiefly of Polish Jews. A handful of people from each transport might be selected for labour around the camp, in workshops which handled the victims' stolen property or as the *Sonderkommando* who disposed of the bodies, but they too would eventually be killed. The existing Auschwitz concentration camp complex became an additional killing centre, primarily in its massive Birkenau satellite, for Jews from across occupied Europe; most were gassed on arrival although a minority were selected for forced labour. The Majdanek concentration camp also had gas chambers (which, like Auschwitz-Birkenau's, used the pesticide Zyklon B) in which thousands of Polish Jews were murdered. However, many victims of Majdanek were shot (including 18,000 in one day in November 1943), which illustrates that it was not so much the use of gas in itself as the use of mass murder which surely defines an extermination camp. Outside Poland, there were two other camps, often overlooked even by historians, where victims were killed in gas vans (Maly Trostenets in Belarus and Sajmište in Serbia) whilst Janowska in Ukraine had no gas chambers but was the site of the murder of between 100,000 and 200,000 Jews.

The emergence of the extermination centres facilitated the creation of transit camps. Whilst Polish and surviving Soviet Jews were largely already imprisoned in ghettos, those in other countries were generally congregated in large holding centres from where most were deported to Poland after a few days or even hours. Transit camps were generally under direct German control but some, such as Drancy in France, were administered by the local regime for much of their history. This highlights another frequently overlooked facet of the Holocaust: the role of Germany's allies. Italy and Hungary refused to deport their Jews (in each case, transports began only after German invasion) but others were willing participants. The most extreme examples were the Croatian *Ustaše* regime, whose large Jasenovac camp complex was responsible for the deaths of tens of thousands of people, and the Romanian occupiers of the Transnistria region of Ukraine, where more than 100,000 people died in a series of makeshift camps and ghettos.

The extent to which the camps survive varies considerably, ranging from the almost entirely intact Auschwitz I to the empty field of Maly Trostenets. The latter, like most of the extermination camps, was destroyed in an attempt to hide the evidence. In *Aktion 1005*, carried out between 1942 and 1944, bodies were exhumed from the pits in which they had been buried and burned on large pyres. More remains of the former concentration camps as they were still in use when captured by the Allies although most barracks were destroyed after the war. In fact, almost the only camps other than Auschwitz to remain more or less complete are those such as Sered' in Slovakia which are rather shockingly still in use today, often as military bases.

Massacre sites

The genocide of the Jews began not with the extermination camps, but with mass shootings in Lithuania, Latvia, Belarus and Ukraine. The crucial escalation of Nazi policy to systematic murder came with the invasion of the USSR in June 1941, the German military being followed by *Einsatzgruppen*. In the first weeks of the invasion, these mobile SS killing squads murdered Jewish men and Communist officials. However, as the summer progressed, their operations expanded to target entire Jewish communities. Victims were taken to locations outside towns and cities, often forests or fields, where they were typically ordered to undress and taken to the edge of large pits to be shot dead. The German murderers were assisted by locals in certain areas such as Lithuania and western Ukraine. Nonetheless, there was growing concern within the SS at the psychological impact of the shootings on the men of the *Einsatzgruppen*, leading to the search for a more 'humane' method of killing – humane, that is, for the perpetrators. This resulted not only in the creation of the extermination camps but also in the delivery of gas vans from late 1941 onwards; by June 1942, 20 such vehicles were operational in the USSR.

More than 1 million people were murdered by the *Einsatzgruppen*, the majority by the end of 1941. As the war turned, *Aktion 1005* operations were carried out at some of the major killing sites but the number of such locations was too great and the advance of the Red Army too swift to allow the evidence to be completely destroyed. The Communists had

5

little interest in commemorating sites of primarily Jewish suffering, however; such places were usually ignored or, at best, marked by simple, non-specific memorials. Some impressive new monuments have been created since 1991 but there are still hundreds of mass grave sites in the former USSR which remain largely unmarked and unknown.

Cities and ghettos

Europe's Jewish population was overwhelmingly urban so most Jews first experienced Nazi brutality in their home towns and cities. As soon as Hitler came to power, German Jews were subjected to violent attacks and an ever increasing range of discriminatory measures, a pattern repeated in each country subsequently occupied by Germany. The most obvious manifestation of the phenomenon was the creation of ghettos. The first were established in Poland in late 1939, and by early 1941 there were ghettos in all major Polish cities. The aim appears to have been to concentrate and isolate the Jewish community prior to its ultimate deportation to some unspecified location, with both the Lublin region of Poland and Madagascar being considered for this purpose in 1939–40. Even during this period, thousands died in the overcrowded and often unsanitary districts to which they had been confined. Following the mass killings, the surviving Jews of the USSR were also forced into ghettos in late 1941 and 1942. In the same period, large numbers of Jews from the Reich were sent to some of the eastern ghettos.

Although there were variations, most ghettos had common features. One was the existence of a Jewish Council (*Judenrat*), or sometimes Council of Elders (*Ältestenrat*), which was responsible for implementing the demands of the Germans. In some, members were elected by the ghetto population; in others, the Germans made the choice. The *Judenräte* are one of the most controversial aspects of the Holocaust but, for the most part, their members did attempt to protect their communities and many developed extensive welfare and educational systems for the increasingly impoverished inhabitants. They were, however, ultimately at the mercy of the Germans. When mass deportations to the extermination camps began in 1942, *Judenrat* leaders were often required to provide lists of names; some refused, others complied (in the latter case, it is worth remembering that most Polish Jews initially had little idea of the destination of transports). Where Jewish leaders refused to cooperate, the SS made the selections themselves. Over the course of 1942 and

1943, ghetto populations were progressively reduced in a series of mass arrests, referred to as *Aktionen*. Some ghetto leaders believed that the remaining Jews could be saved through cooperation with the Germans and put the ghetto's Jewish police force at the Nazis' disposal. Those who remained in the ghettos were increasingly workers employed in war-related enterprises and it was assumed that the Germans would not wish to lose this essential labour. However, ideology outweighed pragmatism and in 1943 Himmler ordered the destruction of the remaining ghettos; only a handful survived into 1944. The *Aktionen* in 1943 were often met with resistance by the underground organisations which emerged in a number of ghettos. The relatively few Jews who survived the liquidations were transferred to labour camps where most were murdered in late 1943 or 1944.

Ghettos were generally not established in other countries with the exception of Theresienstadt in Bohemia (1941–45) and a series of temporary ghettos in Hungary in 1944. Even so, cities elsewhere were still central to the Holocaust. In some countries, they were the places where pogroms took place, most famously *Kristallnacht* in Germany and Austria in November 1938. Although this example was orchestrated by the Nazis, violent attacks on Jews sometimes arose spontaneously from sections of the local population, as when the Germans had marched into Vienna eight months earlier (the same was true in some cities in the USSR in 1941). Cities were where synagogues were destroyed and cemeteries desecrated. Above all, they were the places where millions of Jews lived and where they were arrested and imprisoned before being sent to a transit camp or directly to a murder site in the east. Apparently innocent buildings – a cycling stadium in Paris, a theatre in Amsterdam, an exhibition hall in Prague – became stations on this sorrowful journey.

Cities also bring home the scale of the Holocaust in another way. The Holocaust was not only about the grisly mechanics of mass murder but also about the attempted destruction of both individuals and an entire civilisation that had flourished in Europe for centuries. Although the extent to which traces of this civilisation survive varies considerably, one can still find fragments of the past – a former prayer house, for example, or perhaps a faded Yiddish sign on a wall – in every city included in this book, fragments which may offer some connection, however fleeting, with the pre-Nazi world whilst also serving as a reminder of its loss.

'Euthanasia' centres

Even before the mass murder of Jews commenced, the Nazis had already embarked on a policy of genocide – a systematic attempt to destroy an entire supposedly biologically defined group of people, including even children and the elderly – against people with disabilities. The term 'euthanasia' was employed by the Nazis themselves but in a manner totally different to the common understanding of the word today. Even before Hitler, there was significant support within German scientific and medical circles for the eugenicist idea that the disabled represented 'life unworthy of life', a shockingly callous term which gained widespread usage. From 1933, such theorists had a government receptive to their beliefs; in July of that year, a new law introduced compulsory sterilisation for sufferers of a variety of allegedly hereditary diseases (including schizophrenia, epilepsy, deafness and severe alcoholism). Around 375,000 people fell victim to this law up to 1945. Yet both Hitler and some scientists aimed to go further; as early as 1935, the Führer privately remarked that 'compulsory euthanasia' would be introduced once war came.

In fact, the planning began in early 1939 with the decision to murder disabled children. The first killings probably took place in October and continued in selected hospitals throughout the war, beginning with infants aged three or under but escalating to include all children. Some doctors used starvation but the most common method was to administer overdoses of medicines; around 5,000 children were thus murdered. At some point in 1939, Hitler decided to progress to adults with disabilities, logistically a far larger operation. In fact, there were two separate but parallel campaigns. In occupied Poland, where public opinion was of no concern to the Nazis, special SS units cleared mental institutions simply by shooting patients. Within the Reich, a department of Hitler's Party Chancellery was given responsibility for organising the mass killing of the disabled, coming to be codenamed T4 from its address at Tiergartenstraße 4 in Berlin. Six institutions were selected as killing centres although only four operated at any one time. Victims were chosen on the basis of questionnaires filled out by staff (who were unaware of the forms' true purpose) in their current institutions which were then briefly viewed by a panel of three T4 doctors. Jewish patients were killed as a matter of course, their relatives having been informed that they had been sent to a clinic in Poland from where fake death certificates were posted.

Although each site was slightly different, the basic procedure was the same. Patients were brought in large grey buses provided by the SS. On arrival, they were ordered to undress, registered and then seen by two doctors. This cursory examination was not to decide their fate (which was already sealed) but to determine a plausible fake cause of death for the death certificate. They were then led to gas chambers. Similarly, gas was increasingly used in Poland as well: the very first experimental gas chamber had been created in Poznań in October 1939 whilst gas vans, another Nazi innovation, toured psychiatric hospitals in western Poland through 1940.

In August 1941, Hitler officially ordered a stop to the T4 killings, probably because of growing public disquiet (it was increasingly impossible to hide the reality of the murders from local communities). By this stage, some 70,000 men and women had been killed in the T4 centres. This was not, however, the end of Nazi 'euthanasia'. The murder of children was unaffected whilst killings outside Germany continued equally unabated: during the summer of 1941, the *Einsatzgruppen* shot inmates of Soviet clinics. Indeed, during the SS's quest for a 'humane' alternative to mass shootings in the autumn of 1941, experiments were conducted on patients from asylums in Minsk and Mogilev with dynamite and gas respectively. Hitler had not even ordered a cessation to the killing of disabled adults in Germany and Austria; they were simply no longer to be gassed in the T4 centres. The remainder of the war thus became the period of 'wild euthanasia' during which patients were murdered in institutions across the Reich by the methods previously used on children. In at least one hospital, the killings continued into late May 1945; that is, after the war had ended. In addition, the remaining T4 centres were not abandoned. One became a leading site of 'wild euthanasia' whilst the gas chambers of the other three continued to operate with only the victims changing: even before Hitler's stop order, a new operation – given the code 14f13 – had been launched in the spring of 1941 which eventually saw up to 20,000 weakened concentration camp inmates murdered. The combined death toll for the child murders, T4, 'wild euthanasia' and 14f13 is believed to have been around 200,000. The number of people with disabilities murdered in Poland and the USSR is unknown.

The connections between the genocide of the disabled and of the Jews go beyond a common ideology to sharing the same killing methods and personnel. The three *Aktion Reinhard* camps were staffed by people who had served in T4 and Chełmno by the Lange Commando which had previously used its gas vans to murder the disabled in Poland. The killing sites of the 'euthanasia' programme thus served as prototypes for the extermination camps. Most of these sites reverted to their original medical functions after the war and their dark history was largely forgotten. This has changed in the last 20 years, however, and all of the former T4 centres and several other hospitals now house affecting exhibitions.

Sinti and Roma sites

Only three groups were targeted by the Nazis for systematic extermination: Jews, the disabled and 'gypsies'. The latter term is generally rejected by the people it describes so their preferred terminology of Sinti and Roma has been employed in this book. The Sinti and Roma share an origin but are now considered to be separate ethnic groups. The Sinti were particularly concentrated in Germany whilst the largest communities of Roma were to be found in central Europe and the Balkans. Nazi policy towards them was not entirely consistent, with some racial theorists grudgingly admiring their tendency to marry within their own community and thus maintain their racial 'purity'. As a result, those in mixed relationships or products thereof were especially targeted for persecution, a reversal of the situation with Jews. Nonetheless, all Sinti and Roma were seen as racially inferior and this was reflected in Nazi policy. Persecution began with their inclusion amongst the 'asocial' groups subjected to internment in concentration camps; in the later 1930s, specific 'gypsy camps' were created. The war brought a rapid radicalisation of policy which mirrored that towards the Jews, beginning with deportations to Poland in 1940. The *Einsatzgruppen* murdered Sinti and Roma during the invasion of the USSR whilst similar killings were carried out in Serbia and by the *Ustaše* in Croatia. Polish Roma were often interned in ghettos as were a group from Austria who were sent to Łódź. The latter were murdered at Chełmno whilst the Polish Roma together with tens of thousands of Sinti and Roma from elsewhere in Europe were deported to Auschwitz-Birkenau. The final death toll is believed to have been at least 220,000. The level of destruction was so great in Bohemia that even the local variant of the Romani language is now extinct.

Many of the sites associated with the Sinti and Roma genocide (*Porajmos* in Romani) are the same as those associated with the Jewish Holocaust such as Auschwitz-Birkenau or Łódź. In such places, appropriate memorials have often been created in the last decade or so. Sadly, this is generally not the case for sites associated exclusively with Sinti and Roma suffering.

Museums and memorials

There are memorials to the victims of the Holocaust in every country featured in this book and museums in a great many of them but this has not always been so. Memorialisation was especially problematic in eastern Europe where even major sites were often ignored or marked by simple monuments coyly dedicated to 'Soviet citizens' or 'victims of Fascism'. The failure to highlight the specifically Jewish nature of the tragedy reflected the prevailing ideological dictates in which the war was presented as a struggle between Fascism and anti-Fascism, the latter, of course, represented by Communism. The concept that Jews were killed because they were Jews did not fit this narrative, especially in light of the anti-Semitism to which Communist regimes were themselves prone in Stalin's last years and after the Six Day War. Although some Jewish memorials were created in Poland in the 1960s, it was only after the emergence of Solidarity and Gorbachev in the 1980s that a more honest approach to the past was generally possible.

Commemoration was more effective in western Europe but still surprisingly limited. Although most major camps had been turned into memorial sites by the 1960s and Jewish suffering was acknowledged, there was still a tendency for it to be subsumed within memories of collective hardship. Ironically, the one country with a more honest approach, from the late 1960s at least, was West Germany where it was naturally impossible to pretend that the whole population had resisted or suffered under the Nazis (even East Germany had the consoling myth that, as the heir to the Communist victims of Nazism, it represented the 'good Germans').

Thankfully, much has changed in the last two decades although there are still considerable variations between and within countries. Many excellent new museums have been created whilst there are hundreds of new memorials. Not all of the latter have met with universal approval, with evidence suggesting that survivors and victims' families tend to prefer figurative monuments rather than the abstract concepts which have tended to dominate. Nonetheless, the very fact that so many memorials exist is itself a positive sign of a commitment to remember.

11

PRACTICALITIES

The plethora of new museums and memorials is an indication that sites can change, a process which will undoubtedly continue. Equally, opening hours and entry costs alter. Websites have, therefore, been given for each site where possible and it is advisable to consult these before visiting.

Although many sites are in rather remote locations, all are accessible by car and most by public transport. Where the latter is not available, it is normally possible to take a taxi from the nearest town or railway station. A number of companies offer tours to Holocaust sites which can be very well-organised and informative. However, should a guide be required, especially for locations which may not be included in this book such as a specific ancestral *shtetl*, it is often better to contact the local Jewish museum or community; websites have been given in the text where appropriate.

This is not a general travel guide, so visitors can be trusted to find their own accommodation for which many books and websites offer advice. Visitors who require kosher food can find a database of restaurants at www.shamash.org/kosher. As a general rule, the further east one goes in Europe, the less likely one is to find such facilities although many 'Jewish-style' restaurants offering non-kosher versions of classic Ashkenazi dishes have opened in Poland in recent years.

Some visitors may worry about anti-Semitism in Europe. Although it would be foolish to deny that such prejudice exists, one would have to be very unfortunate to have any direct personal contact with it. There may be instances of graffiti in cemeteries or on Holocaust memorials but these tend to be the work of small far-right gangs or teenagers rather than a reflection of society as a whole. In fact, in some countries – notably Germany and Poland – there has been a resurgence of interest in Jewish history and culture, especially from the younger generation. One form of racism that may sadly be noticeable in some countries is against Roma who remain a marginalised and impoverished group.

CHAPTER 1

FRANCE

The history of the Holocaust in France is more controversial and paradoxical than in almost any other country. The wartime Vichy government was one of only two nominally autonomous regimes (the other being Slovakia) to voluntarily hand over Jews from its territory to the Nazis. Yet, despite far greater official collaboration than in most other countries, more than three quarters of French Jews survived.

There is evidence of a Jewish presence in what became France from as early as the first century and the kingdom became a major centre of Jewish life by the Middle Ages. However, rising anti-Semitism brought a recurring pattern of banishment and return until a final decree of expulsion in 1394. The only Jewish communities thereafter were those in territories annexed in the early modern period, primarily Alsace. It was the Revolution which changed their situation with the granting of full civil equality in 1791 – a first in Europe. This transformation created a highly integrated community characterised by assimilation, patriotism and, despite the poisonous Dreyfus Affair of the 1890s, a strong faith in the French state. However, this began to change from the 1880s. Whilst the number of indigenous Jews grew little, the overall population quadrupled between 1880 and 1939 due to immigration. The earliest arrivals were fleeing tsarist pogroms but, unusually, the great majority of immigrants entered the country after the First World War, including from the Third Reich. The Jewish population of around 330,000 in 1939 was thus stereotypically divided into respectable, secular, Francophone, middle-class 'French' Jews and radical, religious, Yiddish-speaking, poor 'foreign' Jews. The reality was inevitably rather more complex, not least because of a relaxation in the naturalisation laws in 1927. However, in the eyes of the state and many Jews themselves, there was a dichotomy between Jews in France which was to be of significance in the Holocaust.

As is well known, France quickly succumbed to the Germans in May 1940; the armistice of the following month divided the country into the occupied zone (the north and Atlantic coast) under direct German control and the 'free' zone (the south) governed by the Vichy regime of Marshal Pétain. It is less well known that Vichy still had sovereignty in the north, able to impose its policies as long as they did not conflict

France

Principal places mentioned in the text

Other sites mentioned in the text

Border between German-administered France and Vichy France

International borders 2010

English Channel

River Seine

River Rhine

BELGIUM

GERMANY

LUXEMBOURG

Compiègne-Royallieu

Drancy

Paris

Natzweiler-Struthof

River Loire

FRANCE

SWITZERLAND
neutral

Bay
of
Biscay

Oradour-sur-Glane

Saône

Izieu

VICHY FRANCE

Le Chambon-sur-Lignon

River Rhône

0   kilometres   100

0   miles   50

© Martin Gilbert 2010

River Garonne

Gurs

Pyrenees

SPAIN
neutral

Le Vernet

Rivesaltes

Les Milles

Mediterranean Sea

with those of the Germans, meaning that Pétain's government had a key role in the Holocaust. This was reflected in the *Statut des Juifs*, anti-Jewish laws introduced in October 1940 without German prompting. German pressure was responsible for the creation of Vichy's Office of Jewish Affairs in March 1941 to oversee anti-Semitic policy and of the Union of French Jews (UGIF) in November of the same year to coordinate and thus control all Jewish organisations. These developments reflected the growing importance of Eichmann's representative Theodor Dannecker, as did round-ups in 1941 of several thousand foreign Jews who were sent to internment camps. Again, however, most of the camps were run by the French authorities. Some pre-dated the armistice, having been used to intern refugees from the Spanish Civil War and supposed 'enemy aliens' who, rather predictably, had been German and Austrian fugitives from Hitler, many of them Jews.

The escalation of Nazi policy in 1942 was assisted by the emergence of Pierre Laval as prime minister in April. Laval was reluctant to allow the deportation of French citizens but fully acquiesced in that of foreign-born Jews, even surprising the Nazis by pressing for the inclusion of children. Mass arrests began in the north in July, extending to the south in August (five months before Allied landings in Africa prompted the Germans and Italians to occupy the region). Most of those arrested passed through Drancy transit camp in the Parisian suburbs before being transported further east: more than 70,000 Jews were deported in more than 70 convoys up to 1944; only 2,566 survived. If we add those who were executed or who died in French camps, at least 77,021 people lost their lives, approximately 24 per cent of the Jews in France in 1939.

Another way of interpreting the figures, however, is to acknowledge that 76 per cent of French Jews survived, one of the highest proportions for any country. Why this should have been so has long intrigued historians. The answer is clearly not to be found in official Vichy policy although it did mean that widespread raids on French-born Jews did not begin until 1943. The Italian occupation of the south-east in November 1942 also provided a relatively safe haven until Italy's surrender in September 1943. By this time, the war had clearly turned and there was thus greater reluctance on the part of French officials to comply whilst many Jews had been able to go into hiding. This latter development was facilitated by the geography of France but more importantly by the efforts of a committed minority of people. They included Jews themselves, through a variety of welfare organisations and rescue networks, along with specific groups of Gentiles, most famously the Protestant communities of the Auvergne and Languedoc. More generally, initial public indifference gave way to growing shame following the arrest of women and children in 1942, generating a greater willingness to help if only through what has been termed 'benign neglect' – officials ignoring suspect documents, townspeople not asking questions of newcomers, and the like.

Memorialisation before the 1990s tended to focus on sites exclusively associated with the Germans, reflecting a narrative in which the Jewish tragedy was seen as simply one part of a wider French tragedy. Public memorials have now been established which acknowledge the French state's role whilst ambitious museums have recently opened or are currently under construction. These are amongst the most impressive in Europe, belated recognition of the horrors which befell French Jews – sometimes at French hands.

PARIS

With a Jewish population of approximately 200,000 in 1939, Paris was home to almost two-thirds of French Jews. It had been a major centre of Jewish life and learning in the medieval period until the fourteenth-century expulsions. Emancipation encouraged nineteenth-century settlement yet the population still numbered less than 50,000 in 1880. It was transformed by the waves of immigration thereafter: 110,000 Jews came to the city up to 1939, 90,000 of them from eastern Europe. The result was one of the continent's most diverse Jewish communities.

The invasion prompted an exodus from the capital yet many Jews decided to return after the armistice, reassured by the stability that Pétain seemed to represent and by reports of the 'correct' behaviour of German troops. Even after anti-Semitic incidents in the summer of 1940, most complied when the Germans decreed a census of Jews in the occupied zone in October: according to the results, there were 149,734 Jews in the Paris region (around 10 per cent did not register). The results provided the basis for the first mass arrests, targeting male 'foreign' Jews, in May 1941: 3,747 were sent to internment camps. Further round-ups followed in August and December. After the Wannsee Conference, the December internees were sent to Auschwitz and plans were made for mass deportations. In the *grande rafle* of 16–17 July 1942, 12,000 foreign Jews were arrested, the largest such operation and one which profoundly affected opinion in the capital. By the end of August, virtually all had been murdered in Birkenau. Round-ups continued into 1943 and 1944 with French-born Jews increasingly likely to fall into the net. Even so, thousands of Jews continued to live in the city, many in hiding but others 'legally', saved by good fortune or the benevolence of bureaucrats. Estimates of the number of Jews in Paris at the time of the liberation in August 1944 range from 20,000 to 50,000.

Most survivors returned after the war. Although around a third of the 1940 population had been murdered, the community grew rapidly, due in part to immigration from France's north African colonies. The result is that Paris today has an estimated Jewish population of 300,000, making it easily the largest community in Europe and one of the very few to have survived the Holocaust with its vitality and diversity intact.

The Marais and around

Jewish communities existed across the city by the end of the nineteenth century but the historic soul of Jewish Paris was the Marais in the third and fourth arrondissements, as it remains today despite gentrification. This was where most Parisian Jews lived at the time of the medieval expulsions. When large numbers returned in the early nineteenth century, they again took root in the Marais; as their children or grandchildren prospered and drifted to more affluent parts of the city, the area was resettled by the new waves of immigrants, giving it a character similar to London's East End or New York's Lower East Side. Even today, it is one of the few places in Europe where one will still hear Yiddish spoken. The heart of this community was and is the *Pletzl* (Yiddish for 'square'), the group of streets around Rue des Rosiers (St-Paul Metro). The pre-war atmosphere is perhaps best preserved on Rue des Ecouffes, a street of tiny prayer houses, kosher butchers and Judaica shops running south from Rue des Rosiers. The Art Nouveau Agudath Hakehilot Synagogue at number 10 on parallel Rue Pavée was dynamited by the Nazis on Yom Kippur 1940 but restored after the war. Amidst the falafel stores, Hebrew bookshops and upmarket boutiques of Rue des Rosiers itself, there are hints of the district's darkest hours in the regular plaques commemorating murdered inhabitants. The youngest victim recorded, Paulette Wajncwaig at number 16, was one month old. Plaques at nearby 8 Rue des Hospitalières-St-Gervais commemorate the 165 pupils of the

Jewish boys' school located at this address who were deported to their deaths and their headmaster Joseph Migneret who saved dozens of his charges before he too was killed.

South of the *Pletzl* is the Mémorial de la Shoah at 17 Rue Geoffroy l'Asnier, site of arguably the most impressive Holocaust museum in Europe (Sun–Fri, 10.00–6.00 (until 10.00,Thu); free; www.memorialdelashoah. org). The complex was originally created in the 1950s as the location of the *Mémorial du Martyr Juif Inconnu*, a now weather-beaten structure inscribed with the names of major camps and surrounded by bas-reliefs of Holocaust scenes by the Lithuanian-born artist Arbit Blatas. The redeveloped site, inaugurated in 2005, has clearly had a lot of thought and money put into it, evident from the moment one passes the open-air Wall of Names listing the names and years of birth of more than 70,000 murdered French Jews. The permanent exhibition covers the history of the Holocaust, displays on parallel walls tracing developments in France and in Europe as a whole. Video is used to good effect, and personal objects and biographies ensure that one never loses sight of individual tragedies. The exhibition exits into the heartbreaking *Mémorial des Enfants*, 2,500 photographs of murdered children. Other floors contain the crypt – a symbolic tomb containing ashes from the extermination camps – and excellent temporary exhibitions. Computer screens on the ground floor enable visitors to search lists of deportees whilst relatives can, by prior appointment, see victims' police files, handed over to the memorial by former president Jacques Chirac. On the exterior wall of the complex, memorial plaques on Allée des Justes list the names of French citizens awarded the title Righteous Among the Nations.

Further south, hidden at the eastern tip of the Île de la Cité, is the Mémorial des Martyrs de la Déportation (daily, 10.00–12.00, 2.00–7.00), entered through a gate by Pont de l'Archevêché. Dedicated to all French citizens deported by the Germans, the 1962 monument contains the tomb of the Unknown Deportee, flanked by 200,000 fragments of lit glass and quotations from noted French writers. Though the memorial is undoubtedly of its time, it is a powerful, haunting place.

Paris's Museum of Jewish Art and History is located north of the *Pletzl* in an elegant mansion at 71 Rue du Temple (Mon–Fri, 11.00–6.00; Sun, 10.00–6.00; €6.80; www.mahj.org), with a statue of Captain Dreyfus in the courtyard serving as a reminder of earlier persecution. The museum's imaginative displays, mixing history, rituals and specific locations, effectively convey the plurality of the Jewish experience, augmented by a stunning array of objects. The wall of a small inner courtyard, visible from the stairs, lists the names of the inhabitants of this building who died – as in Berlin's Große Hamburger Straße, this is the work of artist Christian Boltanski.

The *Vélodrome d'Hiver*

Outside Bir Hakeim Metro station, little noticed by the throng heading to the Eiffel Tower, Place des Martyrs Juifs du Vélodrome d'Hiver recalls one of the most tragic episodes of the Holocaust in France. The *grande rafle* of 16–17 July 1942 was not the first large-scale round-up but was the one which most deeply shocked Parisian opinion due to the preponderance of women and children amongst the victims. Beginning at 4 a.m. on *Jeudi noir* (16 July), 4,500 policemen combed the capital; by 5 p.m. the following day, they had arrested 12,884 people: 3,031 men, 5,802 women and 4,051 children. The final figure, tallied a few days later, was 13,152. This was actually far fewer than the number on the police lists as many Jews, hearing rumours of the imminent operation, had gone into hiding – although the police figures illustrate the widespread belief that only men would be victims, leaving women and children as the majority of those arrested. Almost 5,000 were taken directly to Drancy from where they were sent to Auschwitz in late July. Families with children under 16 were instead interned, in some cases for up to a week, in the *Vélodrome d'Hiver*, an indoor stadium which stood at the junction of Rue Nélaton and Rue du Docteur Finlay. More than 8,000 people were held in appalling conditions, the testimony of the few survivors emphasising the noise, lack of medical care, and, above all, appalling smell. From the '*Vél d'Hiv*' they were subsequently transferred to transit camps in the Loiret. The Germans had originally intended to deport only adults but, in negotiations with Dannecker prior to the round-up, Laval (perhaps seeking to make up the numbers to preclude the arrest of French citizens) had suggested including children. This, however, required permission from Berlin which was received only in early August. The parents and older children were, therefore, deported to Auschwitz from late July whilst the fate of the youngsters was still being decided. This left around 3,500 effectively orphaned and largely unsupervised children in the camps in conditions which can only be imagined. Once approval was given, the terrified and bewildered children – some of the youngest could no longer even

Paris: *Vélodrome d'Hiver* memorial (Photograph by the author)

remember their names – were sent to Drancy. They were then dispatched in seven convoys to Auschwitz, with 500 children and 500 unrelated adults per train, a consequence of Berlin's insistence that transports containing exclusively children should not be sent. Not a single child survived.

The *Vélodrome* was later demolished but its unhappy history is remembered by two memorials. A small garden on Boulevard de Grenelle, south of the Metro line between Rue Nélaton and Rue Saint-Charles, contains a memorial plaque; south-west of Bir Hakeim, up steps between Quai de Grenelle and the Seine, an elevated park contains a beautiful figurative sculpture. The text at the base of the monument acknowledges the French state's complicity.

Elsewhere

The former *Levitan* furniture store at 85–87 Rue du Faubourg Saint-Martin in the tenth arrondissement was turned into a sub-camp of Drancy in July 1943. 'Privileged' Jews – such as those married to

Gentiles – were employed here sifting goods from looted apartments for shipment to Germany. A plaque recalls this history. In the nearby Gare de l'Est, there is a memorial plaque dedicated to Jewish deportees along with other plaques to French political prisoners, forced labourers sent to Germany and the 1945 returnees – the station was the main point of arrival for survivors, just as it had been in earlier generations for thousands of Jewish immigrants.

The Musée Nissim de Camondo at 63 Rue de Monceau in the eighth arrondissement (Wed–Sun, 10.00–5.30; €6; www.lesartsdecoratifs.fr; Monceau or Villiers Metro) is mainly visited for the magnificent collection of furniture and *objets d'art* accumulated by the Jewish aristocrat Count Moïse de Camondo. Its displays also illustrate how the Holocaust affected even the most integrated and prominent of French Jews: Camondo's daughter Béatrice, her husband and their children were all murdered in Auschwitz.

Another Drancy sub-camp, performing the same function as *Levitan*, was established in the elegant corner mansion at 2 Rue de Bassano in the sixteenth arrondissement (Iéna or Alma-Marceau Metro), although there is no indication of its history at the site.

The Hotel Lutetia at 45 Boulevard Raspail (Sèvres Babylone Metro) in the sixth arrondissement, having previously been requisitioned by the Germans, was used to accommodate Jews and political prisoners returning from Germany in 1945. This was where families of deportees came to enquire about the fate of their loved ones. By the entrance a large bulletin board was placed which desperate relatives covered in notices, pre-war photographs and long lists of missing persons; their searches were invariably in vain.

DRANCY

The most significant location associated with the Holocaust in France, Drancy had unlikely beginnings as a large-scale housing project in the northern suburbs of Paris. Constructed between 1932 and 1936 as a model of modernist architectural principles, it only briefly served as municipal housing before conversion into police barracks. An internment camp for foreign Jews was established on the site in August 1941 although its 4,500 capacity was soon stretched. Once deportations commenced in 1942, Drancy became the principal transit camp for the whole of

France: Jews held in other camps or arrested in the provinces invariably passed through it before being transported to the east. They might be held for two or three days although some transports from the south were sent straight on to Poland on their day of arrival: 64,759 people were deported on 64 transports between 22 June 1942 and 31 July 1944; all trains went to Auschwitz except for four that were sent to Sobibór and one to the Baltic. Amongst the last victims were 250 inmates of Jewish children's homes in the Paris region. When the camp was liberated in August 1944, only 1,542 prisoners remained. Although it was under ultimate German control, Drancy was administered by French officials until mid-1943, an embarrassing fact which French governments were for decades reluctant to confront. The SS takeover was engineered by the loathsome Aloïs Brunner, who also played a leading role in the deportations of the Jews of Austria, Greece and Slovakia. Brunner evaded arrest after the war, eventually finding refuge in Syria; in 2001, amidst unconfirmed reports that he was still alive, he was sentenced in absentia to life imprisonment by a French court. Unsurprisingly, conditions in the camp worsened under his leadership. Yet despite the shortages, brutality and high turnover of inmates, Jewish life was maintained with religious services (a synagogue was established in September 1941) and educational and cultural activities. A resistance movement existed throughout Drancy's existence and 41 successful escapes were made. In November 1943, the Germans discovered a tunnel dug by prisoners; given another day or so, the inmates would have been able to dig the final few metres.

The complex reverted to its original role as social housing after the war and would today resemble any other run-down Parisian suburban estate were it not for the large memorial in front of the blocks and the occasional plaque. Despite Drancy's pre-eminent role in the Holocaust, the memorial (a sculpture of contorted figures flanked by two curved columns which explain Drancy's history and honour its victims) was erected only in 1976 on the rather inappropriately named Square de la Libération, by Avenue Jean Jaurès. An SNCF wagon marked with a Star of David stands behind. Deportees would be loaded onto such wagons the day before departure so that the camp manager would not have to wake up too early – if any died overnight, they were replaced by other inmates. Alongside are plaques from the Union of French Jewish Students and the government, the latter, as at the *Vélodrome*, accepting the French state's responsibility. The estate itself looks much as it did in

Drancy (Photograph by the author)

the 1940s, although some outer buildings were destroyed along with the four watchtowers: the 'red castle', a brick building which housed the camp's toilets, originally stood at the open end of the horseshoe-shaped block. By number 22 on the right are plaques to Drancy's Jewish victims and to British and French POWs who were interned here before the site was converted into a Jewish camp in 1941. Number 15 is the base of the *Conservatoire Historique du Camp de Drancy* (www.camp-de-drancy. asso.fr), the organisation which oversees the site and works to preserve its memory despite limited resources. At number 8 on the left of the complex is a plaque to the poet Max Jacob (a convert to Catholicism) who died of pneumonia in Drancy in March 1944, his hiding place in the Loiret having been discovered by the Gestapo.

The easiest way to get to Drancy is to take the RER suburban train to La Courneuve-Aubervilliers and then bus 143 to the Square de la Libération stop. The deportation trains actually left from Le Bourget station (marked by Place des Déportés outside) until Allied bombing in July 1943 when transports departed from the now disused Bobigny station. The latter is a four-storey building visible from the bridge over the railway on Avenue Henri Barbusse, around two kilometres to the south-west of the camp (bus 151 to Gare (Grande Ceinture)); it is currently undergoing restoration as a memorial site.

NATZWEILER-STRUTHOF

It was Albert Speer's desire for pink granite which led to the construction of a concentration camp on a remote Alsatian mountainside in May 1941 although Natzweiler was not fully completed until October 1943 by which time it contained around 2,000 prisoners. They worked in quarries and in underground tunnels intended to house factories. This latter development contributed to rapid expansion of the camp as did its designation in September 1943 as the main internment centre for *Nacht und Nebel* (Night and Fog) prisoners. *Nacht und Nebel* referred to the punishment of Resistance fighters from western Europe; a secret order from Hitler in December 1941 had decreed that they would disappear into 'the fog of the night', more prosaically meaning that they would be worked to death. Of the 51,684 prisoners who went through the Natzweiler complex (only around 17,000 were interned in the main camp) almost 22,000 lost their lives. The camp was evacuated in September 1944: when it was liberated in November, it was found empty.

After a brief post-war interlude as an internment centre for Germans and alleged collaborators, the site became a national monument in the 1950s. Indeed, Natzweiler was for decades the only camp in France to be properly memorialised, a reflection of the fact that it was entirely German-run. It has been augmented since 2005 by the impressive European Centre on Resistance and Deportation (May–Sept: daily, 9.00–6.30; Mar–Apr, Sept–Dec: daily, 9.00–5.00; €5; www.struthof. fr). Built around an SS bunker, the centre makes effective use of audio-visual materials to trace the history of the camp system and the Resistance across Europe. Perhaps the most moving element is the introductory section which contains artefacts from each of the major camps, including a Zyklon B canister from Majdanek and secretly made children's toys from Ravensbrück.

The camp itself is relatively small and its setting perversely beautiful, cascading down the mountainside. Only four buildings remain, the first of which is actually a reconstructed barrack: the original was burnt down in a neo-Nazi arson attack in 1976. This houses the museum which covers Natzweiler's history from its idyllic pre-war existence (illustrated by 1930s tourist brochures) to the brutality of camp life and the post-war quest for justice. Vivid images are provided by the drawings of former inmate Henri Gayot. The building on the other side of the gallows is the former kitchen. Beyond the barbed-wire fence, partially hidden by trees, is the 'death ravine' from which prisoners were pushed. At the bottom of the camp, past the sites of the prisoner barracks (destroyed in storms in the 1950s), the two preserved buildings are the crematorium (also the centre of gruesome medical experiments) and the prison block; the latter includes eight unimaginably small solitary cells hidden in the walls. Between the two buildings, a large cross and a memorial wall mark the pit, originally the site of the camp's septic toilets, where the SS began dumping ashes from the crematorium as the death rate mounted in 1944.

Higher up the hill, above the camp, is the graceful national monument, dedicated to 'heroes and martyrs of the deportation'; a vault in its base contains the body of an unknown deportee. It is surrounded by a cemetery containing the remains of 1,118 French citizens from camps across Europe. Across the main road, a small sand quarry served as an execution site for the Strasbourg Gestapo: a stone commemorates those of all nationalities executed here, including 17 local youths. A kilometre or so further south along the main road is the principal quarry, now overgrown. Off the path which curves away from the road are two intact stone barracks along with the foundations of others.

Taking the main road in the other direction from the camp leads down the mountain to Natzweiler's gas chamber. An alternative pedestrian route is to follow a section of the *Chemin de la Mémoire et des Droits de l'Homme*, an EU-funded trail which runs through locations associated with Nazi persecution in Alsace. This passes the commandant's house; its most notorious occupant was Josef Kramer, whose period commanding Natzweiler served as an apprenticeship to his greater infamy as 'the beast of Belsen'; in between, he was commandant of Birkenau. The gas chamber was not used systematically to kill weakened prisoners as at other camps; its existence was the result of the perverted medical ambitions of August

Hirt, director of the Institute of Anatomy at Strasbourg University. Hirt had approached Himmler about the possibility of assembling a collection of skeletons of Jews and other racial 'undesirables' from amongst the camp population and he was duly installed at Natzweiler to oversee the project. The dance hall of the local hotel was converted into a gas chamber and 87 Jews – 57 men and 30 women – were brought from Auschwitz on 30 July 1943; 86 of them were gassed in mid-August and the other shot whilst trying to escape at the threshold. Kramer himself operated the machinery. Hirt and his colleague Otto Bickenbach also used the chamber to experiment with mustard gas and phosgene on several dozen mostly Roma prisoners. Hirt committed suicide in 1945 whilst Bickenbach was sentenced to 20 years' imprisonment in 1952, extended to life in 1954; the very next year, he was released as part of a general amnesty and allowed to resume his medical career. The remains of the murdered Jews, found in Strasbourg's Anatomy Institute, were buried in the city's Cronenbourg Jewish cemetery in 1945.

The camp is on the D130, accessed from the village of Rothau on the D1420, nearly 40 miles south-west of Strasbourg. Rothau's train station was the point of arrival for prisoners, marked by a plaque in the waiting room. The camp can realistically be reached only by private transport (from Rothau it is a steep two-hour walk).

GURS

The largest camp in the Vichy zone, Gurs was the site of one of the more curious stories of the Holocaust, involving the Jews of south-western Germany. The camp was originally created in April 1939 to house defeated Spanish Republican soldiers – there were 17,000 by the middle of that year – who were joined in early 1940 by around 4,000 mainly Jewish German and Austrian refugees, perversely regarded as 'enemy aliens'. Most of the inmates were released in the course of 1940 but the German Jews remained. Their numbers were swelled in October 1940 at the behest of Robert Wagner, *Gauleiter* of Baden in Germany. Keen to be the first Nazi to clear his region of Jews, Wagner arranged for the deportation to Gurs of the entire Jewish community of Baden, the Palatinate and parts of Württemberg – 6,538 people, mainly women, children and the elderly, were given only a few minutes to prepare two bags before being dispatched on the two-day journey. More than 2,000 were eventually able to leave, either through escape or by securing emigration visas, but the majority remained; more than 1,000 died of dysentery and typhoid within a year. Other foreign-born Jews living under Vichy were also brought to Gurs in the following years (it was the principal transit centre in the southern zone after the closure of Rivesaltes in late 1942), taking the total to 18,185 Jewish inmates from October 1940 to November 1943. Several thousand were deported to Auschwitz or Sobibór via Drancy; by the time the camp was liberated in the summer of 1944, there were only 48 Jewish inmates left. In total, 60,559 prisoners passed through Gurs, mainly Jews and Spanish refugees. After the war, and before its demolition in 1946, it was briefly used to house alleged collaborators, German POWs, and, again, Spanish Republicans.

The site was neglected for many years, only its cemetery recalling its past. However, after pressure from local youth groups and survivors' associations, a memorial area was created on the camp's northern edge in 1994. This is marked by a canopied information centre to the side of the road into Gurs village. Here, as throughout the site, panels outline the camp's history. A little further along the road, the principal memorial, designed by Israeli artist Dani Karavan, consists of a railway track which leads to a small concrete square, surrounded by barbed wire, carrying a floor plaque from the French government. At the other end of the railway, a stylised wooden skeleton of a barrack shelters another plaque listing the different groups of inmates. A path to its right leads to the camp cemetery, passing the foundation posts of the camp water tower and a memorial erected by the Spanish Basque regional government: many of the Republicans interned here were Basques who had fled by sea after the fall of Santander. Just before the cemetery, a lovely stone sculpture of a suitcase bears the inscription '*Camp de Gurs*' on one side and '*Baden*' on the other. The cemetery wall, erected in 1962 by the Jewish community and the towns of Baden, encloses the graves of 1,073 people, some marked by stones listing names and mostly German places of origin. A central obelisk remembers the majority without gravestones as well as the thousands deported to their deaths in Poland. There is also a memorial for the Spanish victims.

To the left of the skeleton barrack, a gate symbolises the northern limit of the camp: the path running south from here was its main road. A stone sculpture by the path honours Elsbeth Kasser, a nurse who worked for the *Secours Suisse*, one of several mostly foreign or Protestant humanitarian groups active in Gurs. Alongside is the preserved small chalet-like barrack in which she lived, the only surviving wooden vestige of the camp.

The road continues, past a field to the right which was the site of the punishment barracks, into the forest which now covers most of the former area of the camp. Wooden signs indicate the different sections. Almost immediately on entering the woods, the foundations of a bath house are to the left, next to a reconstruction of a barrack – there were 382 such blocks in the camp. Around it are a series of 'virtual barracks' indicated by triangular wooden frames and constructed as part of a memorial art project in 2002. The walkway through the reconstructed barrack continues to the foundations of a further block on the western side of the path, marked by fragments of stone whose French and German texts explain the history of the camp to passing walkers. The foundations themselves are surrounded by more fragments stencilled with scenes of camp life. It is possible to continue along the camp road for a further kilometre or so from here until it reaches the D25 road to Mauléon. A reconstructed barrier indicates the southern limit, beyond which stand the metal posts of the original gate.

The memorial complex is signposted south of the village of Gurs, just off the D936 between Oloron-Sainte-Marie and Navarrenx. Access by public transport is not possible. Taxi companies in Oloron are Louis (Tel: 05.59.39.53.01; taxilouis@hotmail.com) and Myriam (06.79.57.82.66). Oloron's Maison du Patrimoine at 52 Rue Dalmais (July–Sept only: daily except Mon, 10.00–12.00, 3.00–6.00; €3) has a room dedicated to Gurs.

RIVESALTES

Rivesaltes is today the most extraordinary Holocaust site in France, perhaps in Europe. The camp was built as a military base in 1938 but became another centre for Spanish refugees. It assumed a more central role under Vichy with 21,000 people interned there in 1941–1942. Although a majority (55 per cent) of prisoners were Spaniards, Rivesaltes eventually became the principal southern camp for the detention of racial 'undesirables', primarily Jews and Roma. Its most notable feature was its use as a 'family camp' where Jewish couples and their children were held. Any idyllic notions this might evoke were belied by the overcrowded and unhygienic reality, and families were generally separated. Indeed, the original idea of keeping them together was partly a ruse to pressure Jewish parents not to send their children into hiding before internment. Once deportations began in 1942, Rivesaltes became the major transit camp in the Roussillon region and, from August 1942, for the whole Vichy zone. In the course of three months, nine convoys departed for Drancy and then Auschwitz, carrying 2,313 people. However, nearly 600 children were saved from certain death by the heroic activities of welfare organisations in the camp, notably the *Oeuvre de Secours aux Enfants* (OSE), a French-based Jewish charity. At great personal risk, young social workers such as Vivette Samuel and Simone Weil-Lipman smuggled out children, who were hidden in homes run by the OSE and then, once Nazi pressure intensified in 1943, amongst foster parents and Catholic clergy. Following the German occupation of the south in November 1942, Rivesaltes became a military base and the remaining inmates were

Rivesaltes (Photograph by the author)

29

transferred to Gurs except for the Roma who were sent to the specially built Saliers camp near Arles. The site gained new notoriety in the 1960s when it housed more than 30,000 *Harkis*, Algerian soldiers who had fought for France in the war of the 1950s. The overcrowding was greater even than that during the war with many Algerian families forced to live in tents, a symbol of the suspicion and ingratitude with which they were received. Thereafter, the site was occupied by the Marines who gradually abandoned it from the 1970s although a section housing alleged illegal immigrants closed only in 2007.

For decades, these multiple histories of injustice were ignored and the site was left to decay. The legacy of this is an astonishing sight. It occupies an enormous area – more than 600 hectares – of arid plain covered with hundreds of ruined concrete barracks and toilet blocks. They were built to a uniform plan but their varying states of decrepitude create an apocalyptic scene, amplified by scattered coils of barbed wire. There were no memorials on the site until the 1990s when three stones were erected – to Jews, Spaniards and Algerians – by the main road. A 1997 proposal to demolish the barracks led to a concerted campaign to establish a more prominent memorial which is currently being constructed; once completed it will be the most ambitious such centre in France. The project has been beset by delays not least because of the immense cost involved (over €18 million), mostly resulting from the high price demanded by the Ministry of Defence for the land. Originally scheduled to open in 2008 (when construction, in fact, began), the inauguration was put back to 2010 and now seems likely to be in 2011. The memorial site encompasses *Îlot F*, one of two sections used as transit camps for Jews during the 1942 deportations. The centrepiece will be a subterranean museum focussing on the varied experiences of the Spanish, Jews, Roma and *Harkis*. Some barracks will be restored to their wartime state but most will be allowed to continue in their steady decline. *Îlot F* is only a fraction of the whole Rivesaltes complex, however. The plan ultimately envisages the replacement of the other areas with enterprises and parkland but this is likely to take time: for the moment, Rivesaltes is a site unlike any other in Europe.

The camp is north of the town of Rivesaltes, reached by taking the D12 westwards off the A9 at exit 41: follow this road, ignoring the turning into the town, as it goes over the railway, bends sharply to the left and crosses a roundabout. Turn right at the next junction onto Chemin de Tuchan à Sainte-Marie; the memorial area is reached via a signposted dirt track at the first right, opposite the three memorial stones. The car park is on the left after the final large wind turbine. Rivesaltes does have a train station but the camp is over an hour's walk away by a circuitous route. A more practical, though expensive, option might be to take a taxi from Perpignan.

OTHER SITES

Aside from Drancy, the major transit camp in the occupied zone was the former Royallieu military base in Compiègne; adjoining camps housed POWs and political prisoners. The very first French transport to Auschwitz carried 1,043 Jews from Compiègne on 27 March 1942. A museum and memorial complex finally opened in 2008 in three former barracks on Avenue des Martyrs de la Liberté, south-west of the town centre (daily except Tue, 10.00–6.00; €5; www.memorial.compiegne.fr).

Le Vernet was a notorious southern camp for 'suspect foreigners' which had held Spanish Republicans and German refugees before the fall of France. Most inmates from 1940 were political prisoners but several hundred foreign-born Jews passed through en route to Drancy. There are memorials (including a train wagon) at the station, north of the village by the N20 road. A water tower and stone gate posts are the only surviving elements of the prisoners' camp, located a short walk north along the N20 by Allée d'Embayonne, opposite former guards' barracks (now private housing). A memorial cemetery is further up the road whilst there is a very small museum on Place Guilhamet back in the village (Mon, Thu, 8.30–12.00, 1.30–5.00; Tue, 1.30–5.00; Fri, 8.30–12.00, 3.00–6.30; free). Le Vernet d'Ariège is 30 miles south of Toulouse between Saverdun and Pamiers.

The only other camp to be significantly memorialised is Les Milles, just south-west of Aix-en-Provence. The former tile factory held German citizens, predominantly refugees, until the armistice: those interned included the artists Max Ernst and Hans Bellmer. Thereafter, it became a camp for aspiring émigrés and finally, in summer 1942, a transit camp for more than 2,000 Jews from Provence. The existing memorial complex includes remarkable murals painted by an unknown internee in 1940–1941 and a train wagon commemorating the deportations (Mon–Fri, 9.00–12.00, 12.45–5.00). The wider site is currently being restored as a memorial museum which is due to open, after years of delays, in 2010–11 (www.campdesmilles.org). The site is signposted on Chemin des Déportés in Les Milles village, off the D9.

An affecting memorial site is the former OSE children's home at Izieu between Chambéry and Lyon (June–Sept: daily, 10.00–6.30; Oct–May (except weekends in Dec & Jan): Mon–Fri, 9.00–5.00; Sat, 2.00–6.00; Sun, 10.00–6.00; €5; www.izieu.alma.fr) where 44 children and 7 adults were arrested in a surprise raid in April 1944; only the teacher Lea Feldblum survived Auschwitz. The arrest of the children was one of the major charges against Klaus Barbie in his 1987 trial. Take the A43 and then the D592 to Aoste from where Izieu is signposted.

A happier story is associated with the celebrated Auvergnat village of Le Chambon-sur-Lignon, the first entire community to be honoured as Righteous by Yad Vashem. The Protestant villagers hid up to 5,000 Jews and refused to betray them even after their inspiring pastor André Trocmé was arrested in February 1943. There is a plaque erected by Jewish survivors opposite the Protestant church whilst it is hoped to create a memorial museum. Le Chambon is a couple of miles north of the D15 between Le Puy-en-Velay and Saint-Agrève, another of the several Protestant communities in the region where Jews found shelter.

Though strictly speaking not a Holocaust site, Oradour-sur-Glane was the scene of the most infamous wartime massacre in France when 642 people were killed – the men shot, the women and children burned alive in the church – by the Waffen SS, and the village itself destroyed allegedly after being confused with nearby Oradour-sur-Vayres where it was believed a German officer was being held by the Resistance. Amongst the victims were seven Jews being hidden by the villagers. The ruins were left after the war and a new village built nearby. There is now a memorial centre by the site (May–Sept: daily, 9.00–7.00; Mar–May, Sept–Oct: daily, 9.00–6.00; Feb, Nov–Dec: daily, 9.00–5.00; €7.50; www.oradour. org). Oradour is on the D9, north-west of Limoges.

BELGIUM

B elgium had a unique Jewish population in that it overwhelmingly consisted of recent immigrants and as such might have been expected to be particularly vulnerable to the Nazis. Many did indeed fall victim yet a majority of Jews survived due in no small measure to their own actions and to those of a significant minority of Gentiles.

Although a medieval Jewish community had existed, it was expelled in the fourteenth century meaning that modern Belgian Jewish history began in the sixteenth century when Portuguese Marranos (Jews who had been forcibly converted to Christianity but who secretly maintained their faith) began to settle in Antwerp. Yet despite an increase in civil rights, culminating in the arrival of the French Revolution in the 1790s, only around 1,000 Jews lived in the country at the beginning of the nineteenth century. Numbers increased significantly in that century but much of this population was transient. It was after the First World War that a large Jewish community developed as a result of large-scale immigration from eastern Europe and Germany. Despite the flight of several thousand in 1939–40, approximately 66,000 Jews remained in Belgium after the occupation began in May 1940; only around 10 per cent were Belgian citizens.

Nazi policy was similar to that in France although it generally proceeded more slowly and, crucially, without any prompting from the indigenous authorities. The first major anti-Jewish initiatives came in the autumn of 1940 in the form of exclusion from the professions and 'Aryanisation' of Jewish businesses, although the latter was implemented rather slowly and, almost uniquely, never completed. Further restrictions followed in the course of 1941 and in November of that year the Association of Jews in Belgium (AJB) was established as an equivalent to the UGIF in France, a central Jewish body through which the Nazis hoped to control the community. The escalation in 1942 led to the use of more than 2,000 Jews in forced labour in the spring, a prelude to round-ups and deportations to Auschwitz which began in August. More than 25,000 people were arrested and interned in barracks in Mechelen before being transported eastward. The Germans initially claimed that only 'foreign' Jews (who were, of course, the vast majority in Belgium) would be deported but in September 1943 there were large round-ups

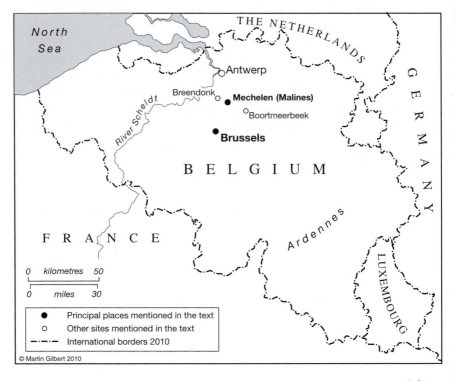

of 'Belgian' Jews. It is estimated, adding those who perished on Belgian soil, that 28,902 died during the Holocaust, close to 44 per cent of the mid-1940 population.

However, the fact that more than half the Jews survived is, in the circumstances, rather astonishing. The rate in Belgium was lower than in France or Italy yet it lacked most of their advantages. Unlike Italy, the occupation was lengthy (more than four years) and, unlike France, the whole of the country was under direct German control for the whole of that time. For the Jews themselves, the fact that most were relative newcomers, often speaking French with an accent and Flemish not at all, further heightened the potential danger. However, this could also have worked as a factor in favour of survival – given that so many Jews were refugees from persecution, many were active in leftist or Zionist politics, enabling them to slip easily into underground activities. Indeed, one distinctive feature of Belgian Jewish responses to the Holocaust was a willingness to think the worst of Nazi intentions and to take action accordingly. There was thus both significant Jewish involvement in the work of the general Resistance and the emergence of a specifically Jewish underground. For example, in the summer of 1942, the AJB's card index of Jews was destroyed in a fire, hampering the round-ups. More strikingly, on the night of 19–20 April 1943, three young Resistance fighters – Robert Maistriau, Georges Livschitz and Jean Franklemon – attacked a convoy travelling from Mechelen to Auschwitz. They succeeded in liberating 231 of the 1,631 Jews on the transport of whom 115 were able to escape; this was the only recorded instance of an armed attack on a death train anywhere in Europe. Survival was also facilitated by the attitudes of parts of the general population. Although there was widespread anti-Semitism in the Flemish-speaking north, most Jews – with the notable exception of the Antwerp community – lived in ethnically mixed Brussels or in the French-speaking south where anti-Jewish prejudice was marginal and where lingering resentment towards the German occupation in the First World War engendered little enthusiasm for collaboration with the Nazis. The exiled Belgian government and the Catholic Church also gave a lead in encouraging non-compliance. For example, following guidance from London, government officials refused to implement anti-Jewish economic measures in October 1940.

Memorialisation of sites associated with Nazi persecution began almost immediately after the war although it tended to dwell on general suffering. Even so, Belgium was one of the first countries to create a prominent national Holocaust memorial. The most obvious omission was rectified in the 1990s when a moving museum was established in the former Mechelen transit camp.

BRUSSELS

With a community of some 33,000, Brussels was home to just over half of Belgium's Jewish population. Although most were recent immigrants, the capital also had the largest number of 'Belgian' Jews. It was thus the location of national communal institutions, charitable societies and political organisations. This was to be of great importance in providing a network of mutual support once persecution commenced, first in terms of financial aid to the needy and later in the life or death question of finding shelter: it is estimated that as many as 12,000 Jews were in hiding in Brussels. Gentile attitudes were also important. For example, when the first major anti-Semitic laws were issued in October 1940, Brussels Free University publicly protested at the dismissal of Jewish academics. When the yellow star was imposed in May 1942, the municipal authorities refused to distribute the badges, an example of defiance almost unique in occupied Europe. Nonetheless, thousands were victims of the deportations with major round-ups of 'foreign' Jews in mid-August and early September 1942. The process continued for a year until the large-scale assault on 'Belgian' Jews in September 1943. That said, the relatively high survival rate meant that the city emerged from the war as home to one of Europe's larger remaining Jewish communities, generally estimated to be between 15,000 and 20,000 today.

Belgium's national Holocaust memorial is located in the south-western Anderlecht district, the major area of pre-war Jewish settlement. Inaugurated in 1970, it is an impressive structure especially for its time. A large hexagonal courtyard is suggestive of a Star of David, a motif echoed throughout the memorial, whilst chains on the wall recall a menorah. Marble tablets list the names of 23,838 Belgian Jews murdered in the extermination camps. The centrepiece podium and crypt were vandalised in 2006 and it has taken some time for the damage to be repaired. The memorial is surrounded by a small park which includes a further memorial to Jewish Resistance fighters on the outer wall of the courtyard. The complex is on Square des Martyrs Juifs, at the corner of

Brussels: Holocaust memorial (Photograph by Elizabeth Burns)

Rue Emile Carpentier and Rue des Goujons (Grondelstraat), half a mile west of the Gare du Midi. There is a gate to the park at this corner which may be closed; an open gate is a few steps further along Emile Carpentier. The memorial itself deliberately has a number of closed gates – the actual entrance is slightly hidden a few steps down on the right.

Nearby is the worthy National Museum of the Resistance (Mon–Tue, Thu–Fri, 9.00–12.00, 1.00–4.00; free) at Rue van Lint (Van Lintstraat) 14. The museum's displays are old-fashioned and mostly labelled only in French and Flemish but interesting nonetheless. There is much 'secret army' material such as weapons, printing presses and fake identity cards spread over two floors. A small memorial room holds urns containing ashes from different concentration camps.

The Jewish Museum of Belgium is at Rue des Minimes 21, near the Palais de Justice (Sun–Fri, 10.00–5.00; €5; www.mjb-jmb.org). The modern displays are very much an introduction to Judaism with exhibits on rituals and family life. The most remarkable feature is the interior of a Hassidic prayer house from the village of Molenbeek. A small top-floor room provides biographies of the Jews of Molenbeek, in the process showing how the Holocaust affected even the smallest of communities. A couple of streets south-east, the Great Synagogue stands at Rue de la Regence.

South-east of the city centre, the tall building at Avenue Louise 453 was the Belgian headquarters of the Gestapo and the centre of anti-Jewish operations. On 20 January 1943, a young Belgian aristocrat serving in the RAF, Jean-Michel de Selys Longchamps, strafed the building from top to bottom before throwing British and Belgian flags into the streets below. Four Germans were killed but the occupiers probably felt the humiliation more deeply. There is now a memorial to de Selys (who lost his life over Ostend in August 1943) in a traffic island opposite and a plaque on the building itself (tram 94, Abbaye stop).

MECHELEN

Mechelen's location between Brussels and Antwerp and at the major axis of rail lines in Belgium made it a natural choice when the Germans decided to create a single transit camp for the deportations in the summer of 1942. The eighteenth-century Dossin barracks were converted into accommodation for Jews with the first inmates arriving in late July. Less is known about conditions in Dossin than in most similar institutions partly because there were relatively few survivors: only 1,218 of those deported lived to the liberation. Transports began on 4 August 1942 and at their peak in the ensuing months left at a rate of two per week. By the time of the last transport on 31 July 1944, 28 trains had carried more than 25,000 people to Auschwitz-Birkenau; more than 16,000 were gassed on arrival.

The barracks reverted to the control of the Belgian military after the war and remained in use until the 1970s. Much of the complex was turned over to housing in the 1980s with a garden and walkways placed in the central courtyard. However, the absence of recognition of Dossin's role as the most significant Holocaust site in Belgium led to growing pressure for at least part of the building to be given a memorial function. This culminated in the opening of the Jewish Museum of Deportation and Resistance in 1995 (Sun–Thu, 10.00–5.00; Fri, 10.00–1.00; closed second & third weeks of Aug; free; www.cicb.be), occupying the north-eastern side of the barracks. There are plans to extend the site to encompass the whole of the eastern wing and into surrounding buildings but even in its present restricted location the museum is a fascinating and moving experience. The most striking section consists of a series of 28 wall panels – one for each convoy – listing the numbers on the transports and the numbers killed. Family photographs are used to personalise the tragedy with those deported (often everyone in the picture) shaded in. The basement section covers the fate of the deportees in Birkenau, one figure in particular standing out: no Jewish child under 13 sent from Mechelen to Auschwitz survived. On the street outside, on the building's exterior wall, there is a memorial plaque dedicated to the deported Jews, in front of which six vertically raised pieces of railway track symbolise the 6 million victims of the Holocaust. A further memorial commemorates Roma victims of Mechelen.

The former barracks are at Goswin Stassartstraat 153, an easy walk north of Mechelen's historic centre. The museum is immediately to the right in the gateway, entered by pressing the buzzer. On the south-west side of the city in a traffic island on Van Benedenlaan, there is a further memorial, this time to political prisoners held in Nazi camps.

OTHER SITES

Breendonk fortress, built before the First World War, was converted by the Nazis into a camp for political prisoners awaiting transit to the Reich. The total number of inmates during the occupation was only about 3,500 but several hundred died from torture, poor living conditions and execution. There are believed to have been 219 Jewish prisoners: 54 were deported to Auschwitz via Mechelen whilst 65 died in the fortress. Breendonk is possibly the most intact of all Nazi camps and became a memorial museum in 1947 (daily, 9.30–5.30; €6; www.breendonk.be) although a recent renovation led to the abandonment of traditional text-based presentations, requiring visitors to use an audio-guide instead. It is next to the A12 motorway on the edge of Willebroek, west of Mechelen (from where there are buses).

Antwerp suffered heavy losses during the Holocaust and was the scene of a particularly nasty pogrom on Passover in April 1941. Nonetheless, the community has recovered to some extent and is often described as Europe's last *shtetl*, possibly the only place in the continent where Yiddish remains the principal language. This reflects the refugee past of Belgium's Jews as does the dominance of Hassidism. The traditional centre of this community of *shuls*, kosher butchers and diamond shops is Pelikaanstraat on the west side of the city's train station. There is a striking memorial to the city's deported Jews on Belgiëlei, further south at the junction with Mercatorstraat. The Great Synagogue is on the other side of the railway bridge at Van Den Nestlei 1.

Boortmeerbeek, off the N26 between Mechelen and Leuven, is close to the site of the 1943 attack on the Auschwitz-bound convoy. A monument honouring Maistriau, Livschitz and Franklemon is by the railway tracks at the village's station.

CHAPTER 3

THE NETHERLANDS

The Netherlands was home to arguably Europe's most secure and prosperous Jewish community yet nowhere in the west of the continent was the Holocaust more devastating. Around three quarters of Dutch Jews were murdered, a figure far in excess of any comparable country.

There was little portent of this fate in 1939, the Netherlands having been seen since the early modern period as one of the safest havens for Jews in Europe. Although the original medieval community had been expelled in the fourteenth century, the late sixteenth century saw the emergence of a significant Sephardic presence as Portuguese Marranos settled in ports such as Amsterdam. Most cities welcomed Jews and they were able to participate fully in economic life during the seventeenth-century 'Golden Age', the diamond trade being only the most celebrated of the many areas of Jewish enterprise. This encouraged further immigration with a large Ashkenazi community also emerging. The perception of the Netherlands as a civilised, open country (indeed, the greatest prejudices Jews encountered were often those between the generally prosperous Sephardim and the poorer Ashkenazim) continued to encourage migration into the twentieth century. Thousands of German Jews sought refuge in the 1930s (the Frank family being only the most famous example), a process which continued even after the outbreak of war. Of the 140,000 or so Jews who lived in the Netherlands in 1940, around 25,000 are believed to have been refugees from the Reich.

The invasion of May 1940 was a profound shock for Jews and non-Jews alike, given that Germany had respected Dutch neutrality in the First World War. The usual spate of anti-Semitic policies began in the autumn of 1940 with exclusion from the civil service and the registration of Jewish assets as a prelude to expropriation. Jews were required to register as such with the authorities in January 1941, and a Jewish Council, the *Joodse Raad*, was established a month later. Over the same winter, hooligans from the previously marginal Dutch Nazi Party (NSB) assisted the Germans in harassing and arresting Jews. After one such incident led to a fracas in an Amsterdam café in February 1941, several hundred

The Netherlands

young Jews were sent to Buchenwald and later on to Mauthausen. This prompted a general strike in major cities, the most prominent public display of solidarity with Jews anywhere in occupied Europe, but the threat of further Nazi reprisals caused it to fizzle out. The strike demonstrated to the Germans that they could not expect the support of the majority of the Dutch public but they calculated, correctly, that fear of force would limit active resistance. Indeed, there were few protests when more young men were dispatched to Mauthausen in June. Further restrictions were imposed in the same summer including expulsion from education whilst thousands were sent to forced labour camps in the autumn. From January 1942, there were round-ups of provincial Jews, many of whom were settled in Amsterdam which essentially acted as a holding centre prior to the deportations. The yellow star was introduced at the beginning of May and transports to the death camps began in July 1942, most via a former refugee camp at Westerbork. It is estimated that, in a little over two years, 107,000 Jews were deported; 5,200 survived. Most of the remainder of the roughly 30,000 Dutch Jews who survived did so through hiding.

The scale of the destruction in the Netherlands may seem somewhat paradoxical given that the country was, by common consent, one of the least anti-Semitic in Europe. Indeed, only Poland (with a larger population) has had a higher number of citizens awarded the title of Righteous by Yad Vashem. However, there were certain factors which worked against Dutch Jews. One was the nature of the occupation under *Reichskommisar* Arthur Seyss-Inquart, a loyal Austrian Nazi. The party and its institutions had a more direct administrative role in the Netherlands than in Belgium where the Wehrmacht prevailed. More controversial is the role of the Dutch administration. Although the Queen and her cabinet fled to London, the heads of the civil service remained in place in the hope of maintaining stability and limiting the German takeover. However, their policy of reluctant compliance with German measures, a contrast to the often obstructive approach of Belgian officials, meant that the efficient Dutch administrative machine was effectively put at the disposal of the Nazis. Even more contentious is the role of the Jewish community leadership, especially of the two chairs of the *Joodse Raad*, Abraham Asscher and David Cohen. A post-war Jewish community tribunal found them guilty of collaboration and barred them from any communal positions. Amongst the criticisms were that they had failed to speak out against the extermination (thus missing a chance to warn the Jewish public), had carried out all German demands including selection for deportation, and had sought to primarily protect themselves and their families and associates. The latter charges were perhaps especially unfair and the men were later exonerated. Even so, despite their invidious situation, Asscher and Cohen's policy of compliance and reassurance did contrast with that of Jewish leaders in Belgium.

Few countries have approached commemoration of the Holocaust as seriously and extensively as the Netherlands. This was not always true for the camps (which remained in use for decades afterwards) but the situation has been remedied by the creation of new museums from the 1980s onwards.

AMSTERDAM

Amsterdam was one of Europe's great Jewish centres, home to the majority of Dutch Jews since the 1590s. '*Mokum*' (from the Yiddish for 'town') was an almost unique example of tolerance and prosperity for much of the early modern period although this must be qualified by awareness of the disparities in wealth and status between the Sephardic and Ashkenazi communities. These really began to be addressed only in the nineteenth century when the rise of industry, education and secularism created a shared Dutch (or perhaps Amsterdam) Jewish identity. The city's historic reputation attracted more than 10,000 refugees from Nazism in the 1930s, giving it a Jewish population of around 75,000 by the beginning of the occupation.

In addition to the legal and economic restrictions imposed across the country, Amsterdam's Jews were especially subjected to attacks by the Dutch far right. It was in this context that Jewish self-defence actions led to the arrest of 389 young men in February 1941 and their subsequent deportation which triggered the general strike. It began on 25 February at the instigation of Communist activists in the docks and quickly spread across the city. For three days, factories, transport and other public services came to a halt. Whilst it made no long-term difference, it was a singular display of support for Amsterdam's beleaguered Jewish community although some survivor testimony and contemporary accounts suggest that public sympathy lessened in the following years as the hardships of the occupation engendered more insularity.

The city played a central role in the deportation process with a January 1942 order that all Dutch Jews should be concentrated there (although this was not fully implemented). In turn, settlement was restricted to certain areas, especially the historic Jewish quarter, meaning that Amsterdam had a de facto ghetto for the first time in its history. Round-ups were then carried out by the Germans with the assistance of NSB members, with the main holding centre being the Hollandsche Schouwburg (Dutch Theatre) from where victims were sent to Westerbork. One of the largest *Aktionen* came in May 1943 when the Germans commanded 7,000 Jews, including employees of the *Joodse Raad* and their families (hitherto largely protected), to assemble for deportation. When only 500 complied, the Jewish quarter was sealed and large-scale raids snatched people at random. Deportations accelerated in the following months with even the leadership of the *Joodse Raad* sent to Westerbork in September 1943. By the end of that year, hardly any Jews were still living openly in Amsterdam.

The modern community is believed to number between 15,000 and 20,000, although the very high level of assimilation and mixed relationships mean that many would not necessarily consider themselves Jewish. Even so, Amsterdam, like Paris, does still have a visible Jewish presence, along with one of the largest collections of Holocaust memorials and museums in Europe.

The Jewish quarter

The historic Jewish quarter lies on the eastern edge of the city centre around Waterlooplein and Jodenbreestraat. The area was never a ghetto until the war; indeed, non-Jews had always lived there as evinced by the fact that the district's most famous resident was Rembrandt. Equally, Jews settled in other parts of Amsterdam. Nonetheless, the quarter remained home to the principal synagogues and commercial life. The latter was particularly evident in Waterlooplein which was the site of a huge pre-war street market. An ill-judged 1980s redevelopment saw the square occupied by the Stopera, a large ugly edifice containing the town hall and opera house; behind it, by the Amstel, are two low-key memorials. At the western corner, a black pillar commemorates the 500 or so Jews who lost their lives serving in the Resistance. Barely noticed in the other corner is a memorial to the Jewish Boys' Orphanage which occupied this site from 1865; almost 100 children and three carers were deported to Sobibór in March 1943. After the war, the building was used as a residence for

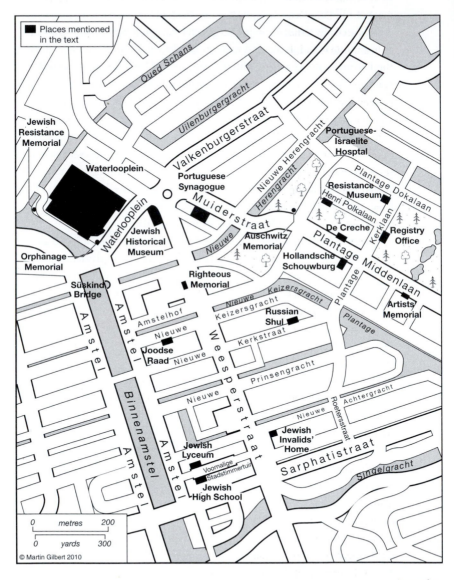

Places mentioned in the text

Oued Schans

Uilenburgergracht

Valkenburgerstraat

Jewish Resistance Memorial

Portuguese-Israelite Hosptal

Waterlooplein

Portuguese Synagogue

Nieuwe Herengracht

Herengracht

Muiderstraat

Plantage Dokalaan

Resistance Museum

Henri Polkalaan

Jewish Historical Museum

Nieuwe

Auschwitz Memorial

De Creche

Registry Office

Kerklaan

Plantage Middenlaan

Orphanage Memorial

Hollandsche Schouwburg

Süskind Bridge

Righteous Memorial

Keizersgracht

Nieuwe Keizersgracht

Russian Shul

Plantage

Artists Memorial

Amstelhof

Nieuwe

Kerkstraat

Weesperstraat

Amstel

Joodse Raad

Nieuwe

Prinsengracht

Binnenamstel

Nieuwe

Roetersstraat

Achtergracht

Nieuwe

Jewish Invalids' Home

Jewish Lyceum

Voomalige Stadstimmertuin

Sarphatistraat

Singelgracht

Jewish High School

| 0 | metres | 200 |
| 0 | yards | 300 |

© Martin Gilbert 2010

Amsterdam

young Jews preparing to emigrate to Israel; it was eventually sold and then demolished to make way for the Stopera. Pale bricks in the paving mark the building's outline; their Dutch text recalls its history.

Located immediately east of Waterlooplein, Mr Visserplein, little more than a traffic island, is named after Lodewijk Ernst Visser, Chief Justice of the Dutch Supreme Court. Suspended from office under the Nazi racial laws, he became the chair of the Jewish Coordinating Committee, a body created by the community in December 1940 to provide leadership and assistance. The Nazis were inevitably unwilling to tolerate such an organisation, effectively replacing it with the *Joodse Raad*. Visser became a fierce critic of Asscher and Cohen, as well as of government officials, for their policy of cooperation. He died of a heart attack in February 1942, within days of being warned that he would be sent to a concentration camp if he continued to publicly confront the Nazis.

On the south-eastern side of Mr Visserplein is the large seventeenth-century Portuguese Synagogue (Sun–Fri, 10.00–4.00 (Fri until 2.00, Nov–Mar); €6.50; www.esnoga.com), one of the world's great Sephardic temples. The synagogue backs onto Jonas Daniël Meijerplein, site of a statue of a hefty dockworker erected as a tribute to the 1941 strike. On the corner of Meijerplein and Nieuwe Amstelstraat, the Jewish Historical Museum (daily, 11.00–5.00; €7.50 or €10 with Portuguese Synagogue; www.jhm.nl) occupies a complex of linked former Ashkenazi synagogues which form a striking backdrop to the exhibits. The blue-ceilinged Great Synagogue, deployed to excellent effect in covering religious traditions and pre-twentieth century history, was used for the registration of 3,000 people caught in raids on 26 May 1943; most had to spend the night and part of the following day in the square outside.

The streets to the north of the main squares emphasise the historic Jewish character of the district. Nieuwe Uilenburgerstraat, which runs directly north of Waterlooplein, is home to the large former Boas diamond factory (recently returned to Jewish ownership) at 173–175 and a synagogue, sheltered behind a large wall at 91. On Rapenburgerstraat to the east, a former rabbinical seminary stands at 175–179 and the Jewish Girls' Orphanage at 169–171 (its residents were deported in February 1943). Recent work has restored the original Hebrew text at the top of the latter.

South of Waterlooplein, the small white bridge over the Nieuwe Herengracht at its junction with the Amstel is named after Walter Süskind, a German Jewish immigrant who was instrumental in organising the rescue of children from the Hollandsche Schouwburg; he is honoured by a plaque on the bridge's south-eastern pillar. On Weesperstraat to the east, between Nieuwe Herengracht and Nieuwe Keizersgracht, a neo-classical memorial in a small garden is dedicated to Gentiles who protected Jews; this was erected shortly after the war. The former headquarters of the *Joodse Raad* is located on the southern side of the next canal at Nieuwe Keizersgracht 58.

The Russian *Shul* at Nieuwe Kerkstraat 149 (the eastern end of the next street to the south) was opened in 1889 to meet the needs of refugees. Restored in the 1980s, it now attracts the latest wave of immigrants from the former Soviet Union. A couple of blocks further south at Nieuwe Achtergracht 100, on the corner with Weesperstraat, is the former Jewish Invalids' Home which moved into these rather drab premises in 1938. The staff and patients were arrested and deported on 1 March 1943, as related by a plaque. Voormalige Stadstimmertuin, accessed by arches at both the Weesperstraat and Amstel ends, is just to the west. Number 2 housed the Jewish High School from 1938. It moved to the suburbs in the 1970s although its post-war name, the Maimonides Jewish Lyceum, remains in a mosaic above the door. Opposite, at number 1, the Jewish Lyceum was established as a secular school in 1941 as a result of the expulsion of Jews from state education; it closed in 1943, its students dead or in hiding. Jacob Presser, who later wrote *Ashes in the Wind*, the classic history of the Holocaust in the Netherlands, was one of the teachers whilst the most famous pupil was Anne Frank. A contorted Star of David, flanked by the dates 1941 and 1943, stands over the door.

The area east of Meijerplein was less traditionally Jewish but still important in the Holocaust. Just across the Nieuwe Herengracht at the start of Plantage Middenlaan, Wertheim Park contains the *Nooit meer Auschwitz* ('no more Auschwitz') memorial (panels of broken mirrored glass), a work by artist Jan Wolkers commissioned by the Dutch Auschwitz Committee. The former Portuguese-Israelite Hospital is at Henri Polaklaan 6–12 around the corner (the image of a pelican feeding its young over 12A is a symbol of the Sephardic community). Most of its patients were deported in 1943 whilst the hospital was also used for the sterilisation of Jewish men in mixed marriages. In the immediate aftermath of the liberation, it accommodated survivors of the camps. Just

Amsterdam: the Jewish Lyceum (Photograph by Elizabeth Burns)

south of Wertheim Park, the building at Plantage Parklaan 9 was a Jewish community office (the original plaque still above the door); this was one of the sites where yellow stars were sold in May 1942.

The Hollandsche Schouwburg (daily, 11.00–4.00; free; www. hollandscheschouwburg.nl) at Plantage Middenlaan 24 is the most significant building associated with the Holocaust in the city. The theatre, constructed in 1892, was one of the most popular in Amsterdam but in September 1941 the Nazis designated it as the Jewish Theatre (i.e., for Jews only). It was then requisitioned and transformed into the main deportation centre in the summer of 1942. Jews were ordered to report there but more often were brought by force and held in appallingly overcrowded conditions, sometimes for weeks, before being dispatched to Westerbork. Despite its historic importance, the building was allowed to decline after the war; by the time a monument was created in 1962, its fabric was such that much of theatre had to be removed. Panels in a side room to the left of the foyer list the 6,700 family names of murdered Dutch Jews whilst the upstairs is given over to an exhibition on Amsterdam Jewish life. The former auditorium is now a large open-air space dominated by a memorial obelisk.

Virtually opposite the theatre, at Plantage Middenlaan 31–33, is *De Creche*, a nursery for babies of the internees and the scene of a remarkable act of rescue, marked by a plaque. Süskind used his position as an employee of the *Joodse Raad* to try to ensure that the infants were not registered on arrival. They were then smuggled out in laundry baskets, bags or even milk churns. The young female staff would wait until a tram passed by, blocking the view of the German guards outside the theatre, and then run alongside the tram until it reached the next stop; passengers kept the conspiracy of silence. It is estimated that more than 600 children were thus saved.

Further along Plantage Middenlaan, a park by Plantage Westermanlaan contains a striking sculpture of a clenched fist emerging from a deconstructed figure, a memorial to artists who served in the Resistance, notably the sculptor Gerrit van der Veen who was executed in 1944. On the other side of the road is Artis, Amsterdam's zoo, which was used as a hiding place by Jews and deserters from labour conscription. Plantage Kerklaan 36, by the zoo's entrance, was the wartime site of Amsterdam's Registry Office. As a plaque relates, on 27 March 1943, a group of Resistance fighters (including van der Veen) disguised as police entered the building and set fire to the identity documents of Amsterdam Jews. Their mission was assisted by the fire brigade who used their hoses to maximise the damage. Unfortunately, the attack came too late for most Jews and the group was betrayed to the Germans – 12 of its members were executed in July 1943.

The late nineteenth-century Plancius building at Plantage Kerklaan 61 once hosted various Jewish cultural and political activities. It is now the site of the Dutch Resistance Museum (Tue–Fri, 10.00–5.00; Sat–Mon, 11.00–5.00; €6.50; www.verzetsmuseum.org) which goes beyond its eponymous topic to provide thorough coverage of everyday wartime life and the choices facing ordinary citizens. A section on the 1941 strike serves as a prelude to an examination of the Holocaust. A later section on hiding has some fascinating objects made to relieve the boredom, including paintings by the husband and son of Eva Geiringer (later to be Otto Frank's second wife) and a chess set in which the black pieces wear German helmets.

Between October 1942 and May 1943, 11,000 Jews were deported to Westerbork from Muiderpoort station (tram 3 to its terminus, then under the bridge). A memorial rose garden in front of the station on Oosterspoorplein faces a bench carrying Victor E van Vriesland's poem *Muiderpoortstation*. The nearby Karel Appel sculpture is unrelated.

Elsewhere

The Anne Frank House is located west of the centre on Prinsengracht: the secret annexe, in Otto Frank's business premises at 263, is accessed through 267 (daily: July–Aug, 9.00–10.00; mid-Mar–May & early Sept, 9.00–9.00 (until 10.00, Sat); Sept–Mar, 9.00–7.00; €7.50; www. annefrank.org). Despite the crowds (the site is the most visited museum in the Netherlands), it is hard not to be moved by the simple displays of personal items such as Margot's Latin exercises and Peter van Pels's board game. The pictures pasted by Anne remain on the wall of the room she shared with Fritz Pfeffer. Other rooms cover the context of the Holocaust in the Netherlands and the history of the diary – a glass case holds 56 copies in different languages. There is a small statue of Anne outside in Westermarkt by the south-west corner of the church. To the east of the church is the Homomonument, a memorial dedicated to gay victims of both Nazism and other forms of persecution. Three pink triangles in the pavement link to form a larger triangle jutting out into the canal.

Museumplein, south-west of the centre, is the site of two contrasting memorials. A metal sculptural ensemble emanating disturbing noises is dedicated to Dutch women sent to Ravensbrück. Around 100 metres further south, a figurative sculpture of a man, woman and child backed by a flame honours Roma victims of the Nazis.

The New South suburb was constructed between the wars and German Jewish refugees were some of its first residents, amongst them the Franks who lived in a modernist housing block at Merwedeplein 37 (trams 12 and 25 to Waalstraat/Churchilllaan or tram 4 and buses 15, 65 and 245 to Waalstraat/Rooseveltlaan). A statue of Anne is in the adjacent park. On the other side of Victorieplein, the Jewish Children's Monument is located by a playground at Gaaspstraat 8. Two days after Jewish children were banned from playgrounds in November 1941, the Nazis turned this site into a market designated as the only place in the district where Jews could buy or sell goods. The monument, which was erected in 1985 by survivors and Resistance fighters after a spate of racist incidents in the area, depicts two children playing whilst two marginalised Jewish children look on. Its main text reads 'play together, live together'.

Further west, two of the most feared buildings in Amsterdam stood on opposite sides of Euterpestraat (now Gerrit van der Veenstraat) by its corner with Rubensstraat (tram 24 to Minervaplein, then walk north). The headquarters of the SD occupied a requisitioned girls' school at 91–109. This was where the Franks and their helpers were held after the arrest as were many other Jews and members of the Resistance. Opposite, in another school, was the *Zentralstelle* (the Central Office for Jewish Emigration) which was established a month after the February strike to control Jewish policy. Both buildings were badly damaged in an RAF air raid in November 1944, the *Zentralstelle* irretrievably so. Its site is now occupied by a small memorial square. The rebuilt SD building bears a plaque commemorating both the air raid and the deported Jews. Many of those who passed through the imposing redbrick, including the Franks' protectors Kugler and Kleiman, eventually found themselves a kilometre to the west in the still functioning Amstelveenseweg prison on the corner of its eponymous street and Havenstraat (tram 16 and many buses to Harlemmermeerstation).

The Amsterdamse Bos, the forest south of the ring road, is the location of the unusual Dachau memorial. Two tall hedgerows flank concrete paving slabs listing the names of the major Nazi camps, beginning with the first. The memorial is a few hundred metres into the park, just off Bosbaanweg, the main road which skirts the south of the lake. The nearest bus stop is van Nijenrodeweg/Amstelveenseweg (62, 166, 170, 171 and 172), just outside the park.

A little-known memorial in northern Amsterdam commemorates the Jewish employees of the now demolished Hollandia Kattenburg rainwear factory who were arrested on 11 November 1942. Of the 367 victims, only 8 survived deportation to the camps: the names of the murdered 359 are listed on a memorial erected by staff of the company's Manchester branch in a park by a school, a short walk from the IJplein ferry stop (catch the free ferry from behind the Central Station). Walk along the IJ embankment until it reaches steps down to a road to the left and turn into this road (IJplein) until it intersects with diagonal Hollandia Kattenburgpad. The monument is on the right.

VUGHT

Vught, constructed in 1942, was officially the only concentration camp in the Netherlands. Strictly speaking, it was actually two institutions. The 'protective custody camp' housed political prisoners from the Netherlands, Belgium and Germany. The 'Jewish transit camp' assembled provincial Jews or those belonging to previously exempt groups; they were deported to Poland via Westerbork or occasionally directly. Inmates, both Jews and politicals, were used as forced labour in workshops, some of which were managed by Phillips. Unlike other major businesses implicated in the Holocaust, the electronics company is generally regarded as having emerged with some credit: it insisted that its Jewish workers be well treated (including receiving a daily hot meal) and attempted to prevent their deportation. These efforts were to prove ultimately futile, however, as the last 'Philips Jews' were deported in June 1944 and the company was expelled from the camp by the SS on suspicions of sabotage. It is estimated that 31,000 prisoners were held in Vught, of whom 12,000 were Jewish. Most of the Jews were murdered in Auschwitz or Sobibór; 750 of the other prisoners died in the camp.

The camp was one of the earliest to be liberated, by British troops in October 1944. After the war, it was taken over by the military and most of the large complex remains in use although very few original buildings survive. In addition to modern barracks and a civilian prison, the site also houses Moluccan veterans of the Dutch army who came to the Netherlands in the 1950s. However, at the bottom of the long road which runs alongside the camp walls, the area around the crematorium has been given over to the Kamp Vught National Monument (Tue–Fri, 10.00–5.00; Sat–Sun, 12.00–5.00; free; www.nmkampvught.nl) which makes effective use of its limited space. The 2002 visitors' centre contains some imaginatively presented exhibits, unfortunately labelled only in Dutch although an English guide (€3) covers some of the relevant material. A large-scale model of the camp in the square outside illustrates what a small fraction is contained within the memorial area. The barbed-wire fence and watchtowers alongside are reconstructions as is the barrack which contains replicas of toilets, a washroom (with original sinks), dining room and dormitory.

The crematorium is the only surviving original building within the memorial area. Along with the furnaces and dissection table, the block contains a reconstruction of cell 115 (the original was in the camp prison), the scene of a particularly shocking incident. A group of female inmates had punished a suspected SS informant by shaving her hair; when one of the women was interned in the prison, the others protested. Commandant Adam Grünewald reacted to the insubordination by forcing as many women as possible – 74 in total – into the cell on the night of 15 January 1944; by the morning, 10 were dead. Because of this incident, the culmination of a series of cruelties, Grünewald was removed as commandant. The *Asputten* outside the crematorium are two symbolic graves containing ashes found around the building.

At the rear of the complex stands the Jewish children's monument. Following arrests in the provinces in spring 1943, the Jewish camp was severely overcrowded. The Nazis' solution was to round up all of the children – infants on 6 June, those up to 16 on the next day – and dispatch them, after a brief stop at Westerbork, to Sobibór; 1,260 children were murdered along with 1,800 parents who chose to accompany them. The names and ages of the children are listed on the memorial; sculpted toys and books are at its base.

Perhaps the most shocking sight in Vught is to be found back in the visitors' centre in the stacks of stones which originally adorned the memorial at the camp's execution grounds. The tablets were defaced with tar on the fiftieth anniversary of the liberation of the Netherlands in 1995, causing national outrage; those responsible have never been caught. The neighbouring memorial room lists the names of those who died in Vught. There is a photograph of Jan Herberts, the youngest of them, who was arrested for attacking a German soldier. Being only 17, he could not be executed under the Geneva Convention (to which the Nazis paid some heed in western Europe) so was held until his eighteenth birthday and then shot. The final section of the visitors' centre is used for interesting temporary exhibitions.

Outside the complex, a path through the woods, indicated by white markers on the trees, leads to the memorial site at the rifle range (*Fusilladeplaats*), set on a small island. The original memorial was established immediately after the war, engraved with the names of 329 Resistance fighters executed here in the summer of 1944. New tablets have replaced the desecrated originals.

The site is signposted off the N65 which runs through Vught village, just south of 's-Hertogenbosch. If one is using public transport, it can be reached through the marvellous Dutch institution of the train-taxi: buy tickets from the special machines in 's-Hertogenbosch station and then phone for a taxi from the train-taxi kiosk outside.

WESTERBORK

Westerbork had ironically originally been created in 1939 to shelter Jewish refugees from Germany, with the costs met by the Netherlands Jewish community. Even after the invasion, it remained under Dutch administration until the deportation era. The camp was expanded (the costs met through expropriated Jewish capital) and then brought under direct German control on 1 July 1942. The first transport of arrestees arrived on 14 July; most were dispatched to Auschwitz the very next day. Between that date and 15 September 1944, there were 93 transports from Westerbork, primarily to Auschwitz-Birkenau (54,930 people) and Sobibór (34,313). The majority of Westerbork's inmates spent only a few days or even hours in the camp but, more so than at Drancy or Mechelen, there was also a relatively privileged semi-permanent population which included the Jewish leadership and their employees, along with various supposedly 'exempt' categories such as certain groups of foreign Jews and war veterans. This community was allowed a considerable degree of autonomy by the Germans which enabled the development of a relatively 'normal' existence illustrated by the establishment of workshops, a hospital (with 1,725 beds and 120 doctors at its peak), a school and a wide range of sporting and cultural activities; the camp even had its own currency. However, the threat of deportation was constant with trains generally departing every Tuesday. Although the quotas for each transport were set by the Germans, their composition was left to the camp's Jewish leadership. This latter group largely consisted of German Jews, often Westerbork's original inhabitants, which inevitably fuelled tensions with the Dutch Jews. In due course, however, nearly all, regardless of background, were deported. When the Germans abandoned the camp in April 1945, in advance of the arrival of Canadian troops, only 876 Jews were left there.

Like Vught, the camp remained in use after the war as a military base and accommodation for Moluccans before being run down in the 1960s. A small national monument was created in 1970 but destruction of barracks continued, the last being removed in 1971. The site was partially taken over by large radio telescopes which still dominate its perimeter,

Westerbork (Photograph by Elizabeth Burns)

and the memory of Westerbork was allowed to fade. However, survivor pressure led to the creation of a museum in 1983, albeit more than two kilometres west of the camp because of the risk of cars interfering with the telescopes. Much of the focus of the exhibition (Mon–Fri, 10.00–5.00; Sat–Sun, 1.00–5.00 (from 11.00, July & Aug); €5; www.westerbork. nl) is on life in the 'city on the heath' with interesting material on the attempts by the SS to make the camp appear like a normal community, as evinced by remarkable footage filmed as late as 1944. The most striking displays, however, are the photographs of families and individuals along with snatches of home movies which form the prelude to the room dedicated to the deportations. As at Mechelen, panels with pictures list each train whilst a voice reads the names and ages of the 1,132 people who formed the first transport to Auschwitz on 15 July 1942.

The territory of the camp, properly transformed into a memorial area only in the 1990s, can be accessed either by a regular bus service (€1.50 single, €2 return) or by walking the trails through the forest or the main road (there is a map in the museum car park). The first sight to greet the visitor is a large poster of a deportation train behind five granite tomb-like blocks representing the main destinations of the transports (Auschwitz-Birkenau, Sobibór, Theresienstadt, Mauthausen, Bergen-Belsen); the numbers of people deported and killed are inscribed on each. A little further along, past a raised bank representing the site of the command building, barbed-wire fence marks the camp's boundaries – this is where the bus stops.

The destruction of the camp in the 1960s and 1970s was so thorough that it is now a large field broken by groups of trees with the radio telescopes lurking incongruously to the south. Nonetheless, imagination has been shown in attempting to convey its topography, with raised earthworks marking buildings and the central track towards the national memorial following the route of the main camp road. Concrete planks mark the site of the ramp where the deportation trains were loaded: they initially departed from nearby Hooghalen station but the line was extended into the camp in November 1942. A small tent-like structure, near a memorial stone from Jerusalem laid by Chaim Herzog in 1993, contains a scale model of Westerbork. The most remarkable element of the complex is the *Appellplatz* which is covered in 102,000 small bricks arranged in barrack-like rows; in an aerial view, they form a map of the Netherlands. Most of the bricks are marked with Stars of David but some carry flames, representing the 245 Roma who arrived on 16 May 1944; they were deported three days later, only 30 surviving. To the left of the main track, small sections of some barracks have been reconstructed in concrete, including Block 67 which formed part of the camp's punishment section. Amongst its inmates were the Franks, interned there on their arrival in August 1944 because they had broken the law by hiding! The 1970 national monument at the eastern extremity of the camp is striking – a piece of railway track whose frayed rails have been wrenched into the air, flanked by a watchtower and a bunker.

The site is close to the village of Hooghalen and is signposted east of the A28 between Beilen and Assen. Train-taxis can be taken from the former's station.

OTHER SITES

Amersfoort, south-east of Amsterdam, was the site of the main internment camp from 1941 until the opening of Vught; it also served as a holding centre for local Jews. Expanded in 1943, it then became a camp for political prisoners in transit to the Reich. The barracks (which were used by the army after the war) were demolished in 1968 and the site is now largely occupied by a police-training college. However, a small memorial complex incorporates an information centre and fragments of the camp (Mon–Fri, 9.00–5.00; Sat–Sun (Apr–Sept), 1.00–5.00; free; www.kampamersfoort.nl). The rifle range opposite, which served as the camp's execution grounds, was turned into a national monument in 1953. The site of the execution of 77 Soviet POWs in 1942 is nearby, marked by a memorial. The complex is on Appelweg, off Laan 1914, just beyond the N221 ring road to the south-west of the town near the junction with the N227.

The first major camp, superseded by Amersfoort and Vught, was at Schoorl, north of Bergen (near Alkmaar) and off the N9. The hundreds of Jewish men who were sent to Buchenwald and Mauthausen in early 1941 were first held there. There is a memorial stone at the site of the former gate by the Het Zandspoor visitors' centre at Oorsprongweg 1 to the north-west of the village.

CHAPTER 4

ITALY

Italy had the highest rate of Holocaust survival of any occupied nation other than Denmark. This may seem curious, given that it also had Europe's first Fascist government, but reflects the unusual history of the country's Jews.

Their presence in the peninsula dated back 22 centuries and was often characterised by misfortune. The Middle Ages brought the same vicissitudes as elsewhere in Europe, culminating in the creation of walled ghettos in most major cities in the sixteenth century. Indeed, the word 'ghetto' is commonly believed to derive from '*getto*', an Italian term for metal casting, in reference to the location of the first such community amidst Venice's former iron foundries. However, the nineteenth century brought a radical transformation when the armies of Piedmont swept away the ghettos as they unified Italy. There then followed a period of remarkably rapid Jewish advancement in public life. It would be wrong to say that anti-Semitism did not exist but, compared to states such as France and Germany, it was strikingly absent from mainstream politics. This is borne out by the fact that Italy had two Jewish prime ministers – Sidney Sonnino (a convert to Protestantism) and Luigi Luzatti – before the First World War. The Jewish community in turn became one of the most assimilated in Europe, characterised by high rates of mixed marriages and widespread devotion to the state, monarchy and liberalism. Even the emergence of Fascism did not significantly change the position of Jews except in the sense that all Italians suffered a loss of democratic rights. Mussolini's movement was nationalistic and xenophobic but, except for a few fanatics, generally free of anti-Semitism. Indeed, Jews joined the Fascist Party in roughly similar proportions to the rest of the population and some rose to senior positions within the regime. Even the Duce himself had a Jewish mistress, Margherita Sarfatti, in the mid-1930s.

The atmosphere changed with an anti-Semitic press campaign in late 1936, a prelude to 1938 racial laws which banned mixed marriages and forced Jews out of the professions. It is generally believed that this was a cynical ploy by Mussolini to impress Hitler as part of his attempt to secure a German alliance. Italy's belated entry into the war in June 1940 brought the internment of foreign Jews (often refugees from France)

and the requirement in May 1942 that adult Jewish men register for forced labour (although implementation was extremely lax). Yet despite the intensifying persecution, no Jews were handed over to the Germans whilst diplomats and military personnel in Italian-occupied territory in Greece, Yugoslavia and France openly defied Nazi policy. Many actively protected Jews by providing hiding places, false documents and even transport to Italy. Hitler fully intended the Jews of Italy and the occupied territories to share the fate of those elsewhere but was content to bide his time, unwilling to alienate his ally.

It was Fascist military failure that ironically brought the Holocaust to Italian soil. The Allied landings in Sicily caused Mussolini's fall from power in July 1943 and Italy's inevitable surrender in September, prompting German occupation of most of the country and the installation of Mussolini as the head of the puppet Salò Republic. German round-ups began in October 1943 and continued in the following months, assisted by a Salò decree in November ordering the Italian police to arrest Jews. The victims of the October seizures were dispatched straight to Auschwitz; those arrested by Italians were held in internment camps, notably Fossoli di Carpi, from where deportations began in early 1944. In total, some 6,800 of Italy's 45,200 Jews were deported; around 15 per cent thus lost their lives in the Holocaust.

Appalling though this figure is, it does mean that a large majority survived. There are several reasons why this should have been so. The most obvious is the relative brevity of the German occupation – nine months in Rome, twice as long in the north – amplified by the fact that Germany was obviously losing the war by this stage. However, the same was true of Hungary which was occupied even later yet with a far deadlier outcome. The fact that the Jewish community was assimilated and comparatively small undoubtedly assisted hiding. Ultimately, however, Jewish survival owed most to the initiative, courage and basic decency of thousands of people. A leading role was played by *Delasem*, a Jewish agency established in 1939 to assist foreign refugees in Italy. Although it went underground after the occupation, it was able to organise hiding places and supplies for thousands of foreign and Italian Jews. Many of the shelters were religious institutions, testifying to the singular importance of large numbers of Catholic priests and religious houses. More generally, a great many authority figures – policemen who tipped off Jews in advance of raids, doctors who hid them in hospitals, municipal officials who destroyed community lists – along with ordinary citizens of every background all played their part. There were, of course, less reputable characters, notably informants – the most notorious, Celeste di Porto in Rome, was herself Jewish – and Fascist thugs. Nonetheless, the level of assistance given to Italy's Jews by their compatriots is one of the brighter stories to emerge from the utter darkness of the Holocaust.

Italy was one of the earlier countries to begin to commemorate sites associated with the Holocaust and there are now a number of impressive memorials whilst the modern Jewish community of around 35,000 people is itself a testament to the failure of the Nazis in at least one country.

ROME

Rome was home to Italy's largest and possibly oldest Jewish community. Indeed, it is believed that the Jews were the only direct descendants of the peoples who inhabited ancient Rome to still reside in the city two millennia later. During the imperial period, the community grew to an astonishing 50,000, more than the Jewish population for the whole of Italy in the twentieth century. Jewish fortunes fluctuated but the most severe blow before the Holocaust was inflicted by Pope Paul IV who ordered the creation of the most notorious and long-lasting of the Italian ghettos in 1555; Jews were further forbidden to own property, subjected to compulsory Christian sermons and obliged to wear yellow badges when outside the ghetto. The abortive Roman Republic of 1849 tore down the walls but the ghetto was finally abolished only when Italian troops took the city in 1870. A period of unprecedented prosperity followed; even after Mussolini's racial laws, most of Rome's 12,000 Jews considered themselves safer than those elsewhere in Europe.

Tragically, this sense of security persisted after the Germans occupied the city. The community's leaders Dante Almansi and Ugo Foà, both former Fascist officials, seem to have believed Rome's Jews would be left unmolested, trusting in Mussolini and the Pope to protect them. Not all leaders were so sanguine, notably Chief Rabbi Israel Zolli who went into hiding after his warnings were ignored. However, most Jews were reluctant to credit tales of Nazi atrocities, an impression reinforced by the apparently decent behaviour of German troops. The first sign that this was mistaken came on 26 September 1943 when Herbert Kappler, head of the SD, demanded a ransom of 50 kilograms of gold to spare the Roman Jews. This extortion was Kappler's own initiative. He later claimed that he believed that hunting Jews was a waste of manpower compared to anti-partisan actions and hoped to persuade Himmler, who had already ordered the deportations, that economic exploitation was preferable. Less charitable observers have suggested that the move was a ploy to reassure Jews that they could be saved, giving Kappler time to prepare the deportation. If the latter was the case, it worked: the gold was raised and most Jews assumed they were secure. They were, therefore, taken by surprise by a massive round-up on 16 October, which began at 5 a.m. and netted 1,259 people. After the release of those belonging to exempted categories (mixed marriages, citizens of neutral countries) and of non-Jews mistakenly picked up, more than 1,000 were sent to Auschwitz. More were arrested in the following months: at least 1,700 Roman Jews were deported to Poland in total. Others fell victim to Fascist violence whilst 75 Jews were amongst the 335 people murdered in the infamous Ardeatine Caves massacre on 24 March 1944. This was a savage reprisal for a partisan attack on an SS police battalion which had left 33 Germans dead. Hitler is said to have ordered that 100 Italians be killed for every German. Kappler reduced the figure to 10 per German and compiled a list of partisans, POWs and other prominent figures; Jews held in Rome's prisons were added to make up the numbers.

Nonetheless, more than 10,000 Jews survived. A particularly important role was played by *Delasem;* its representative in Rome, Settimio Sorani, did not share the faith of men such as Foà in German promises and organised hideouts in the weeks before 16 October. When Sorani himself went into hiding, *Delasem* activities were overseen by the remarkable Father Benoit, a French Capuchin who had already distinguished himself in rescue operations in his homeland. Their efforts helped to save the lives of 4,000 Jews who were sheltered throughout the city. Many of the *Delasem* refuges were churches and convents whilst other Jews also came to such institutions independently. This prominent role for the Catholic Church raises the vexed question of the actions of Pope Pius XII, a subject which has generated heated polemics. It was widely believed after the war, including by many survivors, that he was responsible for the provision of shelter but this has never been proven whilst the Pope's failure to condemn the Holocaust, publicly or privately, even after the arrest of the Jews of his own city has been an especial source

Rome: Largo 16 Ottobre 1943 (Photograph by Elizabeth Burns)

of controversy. Nonetheless, the institution which Pius led, the source of much unhappiness in earlier Roman Jewish history, was undoubtedly significant in saving lives. As a result, the modern community numbers some 13,500, maintaining a unique and unbroken connection with the Jews of the ancient world.

The old ghetto and around the Tiber

Jews settled across the city after emancipation but the former ghetto area remained the home of around 4,000 in 1943 and was the principal target of the great round-up of 16 October. The heart of the warren of narrow streets is Via del Portico d'Ottavia, named after the ancient gate which dominates its eastern end. Victims of the round-up were forced to wait in the rain outside this gate before being taken across the Tiber. On the wall of the adjoining fourteenth-century Casa dei Vallati at 28–30 (now home to the city's Department of Ancient Monuments) there is a plaque to the victims, supplemented by another commemorating babies murdered in the Nazi camps. The small square in front of this building has been renamed Largo 16 Ottobre 1943.

Rome's main synagogue is nearby at Lungotevere dé Cenci 15, its walls inscribed with memorials to the deportees, victims of the Ardeatine Caves massacre and partisans. It was built at the beginning of the twentieth century and replaced five synagogues located in a single building – a result of papal restrictions – which had served the ghetto and which are now recalled by Piazza delle Cinque Scole, a block to the north-west. The synagogue complex also houses Rome's Jewish Museum (Sun–Thu, 10.00–4.15 (until 6.15, June–Sept); Fri, 10.00–1.15 (until 3.15, June–Sept); €7.50; www.museoebraico.roma.it), which contains an impressive range of objects from the original five synagogues and a small section on the Holocaust (entry also includes a guided tour of the temple). Facing the western side of the synagogue, the school at Via del Tempio 5 has a plaque to 112 former pupils murdered by the Nazis. Largo Stefano Gaj Tachè, a small square between the synagogue and the school, is named after a one-year-old killed in a terrorist attack on the synagogue in 1982.

The Isola Tiberina is opposite the synagogue, accessed by Ponte Fabricio. The Church of San Bartolomeo all'Isola on the southern side of the island was often the first point of refuge for Jews fleeing the round-ups – around 400 took temporary shelter here before moving on to more permanent hideouts. Two of the more notable of these refuges are located on the other side of the Tiber, on Via Garibaldi which runs up the Janiculum Hill from a point near to Ponte Sisto. The Augustinian Convent of Santa Maria del Sette Dolori at number 27 sheltered 103 Jews whilst the Convent of Nostra Signora di Sion, hidden behind high walls much further uphill at 28, provided sanctuary for 187, the largest number of any religious house.

Those who were less fortunate found themselves in Via della Lungara, north of the foot of Via Garibaldi. Victims of the 16 October round-up were taken to the Collegio Militare in the Palazzo Salviati at 81c–83 where they were held under armed guard for two nights with little food – most of those arrested early on the Saturday morning had not eaten all day – before being taken in trucks to the awaiting deportation train on 18 October. On the first night in the college, a baby was born in the courtyard, destined to end its short life in Poland with almost all of the other internees. There is a simple memorial plaque on the exterior wall. Most of the 671 Jews arrested in the later operations were held in the notorious Regina Coeli prison, located further south down the same street and encircled by Via di San Francesco di Sales.

Elsewhere

There is a memorial plaque to Sinti, Roma and Camminanti (travellers of Sicilian origin) victims of the Holocaust at Via degli Zingari (Gypsy Street) 13–14, north of the Forum (Cavour Metro). Further north, near Barberini Metro, Via Rasella was the scene of the partisan attack on 23 March 1944 which prompted the Ardeatine Caves massacre. Bullet holes still mark the building at 140–142 on the corner with Via del Boccacio: the gunfire came from the Germans who, thinking they had been attacked from the rooftops, fired upwards; in fact, the bomb had been left in a street-cleaner's cart.

Located east of the centre, Tiburtina station (accessible by the Metro) was the point of departure for the victims of the 16 October round-up, brought from the Collegio Militare and loaded into 18 cattle wagons over a period of eight hours. After each carriage was filled, the prisoners were locked in and forced to wait in the darkness whilst the trucks returned to collect more from the college. The transport, which contained at least 1,023 people, departed on 18 October and arrived at Auschwitz four days later; 15 men and one woman survived. On platform 1 there is a memorial plaque to the convoy as well as to the many other Romans deported to the Reich. Alongside are further plaques to individuals. There is a low-key Holocaust memorial in front of the ceremonial hall of the Jewish section of the Verano cemetery, accessible from the Piazza delle Crociate entrance, a short walk from Tiburtina.

South-east of the centre, Via Tasso 145–155 was the Gestapo headquarters in Rome (Manzoni Metro). This was where the Jewish community leaders had to deliver the 50 kilograms of gold on 28 September 1943. In fact, they brought a further 300 grams in case the Nazis attempted to underweigh the gold (as, indeed, an SS officer did). In the 1950s, a group of former cells became the Historical Museum of the Liberation (Tue, Thu–Fri, 9.30–12.30, 3.30–7.30; Wed, Sat–Sun, 9.30–12.30; free; www.viatasso.eu) which covers the Nazi terror – including the deportations and the Ardeatine Caves massacre – and the Resistance. The graffiti left by prisoners has been preserved.

From nearby Piazza San Giovanni in Laterano, one can catch bus 218 to the Ardeatine Caves (Fosse Ardeatine). The Germans had attempted to seal the caves with explosions in an effort to hide the location of the massacre but rumours brought pilgrims to the site within days although exhumation of the bodies was possible only after the liberation. They were found buried under rubble in piles – in order to save time, the Germans had ordered the victims to climb on top of those who were already dead so that they would not have to pile them up themselves later. In 1948, the site became a haunting national memorial (Mon–Fri, 8.15–3.15; Sat–Sun, 8.15–4.45; free). A section of the cave complex, visibly damaged by the German explosions, can be visited; the site of the killing is hidden behind a twisted metal gate. The victims are now buried in a concrete mausoleum outside, each grave bearing the individual's name, age and profession. The beautiful grounds also contain a small museum as well as a striking array of memorial sculptures.

FOSSOLI DI CARPI

Hastily constructed by the Fascist authorities in 1940, Fossoli di Carpi properly came into operation in 1942 as a camp for Allied prisoners of war. It was captured by the Germans a day after the surrender of 8 September 1943; they deported the POWs to the Reich to enable Fossoli's transformation into the principal transit camp in Italy. Between December 1943 and March 1944, its sole purpose was the internment of Jews, necessitating the construction of more barracks. In this period, Fossoli was officially controlled by the Salò Republic but in March 1944 the SS took over the 'new camp' (the newer barracks) which continued to hold Jews as well as political prisoners destined for deportation (mostly to Mauthausen). The 'old camp' remained under Salò control and held prisoners arrested by Mussolini's regime and civilians from enemy states. The exact numbers of those interned or deported are unknown as there are no surviving records but it is believed that more than 5,000 people were carried northwards on nine convoys. At least six transports were 'Jewish' (five to Auschwitz-Birkenau; one to Bergen-Belsen), comprising more than 40 per cent of all Italian Jews deported. Amongst them was Primo Levi who was included in the more than 600 people dispatched on the first transport to Auschwitz on 22 February 1944; he was one of only 20 who survived. The advancing front line led to the transfer of operations to Bolzano in August 1944 but the Germans continued to exploit the site, using it as a collection centre for Italian forced labourers until final evacuation in November.

The 'old camp' was destroyed in 1946 and turned over to agriculture. The 'new camp' had a colourful post-war history as, successively, an internment site for Fascists, a displaced persons camp, a centre for orphaned and abandoned children, and a home for Italian refugees from Yugoslavia. It was abandoned in 1970 and left to decay, resulting in a state of considerable disrepair. Restoration work began in 1998 and it is now possible to visit the site, albeit at very restricted times (Mar–1st Sunday in July: Sun, 10.00–12.30, 3.00–7.00 (afternoons outside European Summer Time, 2.30–5.30); free; www.fondazionefossoli. org; for visits at other times ring 059 688272). The atmospheric ruined barracks are often taken over by vegetation but one block has been restored, housing simple yet informative exhibitions on Fossoli's history. Another section of the barrack, on the restoration process, illustrates just how much the project has relied on the goodwill of often elderly volunteers.

In Carpi itself is an imaginative attempt to commemorate victims of Nazi terror – the Deportee Memorial Museum (Fri, Sat & public holidays, 10.00–1.00, 4.00–8.00 (afternoons outside European Summer Time, 3.00–7.00); €3; same website), located in a wing of the Palazzo dei Pio which dominates central Piazza Martiri. The initiative for the memorial came from former inmate Ludovico Barbiano at a time when the site of the camp was still in use. It consists of a series of rooms on whose walls are etched quotations from the last letters of condemned Resistance fighters from across Europe along with sketches by artists including Picasso and Léger. The walls of the final room are covered with the names of 14,314 Italian deportees whilst tall concrete slabs in the courtyard are inscribed with the names of camps and ghettos. The fact that the memorial and the camp are not currently open on the same days is obviously a source of some frustration although the former's hours have changed frequently. Carpi's former synagogue, which closed in 1922, is at Via Giulio Rovighi 57, off Via Jacopo Berengario across the square.

Carpi is north of Modena, east of the A22. The memorial museum is in the town centre, a short walk west from the train station. The camp is about 4 miles to the north, signposted off the SP413 (taxis are available in Carpi).

LA RISIERA DI SAN SABBA

La Risiera di San Sabba in Trieste was both the deadliest and most mysterious camp in Italy. A former rice-husking factory, it was taken over by the Germans in September 1943 and initially used as a prison camp for Italian servicemen. La Risiera soon took on a more sinister role, however, following the incorporation of the Trieste region into the Reich. This was reflected not only in its new designation as an internment camp for Jews, partisans and political prisoners in late October but also in the arrival from Lublin the previous month of Odilo Globocnik and his *Aktion Reinhard* personnel, including Christian Wirth and Franz Stangl. These were the men who had overseen the extermination of Polish Jewry and, earlier, of the disabled in Germany and Austria. Officially their role was to lead the fight against the Yugoslav partisans but the presence of the most experienced Nazi killers in Trieste has given rise to speculation that La Risiera was, or at least was intended to become, a death camp. Much is unknown about its exact functioning but the camp was commanded by Joseph Oberhauser, formerly Wirth's right-hand man in Bełżec, and staffed by the same SS personnel and Ukrainian auxiliaries who had served in Poland. It is estimated that more than 20,000 people passed through the camp; many, including more than 700 Jews, were deported to Auschwitz, Dachau and Mauthausen. However, La Risiera also became a killing centre in its own right. Eyewitness estimates suggest that 3,000 to 5,000 were murdered there, including Yugoslav partisans and Jewish mental patients from north-eastern Italy. In many cases, victims were strangled or clubbed to death by the Ukrainian guards but it seems that gas vans were also used, a chilling echo of the previous activities of Oberhauser's team. Like the Polish camps, La Risiera also became a vast centre for plunder, storing goods stolen from inmates and local Jewish communities.

The retreating Germans dynamited part of the complex during the evacuation in April 1945 but, after a period first as a refugee camp and then of neglect, the remaining buildings were incorporated into an impressive memorial site which opened in 1975 (daily, 9.00–7.00; free; www.retecivica.trieste.it/triestecultura/musei/civicimusei/risiera/risieraframe.htm). It is entered by a narrow passageway at the end of which, on the left, stands the 'death cell'. This was where condemned prisoners were held, often sharing the cell with the bodies of previous

La Risiera di San Sabba (Photograph by Elizabeth Burns)

victims. The adjacent building mainly housed the SS and workshops but the ground floor, open to visitors, contains 17 shockingly small cells which held up to six prisoners each. The interior of the adjoining building is now known as the 'room of crosses' because of the shapes formed by the large wooden beams which once separated the floors and rooms. This was where Jews and other prospective deportees were held, their memory recalled by small alcoves in the walls containing objects stolen from Trieste Jews and an urn of earth from Jerusalem. In the courtyard outside, metal plates mark out the site of the destroyed crematorium – the outline of its eastern wall is still visible on the main building whilst metal pillars indicate the location of the chimney. The Germans initially used the existing rice-drying facility for burning bodies but created a larger crematorium in April 1944 in line with the expansion of the murder operation. This was designed by Erwin Lambert, who was also responsible for the gas chambers in the T4 programme and at Treblinka, further arousing suspicion about the ultimate purpose of the Trieste camp. The liberators found three cement sacks full of bones and ashes amidst the rubble. A small exhibition of photographs and artefacts from La Risiera and other camps in the main building includes a replica of the club with which the Ukrainian guards killed prisoners – the original was found in the crematorium ruins in 1945. Around the back of the main building, past walls lined with plaques to groups and individuals, is a commemoration room with an exhibition on the history of the camp, the region and the partisans.

La Risiera is at Via Giovanni Palatucci 5 in the southern suburbs of Trieste. It can be reached by taking the regular number 10 bus to Via di Valmaura (past the football stadium) from where it is a short walk.

Trieste's large Byzantine-style synagogue at central Via San Francesco d'Assisi 19 was the victim of violence in October 1941 and July 1942 (i.e., before the German occupation), an illustration of the ethnic tensions in Trieste. On the first occasion, anti-Semitic graffiti was daubed on the walls; the second attack culminated in the destruction of sacred objects inside the building. The city is also home to the Carlo and Vera Wagner Jewish Museum (Tue, 4.00–7.00; Wed–Thu, 10.00–1.00, 4.00–7.00; Sun, 10.00–1.00, 5.00–8.00; €5.50), a collection of ritual objects, at Via del Monte 5/7 below the Castello.

OTHER SITES

Following Fossoli's evacuation in the summer of 1944, the main transit camp was located in the Dolomite town of Bolzano. Given the course of the war at this stage, most of those who passed through were partisans and other political prisoners although several hundred Jews were deported to Auschwitz. The camp was demolished in the 1960s; all that remains today is the perimeter wall, surrounding modern apartment blocks. Facing one side of the wall are six information panels, erected in 2004, which can be found in an alley running off Via Resia, opposite Via Piacenza, in the western suburb of Gries.

The original *getto* in Venice contains an affecting memorial in the form of a wall listing the names and ages of 247 murdered local Jews, accompanied by reliefs of Holocaust images by artist Arbit Blatas. It is located in Campo Nuovo Ghetto by the Casa di Riposo Israelitica (Jewish Old Age Home) from where the victims were taken. The city's

Jewish Museum (Sun–Fri, 10.00–6.00 (until 7.00, June–Sept); €3; www.museoebraico.it) – essentially a collection of Judaica – is in the same square.

One of the most remarkable stories of rescue occurred in Nonantola, north of Modena on the SP255. The elegant Villa Emma, on Via Mavora west of the centre, was used by *Delasem* to shelter orphaned Jewish children, mainly refugees from central Europe, who had been found hiding in Slovenia in 1942. They were later joined by child refugees from Croatia. Within 24 hours of the German occupation, all 73 had disappeared, sheltered within the community, so that the Nazis were unable to find a single child. Most were later smuggled into Switzerland with the help of two priests from Nonantola's seminary (part of the San Silvester Abbey in the centre of the town on Piazza Abbazio), where many of the children had been hidden. In 2004, the Villa Emma Foundation was created to preserve the memory of the solidarity of the people of Nonantola. The foundation's activities are very much a work in progress (www.fondazionevillaemma.org); in due course, it should be possible to visit the Villa.

CHAPTER 5

GERMANY

The Holocaust was, of course, initiated, planned and organised in Germany. Although the majority of murders occurred to the east, Germany was also the scene of the first and last chapters of the genocide, respectively the progressive marginalisation and terrorisation of its Jews and the appalling tragedy of the death marches.

Jews first settled in Germany in the Roman period but it was in the early Middle Ages that the country became a Jewish heartland with cities such as Mainz and Worms acquiring a global reputation as centres of learning. However, the era of persecution ushered in by the Crusades left these communities increasingly vulnerable to pogroms and expulsions. Growing numbers migrated eastwards, taking with them the Yiddish language as a permanent legacy of the German-Jewish experience. The situation of those Jews who remained further deteriorated as a result of the Protestant Reformation, most vividly expressed in Luther's shocking treatise *On the Jews and Their Lies*. The tide began to turn only in the eighteenth century when the ideas of the Enlightenment generated a more favourable climate, culminating in full emancipation in the nineteenth century. The new intellectual currents also had a significant impact within the Jewish community with Germany becoming the centre of the *Haskalah* (Jewish Enlightenment), manifested in the emergence of Reform Judaism, a high degree of assimilation (including extraordinary rates of mixed marriage), and a strong sense of loyalty to the newly united country.

Sadly, Jewish advancement was accompanied by a resurgence of anti-Semitism on the political right in the 1870s and 1880s. What differed from the past was a focus on race rather than religion, drawing inspiration from Social Darwinism to argue that Jews were an inferior people whose integration threatened Germany with degeneracy. The anti-Semites particularly targeted *Ostjuden*, the tens of thousands of refugees from the Russian Empire whose poverty, piety and political radicalism were easier targets than the bourgeois respectability of German Jews (regrettably, the latter were themselves often hostile towards the immigrants). Although the racists had little direct influence, their ideas gained some acceptance amongst the empire's elites. The most shameful manifestation was the army's 1916 census of Jews following baseless accusations that

they were avoiding military service; when the results proved to counter expectations, they were never published.

The ambiguities of German Jewish existence intensified in the Weimar Republic. On the one hand, the 1920s were a time of unprecedented equality and Jewish achievement. On the other, this encouraged the far right to blame Jews for the problems which beset the fledgling democracy; one very public demonstration of this hatred was the assassination of Foreign Minister Walter Rathenau in 1922. That said, the Nazis and other *völkisch* parties remained a marginal force electorally and it is inconceivable that Hitler could have come to power without the Depression. Even after 1929, there is little evidence that anti-Semitism was a major reason for the surge in Nazi support. Nonetheless, the idea that Germany had a 'Jewish problem' gained widespread currency in conservative circles whilst Nazi thugs were increasingly emboldened to assault Jews and their property, the violence escalating after Hitler's appointment as chancellor in January 1933. The first coordinated national action was the infamous shop boycott of 1 April 1933 which was swiftly followed (7 April) by the Law for the Restoration of the Professional Civil Service excluding Jews from government service (amongst them teachers, professors and judges). More than 60,000 Jews decided to emigrate in the first year of the Nazi regime, representing more than 10 per cent of the community which had stood at 522,000 by religion or 566,000 by race (the Nazi definition) in January 1933. Incidentally, the alleged authors of Germany's misfortunes formed less than 1 per cent of the national population.

A new phase of persecution began in 1935 with local campaigns of violence initiated by Nazi radicals. Their pressure for more far-reaching measures was one factor behind the notorious Nuremberg Laws of September which banned mixed relationships and effectively deprived Jews of their German citizenship. Jews were defined as those with three or four Jewish grandparents or with two Jewish grandparents and married to a Jew or practising Judaism. The considerable bureaucratic debate over such tortuous definitions – and, even more so, over those for the so-called *Mischlinge* with fewer Jewish ancestors – contrasted with the absence of any significant protest against the laws themselves. The more optimistic Jews hoped that their legal separation might usher in a period of stability, assuming that the Nazis would now consider the 'problem' solved. This impression appeared to be strengthened when overt anti-Semitism was toned down during the 1936 Olympics. However, plans were already being made to drive Jews further out of German life. Their fruits became evident in 1938 with a tranche of discriminatory laws (including bans on practising medicine and law and an order that all men take the name Israel and women Sara) accompanied by the imprisonment of 1,500 Jews in concentration camps and renewed local terror actions.

More than 15,000 Polish Jews were expelled from Germany in October 1938 and dumped in the no man's land between the two countries until Poland finally agreed to take them in. The assassination of a German diplomat in Paris by Herschel Grynszpan, the son of two deportees, in a revenge attack was then used as the excuse for a pogrom of as yet unprecedented ferocity on 9–10 November. The term *Kristallnacht* (Night of Broken Glass) fails to adequately describe the horror of what took place (*Novemberpogrom* is preferred in Germany today): at least 91 people were murdered, 200 synagogues burned down and tens of thousands of homes and businesses attacked. In the aftermath, 30,000 Jews were sent to camps and the community forced to pay a collective fine of 1 billion marks. Further laws in the ensuing days forbade Jews from owning businesses and expelled Jewish children from state schools. The Nazis' intention was clearly to intimidate Jews into leaving Germany whilst simultaneously denuding them of their assets. A further incentive to leave was provided by Hitler's chilling 'prophecy' to the Reichstag in January 1939 that world war (which would, of course, be the fault of the Jews) would result in 'the annihilation of the Jewish race in Europe'. In the course of 1938–39, almost 120,000 Jews emigrated.

War brought yet further restrictions. Jews were increasingly expelled from certain neighbourhoods of cities and subjected to forced labour. The Nazis, meanwhile, almost immediately launched a campaign of systematic mass murder in the form of the T4 programme. By late 1941, it was clear that German Jews would share the fate of the disabled. The yellow star was introduced in September and emigration (which had become increasingly impractical) was finally banned in October. Although several thousand Jews had already been deported in 1940, some as part of the Nisko Plan, others to Gurs in France, these actions were localised and did not yet have murder as their aim. By contrast, October 1941 saw the beginning of the deportation of all German Jews. The first were sent to Łódź, Minsk, Riga and Kaunas; almost all were killed in the course of 1942 although some of those taken to the Baltic in late 1941 were shot on arrival. Transports in 1942–43 went directly to

Auschwitz with the exception of around 40,000 mainly elderly Jews sent to Theresienstadt, itself an antechamber to Birkenau. By early 1943, the only Jews legally remaining in Germany were those in mixed marriages or working in essential industries. They were targeted in the *Fabrikaktion* of February 1943 which prompted protests in Berlin, an act of resistance whose rarity highlighted the prevailing attitude of indifference of most citizens. Although the more visible manifestations of persecution such as *Kristallnacht* caused some unease, there were no large-scale protests in contrast to those against the T4 programme.

Germany was declared free of Jews in July 1943. This was not the end of the Holocaust in the country, however. As defeat drew closer, inmates of Polish camps were transferred to Germany; even when Allied armies entered the country, prisoners were still being forced from camp to camp in increasingly futile death marches. Thousands were shot or died from exhaustion whilst the ever more crowded camps were engulfed by epidemics and starvation, most graphically illustrated by the infernal scenes which greeted the British liberators of Bergen-Belsen.

Ironically, Germany's Jews had one of the higher rates of survival of the Holocaust, because of pre-war emigration. Some 70,000 of those who fled were then caught in countries later occupied by the Nazis but around 300,000 reached safety. The majority of those who stayed were murdered, bringing the total death toll to approximately 200,000. Only around 20,000 Jews chose to remain in West Germany after 1945 (less than 1,000 lived in East Germany), but there has been an astonishing revival of Jewish life since reunification, largely because of immigration from the former USSR. The fact that Germany should again be seen as a haven for Jews – by the early twenty-first century more ex-Soviet Jews were migrating to Germany than to Israel – is an indication of how far the country has changed. For much of the Cold War, the reality of the Holocaust was obscured by the platitudes of Communist dogma in East Germany whilst there was a marked reluctance to fully confront the past in the Federal Republic, attested to by the failure to bring most of the murderers to justice. However, from the late 1960s, a younger generation of West Germans sought a more honest understanding of the Holocaust and proper commemoration of it, a process which has accelerated since unification. There are thus few, if any, countries in Europe where there is greater awareness of the Holocaust or such public memorialisation of it.

BERLIN

The heart of the Nazi empire was also home to Germany's largest Jewish population, some 160,000 people by 1933. A small community had existed in the Middle Ages but the familiar pattern of pogroms and expulsions culminated in the banishment of all Jews in the 1570s; it was to be another hundred years before they were allowed to resettle. As the capital of the increasingly powerful Prussian state, Berlin's intellectual influence spread in the eighteenth century and the city became the centre of the *Haskalah*. Even so, the community numbered less than 10,000 as late as the 1840s. Its astonishing growth thereafter was primarily the result of immigration from eastern Europe which continued in the inter-war period. This development also gave Berlin Jewry a character different to that of communities in the rest of Germany. Whilst there were certainly thousands of educated, middle class and highly assimilated Jews, the new arrivals tended to be poor and more likely to be drawn to Orthodox Judaism or radical politics.

The size and nature of the Berlin community made it especially vulnerable to the emergence of the Nazis even before 1933, the *Ostjuden* being a highly visible target for SA thugs. As the capital, Berlin was naturally the first city to be subject to the ever-increasing restrictions. The violence of 1938 was particularly severe in the city, with attacks on synagogues as early as May. The largest number of Polish Jews rounded up in October were from Berlin whilst the name *Kristallnacht* itself derived from the broken glass from the Jewish stores of Leipziger Straße. In the aftermath, several thousand people were sent to Sachsenhausen and Jewish homes in wealthier districts were confiscated. The result was a surge in emigration to the extent that around 90,000 people had left the city before the 1941 ban. Through that year, Goebbels, as *Gauleiter* of Berlin, had pressed for the deportation of the remainder, arguing that the capital should be the first city in the Reich to be free of Jews. This process began on 18 October when 1,000 people were sent to Łódź; around 60,000 were deported in the next 18 months and the city was declared *Judenfrei* in June 1943. There were, in reality, still somewhere between 6,000 and 7,000 Jews (in mixed marriages, in hiding or pretending to be non-Jews), but they represented less than 5 per cent of the 1933 population.

It was expected that survivors would not wish to stay after the war but a few thousand remained, almost entirely in West Berlin. The community has been transformed, however, since 1989 by the influx from the former

Berlin: Neue Synagogue (Photograph by Elizabeth Burns)

Soviet Union. Although it may not be on the scale of a century earlier, this wave of migration has more than doubled the estimated Jewish population to more than 20,000. Little of the pre-war city survives but the period since the fall of the Wall has also seen a dramatic renewal of interest in Berlin's Jewish heritage, most vividly expressed by its 2001 Jewish Museum.

The Jewish quarter and eastern Berlin

Jews resided throughout Berlin by the 1930s but the highest concentration lived in the Spandauer Vorstadt and Scheunenviertel neighbourhoods to the north and east of the Museum Insel. The most visible reminder of their presence is the celebrated Neue Synagogue at Oranienburger Straße 28/30, inaugurated in 1866 to serve the rapidly growing community. The temple was one of the few to survive *Kristallnacht,* thanks to the district police chief Wilhelm Krützfeld who drove the mob away with his revolver; he was later removed from his post. The building (used as a Wehrmacht store from 1940) was less fortunate in 1943 when it

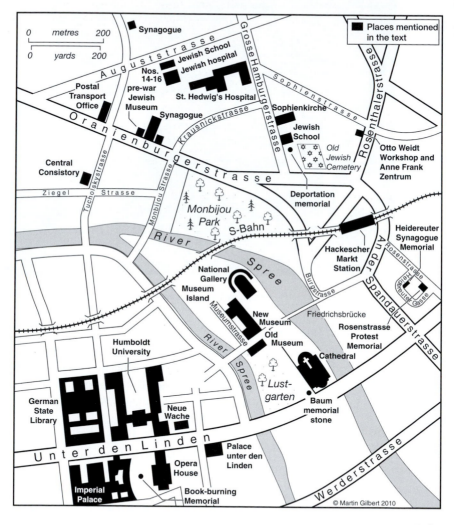

Berlin

was badly damaged during an RAF bombing raid. It was unsurprisingly neglected by the DDR until 1988 when partial restoration began, a process completed in 1995. The remnants have been impressively renovated, notably the spectacular Moorish dome, and the synagogue is now one of Berlin's major tourist attractions (Sun–Mon, 8.00–8.00 (until 6.00, Nov–Feb); Tue–Thu, 10.00–6.00; Fri, 10.00–5.00 (until 2.00, Oct–Mar); €5; www.cjudaicum.de). A ground-floor exhibition covers the history of the building and community, its final room looking out onto the outline of the destroyed sections. The most poignant feature is a map of the district on the floor, the streets represented by metal bars and prominent Jewish buildings by cabinets whose cases and draws reveal the story of each. There are temporary exhibitions upstairs along with a screen carrying the names of 50,576 deportees; only 4,641 survived.

Tucholskystraße to the west is named after Kurt Tucholsky, a Weimar-era Jewish satirist and socialist activist who committed suicide in Sweden in 1935. Number 9 is the home of the Central Consistory of Jews in Germany whilst 40, to the north of Oranienburger Straße, was the site of the Adass Yisroel Orthodox Synagogue which was closed after *Kristallnacht* and destroyed by wartime bombing. The new building on the site was restored to Adass Yisroel in 1989 and today again houses a synagogue. The organisation had originally been founded in the late nineteenth century as a reaction to the prevailing Reform and Liberal tendencies, reflecting the growing presence of eastern European immigrants.

Around the corner, Auguststraße was home to a number of communal institutions. The dilapidated redbrick at 11–13 was a girls' school (closed in 1942) whilst 14–16 next door housed a Jewish hospital until 1914 and then several organisations including *Ahawah*, a home for refugee children from the east; from 1941 to 1943, it was turned into an assembly site for elderly and sick Jews. Both buildings have been returned to the community but a shortage of funds means that much restoration work remains to be done. Number 17 also housed a variety of offices including those of the Association of Eastern European Jews.

A left turn leads to two interesting memorials on Koppenplatz at the top of Große Hamburger Straße. A sculpture of a table and two chairs, one knocked over, is intended to represent the deportees' enforced departure. In the courtyard of number 6, accessible through the Herrmann & Wagner Gallery, is a memorial to Ilse Goldschmidt, the house's murdered former owner. Returning down Große Hamburger Straße to Oranienburger Straße, one will notice a number of metal cobbles carrying the names of former residents and their fate, some of the more than 1,000 such memorials in Berlin installed as part of the *Stolpersteine* project which attempts to honour victims of Nazism in dozens of German cities (www.stolpersteine.com). The empty space at 15/16 was the site of a house destroyed by a bomb in 1945. Plaques on the walls list the names and occupations of former residents, a project by the artist Christian Boltanski. However, this is not – as is often assumed – solely a Holocaust memorial, Jewish victims of the Nazis mixing with Germans killed in air raids or the Battle for Berlin. Number 27 opposite was a Jewish school, its original inscription ('Boys School of the Jewish Community') still above the door (girls were admitted from 1931). The number of students doubled within the first year of Nazi rule, a testament to the growing problems faced by Jewish children in state schools. The school was closed in 1942 and held the residents of the home for the elderly next door prior to their deportation. It is once again a Jewish school, having been restored to the community in 1992. The old people's home, now marked only by traces, was itself one of the principal holding centres for prospective deportees, secured by barred windows and armed guards (although some inmates escaped during an air raid on 31 December 1942). It adjoined the oldest Jewish cemetery in the city which was used until the nineteenth century. The graves were destroyed in 1943 but the site was converted into a memorial park in the 1970s and has recently undergone restoration. By the entrance is an ensemble of sculpted figures representing the deportees; this was originally designed for the Ravensbrück memorial but sat uneasily with Communist representations of the Holocaust. There is also a gravestone for the reformist philosopher Moses Mendelssohn which replaces the original destroyed by the Nazis.

On parallel Rosenthaler Straße, Hackesche Höfe is a series of interlinking Art Nouveau courtyards built for Jewish tenants and businesses; it now houses upmarket shops, restaurants and cultural institutions. The next passageway at Rosenthaler Straße 39 contains two contrasting museums. That on the left of the courtyard is based in the workshop of the brush manufacturer Otto Weidt (daily, 10.00–8.00; free; www.museum-blindenwerkstatt.de). A committed pacifist and opponent of Nazism, Weidt employed mainly blind and deaf Jews in his enterprise (he was almost blind himself) and saved many from deportation by bribing and misleading the authorities. A series of rooms labelled in both type and Braille tell the story amidst the machines and products of the workshop. At the back is the concealed room where Weidt hid the Horn family; they were discovered and sent to Auschwitz in 1943 although Weidt himself survived his interrogation. The Anne Frank Zentrum at the back of the courtyard (Tue–Sun, 10.00–8.00 (until 6.00, Oct–Apr); €4; www.annefrank.de) is primarily aimed at school parties with interactive displays promoting a general message of tolerance alongside the story of Anne's life.

Located on the other side of Hackescher Markt S-Bahn, Rosenstraße was the site of a remarkable act of defiance during the *Fabrikaktion* of February 1943 when a former Jewish community building at 2–4 (now destroyed) held some of the arrested men. Their non-Jewish wives and other relatives came to the street in increasing numbers until the men were released on Goebbels's orders. Recent research has suggested that most of the men were not actually about to be deported but the demonstrations were nonetheless an all too rare example of protest against Nazi anti-Semitic policy. They are marked by large stone sculptures of the women in a small grassy square and kiosks carrying information panels at either end of the street. Most visitors miss another memorial, slightly hidden behind the trees, in the western corner of the square: foundations discovered in 2000 mark the site of the Heidereutergasse Synagogue, the oldest in Berlin, which was badly damaged on *Kristallnacht*; the ruins were pulled down by the Communists in the 1960s.

Beyond Scheunenviertel, the former East Berlin is largely dominated by concrete tower blocks and vast Stalinist highways but a few relics of the Jewish past survive, mainly concentrated around Kollwitzplatz near Senefelderplatz U-Bahn. An information board by the station's northern exit explains the area's Jewish history. The large redbrick building to the right at Schönhauser Allee 22 was a home for the elderly; its residents were deported to Auschwitz and the site taken over by the SS. The cemetery next door was surprisingly left largely unmolested although some stones were destroyed during the Battle for Berlin. At its rear is the closed gate to the *Judengang*, a 40-metre passageway which exits onto Kollwitzplatz between Knaackstraße 39 and 43 (where there is a gate marked with Stars of David). The origins of the passage are unclear: one legend is that Jews were forbidden to use the cemetery's front entrance because the Prussian king did not wish to be disturbed by funeral processions on the way to his summer residence. A little to the east is the Rykestraße Synagogue (number 53), the largest surviving temple in Germany (Thu, 2.00–6.00; Sun, 11.00–4.00; €7). It was attacked on *Kristallnacht* but was spared due to the fire risk to

Berlin: Memorial to the Murdered Jews of Europe (Photograph by Elizabeth Burns)

the densely populated neighbourhood. One of the few synagogues to return to use after the war, it was starved of funds by the Communists, a situation rectified by a 2007 restoration. The water tower opposite the bottom of Rykestraße was used as an improvised concentration camp in the early months of the regime.

The Weißensee Jewish cemetery is one of the largest in Europe and was used as a hiding place by Jews and deserters during the war. It is located further north-east, at the end of Herbert-Baum-Straße (a short walk back along Berliner Allee from the Albertinenstraße stop for tram M4). The street is named after a Jewish Communist who led an attack on an exhibition of anti-Semitic and anti-Soviet propaganda in May 1942; he and his associates were soon captured and murdered whilst 500 Jews were rounded up as a 'reprisal'. His gravestone is on the honour row. There is a Holocaust memorial in front of the ceremonial hall whilst field G7 contains the 'urn field' in which the ashes of camp victims are buried.

Central Berlin

At the corner of the Lustgarten, opposite the Berliner Dom, is a DDR memorial to Herbert Baum at the site where his attack took place; modern perspex panels on the stone cube explain the specifically Jewish dimension which the Communists omitted to mention. Nearby Bebelplatz, opposite Humboldt University, was the site of the infamous book burning encouraged by Goebbels in May 1933: more than 20,000 books by Jewish, left-wing and 'degenerate' authors were destroyed, a move copied by students in other German cities. There is a symbolic memorial at the heart of the square where a glass panel looks down onto empty book shelves. Surrounding plaques carry Heine's famous quote: 'Where they burn books, they will also in the end burn people'.

The largest cluster of memorials in Berlin is at the other end of Unter den Linden by the Tiergarten. The most prominent is the Memorial to the Murdered Jews of Europe, a 19,000-square-metre site covered in an undulating field of 2,711 large concrete blocks which rather resembles an enormous Jewish cemetery from afar. Its location in the centre of the city (the north-eastern corner is on the site of Goebbels's bunker) is a clear statement of intent to remember but one can see why the monument, inaugurated in 2005, has been criticised. Unlike the two designs vetoed by Chancellor Kohl in the 1990s (one of which would have created a large concrete plate on which all known names of Holocaust victims would have been inscribed), the memorial is starkly anonymous: nothing, other than the visitor's prior knowledge, indicates its purpose. More depth is given to the site by the presence of the 'information centre' – essentially a Holocaust museum – underneath the memorial (Tue–Sun, 10.00–8.00 (until 7.00, Oct–Mar); free; www.stiftung-denkmal.de) which was added to the design only at the insistence of the Bundestag. Amongst the several other controversies which beset the construction, the most serious was the revelation that a subsidiary of the company providing the anti-graffiti spray had manufactured the Zyklon B pellets used in some of the death camps. In a further twist, a survey in 2008 revealed that over half of the blocks were already cracked, an embarrassment for a project which cost over €25 million.

Some critics of the memorial argued that it was wrong to commemorate only Jewish victims of the Nazis with the result that two new initiatives have been undertaken. In the south-eastern corner of the Tiergarten, opposite the bottom of the Holocaust memorial, is a 2008 monument to homosexual victims in the form of a similar concrete block with a window through which visitors see a looped film of two men kissing (this will rotate every two years with a video of women). In the north-eastern corner of the park, opposite the Reichstag, construction finally began in 2008 (after many years of delays) on a memorial fountain to the murdered Sinti and Roma. Perhaps the most effective monument in the area, however, is also the simplest: a row of more than 90 iron plates outside the Reichstag, each carrying the name of a parliamentarian murdered by the Nazis. By contrast, little has been done to commemorate disabled victims. Outside the Berlin Philharmonie, built on the site of the confiscated Jewish villa where the murders were orchestrated at Tiergartenstraße 4, there is only a simple plaque. The abstract Richard Serra sculpture alongside was not created as a memorial although it was later designated as one after activists had drawn attention to the history of the site.

The Bendlerblock at Stauffenbergstraße 13–14, a short distance from the Philharmonie, housed the high command of the German armed forces and as such was where Count von Stauffenberg and other officers formulated the doomed July Bomb Plot of 1944. After planting his bomb at Hitler's Wolf's Lair headquarters in East Prussia on 20 July, Stauffenberg returned to Berlin assuming the Führer was dead. That same night, he and his fellow conspirators were executed in the courtyard, marked by a statue and a memorial plaque. The building is still used by the Ministry of Defence but a section is given over to the German Resistance Memorial Centre which provides a thorough overview of anti-Nazi movements, including Jewish resistance (Mon–Wed, Fri, 9.00–6.00; Thu, 9.00–8.00; Sat–Sun, 10.00–6.00; free; www.gdw-berlin.de).

The Gestapo headquarters were located at Niederkirchnerstraße 8 in the heart of the government district to the south of the Holocaust memorial. Badly damaged in the war, the buildings were demolished in 1956 but sections of the basement were rediscovered during excavations in the 1980s. The site, next to a section of the Berlin Wall, was converted into an open-air exhibition, the Topography of Terror (daily, 10.00–8.00 (until dusk, Oct–Apr); free; www.topographie.de), which details the development of the police state through placards on the surviving walls (English information sheets are available from the small information centre). It was announced in 2007 that construction would finally start on a museum at the site after years of delays.

Almost directly east along Zimmerstraße (or a few minutes from Spittelmarkt U-Bahn) is the site of the Lindenstraße Synagogue. Badly damaged on *Kristallnacht*, the ruined temple was pulled down after the war and an office block built. Through the latter's archway at Axel-Springer-Straße 50, concrete benches have been placed to indicate the location of the pews. Further down the street at Lindenstraße 9–14 (also accessible from Hallesches Tor U-Bahn) is Berlin's justly celebrated Jewish Museum (daily, 10.00–8.00 (until 10.00, Mon); €5; www.jmberlin.de). Daniel Liebeskind's stunning building is the chief reason for its fame but the imaginative exhibition makes good use of the space to relate the course of German Jewish history. The Shoah inevitably intrudes, notably in the form of the Axis of the Holocaust in the basement, a passage lined with the names of murder sites and pictures and personal effects of victims which leads to the darkened Holocaust Tower, and the unnerving *Shalechet*, an installation by Israeli artist Menashe Kadishman on the ground floor. The relevant section of the main exhibition uses the building to good effect to trace the development of Nazi persecution and the responses to it. There is a particularly moving collection of pictures taken by the American photographers Meyer Levin and Eric Schwab in 1945; the latter found his mother in Theresienstadt.

The Fraenkelufer Synagogue was mostly destroyed by *Kristallnacht* and air raids but a wing survives, accompanied by a small memorial, at Fraenkelufer 10 (Kottbusser Tor U-Bahn).

Western Berlin

On the south-western exterior wall of Nollendorfplatz U-Bahn station, a pink triangle commemorates gay victims of the Nazis. Outside the next stop, Wittenbergplatz, a very basic memorial lists major Nazi camps. Close to Kurfürstendamm station, the modern synagogue at Joachimstalerstraße 13 occupies a hall in a pre-war Jewish school building. The nearby Fasanenstraße Synagogue (at 79–80) is a modern functional building on the site of the original destroyed in 1938. Remnants of the masonry stand outside along with a huge sculpted Torah roll and a memorial wall with names of camps and ghettos. The Pestalozzistraße Synagogue (in the back courtyard of 14, a few minutes from Wilmersdorfer Straße U-Bahn) survived the pogrom after the fire department, fearing the spread of flames to other buildings, intervened.

The Bayerisches Viertel in Schöneberg was an area of significant Jewish settlement, especially by the wealthy (hence its nickname of 'the

Jewish Switzerland'). Eighty street signs in the district quote different anti-Semitic laws in an attempt to illustrate the pervasiveness of Nazi discrimination; there is a map of the locations in Bayerischer Platz, opposite the U-Bahn station of the same name. When the panels were unveiled in 1993, many local residents initially assumed they were the work of neo-Nazis and complained to the police. There is a simple memorial at Münchener Straße 37 to the former synagogue which stood here. It survived 1938 and was used as a storehouse for stolen Jewish goods in 1941 but was destroyed later in the war.

There is a memorial to a former Adass Yisroel synagogue on Siegmunds Hof by the Spree (Tiergarten S-Bahn). One of the most striking Holocaust memorials in Berlin is a little further north at the site of the Levetzowstraße Synagogue (on the corner with Jagowstraße) which was used as an assembly point for 37,500 people during the deportations. Having survived *Kristallnacht* and the war, it was astonishingly demolished in the 1950s. The memorial consists of three connected elements: chained roughly sculpted marble figures entering a stylised cattle wagon, floor plaques with images of Berlin's synagogues and a giant metal sheet listing the deportation trains. These transports departed from Moabit freight station to the north; a memorial on the Putlitz Bridge (Westhafen S-Bahn) overlooks the station. An additional plaque documents the repeated attacks to which the memorial was subjected in the early 1990s.

One of the first memorial sites to be established to the victims of Nazism (1952) is within the grounds of Plötzensee Prison on Hüttigpfad (daily, 9.00–5.00 (until 4.00, Nov–Feb); free; www.gdw-berlin.de; bus 123 to Gendenkstätte Plötzensee). Between 1890 and 1932, 36 people were executed at the prison (all murderers); between 1933 and 1945, the number was 2,891. They were primarily political opponents, amongst them dozens of people associated with the July Bomb Plot. Although the site was not directly connected with the Holocaust, the memorial – a wall and the remaining sections of the execution buildings – is dedicated to all victims of the dictatorship.

The Charlottenberg Jewish cemetery in the far west of the city was established after the war. Ashes from Auschwitz are buried in front of a simple memorial which is surrounded by stones erected by survivors to relatives and friends. The grave of Heinz Galinski, who survived Auschwitz and Belsen to become the Jewish community's post-war

Berlin: Grunewald station (Photograph by Elizabeth Burns)

chairman, is nearby. His original gravestone, smashed by neo-Nazis in 1998, has been kept alongside. The cemetery is accessed by a path from Scholzplatz on the corner of Heerstraße and Am Postfenn (Pichelsberg S-Bahn, then walk south).

The Jews of the southern suburb of Steglitz are commemorated by the *Spiegelwand*, a mirrored wall listing the names and addresses of the 1,723 people deported from the district along with a brief history of the community, on Hermann-Ehlers-Platz, a square used as a market by day (Rathaus Steglitz U- & S-Bahn).

Grunewald station (S-Bahn and regional trains) to the south-west of the city was the departure point for most transports. Metal sheets listing the date of departure, number of passengers and destination of each train have been placed on the deportation ramp to form the excellent *Gleis 17* memorial. Outside the station entrance is a further memorial, a concrete wall out of which haunting silhouettes have been hewn.

WANNSEE

A former industrialist's mansion overlooking a beautiful lake was the site of the notorious Wannsee Conference of 20 January 1942 at which the 'final solution of the Jewish question' was discussed. The meeting was not, as is sometimes supposed, the place where the Holocaust was decided upon; by the time it convened, probably more than 1 million Jews had already been murdered. Rather, its purpose was to determine how to implement the genocide, in particular its extension from the Jews of Poland and the USSR to those of the rest of Europe. Reinhard Heydrich, Himmler's deputy and the man charged by Hitler and Göring with responsibility for the 'final solution', therefore brought together representatives of the agencies which would be involved in this process (the conference was originally scheduled for 9 December 1941 but was postponed due to Japan's attack on Pearl Harbor). The issues discussed were recorded by Adolf Eichmann in the official minutes albeit euphemistically; at his trial in Jerusalem, Eichmann explained that Heydrich had instructed him to 'clean up' the record to avoid explicit language. Heydrich, after reviewing Nazi policy up to this point, explained the agreed policy of 'evacuation to the east' which would include all 11 million Jews that the Germans believed to be living in Europe (including those in Britain and neutral countries). Stronger Jews would be put to work in which most would 'fall away'; there could be few illusions about the fate of those unable to work. Much of the subsequent discussion was taken up with bureaucratic wrangling over the status of Jews in mixed marriages and their offspring. As the meeting drew to a close, cognac was served and the participants discussed, in the words of the minutes, 'different types of possible solutions'.

For most of the post-war period, the elegant villa was used as a hostel for schoolchildren but it was converted into a memorial and educational site (daily, 10.00–6.00; free; www.ghwk.de) on the fiftieth anniversary of the conference. The heart of the well-labelled permanent exhibition (which covers the evolution of the Holocaust) is room 9 where the meeting took place: panels provide biographies of the participants and highlight the issues discussed. An excellent library and a media centre are upstairs.

The villa can be easily reached by taking the Berlin S-Bahn to Wannsee and then bus 114 to the Haus der Wannsee-Konferenz stop. The address is Am Großen Wannsee 56–58, a short walk back.

BRANDENBURG

Brandenburg was the site of the first T4 centre to commence its murderous operations and the only one not to be located in a medical facility; the site chosen was a former prison which had briefly served as a concentration camp in the early months of the regime. A brick barn was converted into a gas chamber and the first 'demonstration' took place in December 1939 or January 1940 when around 20 patients were gassed in the presence of an invited audience of officials and doctors. The 'success' of this operation established carbon monoxide as the method of killing for T4; it was later employed by the same staff in *Aktion Reinhard*. Amongst them were physician-in-chief Dr Irmfried Eberl (first commandant of Treblinka), cook Kurt Franz (the most feared officer in Treblinka and its final commandant), and policeman Christian Wirth (ultimately overseer of all T4 centres and later of the *Aktion Reinhard* camps). The murders continued until October 1940 when the operation was transferred to Bernburg, probably because the local population was increasingly aware of what was happening. It is believed that 9,772 people had been killed by this time.

The complex served as a detention facility for forced labourers for the remainder of the war. Although some buildings were destroyed in this period, it was the Communists who, with customary sensitivity, demolished most of the remainder and constructed a car park over much of the site. The only indication of Brandenburg's gruesome history was a wall plaque erected in 1962. However, pressure from victims' families and disability rights groups finally led to a more substantial reminder in 1997 with a series of information boards, a low-key but oddly touching commemoration. Behind the main group at the rear of the car park are the partial foundations of the barn where the gas chamber was located. The site is on the southern side of Nicolaiplatz (trams 1, 2 and 6; buses F, H and W). The first panel is on Plauer Straße and the second to the left in the courtyard of the municipal administration building which was the main block in the prison. The remaining panels are in the car park.

The Brandenburg-Görden clinic at Anton-Saefkow-Allee 2 in the north of the city (tram 1, Asklepios Klinik stop) also played a key role in the medical murder. Almost 2,000 women were sterilised there before the war; in 1940, it became the first specialist centre for the murder of disabled children whilst also serving as a transit facility for adults being sent to the T4 centre (where some of Görden's child patients were also murdered).

Hans Heinze, head of the clinic's paediatric department, was one of the three medical assessors whose judgements determined the fate of disabled children across the Reich. At Görden, he established a research department in which the brains of the victims were studied; the clinic also served as a training institution for young doctors involved in the murder programmes. There is a small memorial close to the entrance on the right of the main path whilst the Psychiatric Museum (in house 23 at the rear of the complex) contains an exhibition on the hospital's role in the Nazi period although its opening hours are unpredictable (brandenburg@asklepios.com). Brandenburg prison (next door to the clinic) housed political prisoners.

Brandenburg is on the B1, west of Berlin from where there are regular trains. Around the corner from the station, a memorial marks the empty space of the former Jewish cemetery (destroyed in 1938) on Geschwister-Scholl-Straße.

SACHSENHAUSEN

Sachsenhausen concentration camp was created in 1936 in Oranienburg to the north of Berlin. There had already been a makeshift camp in the town in 1933–34 but the new institution was destined to be far larger and more important. Its proximity to the capital led to it becoming the administrative centre for the whole camp system and it was used as a training facility for SS officers; amongst its graduates was the future Auschwitz commandant Rudolf Höss. Most pre-war inmates were political prisoners and Sachsenhausen became the principal internment centre for high-profile opponents of the Nazis, amongst them Pastor Martin Niemöller and Herschel Grynszpan (captured in France in 1940). More than 5,000 Jews were sent to the camp after *Kristallnacht* whilst a further 900 (mainly Polish citizens living in Berlin) were interned there after the outbreak of the war. Nearly all remaining Jewish inmates were deported to Auschwitz in 1942; an exception was made for 142 prisoners, many of them from Auschwitz, engaged in Operation Bernhard, a plan to produce fake British banknotes in an attempt to destabilise the enemy's economy (depicted in the film *The Counterfeiters*). However, most wartime prisoners were Poles and Soviet POWs; amongst the latter was Stalin's son Yakov Dzhugashvili, who died (probably while running into the electric fence) in 1943. More than 10,000 Red Army soldiers were murdered in the camp: most were shot but others fell victim, in September 1941, to tests that the SS carried out of its

Sachsenhausen (Photograph by Elizabeth Burns)

newly developed gas vans (a small gas chamber was constructed in the camp itself in 1942 or 1943). There were further mass murders in advance of the evacuation but most prisoners were forced westward on death marches: when the Red Army arrived on 22 April 1945, only 3,000 were left in the camp. It is estimated that 200,000 people passed through Sachsenhausen and its satellites; around 30,000 died, most of them Soviet POWs.

The camp was taken over by the NKVD between 1945 and 1950. Around 60,000 people were interned, some of them Nazis, many not; 12,000 died. The site became a memorial in 1961 and inevitably reflected the DDR's ideological preoccupations but reunification has enabled a more effective and honest presentation of the past (daily, 8.30–6.00 (until 4.30, Oct–Mar; indoor facilities closed on Mon); free; www.stiftung-bg.de), beginning with the useful visitors' centre by the car park (built on the site of a weapons' maintenance workshop). A scale model outside gives a sense of the huge size of the wider Sachsenhausen complex, which stretched well beyond the memorial area. The route from the visitors' centre leads along the *Lagerstraße* which separated the SS barracks to the right from the command buildings and inmates' camp on the left. A museum building to the right of the entrance to the latter covers the first Oranienburg camp and the history of Sachsenhausen in East Germany alongside temporary displays. To the left, near memorials to a range of inmates, is the former commandant's house. This will eventually house an exhibition on the SS whilst the solid gatehouse will cover the organisation of Sachsenhausen.

These planned new exhibits are indicative of the ongoing transformation of the site. The original 1961 memorial concept focused on the victory of 'anti-Fascism' and saw little need to preserve the original camp: most buildings were destroyed and those that remained not well cared for. The results are apparent in the semi-circular *Appellplatz*, only a concrete wall representing the barracks which once surrounded it. Few original structures remain so the aim of the current administration is to use them to maximum effect. This is the case with Blocks 38 and 39 in the 'small camp' (where most Jewish prisoners were held) to the right; both were reconstructed from original materials in 1958–60, and again after a 1992 arson attack, traces of which are still visible. Barrack 38 houses an exhibition on Jewish prisoners. The centrepiece is a glass case with scraps of shoes and other artefacts discovered during drilling in 1996. There is a fascinating section on the counterfeiting group. Barrack 39 addresses daily life with a multimedia display based on the recollections of 20 former prisoners. The surviving wing of the nearby prison block adjoins memorials in the execution yard.

The only surviving buildings behind the concrete wall (past a plaque marking the site of the gallows) are the laundry to the left (housing a cinema and meeting room) and the kitchen to the right. The latter is given over to a new exhibition covering the camp's history. The bombastic obelisk behind was the original centrepiece of the memorial. At the northern point of the triangular camp, Tower E (which houses a small exhibit on the relationship between the camp and the town) overlooks the entrance to Sachsenhausen's 'special section' where Soviet POWs were held and where Germans were later interned by the NKVD. A new museum and surviving barracks relate the history of the latter period near to the mass graves of its victims.

An exhibit on the western wall of the main camp marks the site of 'Station Z', the centre of killing operations from 1942. The foundations of the crematorium and gas chamber are under a canopy behind the wall, near ash pits and an execution trench. The extermination facilities were intact when the camp was liberated but were blown up by the East Germans in the early 1950s and the site used as a dumping ground (it was originally intended to have a police firing range there!) until the creation of the memorial. The gas chamber appears to have been used to supplement rather than replace the mass shootings; its main victims were probably prisoners (often foreign forced labourers) brought to Sachsenhausen to be executed and, in the last months, weakened inmates. A plaque further south along the main wall marks the site of the first crematorium.

The surviving infirmary barracks are to the left of the *Appellplatz*; displays address medical care as well as the crimes committed by Sachsenhausen's doctors, including the murder of Red Army soldiers by lethal injection. A section of the pathology building also survives. This had close links with Berlin's universities and SS medical academies: skeletons and skulls were passed on to their 'racial-anthropological' collections. By the camp wall are the mass graves of infirmary patients who died after liberation.

A short walk from the visitors' centre is the 'T-Building' on Heinrich-Grüber-Platz; it was the headquarters of the Inspectorate of Concentration Camps from 1938 and thus supervised the entire camp system within the Reich. There is an exhibition on its role in one of the largely unchanged rooms.

Oranienburg is off the B96 north of Berlin; the camp is signposted. To reach the site by public transport, take the train or S-Bahn to Oranienburg and then bus 804 or follow the signs from the station for 20 minutes. There is a death march memorial on the approach to the camp at the corner of Straße der Einheit and Straße der Nationen.

RAVENSBRÜCK

Ravensbrück was the only large concentration camp for women. Before its creation in 1939, female prisoners were held in special sections of men's camps or in a small camp at Lichtenburg. They were overseen by female guards although command and administrative positions remained in the hands of men. There were also children in Ravensbrück, brought with their mothers or born there, whilst the special Uckermark camp for teenage girls was created nearby. An adjacent camp for men (officially a Sachsenhausen satellite) was established in 1941. Ravensbrück's earliest inmates were political prisoners, criminals and 'asocials' (such as prostitutes) but the population mushroomed during the war with the influx of Polish and Soviet

Ravensbrück (Photograph by the author)

women and increased even further in its last year with the arrival of death marches. Jews formed approximately 15 per cent of the more than 130,000 women who passed through Ravensbrück and its sub-camps and Roma around 5 per cent; both groups were unsurprisingly targeted for the worst treatment. Thousands died as a result of the conditions in the camp whilst weakened inmates were sent to Auschwitz or Bernburg. A small gas chamber was constructed in late 1944 in which several thousand women were murdered prior to the camp's liquidation. Although up to 7,500 western European prisoners were handed over to the Red Cross and several hundred Germans released, the majority of inmates were forced on a death march northwards in late March 1945. When the camp was liberated on 30 April, it held less than 3,500 sick prisoners; the death march was intercepted by the Red Army a few hours later. Estimates of the total number of Ravensbrück's victims vary but the figure may have been as high as 90,000.

The site was utilised by the Red Army after the war. Although a small memorial area was created in 1959, the majority of the complex remained in use as a military base until the Russian withdrawal in the 1990s. The current memorial site (Tue–Sun, 9.00–5.00; free; www. stiftung-bg.de) occupies most of the area of the camp although very few buildings remain. The most prominent is the command building by the car park which houses the principal exhibitions on its first floor. The two displays – on the history of the camp and the women who were interned in it – are only in German although there are English information folders. More immediately comprehensible are the vivid sketches of French prisoner Violette Lecoq and preserved artefacts, including children's toys. The SS garage behind addresses the history of the camp after 1945 and also houses temporary exhibitions. Next to the camp entrance to the north of these buildings, a surviving block (which housed the waterworks) is now used for special exhibits. Eight emaciated sculpted figures, created by British artist Stuart N.R. Wolfe, stand outside, their coloured triangles representing different categories of prisoner. The small guardhouse by the entrance holds a huge book listing the prisoners.

The camp itself is a large open space with only depressions in the gravel and small signs to indicate where barracks once stood. That nearest the gate, behind the plaque indicating the *Appellplatz*, was the infirmary. The barbaric experiments performed here included forced sterilisation by Dr Carl Clauberg, who was relocated from Auschwitz late in the war. To the right are the foundations of the kitchen and shower building. The function of the two long surviving buildings to the left was unknown. There is more substantial preservation of the industrial sector at the rear, partially enclosed by a remaining section of the camp wall. The principal building was a large textile workshop. The men's camp was immediately to the south of the industrial area whilst the girls' camp was some distance away to the south-east; both are inaccessible. An overgrown section of the women's camp, containing one surviving barrack, is also fenced off; this was the site of a large tent erected in late 1944 to accommodate Jewish and Roma women evacuated from Auschwitz.

The only other remaining building is the former prison south of the kitchen foundations. Its cells were turned into memorial rooms in the 1980s: each nation represented was responsible for the content of its cell with many reflecting the ideological considerations of the time, most notably the USSR's. After some debate, it was decided to preserve these Communist memorials as historical artefacts in their own right. They have, however, been supplemented by others: to Jews, Sinti and Roma, and the July Bomb Plotters.

Outside the prison, south of the car park, is the original memorial area by the crematorium. It is believed that the gas chamber was next to it although some accounts suggest that it was in the Uckermark girls' camp (which had been emptied in 1944). The rose garden alongside is planted on the mass grave of 300 inmates who died just before or after liberation. An information panel on its southern side relates the history of the Siemens factory which lay beyond the trees. The monument by the lake was erected by the Communists.

The buildings to the north of the car park and along the approach road were SS accommodation; some are now used as holiday homes. The commandant's house was the first in the row of four villas overlooking the camp near the waterworks building. The first barrack on the opposite side of the road is now used for international youth conferences, the second houses an exhibition on the female guards and the next a youth hostel.

Ravensbrück is located in the east of Fürstenberg/Havel, about 50 miles north of Berlin. Fürstenberg is on the B96 and can be easily reached by trains from the capital. Unfortunately, the camp is poorly signposted for both drivers and pedestrians – follow the signs for the youth hostel (*Jugendherberge*) instead. These will lead onto the L15 (Dorfstraße) from where traces will be more visible: a memorial sculpture of emaciated women at the turning into Himmelpforter Weg; a Soviet tank and a memorial of caged rocks at the turning into Straße der Nationen which leads to the camp. It may be possible to get a taxi from the station as an alternative to the two-kilometre walk.

NEUENGAMME

Neuengamme concentration camp was established in late 1938 around a brick factory outside Hamburg. Originally a satellite of Sachsenhausen, it became a camp in its own right in 1940 following a deal between the SS and the city to produce materials for construction projects, prompting a huge expansion of the camp and of a satellite network in the Hamburg region. The largest groups to pass through Neuengamme were Soviet POWs and Poles. There were few Jews until the arrival of transports from Hungary and Poland, numbering some 13,000 people, in the summer of 1944. During the death march era, several thousand prisoners were loaded onto boats moored in the Bay of Lübeck. On 3 May 1945, the RAF hit the *Cap Arcona* and *Thielbeck*, mistaking them for German military transports. Some 7,000 prisoners died (many shot by the SS whilst trying to save themselves); SS men and the crew were rescued by German ships. In total, more than 40,000 of the 100,000 people imprisoned in the Neuengamme camp system lost their lives.

The camp was liberated by the British on 4 May 1945 and held suspected Nazis until 1948 when it was transferred to the city of Hamburg. A large prison was constructed on the site of the inmates' camp in 1949, later supplemented by a juvenile detention centre. Although a memorial area was created in the 1960s (replacing a 1953 monument which made no mention of the site's history), the presence of the penal facilities meant that the camp itself was not accessible, a cause of increasing protests. The prisons were finally demolished in 2002–06, enabling the whole territory of Neuengamme to be included in what is now an impressive memorial site (Mon–Fri, 9.30–4.00; Sat–Sun, 12.00–7.00 (until 5.00, Oct–Mar); free; www.kz-gedenkstaette-neuengamme.de).

The modern southern entrance was, from 1941, the site of the simple camp gate; a large gatehouse of the type found elsewhere was planned but never built. To the right is a small information centre, to the left the *Appellplatz*. The current square is a reconstruction although a panel marks a fragment of the original, discovered after the prison's demolition. The inmates' barracks were to the left of the *Appellplatz*; the only surviving elements are two large brick buildings constructed in 1943–44 (six more were planned) and the foundations of the latrine between Blocks 7 and 8. The western brick building now houses the memorial administration and archive. To its north, by the road, is the main SS guardhouse next to a large watchtower.

The sites of the wooden barracks are indicated by bricks and stones with panels explaining the purpose of each. For example, the long blocks immediately after the information centre formed the infirmary where Dr Kurt Heißmeyer carried out experiments with tuberculosis on Jewish children (see Hamburg in 'other sites' below). A weeping willow to the right is the last remnant of the 'oasis', a garden which prisoners were forced to maintain for the SS; two monkeys were kept there for a time. Further up to the right is the site of the camp brothel, established in 1944 for privileged prisoners.

The site of the kitchen lies at the top of the main path near the exposed foundations of the camp prison; the latter was temporarily converted into a gas chamber in the autumn of 1942 for the murder of 448 Soviet POWs. The eastern brick building, which accommodated up to 3,000 prisoners and a basement workshop, now houses the main museum which traces Neuengamme's history over two floors with the principal focus on the prisoners, illustrated by biographies and photographs. The exhibition also covers the site's contentious post-war history.

Behind the museum, against a backdrop of wind turbines, is the Walther factory where up to 1,000 prisoners manufactured weapons from 1943. As a relatively comfortable position (working indoors with fewer beatings), employment here was much sought after. It now houses an exhibition on slave labour. The right of the building (with a mosaic of Europe by its entrance) is used for special exhibitions. The building opposite was intended to be a foundry but construction was never completed. The coach park further to the right was the site of more armaments workshops.

The crematorium, constructed in late 1944, was in front of the industrial buildings; its site is marked by a plaque. A path curves from here to a reconstructed stretch of the railway which, from 1943, ran into the camp; a Reichsbahn wagon stands as a memorial. The cement surface opposite, the same size as the wagon's interior, contains 80 pairs of footprints to indicate how tightly prisoners were packed in. The field on the other side of the coach park access road was the site of the SS shooting range where executions took place.

Returning to the museum, the main path leads northwards past a remnant of the post-war prison to the field which held the SS camp. The main surviving structure ahead served as a garage (the two buildings behind it were air-raid shelters) and now houses an exhibition on the SS men of Neuengamme. The building to the right (east) of the garage was the commandant's villa.

The juvenile detention centre occupied the space north of the garage. The site has been restored to its wartime state of exposed clay pits; hundreds of prisoners died here in what was considered the most lethal work detail in the camp. The clay was used in the large brickworks across the pits, built between 1940 and 1942 by inmates (there is an exhibition in the eastern wing on the building's history). Relatively few prisoners worked in the largely automated complex, in contrast to the thousands deployed in the construction of the canal to the east, another of the deadliest brigades. The moored barge on the canal carried waste material during the construction and later sand, coal and bricks, all of which had to be loaded or unloaded by inmates. The building to the west of the brickworks was the office of the DESt, the SS company which oversaw production.

The original memorial area is north of the DESt office, past a prefabricated house, a reconstruction of the many such buildings built in Hamburg from concrete produced at Neuengamme; on Sundays (11.30–5.00), helpful Lutheran volunteers provide information to visitors. A house of remembrance whose interior walls carry victims' names is ahead by the site of the SS vegetable gardens where ashes from the crematorium were used as fertiliser. The now wooded area is marked by a series of memorials including one to gay victims of the Nazis, erected in 1985 and thus one of the first to acknowledge what had previously been a rather taboo subject. There is also a monument to the 1944 Warsaw uprising: 6,000 Poles were brought to Neuengamme in its aftermath.

Neuengamme is 12 miles south-east of Hamburg, signposted off the A25 from the Curslack exit. To reach the site by public transport, take the S-Bahn to Bergedorf and then the 227 or 327 bus. There are bus stops and car parks by both the southern entrance and the northern memorial area.

BERGEN-BELSEN

No place other than Auschwitz is more connected with the Holocaust in the public mind than Belsen, yet there was little indication of such notoriety for most of the war, the site having been established as a camp for French and Belgian POWs in 1940. It was extended in 1941 to accommodate captured Soviet soldiers, 14,000 of whom died over the following winter, but even this death toll did little to distinguish Bergen-Belsen from dozens of other camps. Jews were interned there only from April 1943 and the POWs mostly sent elsewhere. Even at this stage, Belsen bore scant resemblance to the hell it would become. The majority of Jewish prisoners belonged to various special categories: citizens of neutral countries, holders of visas from such countries, and, above all, 'exchange Jews' who were held in readiness for potential trade for German prisoners in Allied countries or cash payments. Few of these deals ever occurred whilst 2,000 Polish Jews with entry papers for neutral countries were deported to Auschwitz after a few months. Nonetheless, Belsen seemed safer than any other camp in the Nazi system. All changed in the camp's catastrophic last year. The first

Bergen-Belsen (Photograph by Elizabeth Burns)

sign came in the spring of 1944 when it was designated as a 'rest camp' for sick prisoners from other camps – in short, they were brought to Belsen to die. However, it was the death marches which transformed the site. The first major arrival was a transport of 8,000 women from Auschwitz, Anne and Margot Frank amongst them, in the autumn of 1944. There were insufficient barracks so the women were accommodated in specially erected tents which blew down in heavy storms in November. That same month, the brutal Josef Kramer was transferred from Birkenau to become commandant of what was now officially a concentration camp. From January 1945 onwards, tens of thousands were brought to Belsen which was totally incapable of accommodating the influx. Lack of food, shelter and sanitation and a consequent typhus epidemic caused the deaths of 18,000 people in March alone. By the time the British arrived on 15 April, there were 60,000 prisoners, most of them seriously ill, whilst the camp was littered with thousands of unburied corpses: it is estimated that 35,000 prisoners had died since the start of the year. Thousands more died after liberation, many because their bodies could not cope with the food that the well-meaning British soldiers gave them. The footage filmed by the liberators is perhaps the most shocking of the Holocaust: most other camps had been evacuated before the Allies arrived but here was the most visible proof of Nazi crimes. An estimated 50,000 people died in Belsen from 1943 onwards.

The typhus epidemic was so severe that the entire camp was burned down by the British, the survivors having been relocated to hospitals and nearby army barracks which became the largest Jewish Displaced Persons (DP) camp in Germany. As a result, essentially nothing survives and the memorial site, established in 1946, rather resembles a large park (daily, 10.00–6.00 (until 5.00, Oct–Mar); free; www.bergenbelsen.de). With this in mind, the authorities are undertaking an ambitious overhaul which may take many years to complete. The most significant change has already been accomplished with the creation of a new museum in 2007 which runs from the car park to the edge of the camp. Much use is made of video, in particular the memorial's extensive archive of interviews with survivors and other witnesses, to supplement the sometimes sparse text whilst cases display artefacts discovered during excavations.

The museum exits by the camp perimeter, the path leading to the former *Appellplatz* in the heart of the 'Star Camp', so named because its inmates, mostly Dutch exchange Jews (4,100 by July 1944), did not have a uniform but were still obliged to wear the yellow star. By the path here is a heather-covered bank of earth, the mass grave of 1,000 people, one of many around the site. The former main road through the camp, which is intended to become the centrepiece of the new memorial concept, was just to the north. This is as yet underdeveloped although just off the 'road' to the north-east of the *Appellplatz* are the excavated foundations of Blocks 9 and 10: the former housed prison cells and a pigsty, the latter Hungarian Jews brought to Belsen in 1944 as part of the Kasztner transport (see chapter 9). The names of some have been written on bricks.

The post-war memorial area is skirted by a circular path west of the *Appellplatz*. Following it clockwise, past more mass graves, leads to the simple but affecting Jewish memorial, erected on the first anniversary of the camp's liberation. Around it are stones to individuals, amongst them Anne and Margot Frank: both sisters died during the typhus epidemic in March 1945. These memorials are in the area of the tent camp where they and thousands of other women were held until the November storms;

they were then moved to inadequate barracks just to the north. There are further memorials in a small glade near the diamond-shaped House of Silence, whilst the principal memorial and wall to the west were created by the British administration in 1947. The timber cross alongside was, rather insensitively perhaps, the very first memorial, erected by Polish female prisoners just after liberation. A turning off the path to the north leads through woodland and a military training area to the Soviet military cemetery which holds the mass graves of thousands of POWs.

Back on the main circuit, more mass graves face the site of the crematorium which will become the start of the memorial route along the camp road. The small crematorium was completely unable to cope in early 1945 and bodies were left to rot in the open air. The path continues its circular route from here through the woods into the former POW camp where the French and Belgian prisoners had been held. Following their evacuation in 1943, a hospital for the remaining Soviet inmates (who had been in what became the Jewish camp) was established here. This too was dissolved in January 1945 and thousands of women, many of them Sinti and Roma, were placed in the overcrowded barracks. A detour (marked on the free plans of the site) leads to wooden frames marking the sites of some of the barracks as well as one of the original reservoirs which proved so inadequate. In fact, retreating SS men cut the water supplies just before the British arrived to hinder the rescue efforts.

The site is by the L298 north-west of Celle and signposted from the A7 between Hannover and Hamburg. To reach the site by public transport, take a train to Celle and then one of the infrequent buses (latest timetables are on the memorial's website).

BERNBURG

Following the decision to close the Brandenburg facility in the autumn of 1940, a new T4 centre was established in Bernburg. The site was one block of a mental institution on the edge of the town; incredibly, the other buildings in the large complex continued to operate as normal throughout. The Brandenburg staff moved en masse to Bernburg and killings commenced in late November 1940: 9,385 patients were murdered by August 1941. Even after the supposed cessation of T4, Bernburg continued to function as a killing centre, taking a leading role in the 14f13 murders of sick concentration camp inmates. Approximately

5,000 prisoners, mainly Jews from camps such as Buchenwald, Flossenbürg and Gross-Rosen, were murdered up to April 1943.

After decades of neglect, there is now an effective memorial complex in Haus Griesinger, the building where the murders took place (Tue–Thu, 9.00–4.00; Fri, 9.00–12.00; 1ˢᵗ Sun of the month, 11.00–4.00; free; www.bernburg.meyersch.de). A door to the right, past a memorial stone to the more than 14,000 people who lost their lives in the building, leads down to the basement where the killing facilities were located. Although some elements are reconstructions – the shower heads in the gas chamber and the dissection table, for example – Bernburg is the most intact of the T4 sites. The original door to the gas chamber and the small window through which the killing personnel could check the 'progress' of their operation were discovered during the creation of the memorial. In the crematorium – the ovens represented by photographs – are two memorial stones and representative photographs of the victims. The exhibition (in German only) is well-presented, addressing the development of 'racial hygiene' through the sterilisation, T4 and 14f13 programmes and Bernburg's role in each. An interesting section highlights the failure of the East German authorities to bring the perpetrators to justice. The floor above is where victims were registered and photographed on their arrival from the bus garage and a suitable fictitious cause of death was decided on. A space on this floor is used for temporary exhibitions; the remaining floors still house psychiatric wards.

Bernburg is between Magdeburg and Halle, off the A14. Follow the signs marked '*Fachkrankenhaus*'. The large complex is at Olga-Benario-Straße 16/18, the memorial signposted from the entrance. To reach the site by public transport, take bus 553 to the Landeskrankenhaus stop. This runs directly from the train station in the morning and late afternoon; at other times, walk or take one of the many other buses from the station to Karlsplatz to catch the 553.

MITTELBAU-DORA

Mittelbau-Dora was the largest of the many camps created late in the war to utilise prisoner labour for arms production. It was established as a satellite of Buchenwald in August 1943, becoming a camp in its own right in October 1944. Inmates excavated tunnels in the Harz mountains to house V-2 rocket and aircraft factories. Until barracks were constructed in

Mittelbau-Dora (Photograph by the author)

the spring of 1944, they also had to live in these tunnels. The construction work was mostly performed by political prisoners (a large proportion of them French) but thousands of Jews were brought to Dora and its sub-camps once the facilities were operational in mid-1944. Their life expectancy was short even by the overall standards of the camp and many weakened Jewish inmates were sent to the gas chambers of Auschwitz and Mauthausen. More Jews arrived in early 1945 following the evacuation of Auschwitz and Gross-Rosen before Dora was itself abandoned in April with thousands marched in the direction of Belsen; many were murdered en route. It is estimated that around 60,000 prisoners passed through Dora and its sub-camps of whom around one-third died.

The current memorial complex (grounds: daily until sunset; museum: Tue–Sun, 10.00–6.00 (until 4.00, Oct–Mar); free; www.dora. de) is accessed via a road which runs through the industrial and SS areas of the camp, the parking area being next to the site of the commandant's office. Virtually nothing of the SS camp remains although maps indicate where buildings were. The modern visitors' centre (2006) houses the fairly small museum.

The entry to the prisoners' camp is marked by two concrete posts. Dora had no gatehouse; a barbed-wire gate stood here instead. The concrete building to the right, now used as a seminar room, stands on the site of the former Gestapo building. The concrete structure to the left, in front of which stands a small steam engine, was a former SS shelter reconstructed in the 1970s. As this suggests, very little of the camp survives, a point which becomes even more apparent standing in the *Appellplatz*. The gently rising banks of earth on which the barracks stood are now largely covered by grass or, further ahead, forest. Behind the main 1974 memorial is the camp's sports field beyond which are the foundations of the prison. The single-storey barrack, comprising 30 cells and an interrogation room, was separated from the rest of the camp by an electric fence. Mass arrests in late 1944 saw up to 20 prisoners being crammed into each cell. The adjoining storehouse stands on the site of the carpentry workshop

Back at the *Appellplatz*, the foundations of the inmates' canteen and food storehouse are on the left past the memorial followed by those of the kitchen. At the point where the path comes to a junction, set back on the right, are the foundations of a barrack in which more than 1,100 Italians were held from December 1943. Only around half of them were soldiers but all were arrested following Italy's surrender to the Allies. Such was Hitler's fury that they were designated 'Italian military internees' rather than prisoners of war in order to bypass the Geneva Convention. About half died.

Small fragments remain in the woods which have enveloped most of the site. The most notable are the ruins of the camp cinema, a corner wall still surviving. Completed in the autumn of 1944, this barrack was intended for privileged prisoners but proved to be short-lived as it became a quarantine block for transports from the east in early 1945. Following the curving path through the woods, one eventually reaches the intact crematorium, its two ovens surrounded by memorial plaques. The building operated from late summer 1944; bodies had previously been burned at Buchenwald or in a mobile oven. A sculpture of five weakened inmates overlooks the camp: this 1964 work was originally intended to be the DDR's memorial at Auschwitz but was considered insufficiently heroic. There are also modern plaques to Jewish as well as Sinti and Roma victims. New stairs lead down to the only two other standing buildings. The wooden block on the left (a

1991 reconstruction using materials from former forced labour barracks in Nordhausen) was the camp's first museum but its future role is unclear. The concrete building was the camp fire station, so solid that it escaped destruction; it is now used for special exhibitions.

Beyond the SS camp, around the road out of the memorial area, was the large Mittelwerk industrial zone. On the northern side of the road were two transport tunnels connected to the underground complex. The Americans removed machinery and documents before handing the facilities over to the Soviet authorities who blew them up in 1949. However, it is possible to see a fraction of the tunnel system through a guided tour in German which leaves from outside the museum (Tue–Fri, 11.00 & 2.00; Sat–Sun, 11.00, 1.00 & 3.00 (also 4.00 in summer)). A model suspended from the ceiling gives some sense of the astonishingly large scale of the underground network. The side tunnels are strewn with rubble from the detonation and pieces of equipment, including V-2 parts.

Opposite the entrance to the tunnels lie some foundations of industrial buildings along with the ramp of the camp station. This was where the transports from Poland arrived in early 1945 and where the transports to Belsen departed from a few weeks later. Further to the east, a cattle car stands by the road as a memorial, opposite a brick wall carrying a map of the death marches. By the sign marking the entrance to the memorial complex, a path leads north of the road to the pillars of the bridge which linked the camp to the railway network.

Dora is signposted off the B4 Nordhausen to Magdeburg road. To reach the site by public transport, take the number 10 Harzquerbahn service from the tram stop outside Nordhausen train station to Nordhausen-Krimderode. Signs from the left of the latter point the way; it is about a 10 minute walk to the edge of the complex.

BUCHENWALD

Buchenwald, one of the largest concentration camps, was established in 1937, its earliest inmates being political prisoners and criminals. The first transports of Jews arrived in the spring of 1938 but it was in the aftermath of *Kristallnacht* that it took a more central role when more than 10,000 were interned; most were released by the end of the year having promised to emigrate. Several hundred Czech Jews received the same treatment when the war began. By this stage, most inmates were German and Polish political prisoners and the remaining Jews were deported to Auschwitz in 1942. However, this process was reversed when transports of Hungarian Jews were redirected to Buchenwald in 1944 as slave labour for its armaments factories. The subsequent arrival of evacuees from Auschwitz and Gross-Rosen pushed the camp population above 85,000: overcrowding was so bad that 13,969 people died in the first 100 days of 1945. Death marches began to depart in early April but the evacuation was not completed due to the well-organised resistance movement within the camp. When the SS fled on 11 April 1945, the remaining 21,000 prisoners were able to liberate themselves and greet the US troops who arrived a few hours later. Close to a quarter of a million people had passed through Buchenwald by this stage; around 50,000 lost their lives.

Although the Americans captured Buchenwald, it lay within the Soviet zone and thus predictably became an NKVD camp until 1950 (7,000 of 28,000 inmates died). Its conversion into the principal East German commemorative site in the 1950s came with the usual ideological constraints but it is now an impressive memorial (grounds: daily until sunset; exhibitions: Tue–Sun, 10.00–6.00 (until 4.00, Nov–Mar); free; www.buchenwald.de).

The car park is in the former SS camp; the large buildings which circle it were SS barracks, mostly now private accommodation. The left of two smaller buildings houses the memorial's information centre from where a path leads to the main camp. Most of the buildings along the route are post-war although the long single-storey block opposite the gate incorporates a part of the command building. One can also see remnants of the SS zoo where bear cubs were kept. The gatehouse, whose clock is stopped at 3.15 (the time of the Americans' arrival), contains prison cells in its left wing; cell 1 was where condemned inmates spent their last night. The gate itself is marked with the motto '*Jedem das seine*', often translated as the apparently innocuous 'to each his own'; a better sense of its meaning is 'everyone gets what he deserves'.

From the *Appellplatz*, one can appreciate Buchenwald's size although it was actually larger than it seems, trees having taken over the north of the complex (it is possible to walk the SS guards' path around the perimeter of the main camp – see the leaflet in the information centre). The most immediately noticeable feature is the paucity of buildings: as at Sachsenhausen, most were demolished to fit the memorial concept. The first surviving structure, past a memorial to 2,098 Poles brought to the camp in October 1939 (1,650 died in five months), is the crematorium to the right, built in 1940 and enlarged in 1942. It also included pathological facilities which were initially used to establish a plausible cause of death to give to families of inmates and later to extract gold teeth from the dead. The mortuary contains 700 open urns which were discovered during restoration work in 1997. Ashes were initially sent to relatives but increasingly dumped outside the camp. Behind the crematorium is the toilet block, constructed following a dysentery epidemic in the winter of 1939–40. It contains a reconstruction of parts of a stable outside the camp where 8,000 Soviet POWs were murdered in 1941–44. The gate to the right of the crematorium led to an armaments factory. Following heavy damage in a 1944 air raid, the facilities were used as an assembly camp for 6,000 Jews about to be dispatched on a death march in April 1945.

The main path from the crematorium to the camp depot (the large building at the rear) leads past the site of barracks, some marked by memorials: to the 2,700 women held in Buchenwald (Block 5), hanged British and Canadian soldiers (17), and Jews (22). This latter was the main Jewish barrack until October 1942: between *Kristallnacht* and that date, 2,795 Jews lost their lives, the largest group of prisoners to die in this period. Instead of the piles of rubble which indicate the other blocks, this is marked by a depression filled with rocks from the camp quarry, as if the earth has caved in. To the right of the main path is the stump of a tree, nicknamed the 'Goethe oak' by inmates, which was damaged in a 1944 air raid.

The depot, the largest extant building, was where new arrivals were brought after passing through the disinfection building next door. Here they received their uniform, shoes and eating utensils and surrendered their civilian clothes and possessions. It now houses the museum whose main exhibition covers Buchenwald's history in great detail. There is a large range of artefacts, including even a section of the portable gallows used to hang prisoners in the woods around the camp from 1942 onwards. On the top floor, there is a new large display of photographs selected from the more than 10,000 in the Buchenwald archive. The disinfection block exhibits the memorial's art collection, the works by inmates rather overshadowing some fairly banal contemporary pieces.

In the woods behind the disinfection building and the ruins of the SS vegetable garden, the mass graves of inmates of the NKVD camp are marked with poles and by a memorial exhibition. Further Nazi victims – Bulgarians, homosexuals, Jehovah's Witnesses and conscientious objectors – are memorialised at Block 45 to the left of the depot. Behind Block 45 are the ruined foundations of Block 50 where the Waffen-SS Hygiene Institute produced typhus serum. The 'little camp', which was established as a quarantine area in 1942, was further to the left. This was where new arrivals were sent from the depot before being assigned to work detachments. The barracks had originally been stables, each accommodating 50 horses; they eventually held up to 1,900 prisoners each in Buchenwald's horrific last months when the large transports arrived from Auschwitz. The little camp included a special block for hundreds of Jewish children and Block 61 where the sick were murdered by lethal injection. As a site of predominantly Jewish suffering, this area was ignored under the DDR. However, a section was reconstructed in 2002 as a memorial designed by New York architect Stephen Jacobs who, as Stefan Jakobowitz, was prisoner 87900.

The infirmary was next to the little camp, in the north-western corner. The only building now standing was a barrack created in 1945, dismantled for use by a local company in the 1950s and then returned and reconstructed in 1994 (foundations of other buildings can be seen in the woods behind). Opposite, marked by a new brick wall, was Block 46, the Hygiene Institute's experimentation centre where its typhus serums were tested on prisoners. Returning uphill, a mound of stones and a row of small columns on Block 14 commemorate Sinti and Roma inmates of Buchenwald; most were brought, like the Jews, in early 1945. The block to the right and the next two up housed Soviet POWs. The grassy area above this group was the site of the 'Jewish camp' for those arrested after *Kristallnacht*; although most were released, 600 died in Buchenwald before February 1939. The remaining building ahead was the inmates' canteen which now houses lecture and exhibition rooms. Returning towards the gate, a memorial stone lists the nationalities of those interned in the camp.

Outside the prisoners' camp, various paths lead through the area of the SS camp which mostly contains moss-covered foundations (all routes are shown on the plan available from the information centre). Just to the south-west of the main camp were the horse stables where Soviet prisoners were executed in 1941. From here, or from the car park, one can walk to Buchenwald's large quarry and the partially reconstructed basement of the SS barrack which is now the Dietrich Bonhoeffer memorial site: the famed Protestant pastor and other opponents of Hitler were held here before being sent to Flossenbürg for execution. The site where ashes were thrown in 1944–45, marked by large stones spelling out the word '*memento*', is further south. East of the car park are the remnants of the camp's railway station next to the foundations of the large industrial facilities.

Back down the road from the camp is the East German memorial, created in 1958 by the cemetery where the bodies of 400 prisoners who died after liberation are buried along with 1,286 urns found in the camp. The simple graves are rather overshadowed by the didactic Communist monuments which were the location of political demonstrations under the DDR. From the entrance, stairs descend past large friezes of camp life to three huge pits in which the SS buried 3,000 corpses just before the liberation. The route returns up to the main element – the 'bell tower', which houses ashes from other camps. In front is a typically Communist sculpture of a group of muscular prisoners standing in resistance.

Buchenwald is about 6 miles north-west of Weimar off the L1054 road to Ettersburg, the turning marked by an obelisk. The hourly route 6 bus runs from Weimar station to the car park.

SONNENSTEIN

Sonnenstein asylum, located in the grounds of the castle which overlooks the city of Pirna near Dresden, was renowned as a world leader in the care of the mentally ill – established in 1811, it was the first major institution of its kind in Germany to seek to treat its patients rather than just confine them. Under the Nazis and Sonnenstein's eugenicist director Hermann Paul Nitsche, all such humanist principles were inverted. Following the hospital's closure in October 1939, three of its buildings were converted into a T4 killing centre in early 1940. Between June 1940 and August 1941, 13,720 patients were murdered whilst Nitsche eventually became T4's senior medical director. Sonnenstein was also used in the 14f13 killing of concentration camp inmates, taking the estimated death toll to 14,751. It is a little-known fact that the first Auschwitz prisoners to be gassed were 575 Polish citizens (Jews and Gentiles) brought to Sonnenstein on 28 July 1941, a month before the first experiments with Zyklon B in the future extermination camp.

The murder machinery was dismantled in 1942 and the buildings became a military hospital. After the war, they were used for commercial purposes and their history remained hidden. It was only in 1989, two months before the collapse of Communism, that an exhibition in Pirna organised by the historian Götz Aly prompted a campaign for the site to be properly memorialised. As a result, a memorial and exhibition (Mon–Fri, 9.00–3.00; 1ˢᵗ Sat of the month, 10.00–3.00; free; www.stsg.de/main/pirna/ueberblick/einfuehrung/index_en.php) now occupy C16 (the building in which the murders took place), sharing the premises with a workshop for the disabled run by the AWO charity; the basement is accessed through the door marked '*Gedenkbereich*'. A room of reflection contains memorials, including one erected by the Polish government in 2005 to the Auschwitz prisoners. Twenty-two placards in the adjacent room provide photographs and biographies which illustrate the range of victims. The murder facilities are marked by steel structures which suggest the original stone wall of the gas chamber, one of the two ovens and the crematorium chimney. The small top floor exhibition in German (there are English leaflets) sets out the history of Sonnenstein along with a general overview of Nazi medical murder.

The memorial site is located at Schloßpark 11. Follow the signs to Schloßpark and then for '*Gedenkstätte*'. Bus H/S stops on Struppener Straße on the edge of the Schloßpark complex. An alternative way to reach the site from the centre of Pirna is to follow one of two memorial routes. The *Gedenkspur*, which runs from the Elbe to C16's basement, consists of 14,751 small coloured crosses drawn on cobblestones by local youth groups although many have begun to fade. In the *Vergenagenheit ist Gegenwart* (Past is Present) route, designed by the German artist Heike Ponwitz, 16 glass panels run from the station to the memorial. Each features a Canaletto painting of Sonnenstein castle inscribed with a keyword or phrase associated with the 'euthanasia' programme. Maps of both routes can be picked up from Pirna's tourist office on the central Am Markt square through which they both pass. There is a DDR memorial plaque, predictably dedicated to 'victims of Fascism', on the steps up to the castle from Obere Burgstraße.

HADAMAR

Hadamar was the last T4 centre to be created, the town's former mental hospital replacing Grafeneck. The murders began in January 1941; by August, Hadamar had cremated its ten thousandth victim. This milestone was celebrated by a macabre party which began with all personnel, led by a member of staff dressed as a priest, attending the cremation, and culminated in a drunken procession around the grounds of the hospital. The killing was officially terminated in the same month on Hitler's order. However, to the minimum 10,072 patients gassed under T4 must be added at least 4,000 people murdered in the 'wild euthanasia' through lethal injections: amongst those killed in this way were Jewish children of mixed marriages. They were exempt from the deportations to the east so an 'educational home' for these children was established at Hadamar in April 1943 as a cover for their murder.

The building where the killings occurred is now block 5 of the Centre for Social Psychiatry and home to the oldest (for many years the only) memorial exhibition dedicated to T4 (Tue–Thu, 9.00–4.00; Fri, 9.00–1.00; 1st Sun in the month, 11.00–4.00; free; www.gedenkstaette-hadamar.de). In the main entrance hall is a 1953 plaque, the first such memorial to be created, whilst the exhibition is situated in the rooms where victims were registered and photographed. The information is in German but it is possible to borrow or buy (€7) an English catalogue containing the full text. One section addresses the little-studied murder of foreign forced labourers: Poles and Russians suspected of having tuberculosis were brought to Hadamar and automatically killed without even the pretence of a medical examination. The exhibition also examines reactions to the killings: one Hadamar citizen who protested, Paula F, was sent to a camp as a warning to other locals. The display concludes with the post-war trials – most of those involved, if sentenced at all, never served full terms – and the contrastingly lengthy struggle of victims' families for recompense. A simple memorial room is decorated with works produced by the art therapy programme which now occupies part of the building.

The killing apparatus was located in the basement, currently accessed by an exterior door on the right of the building, past a memorial bell in the gardens. The rooms are mostly bare although the check tiles of the gas chamber and the dissection table remain. Panels provide biographies and photographs of representative victims. Around the back of the building is the wooden bus garage where the victims arrived, the only one to have survived. Structural damage meant that it was dismantled in 2003 for repair work and reconstructed in 2006. Steps lead up the hill behind to the memorial cemetery where a series of stones act as symbolic markers for the mass graves of those buried during the 'wild euthanasia' years.

The memorial complex is at Mönchberg 8 in the west of Hadamar which is on the L3462 north of Limburg an der Lahn. Trains run from Limburg to Hadamar's small station from where one should exit northwards (left) onto Am Bahnhof, take the second road on the left (Brückenvorstadt) and then turn right at the junction after the railway bridge. The site is signposted from there. Hadamar also has a relatively rare example of a surviving synagogue, which is located at Nonnengasse 6, just beyond the market square to the east of the station.

FLOSSENBÜRG

Flossenbürg concentration camp was established in 1938, initially for criminals and 'asocials'. They were put to work in the nearby granite quarries which drew the SS to the site (although Flossenbürg's hilltop ruined castle, a site of great appeal to *völkisch* groups, doubtless further recommended the village to Himmler). The balance of inmates shifted in the war, with political prisoners (from the Reich and Poland) and Soviet

Flossenbürg (Photograph by the author)

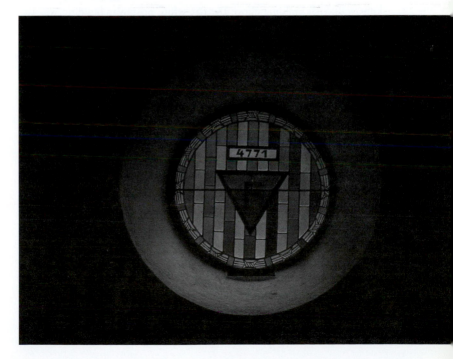

POWs predominating. A large network of sub-camps also developed across southern Germany and western Bohemia. Flossenbürg's connection with the Holocaust primarily stems from its role as one of the principal destinations for the death marches, illustrated by the expansion of its population from 3,300 at the end of 1943 to 15,445 in March 1945 with up to 1,500 prisoners crammed into a single block. Flossenbürg was itself evacuated in April 1945 so that the Americans found only 1,600 critically ill prisoners when they arrived on 23 April 1945. Almost 100,000 people are believed to have passed through the Flossenbürg camp system between 1938 and 1945; around 30,000 died.

Little of the camp remains but what does has been used to good effect (daily, 9.00–5.00 (museum until 4.00); free; www.gedenkstaette-flossenbuerg.de). The car park is within the SS area, next to the large command building which now houses the memorial administration. The building's archway was intended to be the gate to the prisoners' camp but these plans fell through: the camp actually began further back. Further SS buildings are visible on the hills on either side. To the left, a long building (now a restaurant) was the officers' club. On the opposite hill, a fairly long yellowish building above the flat white post-war building was the locksmith's shop. Houses were built further back on this hill for senior SS men. They are hard to see from the car park but the dark wooden buildings with stone foundations are soon obvious walking along Unterer and Oberer Plattenberg around the corner.

The entry to the inmates' camp was marked by two stone pillars which were relocated after the war to the memorial area. The *Appellplatz* beyond looks bigger than it actually was due to the destruction in the 1950s of most barracks. Only two original buildings remain intact: the recently renovated camp kitchen to the left (now used for seminars) and the laundry to the right which houses an excellent new museum. An interesting section deals with the still often taboo subject of the camp's relationship with local civilians whilst a substantial part is dedicated to the horrendous last year. Individual death marches are highlighted and the exhibition finishes with a selection of films from 1945, one of them containing astonishing footage of Litoměřice prisoners secretly filmed at Roztoky near Prague. The Czech citizens halted the train, fed the prisoners and helped more than 300 to escape before the SS decided to carry on with the futile journey. The basement, which served as a bathhouse, includes representative biographies of prisoners.

The infirmary buildings were to the right of the laundry. Dr Alfred Schnabel castrated inmates and later administered lethal injections to weakened prisoners and Soviet POWs following the cessation of killing operations at Bernburg. A path leads past the site to the remnants of the detention block where a plaque on the surviving courtyard wall honours Pastor Dietrich Bonhoeffer, Admiral Wilhelm Canaris and others linked to the 1944 July Bomb Plot who were executed here in April 1945; 15 British SOE agents and three young women of the French Resistance are similarly commemorated. Inside the surviving section is the original museum exhibition, in German only and rather superseded by that in the laundry.

The isolation barracks, built in 1942 to house Soviet prisoners but, in fact, used as quarantine blocks, were behind the prison. In the late 1950s, the area was turned into a cemetery for death march victims from across Bavaria. One of three surviving stone watchtowers overlooks the small crematorium (closed Dec–Mar) behind. As the death toll increased in late 1944, a ramp was constructed by this tower to send bodies down to the ovens. Steps alongside the now grassed over ramp lead into the memorial area (created in 1946 by former inmates), passing through the relocated stone camp gateposts. Two memorials to Jewish victims are by the bottom of the ramp, above the crematorium. The central memorial area, the 'Valley of Death', contains tributes to victims from many countries. The execution site is marked by a paved triangle whilst ashes are interred in a pyramid of earth behind. Steps on the other side lead back up to the cemetery and the 'Jesus in the Dungeon' chapel built by ex-inmates using bricks from the demolished watchtowers; another watchtower is incorporated as if it were the church's belfry. Nearby is a Jewish memorial building, listing the 319 known names of the more than 3,000 Jewish victims of Flossenbürg.

The quarry in which inmates slaved is west of the camp. From the camp car park, walk back along Birkenstraße to the main road, turn left and then almost immediately right onto Bocksbühlweg which comes to a T-junction with Wurmsteinweg. The large yellow building on the right housed the administration of the DESt, the SS company which managed the quarry. A left onto Wurmsteinweg and then right onto Rumpelbachstraße leads to the quarry which is still in use and thus inaccessible. However, the four stone buildings before the entrance were masons' workshops.

In the centre of the village is a cemetery for 121 prisoners buried here on US orders in May 1945; all local men were compelled to take part in the ceremony. In 1946, Polish survivors erected a large monument which stands by the roadside. To get to the cemetery from the camp, take Birkenstraße and turn left onto the main road (which continues under the name Birkenstraße until it turns and becomes Hohenstaufenstraße by the town cemetery). Continue down the hill for a few hundred metres to find the prisoners' cemetery on the right by Schulweg.

Flossenbürg is about 60 miles north-east of Nuremberg, close to the Czech border. To reach the site by car, take the exit for Neustadt an der Waldnaab off the B93 and follow the signs eastward. To access it by public transport, take a train to Weiden in der Oberpfalz and then the hourly 6272 bus (much less frequent at weekends) which stops in the memorial's car park. Whether by car or bus, as one drives through the village the dark SS houses will be visible on the hill in the background.

DACHAU

Dachau was the first proper concentration camp, established on 22 March 1933 as a highly public symbol of the new regime. Much of its tone was set by Theodor Eicke who was appointed as Dachau's second commandant in June 1933 despite recently having been sectioned in a psychiatric institution by the *Gauleiter* of Rhine-Palatinate. Eicke devised the system of regulations and punishments intended to humiliate prisoners and deprive them of any sense of either individualism or solidarity. Dachau thus became the model for subsequent camps, a point reinforced by Eicke's appointment as inspector-general of concentration camps in 1934 and Dachau's use as a training facility for the SS – many commandants of other camps served there. In line with developments across the camp system, it was substantially remodelled and expanded in 1937–38 to increase its prisoner capacity and allow the development of economic enterprises.

The first inmates were primarily Social Democrats and Communists, joined in due course by 'asocials' and common criminals. Early Jewish inmates were those arrested for their politics rather than their ethnicity but from the very beginning they were singled out for the harshest treatment: as early as 12 April 1933, four were shot simply for being Jews. Increasing Nazi persecution brought more Jews, culminating in the incarceration of more than 10,000 after *Kristallnacht*. Most were allowed to leave after they had made the requisite arrangements to emigrate; the remainder were deported to Poland in 1942. For most of the war, the

Dachau (Photograph by the author)

principal populations were German and foreign political prisoners; the camp was also used for the execution of Soviet POWs. However, the increasing importance of arms production led to the redirection of Jewish prisoners from Auschwitz from the summer of 1944, and numbers were swelled during the death marches. When the Americans arrived on 29 April 1945, they found more than 60,000 prisoners of whom around 30 per cent were Jewish (a further 7,000 forced on a death march a few days earlier were overtaken by US forces in early May). More than 200,000 prisoners were registered as having passed through Dachau during its 12-year history; 31,000 were recorded as having died. The real figures were almost certainly higher due to the chaos of the last weeks. The camp was ravaged by a typhus epidemic and the SS were shooting prisoners even as the Americans occupied the camp, prompting furious reprisals.

The camp

The Americans used the camp for the internment of former Nazis until 1948 when it was handed to the Bavarian state government. It was converted into a memorial site (Tue–Sun, 9.00–5.00; free; www.kz-gedenkstaette-dachau.de) only in the 1960s, largely as a result of pressure from former inmates. Dachau is now a major tourist attraction which means that it is sensible to visit the site in the morning before the large tour groups arrive.

The path towards the main camp from the new visitors' centre leads through the 'political section' where the Gestapo building was located (the corners are marked). This was where new prisoners were photographed, where interrogations took place and where deaths were recorded. A section of the large SS camp, which stretched much further to the west, can be seen behind the fence by the surviving stretch of railway to the left, notably the command building in the foreground. This area is inaccessible, however: used by the Americans after the war, first as the internment camp and then as a military base, it was taken over by the Bavarian police in the 1970s. When the Americans arrived at the railway halt within the SS compound, they found 50 cattle trucks piled with the corpses of over 2,000 Jews who had been transported from Poland and left to die.

The infamous '*Arbeit macht frei*' on the gate to the right was Eicke's contribution to Nazi iconography, copied at several other camps. The phrase – widely assumed to have been invented by the Nazis – had actually been current in German nationalist circles since the late nineteenth century and was used by the Weimar government to promote its public works programmes. Two plaques on the gate walls commemorate the US liberators. The large maintenance building to the right of the gate was built by prisoners during the 1937–38 reconstruction. In addition to workshops, it housed the prisoners' baths and kitchen as well as the *Schubraum* (shunting room) where new inmates were admitted. A didactic message was painted on the roof of the building: 'There is one path to freedom. Its milestones are: obedience, honesty, cleanliness, sobriety, diligence, orderliness, sacrifice, truthfulness, love of the fatherland.' It is now the museum, which thoroughly addresses the camp's history. One interesting section – 'Dachau in propaganda and reality' – contrasts the Nazi image with the harsh truth whilst also demonstrating that the camps in the Reich were not hidden away but actively publicised as a means of both intimidating potential opponents and reassuring conservatives that the Nazis were restoring order.

Behind the maintenance building is the prison block, constructed at the same time. The eastern wall connecting the two buildings was where executions by firing squad took place. Cells 63–65 look normal now but in 1944 they were subdivided into 'standing cells', spaces of roughly 2½ square feet in which prisoners could be kept for up to 72 hours. In the eastern wing, cells 81 and 82 relate the story of Georg Elser who attempted to assassinate Hitler in Munich in November 1939.

The *Appellplatz*, in front of the maintenance building, is dominated by a memorial of contorted bodies designed by Serbian artist and camp survivor Nandor Glid. The facing wall carries a sculpture of chains covered with coloured triangles to represent the range of prisoners. The structure also includes a concrete block containing the ashes of unknown victims. Two surviving barracks flank the camp road (whose poplars were planted by prisoners); others are marked by beds of rubble. The surviving block on the left had various functions: canteen, orderly room, library, SS museum and armaments workshop. The barrack to the right (Block A) was part of the infirmary although its interior was reconstructed in 1965 to show the different stages of camp life. Those prisoners who could not regain their health quickly were left to die in a room known as the 'death chamber'. Block B behind was also an infirmary barrack. The next three barracks (1, 3 and 5) were used for medical experiments from 1942, supposedly intended to help the German war effort. For example, in the summer of 1944, 40 Sinti and Roma prisoners were forced to drink only seawater in order to ascertain the possible effects on sailors should their ships be torpedoed. In a similar vein, 90 prisoners died in hypothermia experiments, often being plunged into icy water to determine which organs were paralysed first. More than 70 were killed in experiments simulating the effects of high altitude in 1942.

Beyond the barracks was a detached area which encompassed various buildings, including hutches for Angora rabbits bred at the camp. In early 1944, a camp brothel was established here for privileged prisoners, the women having been brought from Ravensbrück for the purpose. All of these structures were pulled down in the 1960s and replaced by three religious memorial buildings (Jewish, Catholic and Protestant). A Carmelite convent is accessed through a doorway behind the Catholic chapel. A path to the left of the Protestant church leads past a moat and a barbed-wire fence (partially reconstructed in the 1960s) as well as an Orthodox chapel built by members of the Russian armed forces, to Dachau's two crematoria, marked by a memorial stone and a statue of 'the unknown prisoner'. A further stone marks the site of the gallows. The small crematorium (in which 11,000 bodies were burned) operated from the summer of 1940 to April 1943 by which time it could no longer cope with the numbers. It was thus replaced by the larger building which also contained a gas chamber. It is not clear if this was ever used – sick prisoners were variously sent to Hartheim and the Polish extermination camps, murdered by lethal injection in Dachau's infirmary or simply left to die. The four ovens, however, worked regularly until February 1945 when the coal ran out. When the Americans arrived, they found 3,000 corpses in 'death chamber II' (the pre-cremation storage area) on the right side of the building; residents of the town were brought here to view what had been done in their name. Behind the building are two execution sites and ash graves. Amongst those murdered here were 92 Soviet soldiers shot for resistance activities in the camp. The area is now a peaceful memorial garden containing several monuments, including one to Jewish victims.

A little-noticed further part of the complex is east of the prisoner camp. This was the 'plantation', the SS herb garden in which up to 1,500 inmates at a time laboured. This can be reached by entering the Carmelite convent and taking the path to the right out to Alte Römerstraße by the camp's eastern wall. The yellow building and its greenhouses (still in use) are just past Hans-Böckler-Straße, a few minutes' walk to the north.

Dachau is easily reached. The town is a short distance north-west of Munich off the A8 and the camp is well signposted. To reach the site by public transport, take the S-Bahn (line S2) to Dachau and then the 726 bus. An alternative is to walk from the train station along a path of remembrance marked by a series of information panels. A little over halfway, by John-F-Kennedy-Platz, there is a death march memorial – a group of small, emaciated figures on a plinth – on Theodor-Heuss-Straße, just south of the junction with Sudetenlandstraße.

Elsewhere

In 1941–42, 4,000 Soviet soldiers were executed at an SS shooting range north of the camp, now marked by memorials. It can be reached by following Alte Römerstraße (which is not designed for pedestrians) north from the plantation; it comes to a junction with Freisinger Straße after about a mile. Turn right and then left down the dirt road marked by the sign '*Gedenkstätte Schießplatz*'. The building to the right of the parking area housed the SS.

When the coal in the crematorium ran out in early 1945, the bodies of several thousand prisoners were buried on Leitenberg hill, around a mile south-west of the shooting range. The site is now a wooded cemetery, flanked by an Italian chapel (western side) and a tower-like memorial hall (eastern side; the key to both can be acquired at the camp). If coming from the shooting range, exit back onto Freisinger Straße (which becomes Leitenweg after the railway bridge), head south-west until the sign for '*KZ Friedhof auf der Leiten*' and then take a sharp turn to the right. A path marked by stones featuring the stations of the cross leads uphill to the Italian chapel from the car park. Bus 725 runs irregularly from the station to Leitenweg stop from where the site is a manageable walk further along the road, but the only return service is at lunchtime.

The bodies of 1,268 prisoners who died after liberation are buried in Dachau's Wald cemetery in a sloping terrace to the right of the main entrance. The simple stones contrast with the often ornate graves of the locals who served as bystanders during the camp's existence. At the bottom of the hill are two memorials, one to all victims, another erected by former prisoners of the Austrian People's Party. If coming from Leitenberg, drivers should stay on Leitenweg/Freisinger Straße as it curves through the town until the turning for '*Waldfriedhof*' appears down Krankenhausstraße. Pedestrians can turn right earlier, onto Weblinger

Weg after the village of Etzenhausen and continue to the cemetery's northern entrance. Alternatively take bus 720 from the station to the Waldfriedhof stop.

A plaque on the wall of the Dachauer Gemäldegalerie, opposite the Rathaus (bus 720, Rathaus stop), commemorates a group of citizens and escaped prisoners who occupied the town hall on 28 April 1945, the day before the liberation; six were killed by the SS.

GRAFENECK

Grafeneck Castle, previously a seat of the Dukes of Württemberg and from 1929 a Samaritan home for the disabled, was converted in late 1939 into one of the two original T4 centres. Special barracks were constructed in the grounds, amongst them the killing block (containing the gas chamber and crematorium) which began its murderous work in January 1940. By December, 10,654 patients had been killed. The complex was then closed and its staff relocated to Hadamar, largely as a result of growing hostility from locals. Despite Grafeneck's relative remoteness, the people of the neighbouring towns and villages were soon aware of what was happening at the castle and there were written protests to the authorities, notably from Theophil Wurm (Bishop of Württemberg) and Else von Löwis. The latter was a leader of the Nazi women's movement and her letter of November 1940 found its way to Himmler who advised the T4 headquarters to close Grafeneck due to the lack of secrecy and the mood in the region. The complex was then used by the Hitler Youth.

After the war, the Samaritans reoccupied the site and the killing block was demolished. Although a small memorial was erected in 1963, it was only in the 1990s that steps were taken to properly commemorate the victims, complemented by a new information centre in 2005 (daily, 9.00–6.00; free; www.gedenkstaette-grafeneck.de). The relatively small exhibition (in German) covers the history of the castle, T4 and the connections between Grafeneck and the Holocaust. The latter encompass Dr Horst Schumann, the chief physician who advanced (via Sonnenstein) to Auschwitz, and the ubiquitous Christian Wirth whose career was to take him to almost every major killing centre of the Third Reich. The path from the north of the information centre leads past modern chalets which house patients and stand on the site of the death block. A tiny brick wall to the left of the path indicates the corner of the gas chamber. The main memorial area is further along the path, its entrance marked by a stone and paving listing 37 locations across southern Germany from which victims were brought to Grafeneck. The memorials include a work by US artist Diane Samuels consisting of 26 small granite stones, each inscribed with a letter to represent the names of the victims, and a small open-air memorial chapel. Beyond the latter is the cemetery. Its graves are of later patients, not T4 victims, but it does contain the 1963 memorial, a simple stone cross by two raised beds of earth holding 270 urns of victims' ashes. Sculptures by modern patients stand by the wall behind.

Grafeneck is west of the small town of Münsingen which lies between Reutlingen and Ulm. Take the L230 out of Münsingen; after about 2 miles, turn left onto the L247 (marked Marbach and Grafeneck). After about a kilometre, a road on the left leads uphill to the complex. A train runs on schooldays from Münsingen to Grafeneck, stopping right next to the road up to the castle, although getting to Münsingen in the first place is itself a challenge. During school holidays and on Saturdays, bus 7606 from Reutlingen sometimes stops at Grafeneck by the train halt (check www.bahn.de).

OTHER SITES

There are so many memorial sites in Germany that it is impossible to list more than a fraction of some of the more significant and interesting. A database is provided at www.ns-gedenkstaetten.de.

A unique institution – little-known until an arson attack in 2002 – is the small Death March Museum (closed for renovation until 2010; www.stiftung-bg.de) in the Belower forest, where 16,000 exhausted Sachsenhausen prisoners were held for a week in late April 1945. The museum is on Belower Damm, a side road through the woods off the L153 north of Wittstock, around 60 miles north-west of Berlin and a little under 30 miles west of Ravensbrück.

Two rather abstract structures commemorate the thousands of Jews deported from Hamburg. On Platz der Republik (Altona S-Bahn, southern exit), a clinical black wall designed by artist Sol LeWitt is dedicated to the long-established Jewish community of this suburb (there is also a stone to the Polish Jews expelled in October 1938 by the station exit). On Edmund-Siemers-Allee (Dammtor station), Platz der Jüdischen

Deportierten is marked by a similarly anonymous granite block. A more expressive memorial on nearby Joseph-Carlebach-Platz (named after the city's chief rabbi who was murdered in Riga in 1942) traces the outline of the High Synagogue, which was destroyed on *Kristallnacht*, in the square. The most moving site in the city, however, is the Bullenhuser Damm school (Rothenburgsort S-Bahn). In November 1944, Dr Kurt Heißmeyer had 20 Jewish children brought to Neuengamme from Auschwitz in order to conduct experiments with tuberculosis. As the British approached in April 1945, the children and their four carers were brought to the building and murdered in an attempt to destroy the evidence. Twenty-four Soviet POWs were also killed. The basement where the murders took place is now a touching memorial site (Sun, 10.00–5.00; free; www.kz-gedenkstaette-neuengamme.de), accessed through a memorial rose garden on Großmannstraße (open at all times).

More than 1,000 mostly Jewish prisoners on a death march from Mittelbau-Dora were forced into a barn and burned to death in April 1945 at Gardelegen, roughly halfway between Berlin and Hannover. The Americans, who discovered the atrocity two days later, forced the townspeople to bury the corpses in a specially created military cemetery which now adjoins a memorial at the site of the barn. The complex is to the north-east of the town by the new B71 bypass.

Zeithain, 40 miles east of Leipzig, was the site of the deadliest POW camp in Germany: 25,000 to 30,000 Soviet soldiers died there. Although the camp was largely destroyed, two large mass graves and an exhibition complex make up the Zeithain Memorial Grove (Mon–Thu, 10.00–4.00; Fri, 10.00–2.00, Sun (May–Nov only), 11.00–5.00; free; www.stsg.de/main/zeithain/ueberblick/einfuehrung/index_en.php), signposted off Gröditzer Straße, north-east of the village.

Heidelberg's excellent Documentation and Cultural Centre of German Sinti and Roma houses Europe's first permanent exhibition devoted to the Nazi murder of Sinti and Roma at Bremeneckgasse 2 (Tue–Wed, Fri, 9.30–4.30; Thu, 9.30–8.00; Sat–Sun, 11.00–4.00; free; www.sinti-und-roma.de) on the eastern edge of the city.

Stuttgart's *Zeichen der Erinnerung* (Signs of Remembrance) is an impressive memorial near to the Nordbahnhof from where deportation trains left. Walls listing the transports and the names of the deportees enclose railway tracks. The memorial is accessed by a path between Nordbahnhofstraße 67 and 69 (U15 tram to Mittnachtstraße).

Nuremberg's former Nazi Party Congress Hall at Bayernstraße 110 (Dutzendteich S-Bahn) houses the exhibition *Fascination and Terror* focussing on the history of the Nazis and their relationship with the city (Mon–Fri, 9.00–6.00; Sat–Sun, 10.00–6.00; €5; www.museen.nuernberg.de). Guided tours of the Palace of Justice, accessed from Bärenschanzstraße 72 (Bärenschanze U-Bahn), are also possible (weekends, 1.00–4.00; €2.50; www.museen.nuernberg.de) although Courtroom 600, where the post-war trials occurred, is inaccessible until 2010 when a new memorial will be unveiled. The Deutsche Bahn Museum (Tue–Fri, 9.00–5.00; Sat–Sun, 10.00–6.00; €4; www.db.de/site/dbmuseum/de/start.html) at Lessingstraße 6, south of the centre, covers the Reichsbahn's role in the Holocaust.

Munich has a significant number of memorials. Perhaps the most effective is a large stone marking the site of the High Synagogue (destroyed on *Kristallnacht*) at the top of Herzog-Max-Straße near Karlsplatz. Central Platz der Opfer des Nationalsozialismus contains a plaque to murdered Sinti and Roma along with the rather cold main monument. Lindwurmstraße 127 (Goetheplatz U-Bahn) has an easily missed plaque to another destroyed synagogue, whilst the facing Hermann-Schmid-Straße has a memorial (between 5 and 7) to the patients and staff of a Jewish nursing home who were deported to Theresienstadt in 1942. In the north of the city (Am Hart U-Bahn), on the corner of Knorrstraße and Troppauer Straße, a memorial marks the Milbertshofen camp which the Jewish community was forced to construct at its own expense in spring 1941; 1,100 Jews were held there until their deportation in November of the same year. These and other memorials are comprehensively catalogued in a three-volume study available (in German) on the website of the Munich Documentation Centre for the History of National Socialism (www.ns-dokumentationszentrum-muenchen.de: follow the links through 'National Socialism in Munich'). The centre itself, currently at the planning stage, will be located at the site of the destroyed Brown House, the Nazi Party headquarters. One museum that has recently been completed is the Munich Jewish Museum (Tue, 10.00–6.00; €6; www.juedisches-museum-muenchen.de) at Sankt-Jakobs-Platz 16.

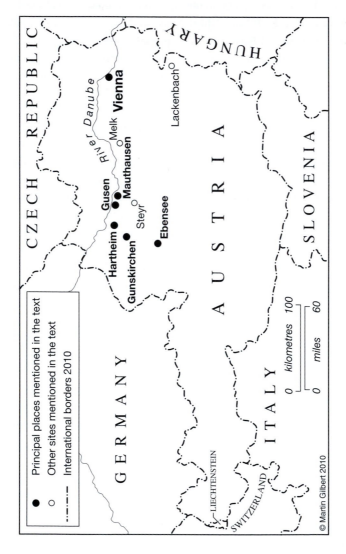

Austria

© Martin Gilbert 2010

CHAPTER 6

AUSTRIA

A s a full part of the Nazi state from 1938, Austria played a significant role in the Holocaust. Indeed, historians often note the preponderance of Austrians in the extermination process: it has been estimated that they comprised one-third of the key personnel even though they accounted for only 8 per cent of the Reich's population. As well as Hitler himself, examples include Eichmann, Ernst Kaltenbrunner (Heydrich's replacement as Himmler's deputy), Odilo Globocnik (overseer of *Aktion Reinhard*), Franz Stangl (commandant of Sobibór and Treblinka), Arthur Seyss-Inquart (*Reichskommissar* of the Netherlands) and Amon Goeth (commandant of Płaszów).

This may, in part, reflect the uneasy history of the Jews in Austria. Jewish settlement in the Middle Ages was punctuated by persecution, renewed during the seventeenth century when Austria's Habsburg emperors became the political leaders of the Counter-Reformation. It was only under Joseph II in the 1780s that religious toleration was granted and only in the mid-nineteenth century that full civic equality was achieved. These latter developments, and Austria's position at the heart of Europe's most multi-national empire, brought a rapid growth in the Jewish population, peaking at almost 250,000 in the First World War. However, Austria became a major centre of modern anti-Semitism; indeed, anti-Semitic parties generally performed far better there before the First World War and in the 1920s than in Germany. The rise of Nazism across the border further darkened the horizon with a three-way struggle for power in 1933–34 between the Socialists, Austrian Nazis and the increasingly Fascist-influenced Christian Social Party of Englebert Dollfuß. The latter prevailed only to be assassinated by Nazis in 1934. Although Mussolini initially acted as a barrier, Italy's increasing diplomatic proximity to Hitler left Austria vulnerable to German ambitions, culminating in the *Anschluß* of March 1938, an event enthusiastically welcomed by probably the majority of the population.

Whereas in Germany Nazi policy had been a process of gradually escalating persecution, in Austria it took the form of instantaneous and fanatical violence. Acts of humiliation were accompanied by a rapid removal of rights and the confiscation of Jewish property. The goal at this stage was emigration, a process assisted by the creation of the Central Office for Jewish Emigration under Eichmann in August 1938. Thousands were sent to camps after *Kristallnacht* and released only on condition that they leave the country. These policies had the desired effect in that around two-thirds of Austria's Jews – 126,445 – had fled abroad by September 1939, paradoxically ensuring that a far higher percentage survived than in many other countries once Nazi objectives turned to extermination. Of the 58,000 who stayed, only around 2,000 were able to escape before the final ban on emigration in late 1941. The remainder were largely deported to ghettos and camps in Poland and the USSR or to Theresienstadt. A mere 7,000 Jews remained in Austria, most in mixed marriages; they were made to carry out forced labour. It is estimated that more than 65,000 Austrian Jews were killed in the Holocaust, taking into account the deportees, those who died in Austria, and those who fled to other countries only to once again fall into Nazi hands. Less well-known is Austria's role in the fate of the Hungarian Jews, more than 20,000 of whom were employed in the construction of defensive fortifications on the eastern border from the summer of 1944. As the Soviets approached, many were sent west, first to Mauthausen and then, catastrophically, to Gunskirchen. Thousands died, their graves scattered across rural Austria.

Proper commemoration was slow to emerge, certainly slower than in Germany. Although Mauthausen was soon established as a memorial site, the Holocaust was generally overlooked in public debate and many sites were ignored or put to other uses. The situation was not helped by the Allies' 1943 Moscow Declaration which presented Austria as Hitler's first victim, a description not entirely justified by the public reaction in 1938; this enabled post-war politicians to avoid any serious focus on complicity in Nazi crimes. It was really only during and after the Waldheim affair in the late 1980s that a serious debate began about Austria's role in the war. In the two decades since, the country has done more to confront its history as demonstrated by a range of new memorials. Although the far right's intermittent electoral success in recent years is a cause for concern, it too has stimulated a renewed examination of Austria's troubled relationship with the Nazi era and the Holocaust.

VIENNA

By the early twentieth century, Vienna was home to the largest Jewish community in the Germanic world. Jewish settlement had been recorded as early as the tenth century but periods of prosperity alternated with those of persecution and there were expulsions in 1420–21 and 1670. As late as 1846, there were less than 4,000 Jews in the city. The population mushroomed thereafter, encouraged by equal civil rights and swelled by immigration from other Habsburg provinces and from the Russian Empire, exceeding 200,000 by 1923. In this period of growth and self-confidence, the city became a centre of Jewish learning and Hebrew literature yet also the home of the Zionist movement. The latter is perhaps not surprising as dark currents existed within the city even during the golden age of Viennese Jewry, most notoriously demonstrated by the success of the rabidly anti-Semitic Karl Lueger, the Christian Social Party's mayor from 1896. It was in this poisonous atmosphere that the young Hitler, then a failed artist and down-and-out, began to develop his racist philosophy.

Although the Jewish population declined between the wars, as much a result of First World War refugees returning home as of fear of Nazism, there were still around 170,000 Jews in Vienna in 1938, the overwhelming majority of Austria's 185,000 strong community. The effects of the *Anschluß* were immediate, thousands of citizens eagerly joining stormtroopers in attacking and humiliating Jews, most famously forcing them to scrub pavements. In fact, the German occupation only intensified persecution: local Nazis had already begun to harass the Jewish community in early 1938. At the end of May, 2,000 members of the intelligentsia were sent to Dachau whilst even before *Kristallnacht* there were concerted attacks on synagogues. During the pogrom itself, 49 synagogues were destroyed and 3,600 Jewish men sent to Dachau and Buchenwald. The majority of Viennese Jews emigrated in the following year or so.

There were still more than 50,000 Jews in the city at the outbreak of war, however, and deportations began soon after the invasion of Poland: more than 1,000 Polish and stateless Jews were sent to Buchenwald whilst Viennese Jews were part of the ill-conceived Nisko transports in October 1939 (all but 198 of the 1,584 sent east were driven across the river San into the Soviet zone). Mass deportations began in earnest in 1941, first to Kielce in February, and then the final, systematic deportations from October 1941 into 1942. The principal destinations were Łódź, Riga, Izbica, Minsk and, increasingly in 1942, Theresienstadt. The operation was so comprehensive that the Jewish community was disbanded on 1 November 1942. The only remaining Austrian Jews in the city, apart from a small number in hiding or in privileged occupations, were the less than 6,000 in mixed marriages. That was not the end of Vienna's role in the Holocaust, however: around half of the Hungarian Jews who arrived in Austria in the summer of 1944 were put to work in camps around the capital.

The city's Jewish community, like so many others, could never properly recover from the devastation. Indeed, many survivors, numbed by their losses and disillusioned with the local response to their return, opted to emigrate and it seemed as if Viennese Jewry might disappear altogether. In addition, public memorialisation of the Holocaust was slow to develop. However, there has been significant progress since the 1980s to the extent that the city now markets itself as a Jewish heritage tourist destination. The contemporary community, concentrated in the historic Jewish district of Leopoldstadt, is undergoing a period of relative growth, its numbers boosted in recent years by immigration from eastern Europe and, more unusually, Iran. It officially numbers around 7,000; this is only a fraction of the 1938 figure but the survival and renewal of a visible and increasingly self-confident Jewish presence in Vienna is itself an achievement.

Central Vienna

Judenplatz, the heart of medieval Jewish life, is the location of the Memorial to the Victims of the Holocaust, designed by the British artist Rachel Whiteread. Like most of Whiteread's work, the 2000 monument is a concrete cast of an interior space, in this case that of a library, intended to symbolise the lost lives as well as the role of the Jews as the People of the Book. Around its base are the names of places where Austria's Jews lost their lives. The design has been rather contentious although the memorial is certainly a striking presence dominating the square. The location was chosen to reflect the history of anti-Semitism in Vienna: following the 1420 expulsion, 210 Jews were kept in the city for the public spectacle of forced conversion; when they refused, they were herded into the square's synagogue which was then burned to the ground in March 1421. Astonishingly, above number 2 in the eastern end of the square, there is a wall relief celebrating this event. On the wall of

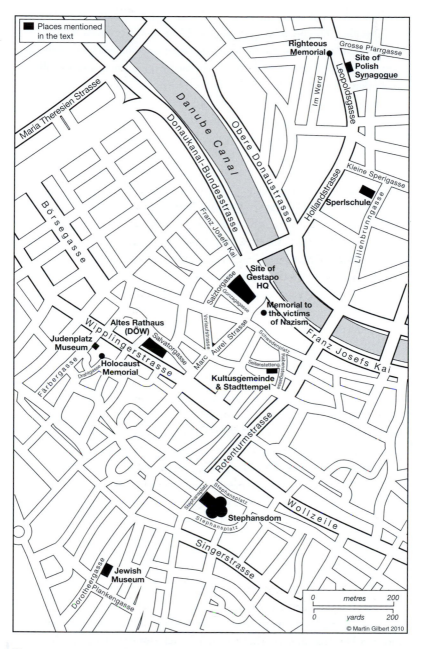

Vienna

number 6 is a more welcome recent addition – a 1998 plaque erected by the Catholic Church which apologises and begs for forgiveness. During the construction of the monument, the surviving foundations of the synagogue were discovered and they can now be seen, along with a small exhibition on medieval Jewish life, in the Judenplatz branch of Vienna's Jewish Museum (Sun–Thu, 10.00–6.00; Fri, 10.00–2.00; €4, or €10 with main Jewish Museum; www.jmw.at) at number 8. The museum also contains the Memorial Room for the Victims of the Shoah whose computer terminals enable one to discover more about the lives and deaths of Vienna's Jews. On the outside wall, there is a plaque to the small number of Austrian Righteous.

Just north of Judenplatz is the Altes Rathaus at Wipplingerstraße 8, which houses the Documentation Centre of Austrian Resistance (DÖW). There is an exhibition at the back of the courtyard (Mon–Fri, 9.00–5.00; free; www.doew.at) covering the Nazi terror and its victims. A thoughtful section covers the post-war period including the less than heroic attitude of Austrian governments to survivors.

A little further east, the elegant corner building at Marc-Aurel-Straße 5 is the former home of the *Palamt* (Palestine Bureau), centre of Zionist activity and de facto social centre for young Jews as persecution increased. Nearby Seitenstettengasse, today as in the 1930s, is dominated by the headquarters of the *Kultusgemeinde* (the Jewish community organisation) at numbers 2–4. As elsewhere, its leaders were later criticised for their alleged passivity and compliance; it is worth noting, however, that they were sent to Dachau almost immediately after the *Anschluß,* so it is hardly surprising that they were reluctant to oppose openly the Nazis once re-established in May 1938. The complex houses the Stadttempel, the only synagogue in the city to survive *Kristallnacht*, allegedly because of fear that fire could spread to the cellars of the nearby Gestapo headquarters. The synagogue, which has a remarkable neo-classical circular interior, can be visited by guided tour only (Mon–Thu, 11.30 & 2.00; €3; www.ikg-wien. at). By its entrance, a Holocaust memorial lists the names of the murdered. Around the back of the *Kultusgemeinde* is Desider-Friedman-Platz, named after the community's president who died in Auschwitz in 1944. Number 1 houses the Holocaust Victims Information and Support Centre.

Descending by the steps next to the Rupert Church to the north, one reaches Morzinplatz. The now destroyed Hotel Metropol, which served as the Gestapo headquarters, faced this square. A monument to victims of Nazism stands on the corner of the small park, the figure of a prisoner surrounded by concrete slabs topped with a Star of David and a red triangle. The site of the hotel itself is occupied by the Leopold-Figl-Hof, named after Austria's first post-war chancellor. On the Salztorgasse side of the building, at number 6, is the Memorial for the Victims of the Struggle for Austrian Freedom (the standard post-war formulation for victims of Nazism), a room with an altar-like memorial and a small exhibition (Mon, Thu & Fri, 10.00–1.30, 2.00–5.00; free). The same building also houses the Simon Wiesenthal Documentation Centre, home to the Nazi-hunter's work until his death in 2005, which is closed to the public. Much of the material has been transferred to the Wiesenthal Center in Los Angeles but there are plans to develop a major Holocaust research institute in Vienna in his honour.

South of Judenplatz, the Barbara Chapel in the north transept of the Stephansdom cathedral, is a Christian memorial to camp victims with a large crucifix containing earth and ashes from Auschwitz and Mauthausen. The tourist office opposite the cathedral at Stephansplatz 10 houses the Jewish Welcome Service (www.jewish-welcome.at) which provides information for Jewish visitors.

Further south is the Jewish Museum at Dorotheergasse 11 (Sun–Fri, 10.00–6.00; €6.50, or €10 with Judenplatz branch; www.jmw. at). Vienna was the site of the world's oldest such institution, inevitably closed in 1938. The modern version (opened in 1993) is more a centre of conceptual art than historical museum, with much space devoted to temporary exhibitions, but the third floor houses the *Schaudepot* (storage depot), glass cases containing a large collection of ritual objects; some still bear scorch marks from *Kristallnacht*.

Standing a little further south, the Monument Against War and Fascism on Albertinaplatz is an immensely controversial sculptural ensemble, unveiled as Austria's first state-sponsored memorial to Nazi victims at the remarkably late date of 1989. The inclusion of war in the concept means that no distinction is made between the different groups of people who died in the Second World War, a point emphasised by the fact that this is built on the site of a 1945 Allied bombing raid in which several hundred people died. Indeed, the only Jewish reference is a small black sculpture of an elderly Jew being forced to scrub the pavement. Many found this degrading, leading directly to the campaign for the Judenplatz memorial.

Leopoldstadt

The city's second district, north-east of the Donaukanal, has been the historic centre of Jewish Vienna since Ferdinand II sanctioned the creation of a ghetto in 1624. Despite expulsion in 1670 by Leopold I, after whom the district became known, Jews again settled in this area when permitted to return in the eighteenth century. Leopoldstadt remained home to most synagogues and communal institutions even after emancipation and assimilation had spread Jewish residence across the city. Following the Nazi takeover, the community was again increasingly restricted to the district and it was here that people were held prior to deportation.

The *Sperlschule*, at Kleine Sperlgasse 2a down an alley, was the principal detention centre for Viennese Jews: 40,000 were held there over the course of the deportations, in some cases for several weeks. The building is again a school today and there is a memorial plaque on its wall by its entry gate. Kleine Sperlgasse is right off Hollandstraße, just across the canal from Salztorgasse.

Hollandstraße soon becomes Leopoldsgasse; a sign by the ugly post-war apartment building at number 29 marks the site of the Polish Synagogue, a victim of *Kristallnacht*, whilst a triangular metal and glass column at the junction with Im Werd is a memorial to Austrian Righteous. The Theodor Herzl-Hof at Leopoldsgasse 13 stands on the site of a pre-war building which housed a vocational school for young women and an Orthodox girls' school. This too was used as a holding centre prior to deportation for more than 10,000 Jews; a plaque on the wall commemorates this history whilst others honour Herzl. Around the corner, Malzgasse 16 was the site of a synagogue and a Jewish hospital (the only hospital available to Jews from 1942) which was also used to augment the *Sperlschule* during the deportation to Łódź. Today it is home to a Talmud Torah school, in a courtyard behind guarded gates.

Leopoldsgasse eventually becomes short Kraftgasse which connects Untere Augartenstraße and Rembrandtstraße. At number 33 on the latter, there is a plaque in the doorway listing the names of 27 former Jewish inhabitants who were deported. This plaque was, unusually, erected by the current residents. Parallel to Kraftgasse, at the southern end of Rembrandtstraße, is Förstergasse. Number 7 was the site of a particularly tragic incident, marked by a wall plaque: nine Jews who had survived the war in hiding had taken refuge in the cellar of this building during the fierce fighting of the Battle for Vienna. They were discovered by a Waffen-SS unit in the afternoon of 11 April 1945 and shot in the street later that night; the Red Army arrived just hours later.

In the eastern part of Leopoldstadt, Tempelgasse 5 (Nestroyplatz U-Bahn) was the location of the Leopoldstadt Tempel, one of the city's principal synagogues until *Kristallnacht*. The site is now occupied by a large complex including a synagogue, a school and the Centre for Psychosocial Care (ESRA) which, amongst other things, provides counselling for Holocaust survivors. The metal grid fence carries memorial plaques for the synagogue, individuals and the 30,000 Leopoldstadt Jews (including 1,600 children) who perished. Tempelgasse 2 was occupied by the *Piper Heim*, eventually the only school left open to Jews.

Pazmanitengasse 6, several blocks further north, was the site of another synagogue, now occupied by an apartment block with a wall plaque (tram 21, Rueppgasse stop). West across Taborstraße at Castellezgasse 35, is the *Zwi Perez Chajes Schule* which was used as a detention centre during the deportations, as recorded by another plaque (trams 21 & N, Heinestraße).

Elsewhere

Located on the other side of the Augarten from Leopoldstadt, the *Brigittenauer Gymnasium* at Karajangasse 14–16 (tram 5, Rauscherstraße or 5 & 33, Wallensteinplatz) was used as a Gestapo internment centre in 1938–39. There is a plaque immediately ahead through its front doors (schooldays, 4.00–6.00). Further north is the Anton Schmid Hof, a post-war housing development facing Jägerstraße U-Bahn station on Leipziger Platz (also tram 33). Schmid was an Austrian Wehrmacht officer executed in 1942 for helping Jews in the Vilna ghetto; the entrance at Leipziger Straße 40 has a plaque in his honour.

The elegant building just north of the city centre at Schottenring 25 (trams 1, 2 & D, Börse) was the temporary post-war headquarters of the Jewish community whilst the Seitenstettengasse complex was restored. It was here that the small number of survivors who returned to Vienna congregated, anxiously waiting for the invariably sad news of the fate of their loved ones. The former home of Vienna's most famous Jewish resident, himself forced to flee to London in 1938, is now the Freud Museum (daily, 9.00–5.00 (9.00–6.00, July–Sept); €7; www.freud-museum.at; tram D, Schlickgasse) at nearby Berggasse 19. Two tram stops further north (tram D, Seegasse) is the Rossauer Jewish cemetery, Vienna's oldest, entered through an old people's home at Seegasse 9. The modern home occupies the site of a Jewish old people's home and hospital which were situated here until the 1970s. The other major historic Jewish cemetery, the Währing, was largely destroyed by the Nazis and the subject of its restoration has been a source of ongoing debate within the municipality. For the moment, the site at Semperstraße 64A (U-Bahn, Nußdorfer Straße) is closed – check the Jewish community's website (www.ikg-wien.at) for any changes.

In Vienna's south-west, around the Westbahnhof, are several sites of note. There is a new memorial in the station itself to the *Kindertransport* children sent to safety in Britain in 1938–39; this is opposite a plaque to the first Austrians sent to Dachau. Standing a block north-east at Kenyongasse 4–12 (tram 5, Stollgasse), a Catholic school is one of a number of locations where arrested Jewish men were held after *Kristallnacht* before being sent to Dachau or Buchenwald. Of the men held in this building, 27 were killed and 88 critically injured. South of here, an unprepossessing building at Schmalzhofgasse 3 (U-Bahn, Zieglergasse) has a memorial to the synagogue which stood here until the pogrom. Two more destroyed synagogues are commemorated with plaques south-west of the Westbahnhof at Turnergasse 22 (trams 52 & 58, Staglgasse) and at decaying Storchengasse 21 (U-Bahn, Längenfeldgasse).

Some of the most significant sites in the history of the Viennese Holocaust are south-east of the centre, around the Belvedere Palace. At Prinz-Eugen-Straße 20–22 (tram D, Plößlgasse) once stood the Rothschild Palais, a symbol of the success of the emancipated Jewish elites of late Habsburg Vienna. The building was requisitioned by the Nazis in 1938 to become the headquarters of Eichmann's *Zentralstelle für jüdische Auswanderung* (Central Office for Jewish Emigration). The initiative for the *Zentralstelle* initially came from within the Jewish community itself as a means of easing departure from Austria following the invasion. However, it became a tool of exploitation, aiming to force Jews out of the country whilst making it as financially difficult for them as possible. As a result, the Nazis were able to ensure that most Jewish wealth fell into their hands. The 'success' of this project led to similar institutions being created in Berlin and Prague in 1939 and to Eichmann coming to be seen as an expert on the 'Jewish question'. In due course, the *Zentralstelle* became a means of registering Jews prior to deportation and it closed in March 1943, there being so few Jews left for it to control. The palace was destroyed in an air raid and replaced after the war with a large ugly building which housed the headquarters of the Chamber of Workers and Employees (AK). This building is itself undergoing extensive reconstruction. Around the corner at Theresianumgasse 16–18, another former Rothschild palace became the Vienna HQ of the SD, Heydrich's security police and intelligence service. This too was destroyed by Allied bombing and there is now a modern building housing AK offices; a circular glass panel sticking out from the wall serves as a memorial.

On the eastern side of the Belvedere, a little way down Aspangstraße from Rennweg S-Bahn station, is Platz der Opfer der Deportation, a small park near the site of the Aspang railway station from which deportation trains left. The street sign explains the history without mentioning that the victims were Jewish though a memorial stone in a fenced off grassy area is more explicit.

Further south, Reumannplatz, a small park into which the U-Bahn station of the same name exits, has a grey stone memorial to 'Victims of Fascism 1934–1945', created in 1981 on the initiative of Austria's major political parties. Nearby, on the wall of the *Reno* shoe shop at Leibnizgasse 10 (corner with Quillergasse), is a memorial plaque to Czechs and Slovaks who died fighting the Nazis in Austria.

In the far south-east, Wien-West (or Saurerwerke) was a sub-camp of Mauthausen created in an industrial zone in 1944; directly next to it was a labour camp for Hungarian Jews. There is a memorial stone in the grounds of the *Zur Bast* guesthouse on the corner of Haidestraße and Oriongasse (Haidestraße S-Bahn, then bus 76A to Oriongasse or a 1 km walk).

The massive Zentralfriedhof (Central Cemetery) on Simmeringer Hauptstraße 230–244 (summer, 7.00–8.00; spring & autumn, 7.00–7.00; winter, 8.00–5.00; different hours for new Jewish cemetery below) is even further south-east and so big that each of its four gates has its own tram stop (trams 6 & 71, only the latter goes to the fourth gate). Gate 1 leads to the old Jewish cemetery, with many impressive nineteenth-century tombs. When this section filled up in the 1920s, the community opened the new cemetery, separated from the rest of the Zentralfriedhof by walls and accessed by gate 4 (Sun–Thu, 8.00–5.00 (until 4.00 in winter); Fri, 8.00–2.00). The colonnaded courtyards around the hall contain some stones for families killed in the Holocaust along with a memorial to Jewish soldiers who fought in the Allied armies and the partisans. A large stone, in the form of a stylised Torah roll, marks the 1987 burial spot of remnants of holy books which were torn up and burnt on *Kristallnacht*. Behind the ceremonial hall, on the corner of group 8A, are the graves of the nine victims of the Förstergasse killing. At the very back (group 22 in the southeastern corner) are the mass graves of Hungarian Jews. In the Christian section of the cemetery, entered via gate 2, are a series of memorials to other victims of Nazism, including a grave for the disabled children killed at the *Am Spiegelgrund* clinic (see below) and stones for victims of the Hinterbruhl and Hadersdorf camps. All are located in the eastern section of group 40; the western section contains memorials for air-raid victims. The cemetery also contains a large memorial to Nazi victims in Group 41H, whilst in rows 36 and 37 of Group 28 there are memorials for socialist victims of the 1934 power struggle and for Austrians who fell in the Spanish Civil War.

The Otto Wagner Psychiatric Hospital at Baumgartner Höhe 1 (Bus 48A, Psychiatrisches Krankenhaus) in the far west was originally the Steinhof mental hospital, one of the largest and most prominent institutions of its kind in Europe, which became a major killing centre during the 'wild euthanasia' period. More than 3,000 people were murdered here, including 772 children at the so-called *Am Spiegelgrund* clinic. The children were given cocoa powder laced with poison or lethal injections. The principal doctor Heinrich Gross stored body parts in formaldehyde, a collection which was used as the basis for acclaimed post-war research papers. Only a very lengthy campaign by victims' relatives, aided by the 2001 film *Spiegelgrund*, led to any semblance of justice. The remains of the children (secretly buried in the complex after the war) were given a proper burial in the Zentralfriedhof in 2002 whilst Gross was stripped of his Honorary Cross for Science and Art in 2003. Despite incontrovertible proof of his role in the murders in a 1981 trial, he had continued to enjoy a prestigious career. There is a memorial to the children behind the main entrance hall, in the form of a field of 772 columns which are illuminated at night and carry a powerful presence. Towards the back of the complex in the administration building (Block V behind Block 13) is a small exhibition in German along with heartbreaking pictures of the murdered children (Wed–Fri, 10.00–12.00, 1.00–5.00; free; www.gedenkstaettesteinhof.at). Close by, near the steps up to the chapel, is a memorial stone to all victims of the 'euthanasia' policy.

MAUTHAUSEN

Mauthausen, together with its Gusen satellite, was the deadliest concentration camp within the Reich proper. It was always likely that a camp would be established in Austria but the impetus for Mauthausen came also from the growing economic activism of the SS, the area's stone quarries leading to its development. The camp opened in August 1938 and initially contained several hundred criminals brought from Dachau. The first political prisoners arrived in 1939 and the outbreak of war led to such a rapid expansion that a separate camp was established at nearby Gusen. Prisoners included Czechs, Spanish Republicans, Poles, Soviets and, later, resistance fighters from western Europe. What distinguished Mauthausen and Gusen was their designation by Heydrich as the only Category III 'camps of no return', that is, camps whose inmates were to be regarded as incorrigible and thus to be exterminated through labour. The Jewish population was relatively small for most of Mauthausen's history although

Mauthausen (Photograph by the author)

several hundred Dutch Jews were sent there in 1941. As with the other camps in the Reich, this changed in the war's last year when transports arrived from Poland and thousands of Hungarian Jews were marched from the eastern border, generating inevitable overcrowding. As the war drew to a close, around 20,000 Jewish prisoners were marched westward to Gunskirchen (see below) before the camp was liberated by the Americans on 5 May 1945. It is believed that almost 200,000 inmates were absorbed by the Mauthausen and Gusen system; including those prisoners gassed at Hartheim, around 119,000 died, of whom 38,120 were Jews.

The camp, hidden behind thick stone walls on a hilltop, soon became a memorial site and remains the best-preserved and most-visited Holocaust location in Austria albeit one which controversially charges for entry (daily, 9.00–5.30; €2; www.mauthausen-memorial.at). A memorial to the left of the approach road marks the area where Soviet POWs were originally held; sick quarters were later located here. The visitors' centre, from where entry tickets are purchased, is to the right of the camp entrance alongside a cinema building (also used for temporary exhibitions).

The camp area proper is entered via the intimidating main gate and through the SS garage yard which has recently been restored following storm damage. Facing the gate, at the top of the opposite wall, is the command HQ. The prisoners' camp and memorial area is accessed by stairs, at the top of which stands a monument to Soviet General Dmitry Karbyshev; he and 200 other prisoners were forced to stand outside on the night of 16 February 1945 whilst cold water was poured over them; none survived. Ahead and to the left is a wide area devoted to the 'Memorials of the Nations', the principal site of remembrance.

First, though, it is sensible to visit the prisoners' camp, entered through another imposing stone gatehouse. A sarcophagus in the *Appellplatz* serves as a memorial to the inmates. Their wooden barracks were to the left of the square but most were torn down after the war. The three that remained (1, 6 and 11) were badly damaged during a 2007 storm and are unlikely to be open for the foreseeable future. This means that it is also not currently possible to see the site of barracks 5 (behind barracks 1) where sick prisoners and 2,700 Jews were held between 1941 and 1944; nearly all were killed. Also currently out of bounds, further along to the left, are a series of memorial cemeteries, including those for bodies exhumed from the mass graves in Gunskirchen forest in the 1970s and for Mauthausen and Gusen prisoners who died after liberation. The notorious Block 20 (originally a sick barrack) stood within this area: 4,500 Soviet officers who had escaped from POW camps and been recaptured were quartered here from spring 1944 and left to starve. On 2 February 1945, 495 escaped though only 419 made it past the outer perimeter. Most froze to death overnight or were recaptured the next day; only a dozen are known to have survived. At the far end of the camp, behind the wall, was a special camp, initially created in 1944 for Polish women after the defeat of the Warsaw Uprising. In the spring of 1945, 1,400 weakened prisoners were stationed here; 560 were then killed in the gas chambers.

To the right of the roll-call square are solid stone blocks which form the main part of the modern complex. At the far end, opposite the mass graves, is the main infirmary barrack which now houses the museum. The text is in German but a guidebook (€2.60) is available from the visitors' centre. The exhibition traces the history of Mauthausen and its sub-camps over two floors in the east wing of the block whilst there is an exhibition on Austrians in the Nazi camp system in the ground floor of the west wing. The west wing basement housed the killing machinery; memorials now mark the three crematoria and the gas chamber. The latter was used to murder weakened prisoners between 1942 and 1945 (victims were previously killed at Hartheim). The second crematorium was also used as an execution site: in the corner, a device supposedly for head measurements was set; when the prisoner was in position, he was shot in the neck. Hangings also took place in this room. The third crematorium is actually under the prison block whose entrance hall is open (accessible from outside). The two wooden blocks back towards the gate were the kitchen and the laundry; the latter contains memorials and a chapel. The corner by the laundry and gatehouse was known as the 'wailing wall', the place where new prisoners had to stand to attention, often for hours at a time. A large number of memorials have been placed here, including a modern stone erected by the Vienna Jewish community and a plaque for Sinti and Roma victims.

Back outside the inmates' camp, the 'Memorials of the Nations' occupy a wide area to the west, dominated by an inevitably huge Soviet structure and a rather more effective Czechoslovak sculpture of an emaciated figure. Perhaps the most touching memorial is the Italian, a stone wall with a large number of plaques to individuals, whilst the Dutch memorial in the south-west corner lists the names of all victims from the Netherlands. A large Jewish monument overlooks the quarry behind; nearby is a memorial to Sinti and Roma victims, amongst whom were 450 women and children transported from Ravensbrück to Mauthausen and murdered.

From here a path leads past other memorials (to children and Austrian Jews) towards the Wiener Graben quarry. There are also remnants of SS accommodation buildings and workshops in the trees to the right. Beyond them lay the so-called tent camp, created in 1944 to house the deluge of new arrivals. In early 1945, it was used to accommodate the thousands of Hungarian Jews who were later marched on to Gunskirchen; there were no toilets or running water. The uneven stone path skirts the sheer edges of the quarry, referred to by the SS guards as 'parachutists' cliff' due to their practice of chasing prisoners up the quarry steps and then pushing them when they reached the top: any who survived the fall drowned in the pools of stagnant water below. This is particularly associated with a transport of 348 Dutch Jews which arrived from Buchenwald on 17 June 1941. The following morning, 50 were forced from the bathhouse naked and driven into the fence. The remainder were sent to the quarry and within three weeks all were dead.

Once the camp expanded during the war, only a minority of prisoners were working in the quarry but they still numbered 1,500 to 3,500 at any given time. Before steps into the quarry were constructed in the summer of 1942, prisoners had to make their way down, and more dangerously up, via loosely set rocks; many were killed by falling stones when those in front tripped. The 186 steps were almost as fatal; apart from a couple of breaks where the stairs curve towards the top, they are mostly a steep single flight which even today is challenging. Prisoners were forced to take this route at speed under constant harassment and with the threat of shooting. Members of the *Strafkommando* (punishment detail) had to carry stones of 100 pounds or more on their shoulders. The quarry itself is a huge hollowed out area; in addition to the quarrying work, an arms factory was also established here in 1943.

The camp is signposted off the B123 road east of Linz between Sankt Georgen an der Gusen and Mauthausen village. To reach the site by public transport, take the 360 bus (Mon–Fri plus Sat mornings) from Linz to the Mauthausen Hauptschule stop from where signs point the way up Ufer-Straße which runs fairly gently uphill to the camp; the walk takes about

20 minutes. If travelling back on foot, it is possible to exit the quarry onto Wiener Graben and walk for a similar length of time to the Mauthausen Wasserwerk stop to catch the same service back to Linz or to Gusen. Mauthausen train station is much further from the camp, although it might be possible to catch a taxi from there.

GUSEN

Gusen was established in December 1939, near quarries in which prisoners already laboured, as a result of the overcrowding in Mauthausen. When it came into operation in March 1940, the initial inmates were Poles whilst in 1941 a large number of Soviet POWs were interned there. However, as the other category III camp, Gusen's turnover of inmates was extremely high. Increasing labour demands for the war effort led to further expansion with Gusen II and III opening in 1944, spreading the complex over several miles. In fact, for most of the war, Gusen had a larger population than Mauthausen. There is evidence that the SS planned to blow up all 25,000 inmates in the Gusen II tunnels, prompting the local Red Cross delegate Louis Häfliger to risk his life and bring the Americans on 5 May 1945. It is estimated that close to 70,000 people went through Gusen of whom at least 37,000 died.

Gusen II was destroyed by the Americans to stop the spread of epidemics but Gusen I remained, as Soviet barracks, until the occupation ended in 1955. The municipality then decided to create a housing estate on the site, selling off plots of land to families to do with as they wished. Somewhat ironically, this unintentionally enabled Gusen's survival as a memorial site. Former prisoners had erected memorial stones after the war by the still intact crematorium oven (which had operated from January 1941) to create a small but meaningful place of remembrance. When plans were announced in 1960 to relocate the stones and oven to Mauthausen, a group of Italian and French former inmates bought the land from the council to safeguard the site and to construct a larger structure, which was completed in 1965. This memorial, designed by a Gusen survivor, encloses the crematorium within concrete walls, around which are a large number of plaques to groups and individuals. It adjoins the 2004 visitors' centre (built around the crematorium's foundations) whose exhibition addresses the camp's history and contains some truly shocking photographs of inmates taken at liberation (Apr–Sept:Tue–Sun,

9.00–5.30; Oct–Mar: weekends & holidays only, 9.00–5.30; free; www. gusen-memorial.at). The visitors' centre itself is the result of greater investment following the takeover of the site by the Austrian government in 1997. The KZ Gusen Memorial Committee, which previously ran the site, still plays an active role, and its website (www.gusen.org) is an excellent source of information on Gusen and other Mauthausen satellites.

The visitors' centre is also the place to collect the Gusen Audiowalk, an absorbing way to cover Gusen I and II, available in English and German (free, but leave passport as security). Visitors are given an iPod containing a 96 minute guided walk, interspersed with comments from inmates, eyewitnesses, a candid camp guard and modern residents. The latter – with the exception of a few, mainly younger, inhabitants – do not cover themselves in glory. The tour starts in the triangular space outside the memorial (where there is a relief plan of the camp) by the main road (Georgestraße) which was itself built by Gusen inmates. Standing a couple of blocks to the east, Georgestraße 18 is a substantial two-storey building set back from the road behind a large iron gate: this was Gusen's gatehouse, now converted into a private residence. Around the corner (the next turning on the left) on an unnamed road are two former SS barracks, also now private housing. That nearest to the road was a guardhouse whilst the other contained a bathhouse and a barbershop. Between them, where there were originally two further barracks, is a simple memorial stone erected by persons unknown after the war. Such sympathy is less evident from the current inhabitants who have erected, virtually opposite the memorial stone, a 'stop' sign notifying visitors that this is private land and that entry is strictly forbidden: this was a direct response to the creation of the Audiowalk. Visitors are thus obliged to reverse their tracks back past the gatehouse and turn right onto Mitterweg. The long building on the right near the top of this road (actually Untere Gartenstraße 14) was the camp brothel where from 1942 privileged prisoners could spend RM 2 to visit prostitutes brought from Ravensbrück (the prostitute got 0.50 – the rest went to the SS). Again, it is now a private house. From Untere Gartenstraße itself, standing in what was the *Appellplatz*, one can see the quarries in which prisoners slaved in the hills to the north. One will also see a large concrete building: this was Gusen's stone crusher, apparently the largest in Europe at the time. The two yellowish buildings to its left were Blocks 6 and 7, the only remaining prisoner barracks.

These buildings are all that survive physically of the camp but continuing further gives some sense of Gusen's scale. West along Untere Gartenstraße, passing the back of the memorial, one comes to Parkstraße. The three-storey building at number 1 is built on the site of Block 27, the Pathological Unit headed by Dr Helmut Vetter, who had previously served in Auschwitz; he forcibly injected Gusen prisoners with supposed cures for tuberculosis which were either useless or hastened their deaths. Block 27 also contained the 'Gusen Pathological Museum' made up of 286 organs 'harvested' from prisoners. Parkstraße 3 is on the site of Block 31 which housed the weakest prisoners. On 22 April 1945, 684 seriously ill inmates were gassed here. Soviet, Polish and Spanish prisoners had previously been gassed in other blocks during a typhus epidemic in March 1942. In addition, between autumn 1941 and autumn 1942, a gas van travelled between Gusen and Mauthausen, mainly killing Soviet POWs. Gusen inmates were murdered en route to Mauthausen and vice versa.

Gusen II was a little further west in the area bordered by Spielplatzstraße (Playground Street), Buchenstraße, Georgestraße and Ringstraße. Some survivors recalled this camp as being worse than Auschwitz. Construction began in March 1944 to house slave labour for the Bergkristall underground plant in nearby Sankt Georgen an der Gusen. Inmates had to dig tunnels or work in Messerschmitt jet factories, both tasks where heat and dust had a devastating effect on already malnourished people. To compound matters, the SS left the running of Gusen II in the hands of criminal *kapos* who could abuse or even kill prisoners with impunity. Jews formed the largest single group and were selected for the hardest labour and received the least food. As they grew weaker, they were sent to Hartheim or Auschwitz (from where many had come) to be gassed. In the winter of 1944–45, when large numbers arrived on transports from the east, the SS simply left Jews outside to freeze to death. There is nothing within this quiet residential area to act as a reminder of such horrors, but there are some remnants of Gusen II beyond the village. Where Ringstraße meets Georgestraße, one can cross the main road and take a path which runs westwards. Continuing until the path splits three ways, the middle route (an elevated path lined with trees) was a section of the prisoner-built railway line which ran from the quarry at Mauthausen to the Bergkristall tunnels. Its course crosses the *Schleppbahnbrücke*, a bridge constructed by the inmates at the bottom of Wimmingerstraße and marked by a memorial by local artist Rudolf Berger, and continues to Bahnhofstraße in Sankt Georgen an der Gusen. Turning right, following the curve of the road under the railway bridge and then turning left onto Kellerstraße, one comes to a path to the right into a field over which the hills of the Bergkristall complex loom. The path passes one entrance (now modernised as an air-raid shelter!) and it is here that the Audiowalk ends. A large wall of rock ahead marks another tunnel, on water board property behind a fence. More can be seen by returning to Bahnhofstraße, heading north away from the railway bridge, and then taking the next left onto Brunnenweg: a memorial board stands just past Brunnenweg 5 and one can discern the tunnels behind the water works. If using the Audiowalk, it will take around 25 minutes to walk back to the Gusen visitors' centre from here.

Gusen III, created in December 1944, was located two miles northeast of Sankt Georgen in Lungitz, next to a local brick factory which housed Messerschmitt parts. In February 1945, a bakery went into operation to serve the entire Gusen system. The camp, the first in the complex to be reached by the Americans, was destroyed after the war but a memorial, a triangular stone with a map of the camp, was erected in 2000. It stands in the meadow in which the camp was located.

The main Gusen memorial can be easily reached, visible on the B123 between Sankt Georgen and Mauthausen. It is next to the Gusen bus stop, served by the same 360 service from Linz that runs to Mauthausen. The Gusen I and II sites are within a short distance of the memorial whilst the former railway route to Sankt Georgen is an approximately 2 kilometre walk. To get to the Gusen III memorial, take the short train ride from Sankt Georgen to Lungitz, exit the station left and, after about 200 metres, take the signposted turning to the left (just past the factory) under the railway bridge. Coming by road from Sankt Georgen, the memorial will be signposted on the right.

HARTHEIM

Schloß Hartheim, in the small town of Alkoven near Linz, was the most lethal of the T4 centres and the most significant in the history of the Holocaust. The late sixteenth-century building, a home for disabled children since 1898, was converted into a killing centre over the winter of 1939–40 with the extermination apparatus located on the ground floor around an inner courtyard. The murders began in May 1940; by August 1941, more than 18,000 had been killed, by far the largest number for any of the T4 centres. Hartheim was also the largest killing site in the 14f13 murders of weakened concentration camp prisoners. In two phases – August 1941 to December 1942 and then through 1944 – inmates were brought there to be gassed, primarily from Dachau, Mauthausen and Gusen. Even after Mauthausen's own gas chamber was established in 1942, Hartheim was still used to kill prisoners, especially Jews. It is generally estimated that at least 12,000 concentration camp inmates were murdered, leaving a total in excess of 30,000 deaths. Murder on this scale could not easily be hidden and rumours soon circulated amongst the citizens of Alkoven, unsurprisingly given the dark, foul-smelling clouds that appeared after the buses arrived and the fact that no one brought to the castle ever left it. Disquiet became so severe that the Nazis were forced to create a cover story about contaminated oil being burned although the fact that they still felt compelled to warn of dire consequences should alternative rumours be spread suggests that the explanation was not entirely convincing.

Hartheim's importance in the wider context of the Holocaust lies not just in the numbers killed or in their origins, but also in its staff who formed the nexus of the *Aktion Reinhard* personnel. It was overseen for a time by the brutal Christian Wirth, transferred following the closure of Grafeneck. Wirth, as the commandant of Bełżec and the inspector of all three *Reinhard* camps, had arguably the largest personal role in the destruction of Polish Jewry. Other Hartheim staff who followed him included Stangl, Franz Reichleitner (Stangl's successor at Sobibór), Gottlieb Hering (Wirth's successor at Bełżec), and Kurt Franz (final commandant of Treblinka).

The site was returned to the Upper Austrian Charity Association in 1948 and used to house people who had lost their homes in floods in 1954 (disabled patients have been treated at the nearby Hartheim Institute since the late 1960s). A memorial was created in 1969 but pressure began to grow for the relocation of the residents and the transformation of the whole site into a fitting place of remembrance, something which was accomplished in 2002–03. The new memorial complex (Mon & Fri, 9.00–3.00; Tue–Thu, 9.00–4.00; Sun, 10.00–5.00; free; www.schloss-hartheim.at) is the largest and most impressive of those at the T4 centres. It is entered through a separate gateway building at Schloßstraße 1 on the castle's east side. Approaching the gateway, a metal sarcophagus whose glass panels feature quotations from the Books of Job and Matthew and Austrian poet Franz Rieger marks a site where victims' ashes and ground bones were buried (they were also thrown into the Danube). Some of these remains were discovered during renovations of the heating system in 2000–01; the sarcophagus was constructed to give them a proper burial. There is also a memorial to two locals executed by the Nazis in April 1945 by the gate.

In the centre of the Renaissance-style Schloß, past a bookshop and a memorial stone in the entrance hall, is the beautiful small courtyard; during the height of the murders, a crematorium oven stood here. Three rooms on the far side present the main exhibition, providing an overview of T4 and Hartheim's role in it. The third room includes a computer database of 37 representative victims with photographs, biographies and medical records. This leads into the memorial area, beginning with pictures of victims and cabinets containing their possessions (unearthed during the renovation work). Their names are inscribed on glass panels in the reception room by a large piece of excavated earth containing more buried artefacts. A walkway leads straight into the now bare gas chamber, demonstrating just how short the route to death was; up to 150 people at a time were murdered here. All of the rooms – the gas chamber, technical room, morgue and crematorium – are whitewashed and unadorned: Mauthausen inmates were brought in the last months of the war to destroy the evidence. Exiting the former crematorium into the south-east corner, individual memorial plaques line the walls. Hartheim also includes the multi-media *Value of Life* exhibition which explores attitudes to disability through history and current ethical debates. Beginning in the corner of the courtyard on the ground floor, it continues upstairs.

Back outside the Schloß, the specially constructed wooden shed where the grey buses arrived was on the west side. There is now a memorial installation in the form of steel panels representing the site of the garage and glass screens listing victims' places of origin. On the northern side, by the road, is a memorial to French victims.

Alkoven lies off the B129, north-west of Linz. To reach the site by train, take the Lokalbahn service from Linz to Alkoven, exit the station to the right and then take the first road on the right. The castle is a 10 minute walk away, clearly visible.

GUNSKIRCHEN

The short-lived Gunskirchen camp was, in some respects, the Austrian Belsen. It was created in March 1945 in response to the over-crowding in the Mauthausen tent camp: the Hungarian Jews who had been marched from eastern Austria were then moved on to Gunskirchen. In the second half of April 1945, between 15,000 and 20,000 Jewish prisoners were brought to the camp, which was completely unprepared for their arrival with only seven incomplete wooden barracks, no running water and just one toilet – a room for 12 men and 16 women accessible for only 6 hours a day – for the entire camp. With around 2,500 inmates in each of the huts (to which they were confined for 12 hours at night), typhus and dysentery were soon rampant and 200 to 300 died each day. Prisoners who, unable to wait for the toilet, soiled themselves were immediately shot by the SS. When the camp was liberated by US troops on 4 May 1945, they found only 5,419 surviving prisoners (an unknown number had run away), hundreds of rotting corpses and mass graves in the forests. Estimates of the death toll range from 2,500 to 5,000 whilst possibly thousands more had died on the march to Gunskirchen.

The camp was located in the Hocholz forest, just south of Gunskirchen village. There is a simple triangular memorial stone, erected in 1995 by the US 71st Infantry Division to mark the fiftieth anniversary of the liberation, at the site of the camp entrance. A sign in German alongside outlines the camp's history. As the sign explains, it occupied the woods (through which there are paths) south and east of here. The buildings were destroyed at the end of the war but there were mass graves for 1,227 prisoners in the forest until the 1970s when they were relocated to the Mauthausen cemetery following cases of vandalism as well as fires caused by candles left by the gravestones. There is an additional memorial on the edge of the village, around 600 metres to the north.

The village memorial is located next to the B1 between Wels and Lambach, at the western turning for Gunskirchen (Lambacher Straße). The unnamed continuation of Lambacher Straße south of the B1 leads to the forest memorial, on the left at the exact point where the road curves sharply to the right. From Gunskirchen train station, the village memorial is a 2 kilometre walk (exit station left until the steps down to Lambacher Straße and then continue south along that road). The 2434 Postbus from the station to Fliederstraße significantly reduces the journey but this is very irregular.

EBENSEE

The very last camp in the west to be liberated, Ebensee was created in November 1943 as a satellite of Mauthausen to provide labour for the construction of tunnels in the side of a nearby mountain. The tunnels, originally intended to house rocket research, were used for the manufacture of motor parts and refining petrol. Conditions were appalling from the start with the as yet incomplete barracks ensuring that large numbers died in the freezing first winter; through Ebensee's existence the average monthly death rate was more than 10 per cent. The first commandant Georg Bachmayer delighted in letting his Alsatian attack prisoners suspended from trees whilst his drunken successor Otto Riemer regularly shot at them. Overcrowding in the war's last months – there were more than 18,000 inmates by early 1945, 40 per cent of them Jewish as a result of the death marches – led to a rapid deterioration to the extent that the crematorium could not cope with the number of victims. As the US Army approached on 5 May 1945, the final commandant Anton Ganz ordered the prisoners into one of the tunnels but they refused; when the Americans began to liberate the camp the next day, they discovered that the tunnel contained a water tank full of explosives. Exact figures are unknown, but at least 8,000 people died in Ebensee.

The site of the camp is now occupied by the suburb of Finkerleiten, constructed by the local authority in the late 1940s, and it is hard to imagine such horrors amidst the comfortable houses and the stunning mountain backdrop. The only surviving remnant is the gateway arch, preserved as a memorial, on Aufeldstraße (off Finkerleitenstraße). Some 3,000 corpses were discovered during the housing development, prompting an Italian widow, Hilda Lepetit, to erect a monument in 1948 on the mass grave in which it was believed her husband was buried. This site then became a memorial cemetery, inaugurated in 1952, to which all of the bodies, together with others buried by the Americans in 1945, were relocated. Sadly, not all motives were as admirable as Lepetit's: one of the prime supporters of the cemetery's creation was a former Nazi activist on whose property victims were buried – she wanted its return and even cited the need to accommodate 'tourist traffic' to the memorial as a reason for clearing her land! The cemetery, signposted from the gateway, contains approximately 4,000 bodies including those of 235 survivors of other camps, notably Gunskirchen, who died after liberation. It is located in the former north-west corner of the camp on the site of the sick barracks, including the notorious Block 23 where the weakest prisoners were held. Their plight was so desperate that during the chaos of April 1945 some resorted to cannibalism. Boards by the mass graves explain where named individuals are buried. There are many memorials, both to nationalities and to specific people, with the centrepiece the Lepetit monument, a large concrete cross.

Signs from the cemetery direct visitors to the *Anlage B* tunnels, one of which is open as a memorial exhibition (June–Sept: Tue–Sun, 10.00–5.00; May–mid-June & late Sept: Sat & Sun, 10.00–5.00; €3; memorial-ebensee.at); the camp gate, removed from the arch on Aufeldstraße, stands by its entrance. It was in this chilly tunnel, number 5, that Ganz intended to blow up the prisoners. The *Anlage B* complex included nine tunnels in total and the entrances to the others (except for two which had no exterior exits) line the path on either side of tunnel 5. The four off the track to the left of the exhibition are partially open, though it would be foolish to venture into the dark, rubble-strewn and often waterlogged tunnels. This path leads gently downhill back to Finkerleitenstraße near the gateway. Further down Finkerleitenstraße from the gateway, a path on the right leads to a sign for '*KZ Gedenkstätte Löwengang*', the route along which prisoners were marched to work in the *Anlage A* tunnels. *Löwengang* was a sardonic reference to being treated like lions in a circus due to the barbed wire and barking dogs that marked the journey. Logs laid by the side of the path indicate the route and an original staircase in preserved. This path eventually descends to two of the tunnels, from where steps lead down to Alte Traunstraße. Turn left up this road to return to the camp or right to head to the town centre where the Museum of Contemporary History (Tue–Sun, 10.00–5.00; €4; same website as above), which oversees the camp complex and tunnels, is located at Kirchengasse 5. This is a considerable distance away, however.

Ebensee is on the B145 between Gmunden and Bad Ischl: take the Rindbach exit and follow the signs to the memorials. From Ebensee train station it takes the best part of an hour to walk, although Postbus 2031 to the Schwaigerweg stop covers part of the route. If walking, exit the station to the left and then go left again onto Doktor-Rasper-Straße. There are signs from the end of this road. The narrow gauge railway which runs alongside Doktor-Rasper-Straße continues to two more of the *Anlage A* tunnels, now part of a mine complex, but access is forbidden. Incidentally, train travellers changing at Attnang-Puchheim to get to Ebensee will find a memorial on platform 1b to Ebensee prisoners, employed clearing bomb damage, who were murdered there on 21 April 1945.

OTHER SITES

There were more than 100 camps in Austria, almost half part of the Mauthausen system. Most have been poorly memorialised although visitors can discover more about Hitler's home province with *Memorial Sites for Concentration Camp Victims in Upper Austria*, an excellent book published by the regional authority and available in the bookshops at Mauthausen and Hartheim for the astonishing price of €1.

Until the installation of facilities in Mauthausen and Gusen, the town crematorium in Steyr was used to burn their dead. There are a number of memorials to these victims in the cemetery at Taborweg 6 whilst the adjacent Jewish cemetery at number 4 holds the mass grave of around 100 Hungarian Jews who died on the death marches. A memorial stone opposite a petrol station on Haagerstraße on the B122a out of town marks the site of the Steyr-Münichholz camp.

Melk was the location of one of the major Mauthausen sub-camps from 1944. The crematorium has been preserved as a memorial along with a small exhibition (Thu–Sun, 10.00–2.00) at Schießstattweg off Dorfnerstraße, south-west of the train station.

Lackenbach in Burgenland was the site of the largest 'gypsy' camp. It was established in 1940 and approximately 4,000 Roma passed through it: around half were deported to Łódź and murdered at Chełmno. Hundreds of others were executed in Lackenbach itself or died of typhoid. There is a memorial on the corner of Ritzinger Straße and Bergstraße in the village, east of the S31 near Weppersdorf.

CZECH REPUBLIC

U nlike Austria, the territories of the modern Czech Republic were unambiguously victims of Nazism, incorporated into the Third Reich through the threat of war in 1938–39. Thereafter, their Jews shared in the fate of those of Germany and Austria although there were distinctive features, notably the Theresienstadt ghetto, an institution with no exact parallel elsewhere.

Jews first appear to have settled in Bohemia and Moravia in the tenth century and flourishing communities developed in a number of cities, most famously Prague, through the Middle Ages. However, growing religious tension in the fifteenth century was accompanied by their expulsion from many urban centres. The advent of Habsburg rule in the sixteenth century meant that Czech Jewish fortunes thereafter fluctuated in the same manner as in Austria until the granting of civil equality in the mid-nineteenth century. This latter process was accompanied by a level of assimilation similar to that in Germany or Austria although the question of which culture to assimilate to caused tensions: in the nineteenth century, most Jews tended to gravitate towards the Germanic world but a predominantly Czech-Jewish identity eventually prevailed. This bond was strengthened in the inter-war period by the fact that Czechoslovakia was the sole stable liberal democracy in central Europe. Tomáš Masaryk, president until 1935, was seen as a friend of the Jews, not least for his role in combating accusations of ritual murder in the trial of the 'Czech Dreyfus' Leopold Hilsner at the turn of the century.

The comparative golden age of the first Czechoslovak republic was destroyed by Hitler with the connivance of the western powers in the Munich crisis of September 1938. The Jews of the Sudetenland now found themselves under Nazi rule whilst the remainder of Czechoslovakia (reconstituted as the second republic) lasted less than six months, annexed by the Germans on 15 March 1939. The Czech provinces were incorporated into the Reich as the Protectorate of Bohemia and Moravia thereby bringing a further 118,310 Jews (according to Nazi racial criteria) under German control. More than 10 per cent were, in fact, German or Austrian Jews who had already fled once from the Nazis. They and other exiles from Germany together with prominent indigenous Czech

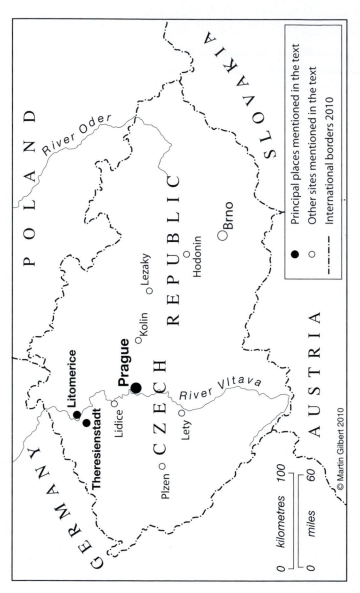

and Jewish leaders were targeted in *Aktion Gitter* which saw the arrest of 5,000 people immediately after the invasion. The first major anti-Jewish decree, on 21 June 1939, initiated 'Aryanisation' of the economy. On the following day, Eichmann, by now regarded as the SD's expert on Jewish issues, arrived in Prague to oversee the creation of a Czech *Zentralstelle*; like the original such institution in Vienna, its role was to force as many Jews as possible to emigrate whilst also extorting their wealth and property. More than 26,000 left before emigration was banned in October 1941 but this was a far lower level than in Germany and Austria, meaning that most Czech Jews remained to face an increasingly ominous future.

As early as October 1939, 3,000 Jews from the east of the country were amongst those sent on the Nisko transports to Poland. An escalating series of regulations followed but the crucial month was September 1941. A census of the community established that there were 88,105 Jews in the Protectorate (another 4,000 were living in hiding); they were now required to wear the yellow star. Later in the month, Reinhard Heydrich was appointed as acting *Reichsprotektor*, thus becoming the effective dictator of the Czech lands at a time when he was also charged with orchestrating the 'final solution' across Europe. The implications were almost immediate: Heydrich ordered the closure of all synagogues, and it was decided to transform the former Theresienstadt garrison into a holding camp in which all Czech Jews would be concentrated prior to their deportation. In the meantime, however, six transports were sent directly to the eastern ghettos in October and November 1941. From the end of November onwards, more than 70,000 were sent to Theresienstadt, most making the further journey on to Auschwitz. Jews were also a significant proportion of the estimated 13,000 citizens murdered in retaliation for Heydrich's assassination in May 1942 by British-trained Czechoslovak soldiers who had been parachuted into the country. It is estimated that around 78,000 Jews from Bohemia and Moravia lost their lives in the Holocaust, close to 85 per cent of the 1941 population.

Effective commemoration was prevented by the anti-Semitism which afflicted the Communist Party in the early 1950s. Whilst this followed Stalin's lead, the anti-Jewish dimension was especially explicit in Czechoslovakia: in the notorious 1952 Slánský show trial of former Communist leaders, 11 of the 14 defendants were Jewish. Any thaw in the 1960s was ended by the resurgence of official anti-Semitism following the

Six Day War and the crushing of the Prague Spring. The situation has been transformed since 1989 with the country rivalling Poland as a centre for Jewish heritage travel and several new memorials being created, although developments have sadly been less positive with regard to remembrance of the several thousand Roma who lost their lives in the Holocaust.

PRAGUE

The Czech capital was one of Europe's great Jewish centres from the Middle Ages when it came to be regarded as a pre-eminent seat of learning, a reputation largely maintained in the following centuries. The community was vulnerable to the same perils which afflicted Jews across Europe – notably a pogrom at Easter 1389 and temporary expulsion in the 1740s – but Prague was generally seen as one of the more stable and welcoming cities in central Europe, although residence was restricted to the traditional Jewish quarter (renamed Josefov in tribute to the reforming Emperor) until the mid-nineteenth century. By the time of the 1930 census, almost half of the Jews of Bohemia and Moravia lived in Prague and the numbers were further swelled by the flow of refugees from Germany. On the eve of the occupation, there were close to 56,000 Jews, including more than 10,000 refugees from the Reich.

The arrival of the Nazis on 15 March 1939 was not accompanied by the spontaneous pogroms which had characterised their entry into Vienna but this did not prevent a similar policy of intimidation and dispossession being rapidly launched. This was accompanied by a concerted propaganda campaign including the Gestapo-organised exhibition *The Jews as the Enemy of Humanity* which Czech workers and children were forced to attend. The creation of the *Zentralstelle* in July 1939, following Eichmann's arrival in the previous month, inevitably brought an escalation of the pressure. Indeed, Eichmann is alleged to have threatened to sweep Prague street by street and send 300 Jews per day to Dachau until the community agreed to mass departures. In this context, Prague was intended to play a role similar to that later performed by Theresienstadt – essentially a transit centre for Czech Jews – with an order in August 1939 for all Jews to settle in the city within one year although the outbreak of war meant that it was never fully implemented. The majority of Prague Jews who did not emigrate were subjected to the escalating series of restrictions imposed on the Protectorate, some of which were specific to the capital such as an

October 1940 decree forbidding them from walking in certain areas of the city, including the Embankment.

Deportations commenced on 16 October 1941 with the first of five transports to Łódź, each carrying around 1,000 people. From the end of November, trains were sent to Theresienstadt. Families were notified by the Jewish community leadership to assemble in the Exposition Hall in the Holešovice district where they were held overnight, or sometimes longer, before being dispatched on the three-hour train journey. According to official figures, 46,067 people were deported from Prague to Theresienstadt or the eastern ghettos; few survived. The last transport, carrying those in mixed marriages, left as late as 16 March 1945.

The return of survivors, including those from other parts of Czechoslovakia who naturally gravitated towards the capital, meant that Prague's Jewish population numbered more than 10,000 after the war but many left the country in the late 1940s before emigration was banned in

Prague: deportation memorial (Photograph by the author)

1950. Thousands more departed in 1968. Since the fall of Communism, there has been a resurgence of interest in the city's Jewish past amongst both Czechs and foreigners. However, the sad fact remains that there are comparatively few Jews in Prague – around 1,500 associated with the religious community, a few thousand more of some Jewish origin – making the contrast between the richness of the city's preserved Jewish culture and the relative absence of modern Jewish life greater than almost anywhere else in Europe.

Josefov

The historic heart of Jewish Prague, the Josefov district in the north of the Staré Město (Old Town) has been celebrated and romanticised through the centuries. However, the character of the quarter was radically altered following the abolition of forced residency in 1852. As wealthier Jews migrated, most of the old passageways and courtyards were demolished to make way for grand boulevards modelled on Paris. Few buildings survived the upheaval but several of those that did now make up the Prague Jewish Museum.

A Jewish museum had been founded in 1906 but was unsurprisingly closed in 1939. However, the Nazis then established the Central Jewish Museum in 1942, accumulating objects from across Bohemia and Moravia to swell the pre-war collection of around 1,000 artefacts to 100,000. It is commonly believed that this was intended to become a 'Museum of an Extinct Race' but the truth is perhaps more complex. The initiative for the new institution actually came from Dr Augustin Stein, founder of the original museum and former chair of the Czechoslovak Council of Jewish Religious Communities, who hoped to save the priceless ritual objects appropriated by the Nazis. The motives of the Germans were clearly different and some scholars have suggested that, instead of planning the exotic museum project, they simply hoped to congregate the relics in one place in order to exploit them financially after the final elimination of the Jews. The items were collected and stored in warehouses across Josefov but primarily in a former Jewish primary school at Jáchymova 3. A plaque commemorates both the school pupils and museum staff who died in Auschwitz.

After the war, the Jewish Museum reopened, albeit subject to restrictions following the 1948 Communist coup. It has been reinvigorated since 1989, becoming one of Prague's major tourist attractions (Sun–Fri,

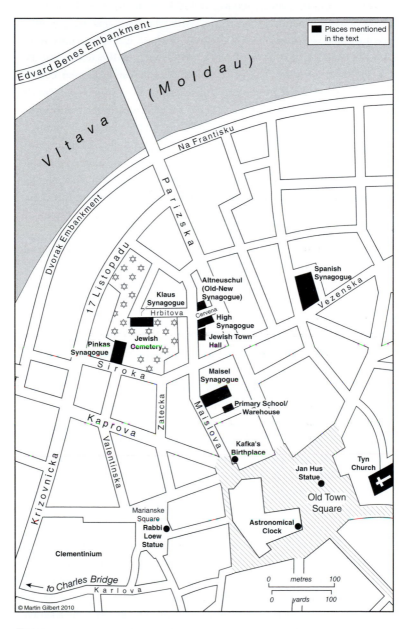

Prague

9.00–6.00 (4.30, winter); 300 Kč, or 480 Kč with Old-New Synagogue; www.jewishmuseum.cz). It begins with the redesigned sixteenth-century Maisel Synagogue at Maiselova 10 whose sparse interior covers Czech Jewish history from the first settlements in the tenth century to the death of Maria Theresa in 1780. An interesting section covers medieval Christian representations of Jews, not all of which conform to the stereotypes one might expect. The story continues in the nineteenth-century Spanish Synagogue, a few blocks east of the rest of the complex at Vězeňská 1, next to a Surrealist statue of Franz Kafka. Its impressive Moorish facade is rather disfigured by an ugly concrete annexe through which one enters; the gilded interior, though, is spectacular. The exhibits address the twentieth century, the Holocaust illustrated by heartbreaking pictures of children in Theresienstadt. There is also a large display of synagogue silver from across the country.

Back in the heart of Josefov, the museum continues with the simple sixteenth-century Pinkas Synagogue at Široká 3 which serves as Prague's Holocaust memorial. In the courtyard, there are plaques to Jews who fought in Czech and partisan forces and to Czech Righteous. The walls of the ground floor and part of the women's gallery are given over to the names of 77,297 Bohemian and Moravian victims, listed alphabetically by their 153 communities; around the ark are listed the locations where they died. All the while, taped voices intone the names of the dead. The names were originally placed on the walls after the war but were removed by the Communists when structural problems necessitated the closure of the building in 1968; they were restored only in the 1990s. Upstairs, room V houses examples of the famous children's art from Theresienstadt, organised by themes ranging from fairy tales and biblical stories to ghetto life and the transports. There is also a small selection of pieces from the contemporary *Art in Extreme Situations* project in which Czech schoolchildren are taught about Theresienstadt and then create their own artwork.

The famously cluttered medieval gravestones of the old cemetery, accessed by a path from the rear of the synagogue, are one of the iconic sights of Prague. The museum concludes in the Klausen Synagogue and adjoining Ceremonial Hall behind the cemetery at U starého hřbitova 3A which address Jewish rituals, festivals and family life. In 1943, the Klausen Synagogue housed the exhibition *Jewish Life from the Cradle to the Grave*, the latter term all too appropriate by that date. Down the street, on the corner of Červená and Maiselova, is the remarkable Old-New Synagogue, claimed to be the oldest in Europe (Sun–Thu, 9.30–6.00 (5.00, winter); Fri, 9.30–5.00; 200 Kč, or 480 Kč with Jewish Museum) and still in use. The building suffered a bomb attack on 20 March 1939, five days after the beginning of the German occupation. Opposite is the fortified High Synagogue, so-called for the fact that the prayer room, also still in use, is located on the upper floor. The Central Jewish Museum's first exhibition (of religious books) was held here in 1942. A room on the ground floor sells tickets for the Old-New Synagogue. Next door is the Jewish Town Hall (Maiselova 18), remarkable for the Hebrew clock on the Červená side. This remains the community headquarters today.

The New Town Hall, further south on Mariánské náměstí, is flanked on its southern side by a large statue of the legendary Rabbi Löw whose grave in the old cemetery remains a place of pilgrimage. Despite his reputation as a great Talmudist and mystic, the sixteenth-century Rabbi is best known in Jewish folklore as the mythical creator of the Prague Golem. According to the most popular version of the story, he fashioned a human form from clay and brought it to life through kabbalistic incantations to protect the Josefov community from anti-Semitic attacks. The Golem, however, became too violent and killed so many Gentiles that Rabbi Löw took its life away and stored its remains in the attic of the Old-New Synagogue.

Centre

In the Nové Město, near the National Museum, the suitably oppressive Petschkův Palác at Politických vězňů 20 (on the corner with Washingtonova) was the Gestapo HQ from May 1939. There is a memorial plaque encompassing a sculpture of a defiant prisoner on the corner wall. A little further north, at Jeruzalémská 7, is the Jubilee Synagogue (Apr–Oct: Sun–Fri, 1.00–5.00; access with ticket for Old-New Synagogue), its beautiful multicoloured exterior suggestive of central Asia or India and matched by the ornate interior. The largest synagogue in the city, it was constructed in 1906–07. A couple of blocks further north, Hybernská 32 housed the *Hadega*, a special company established to deal in Jewish property: Jews were forced to sell jewellery and precious metals to it at discount prices.

South-west of the Nové Město, the baroque Orthodox Cathedral of SS Cyril and Methodius at Resslova 9 (Karlovo náměsti Metro) was where Heydrich's assassins Gabčík and Kubiš, with five comrades, faced their final battle with the Nazis on 18 June 1942. Betrayed by a fellow member of the underground, they were besieged in the church yet the 700 SS troops were unable to take them alive. Three, including Kubiš, died in a gun battle in the loft; the remaining four held out in the crypt until it was flooded with gas and then water at which point they committed suicide. The Germans are estimated to have suffered 14 dead and 21 wounded in the process. On the bullet-scarred wall of the church there is a memorial plaque to the parachutists and to Bishop Gorazd who was executed after taking responsibility for sheltering them. A small exhibition in the crypt (Tue–Sun, 10.00–6.00; 60 Kč), entered around the corner on Na Zderaze, outlines the history of the assassination and the reprisals, including the immediate murder of Jews in custody as well as the more famous Lidice massacre.

Holešovice

Located north of the river, the Holešovice district is where most Prague Jews spent their last hours in the city. The large stark modernist building at Dukelských hrdinů 47 is the Veletržni Palác (trams 5, 12, 14, 15 & 17 to Veletržni), built in the 1930s as the Exposition Hall to house trade fairs. The building was damaged by fire in 1974 and reconstructed in 1995 since when it has housed the National Gallery's modern art collection. In 1941, this was the assembly point for deportations to Theresienstadt: thousands were confined without adequate provisions, medication or sanitation. Opposite the Palác, on the roadside wall of the Park Hotel on Veletržni, there is a memorial in the form of a sculpted relief of emaciated figures, Stars of David clearly visible, marching into the unknown.

Bubny station, off Bubenská to the east, was the departure point for the transports. Jews were usually marched from the Exposition Hall in the early hours of the morning to prevent any displays of Czech sympathy. The rather forlorn building has memorials in its entrance hall to railwaymen who died in the service of the underground, but none to Jews.

North

Heydrich's assassination took place on 27 May 1942 at the corner of V Holešovičkách and Zenklova (trams 10, 24 and 25 to Vychovatelna), now a major traffic junction. As the open-topped car approached, Gabčík stepped into the road and attempted to shoot but his gun jammed. When the *Reichsprotektor* stood up to return fire, Kubiš threw a grenade which hit the car, sending shrapnel and fragments of upholstery fibre flying into Heydrich's body; it was these fibres which caused the blood poisoning that killed him on 4 June. A striking new memorial was unveiled at the junction on the sixty-seventh anniversary of the attack in 2009. The only previous indication of the history of the site was the naming of the streets just to the west Gabčikova and Kubišova. On 27 May, Gabčík fled down the street now named after him with Heydrich's driver Klein in pursuit. He took refuge in a butcher's shop in the house at Valčíkova 22 (the street is named after the look-out), at the junction with Gabčíkova. Unfortunately, the proprietor was an ethnic German and Nazi sympathiser who attracted Klein's attention; Gabčík, however, was able to shoot Klein in the leg and make good his escape. Kubiš got away by cycling south down Zenklova. Near the bottom of Zenklova, off Na Žertvách by the Palmovka Metro station, is the much neglected Libeň Synagogue.

The Kobylisy shooting range (a pre-war military training facility) was employed by the Germans as a mass execution site. It is now a memorial complex entered through an underpass on the edge of a housing estate. Two banks of earth which formed the shooting range remain, opposite a sculpture of a prone woman and a cross. Plaques list the names of those killed, most between 30 May and 3 July 1942 in the aftermath of Heydrich's shooting. The site is signposted ('*Kobyliská střelnice*') off Čumpelíkova, south of Žernosecká (bus 136 from Střížkov Metro to Bojasova). On the other side of the housing complex, between Střelničná and Na Malém klínu (Ládví Metro), is a small walled-in former Jewish cemetery (ring 272 734 609 for keys).

Elsewhere

Most of the old Žižkov Jewish cemetery, in use from the seventeenth to nineteenth centuries, was destroyed by the Communists to make way for the gargantuan TV tower which dominates the neighbourhood. The surviving section on Fibichova (north from Jiřího z Poděbrad Metro) is run by the Jewish Museum and can be visited at restricted times (Mon, Wed, Fri, 9.00–1.00; 40 Kč) although the tombs can be clearly viewed from the square around the TV tower. The new Žižkov cemetery is further east (Sun–Thu, 9.00–5.00 (4.00 in winter); Fri, 9.00–1.00) at Izraelská 1 (Želivského Metro and bus stations). There are a series of

Holocaust memorials near the entrance including one to all Czech Jews and others specifically to victims of Łódź and Theresienstadt. There is also a memorial to those who died in the service of the Allies. The grave of Franz Kafka, buried with his parents, is signposted from the entrance. A plaque at the base of the stone honours the writer's three sisters: Gabriela Hermannova and Valerie Pollakova were deported to Łódź and murdered at Chełmno; Kafka's favoured younger sister Ottla Davidova chose to divorce her Gentile husband in order to protect their daughters. She worked as a nurse in Theresienstadt and was amongst those who tended to a group of 1,260 children who arrived from Białystok in August 1943. She and the other carers were deported with the children to Auschwitz in October; all were murdered on arrival.

In the city's south, behind forbidding walls, stands Pankrác prison on Soudní (trams 18 and 53 to Vozovna Pankrác). Thousands of Czechs were interned here by the Germans; more than 1,000 were executed in the prison itself once a guillotine was installed in the basement in April 1943. The three cells adapted for the executions have been converted into a memorial and are occasionally opened for educational tours (vvpankrac@volny.cz).

There are fewer sites west of the river but the Hrad, traditional centre of power in Bohemia, was the seat of Heydrich and the occupying regime. To the north of the castle (a 10 minute walk from Dejvická Metro), a former Jewish-owned villa at U laboratoře 22 (on the corner with Dělostřelecká) was requisitioned to become Eichmann's residence and the headquarters of the *Zentralstelle* in July 1939. To the south of the Hrad, at Stroupežnického 32 (Anděl Metro), is the modernist Smíchovská Synagogue, a 1930s reconstruction of a nineteenth-century original. After years of neglect, it was restored in 2004 and now houses the Jewish Museum archives.

THERESIENSTADT

The former Habsburg garrison town of Theresienstadt (Terezín to the Czechs) was transformed into an institution unique in the history of the Holocaust, part ghetto, part concentration camp, part Potemkin village. The town was established by Joseph II in the eighteenth century as a fortress and it remained a military base even after losing its strategic importance. The Small Fortress (to the east of the main town) was used as a Gestapo prison from 1940 but it was the 1941 decision to create a collection camp near Prague for the Protectorate's Jews that transformed Theresienstadt. The first transport from the capital, a group of young men sent to prepare the ghetto, arrived on 24 November 1941. Between that date and 16 March 1945, 122 trains from Bohemia and Moravia brought 73,608 people. The Jewish leadership – including Jacob Edelstein, chair of Theresienstadt's Council of Elders – initially believed that deportation could be avoided through productive labour in the ghetto but such notions were soon dispelled: the first eastbound transport (to Riga) departed as early as 9 January 1942. The acute overcrowding (almost 30,000 Czech Jews were sent to Theresienstadt in the first six months of the ghetto's existence) led to deportations directly to the Polish camps from the spring. The first transport to Auschwitz left on 26 October 1942; all subsequent trains had the same

Theresienstadt (Photograph by the author)

destination. The Council of Elders was confronted with the agonising choice of drawing up the lists of deportees.

The character of Theresienstadt changed in two significant respects during 1942. The Czech civilian population was evicted in July enabling the whole town to be incorporated into the ghetto and thus actually improving living conditions. From June onwards, transports of Jews from Germany and Austria began to arrive; more than 40,000 German Jews and 15,000 Austrians eventually passed through the ghetto. This reflected the decision taken at the Wannsee Conference to send certain categories of Reich Jews – primarily community leaders, the elderly and First World War veterans – to Theresienstadt in an attempt to camouflage the true nature of Nazi policy. Although they were still earmarked for extermination, the perception was created, at least within the Reich, that they were being sent to a 'model ghetto' where they would be isolated but allowed to live out their days in relative peace. In due course, Jews from the Netherlands and Denmark were also brought to Theresienstadt.

It was the arrival of the latter group – 481 Danish Jews caught before they could join the mass flight to Sweden – in October 1943 which helped to prompt the most infamous incident in Theresienstadt's history. The uproar in Denmark (and Sweden), together with the world's growing awareness of the Holocaust, led the Nazis to offer to open the ghetto to inspection by the International Red Cross to refute the 'rumours'. In preparation, transports to Auschwitz increased in late 1943 and early 1944 to reduce the congestion: more than 7,000 were deported in May 1944 alone, including the sick and orphans. They were kept in a special section of Birkenau to maintain the deception should the Red Cross decide to inspect there – when it did not, the deportees were murdered in July 1944. The Theresienstadt inspection was preceded by the 'beautification action' from April 1944 in which buildings were cleaned up, new facilities created and entertainments organised. The Red Cross team, which visited on 23 June, was duly impressed and filed a positive report. This propaganda success was capitalised on with a film, commonly known as *The Führer Gives the Jews a Town*, shot in August and September. Objectives achieved, the Nazis restarted the deportations: 18,000 inmates were sent to Auschwitz in September and October 1944. The Danish Jews, incidentally, were transferred to Sweden in April 1945.

The cessation of murder operations in Birkenau saw Theresienstadt's role change: it became a reception centre, first for Jews from Hungary and Slovakia and for those in mixed marriages from the Reich, and then, from April 1945, for death marches. The large influx rather undermined a second beautification programme launched in March as part of Himmler's attempts to negotiate a separate peace with the Americans. Another Red Cross inspection on 6 April produced a less positive reaction and the organisation's representative Paul Dunant remained in the ghetto for the remainder of the war. In fact, he took over the running of Theresienstadt, engulfed by a typhus epidemic, when the SS abandoned it on 3 May 1945. The Red Army arrived on 8 May. In the course of the ghetto's existence, around 155,000 people passed through it (15,000 of them in the last fortnight): more than 35,000 died in Theresienstadt and 83,000 were deported to the extermination camps; only 3,097 of this latter group survived.

After the war, Terezín reverted to being a Czechoslovak garrison town. The Small Fortress, most of whose victims were non-Jewish, became the main focus for memorialisation, a situation which predictably began to change only with the fall of Communism.

The ghetto

Modern Terezín is a rather down-at-heel town, having lost 3,000 inhabitants when the garrison was closed in 1996. Its streets are arranged in a grid pattern, enclosed within large fortified walls. The streets were originally known by letters and numbers (L1–6 for the north-south axis, Q1–9 for the east-west) with each block additionally being labelled with letters and Roman numerals (the Magdeburg barracks, for example, being BV). However, the streets were given German names during the beautification programme. Although these were replaced by Czech names after the war, all plans of the ghetto, including the large map outside the Town Hall, use the German versions so these have been employed here

Buses drop visitors outside the Town Hall on Rathausgasse. A plaque on its wall notes that this was the headquarters of the Red Army command after liberation and pays tribute to the Soviet efforts to combat the typhus epidemic. The building previously housed the ghetto's bank and law courts and was also used for concerts. The corner building to the left, now a post office, was a home for children aged 3 to 10. Such homes were one of the distinctive features of the ghetto. Initially, those under 12 stayed with their mothers whilst older boys were sent to the men's barracks. However, after the Czech civilians left in the summer

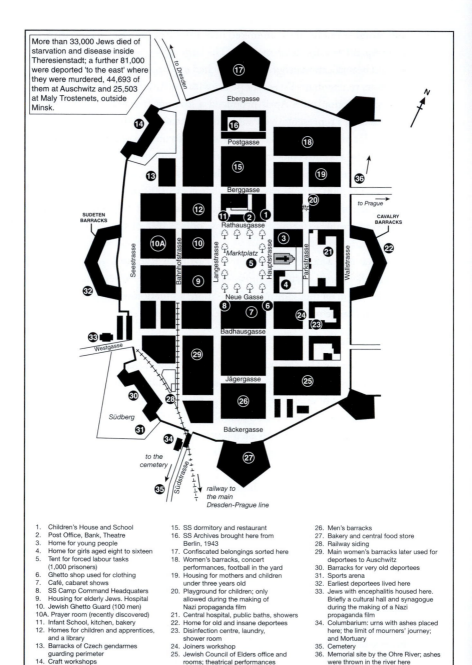

More than 33,000 Jews died of starvation and disease inside Theresienstadt; a further 81,000 were deported 'to the east' where they were murdered, 44,693 of them at Auschwitz and 25,503 at Maly Trostenets, outside Minsk.

to Dresden

⑰

Ebergasse

⑭

⑯

Postgasse

⑱

⑬

⑮

Berggasse

⑲

㊱

to Prague

SUDETEN BARRACKS

⑫

⑪ ② ①

Rathausgasse

⑳

CAVALRY BARRACKS

Seestrasse

⑩A ⑩

③

Bahnhofstrasse

Langestrasse

Marktplatz

⑤

Hauptstrasse

Parkstrasse

㉑

Wallstrasse

㉒

㉜

⑨

④

Neue Gasse

⑧ ⑦ ⑥

㉔ ㉓

㉝

Westgasse

Badhausgasse

㉙

Jägergasse

㉕

㉚

㉘

㉖

Südberg

㉛

㉞

to the cemetery

Bäckergasse

Südstrasse

㉗

㉟

railway to the main Dresden-Prague line

N

㊱

1. Children's House and School
2. Post Office, Bank, Theatre
3. Home for young people
4. Home for girls aged eight to sixteen
5. Tent for forced labour tasks (1,000 prisoners)
6. Ghetto shop used for clothing
7. Café, cabaret shows
8. SS Camp Command Headquaters
9. Housing for elderly Jews. Hospital
10. Jewish Ghetto Guard (100 men)
10A. Prayer room (recently discovered)
11. Infant School, kitchen, bakery
12. Homes for children and apprentices, and a library
13. Barracks of Czech gendarmes guarding perimeter
14. Craft workshops

15. SS dormitory and restaurant
16. SS Archives brought here from Berlin, 1943
17. Confiscated belongings sorted here
18. Women's barracks, concert performances, football in the yard
19. Housing for mothers and children under three years old
20. Playground for children; only allowed during the making of Nazi propaganda film
21. Central hospital, public baths, showers
22. Home for old and insane deportees
23. Disinfection centre, laundry, shower room
24. Joiners workshop
25. Jewish Council of Elders office and rooms; theatrical performances

26. Men's barracks
27. Bakery and central food store
28. Railway siding
29. Main women's barracks later used for deportees to Auschwitz
30. Barracks for very old deportees
31. Sports arena
32. Earliest deportees lived here
33. Jews with encephalitis housed here. Briefly a cultural hall and synagogue during the making of a Nazi propaganda film
34. Columbarium: urns with ashes placed here; the limit of mourners' journey; and Mortuary
35. Cemetery
36. Memorial site by the Ohre River; ashes were thrown in the river here

© Martin Gilbert 2010

of 1942, the Council of Elders, with German approval, instituted the special homes in an attempt to protect children as much as possible from the rigours of adult existence whilst also engendering communal spirit, a concept much influenced by the Zionist ideals of the youth department's leaders Egon Redlich and Fredy Hirsch. Within each home, children were organised into groups which were encouraged to develop a collective identity through activities such as sport and entertainment. Schooling also took place, albeit surreptitiously until the Germans formally permitted education in advance of the Red Cross inspection. This particular home also contained the central kitchen for all the children's blocks in Theresienstadt.

To the right of the Town Hall, entered from Hauptstraße, is another former children's home which accommodated around 350 Czech Jewish boys. In 1991, 50 years after the ghetto's establishment, this was converted into the Ghetto Museum (daily, 9.00–6.00 (until 5.30, Nov–Mar); 160 Kč, or 200 Kč with Small Fortress; www.pamatnik-terezin.cz). The ground floor includes a cinema (which shows surviving fragments of the propaganda film) and a room dedicated to the children which includes a small selection of their artwork. Painting and drawing were encouraged by the youth leaders as a means of expression as well as escapism and were only the best-known facets of the extraordinary creativity generated in the children's homes; poems, songs, theatre and newspapers were also produced. Most of the art is now held in Prague's Pinkas Synagogue but copies cover the wall of the staircase. This leads to the main exhibition which covers the history of the ghetto in detail. Among the most poignant of the many artefacts on display are dolls of ghetto characters, including a Jewish policeman, a nurse, and a boy and a girl making their way to a deportation train.

The Marktplatz stretches south of the Town Hall and Ghetto Museum. This was fenced off from the rest of the ghetto, accessible only to inmates employed in workshops which were incongruously covered by a circus tent from May 1943. In advance of the Red Cross visit, the fences were removed, the grass which still covers the square planted and a stage erected for musical concerts. The first building on the east of the square was the SS headquarters until August 1942 and then converted into a home for German-speaking children. It also contained a post office. The building beyond the church housed Czech-speaking girls. A wall plaque attests to its role in the ghetto's cultural life. To its rear is a small yard, entered from Neue Gasse: a wooden door set within an otherwise walled up archway led to the studio of Friedl Dicker-Brandeis, a Bauhaus-educated painter who took a leading role in teaching art to the children. She was able to hide more than 5,000 of their pictures in two suitcases which were left with a friend before her deportation to Auschwitz in October 1944.

The block on the southern side of Marktplatz housed, from east to west, a shop which sold used clothing, a café and, in the final two buildings, the SS headquarters from August 1942; the basement prison cells were used for the torture of inmates. Moving northwards along the western side of the square, there are two further notable buildings: the first accommodated elderly and sick residents, the second the Theresienstadt Jewish police. On the wall of the latter is a plaque to Dr Ludwig Czech, socialist leader and government minister who died in the ghetto in August 1942. The building on the north-western corner of Rathausgasse and Langestraße housed children and apprentices.

Opposite the entrance to the Ghetto Museum is the Stadtpark which contains a simple 1950 memorial erected by the Red Army. A children's playground was created here during the beautification campaign. In the courtyard of the museum, accessed through a gate on Berggasse, is the 'Children's Park' – a small memorial space with tributes to, amongst others, Fredy Hirsch, Friedl Dicker-Brandeis and Kafka's sister Ottla. To the north of the Stadtpark, the block closest to the wall was the ghetto's infant home but this was destroyed after the war. The Dresden Barracks, the next block to the north (and one of the two largest), was the principal accommodation for women; its basement housed the ghetto prison. On nearby Postgasse, the southern block was occupied by the SS dormitory (demolished at the end of the war); the site is now a hotel. The Bodenbach Barracks on the northern side housed the archives of Himmler's RSHA, relocated from Berlin in 1943; the documents were destroyed as the Red Army approached. The northern bastion behind was, until June 1943, the *Schleuse*, the transfer station where inmates were held prior to deportation; it was later used as the central store for clothing seized from inmates. The nearby north-western bastion housed workshops. A gas chamber was built in an underground passage in this yard in February 1945 although it was never put into use. The mansion to the south of the bastion housed the Czech gendarmes who supervised inmates on tasks outside the ghetto.

Further down Bahnhofstraße, a clandestine prayer room was uncovered during modern restoration work in a storeroom in the yard of the building south-west of Rathausgasse (now Dlouhá 17) which can be visited by ringing the bell marked '*Modlitebna*'. Its ceiling and upper walls still carry Hebrew script and stars. The Sudeten Barracks in the western bastion was a dormitory for the young men sent to construct the ghetto in 1941 and later one of the principal barracks for able-bodied men until 1943 when it was used for RSHA storage. Just beyond here, a road leads out of the fortress to a pre-war sports club converted to house encephalitis sufferers. In the beautification campaign it was turned into the ghetto's 'community centre' complete with library, culture hall and synagogue. In the south-western corner, the dilapidated Jäger Barracks accommodated the elderly. In the Südberg bastion yard behind, a sports area was constructed in 1943.

Seestraße broadens out at this point into an open area which was the departure point for most inmates. Deportees were originally marched to the station in nearby Bohušovice but from June 1943 a railway came directly into the fortress. A section has been preserved as memorial. Alongside is a haunting plaque depicting the deportees; this was originally intended to be placed in Prague until blocked by the Communist authorities (although a similar memorial does now stand by the Park Hotel). The large Hamburg Barracks on Bahnhofstraße, previously the main accommodation for women, became the site of the *Schleuse* once the railway was built: deportees would thus not be seen marching through the ghetto. The block also housed Dutch Jews. Opposite is a small stone hut which stood at the railway terminal.

The rail tracks accompany the road out of the fortress through the Bohušovice gate to the mortuary and columbarium (both daily, 9.00–6.00 (until 5.00, Nov–Mar)). The latter was established in 1942 to store the ashes of those who died in the ghetto – they were shelved in cardboard 'urns'. The cartons were taken by the Germans in November 1944 to the Ohře river and Litoměřice concentration camp and the ashes dumped. The mortuary opposite has been turned into an affecting memorial, its central tunnel leading past preserved artefacts to a rear chamber where a large menorah stands alongside six glass cases arranged in the form of a Star of David containing earth from places where Theresienstadt inmates were murdered. A little further down the Bohušovice road, a path to the left leads to the crematorium and cemetery. The latter, dominated

Theresienstadt: cemetery (Photograph by the author)

by a stylised menorah, contains the remains of some 9,000 people who died in the first year of the ghetto's existence. Thereafter, victims of the ghetto, as well as those of the Small Fortress and Litoměřice, were cremated (except for a brief cessation during the Red Cross visit). The crematorium (daily, 10.00–6.00 (until 4.00, Nov–Mar)) contains an exhibition on death and burial in the ghetto around the four large ovens. In its entrance is a memorial stone laid by Chaim Herzog in 1991. The cemetery was used by the garrison before the war, hence the apparently incongruous memorial to Russian World War I dead. There is also a Soviet cemetery for the soldiers who died fighting the typhus epidemic at liberation.

Back within the fortress, the southern bastion housed the ghetto's bakery and central food store whilst the Hannover Barracks opposite was a male dormitory. The Magdeburg Barracks to the east was the seat of the Council of Elders and now houses a branch of the Ghetto Museum (same hours & ticket) which focuses on cultural life. Amidst rooms devoted to theatre, literature and music, the centrepiece is a multi-room display of ghetto art. The children's work may be more famous but that produced by the adults, exhibited here, is impressive. A section includes 'illegal' art which realistically depicted ghetto life – some of the artists responsible were sent to the Small Fortress, tortured and eventually murdered. Located a block north, the garrison's former brewery, distinguished by its large chimney, was converted into the disinfection centre through which all new arrivals passed. In August 1943, a party of 1,260 children arrived from Białystok in appalling condition. When brought to the shower rooms, they became hysterical and refused to enter until Jewish workers showed them that the rooms indeed contained showers. The fact that the children's alarm was bewildering to the Theresienstadt inmates is a telling commentary on the extent to which the Germans succeeded in insulating the ghetto. The run-down building on the other side of Parkstraße was a joinery workshop. The eastern bastion, accessible from Rathausgasse, was where elderly and mentally ill patients were brought and, increasingly, left to die. The Hohenelbe Barracks opposite served as the ghetto's main hospital.

Returning to the Stadtpark and exiting through the eastern gate, signs point the way to the site by the Ohře where the ashes of 22,000 ghetto victims were scattered by the Germans in November 1944. The central memorial takes the form of a large stylised funeral urn; alongside is a small gravestone.

Terezín is a little over 30 miles north of Prague, signposted off the 8 / E55. Reasonably regular buses run from the capital's Florenc and Nádraží Holešovice bus stations.

The Small Fortress

The Small Fortress (daily, 8.00–6.00 (4.30, Nov–Mar); 160 Kč, or 200 Kč with Ghetto Museum) is located a few hundred metres east of the Ohře along the main road. It was used as a prison from the eighteenth century, initially for errant soldiers but later for opponents of the Habsburgs, and was a natural choice for the Nazis as an internment site for political prisoners. Approximately 32,000 inmates passed through it during the war: most were sent onto prisons or camps elsewhere although around 2,600 died within its walls. It was separate from the ghetto but more than 1,500 Jews spent time in the fortress, usually for infractions of ghetto rules; a third lost their lives there. However, it was the multi-national nature of the victims (who included Czechs, Poles, Soviets and Germans) that ensured that the Small Fortress, rather than the ghetto, would be the main focus of memorialisation under Communism.

Along the entry road to the fortress is the national cemetery where both Jewish and Gentile victims are buried. There is a large Star of David by the walls but this is rather dwarfed by a huge cross. The Small Fortress has much more of the feel of a concentration camp than the ghetto does, with a series of prison yards grouped around the main central courtyard. The point is emphasised by the so-called first yard to the left (north) of the entrance which is entered through a gate marked '*Arbeit macht frei*'. The cells straight ahead were normally used for Soviet and Jewish prisoners who predictably received the worst treatment; there is a plaque erected by the Israeli Embassy to the Jewish victims. Block 12 contains the former cell of Gavril Princip, the Bosnian Serb assassin of Archduke Franz Ferdinand who spent most of the First World War here and died in the Hohenelbe Barracks in the main town. From the first yard one can return to the central courtyard or follow the long, winding tunnels built into the fortifications to the execution grounds outside: the former practice range was used for the shooting and hanging of around 250 prisoners from 1943 although a great many more died from torture or starvation.

To the east of the central courtyard, through the block which housed the SS cinema (now used for documentaries about the site) and past a memorial containing earth from different camps, is the large fourth yard, constructed by the Nazis in 1943. Mass cells to the left held 400 to 600 prisoners at a time. When the fortress was liberated, more than 3,000 were found here in shocking conditions.

The museum, located in former SS barracks south of the central courtyard, covers the history of the occupation as well as that of the Small Fortress. Exhibits include items made by the prisoners, amongst them several paintings from the ghetto (although not marked as such). In the south-west corner of the complex, the third yard includes a little-noticed display on the history of nearby Litoměřice concentration camp – the first detachments of prisoners sent to construct the camp were accommodated in this yard.

LITOMĚŘICE

Located little more than two miles north of Terezín, the town of Litoměřice (Leitmeritz in German) was the site of a short-lived but brutal concentration camp, established as a result of the relocation of war industries to underground tunnels in response to Allied air raids. The programme, codenamed *Richard*, commenced in March 1944 with the camp opening two months later as a sub-camp of Flossenbürg from where inmates were brought to be used as slave labour in the construction projects. In the latter stages of the war, Litoměřice, lying in one of the last areas of territory to be liberated, also became a major focus for the death marches with 4,000 Jews from Auschwitz and Gross-Rosen amongst the thousands brought there. This huge influx triggered a typhus epidemic which added to the effects of malnourishment and overwork. Although the camp existed for a little less than a year – it was liberated on 5 May 1945 – 4,500 of the 18,000 inmates died.

Despite its proximity, and the fact that there is an exhibition devoted to it hidden in the Small Fortress, few of the hundreds of thousands who travel to Terezín are seemingly aware of Litoměřice's existence and even fewer visit it. There is, though, a striking and rather disturbing memorial next to the camp's crematorium which takes the form of a large wire cage resembling a factory in which chained mannequins are bound to a railway cart or suspended by pulleys. At the top of the 'chimney' a lone prisoner climbs to freedom. Alongside is a symbolic urn similar to that by the banks of the Ohře at Terezín. The crematorium itself is maintained by the Terezín Memorial and can be accessed only by prior arrangement in writing (email via the website) although it is possible to peer in through the barred windows. The memorial site is to the west of Litoměřice on Michalovická, off the main 261 road which skirts the town centre. The site is around 500 metres along Michalovická, just after it crosses the railway and immediately recognisable due to the giant chimney. Shortly before this point is the town's cemetery, on the southern side of the road, which contains a memorial to murdered local Jews just by the entrance.

Less publicised is the fact that sections of the camp itself remain intact. After liberation, it was taken over by the Red Army and, although the Soviets have departed, the site, albeit run down, remains a military base today. Access is unsurprisingly forbidden but the large complex can be seen from Kamýcká to the north-west of the centre, accessible from Liškova off the 261 (the base and crematorium are separated by a factory complex). The tunnels also survive in the hills to the west and are maintained by the Terezín Memorial but are not open to the public.

Litoměřice is a short ride from Terezín across the Elbe either by car or frequent buses.

OTHER SITES

One of the more notable Holocaust memorials is Plzeň's 'Garden of Memories', located in the ruins of the Auxilary Synagogue adjoining the Old Synagogue at Smetanovy sady 5. In April 2002, local volunteers wrote the names of Holocaust victims from the city on more than 2,600 stones which now line its floor. The Great Synagogue, a short distance away at Sady pětatřicátníků 11, is the third largest in the world.

Most memorials are located in Jewish cemeteries, a notable example being in Kolín, east of Prague. The fate of the city's Jews is one of the lesser-known elements of the brutal reprisals which followed Heydrich's assassination. A thousand people were rounded up from Kolín and the surrounding area on 10 June 1942 and dispatched on a special transport which, uniquely, was not sent directly to Theresienstadt but held in Bohušovice station whilst the numbers were checked. When it was discovered that there were 1,050 people on the train, 50 were marched to the ghetto; the remaining 1,000 were never seen again. The cemetery on Veltrubská, to the north of the city, includes a memorial listing the names of 487 victims. The more celebrated old cemetery, one of the most venerable in central Europe, is on Kmochova, just west of the city centre. Access to both can be arranged through the tourist office located next to the restored synagogue on Na Hradbách.

The most famous victim of the Heydrich reprisals was Lidice, just north-west of Prague. The SS descended on the village on the evening of 9 June 1942, the day of the *Reichsprotektor*'s funeral: all men were shot, the women sent to Ravensbrück (where more than 50 died) and 82 children were dispatched to the Łódź ghetto before being gassed at Chełmno – 340 Czechs lost their lives in total. The village itself was destroyed. It was decided after the war to leave the ruins as a memorial site whilst building a new Lidice adjacent to them. The result is a haunting testament to the horrors of Nazism, accompanied by a new museum (daily, 9.00–6.00 (until 5.00, Mar, & until 4.00, Feb–Nov); 80 Kč; www.lidice-memorial.cz).

Two weeks after the destruction of Lidice, a similar fate befell Ležáky. In fact, although the numbers were smaller, the murder was even more complete with all 33 adults shot and 11 children gassed at Chełmno. Unlike Lidice, a new village was not built; only memorials and a small museum (May–Sept: Tue–Sun, 9.00–5.00; 10 Kč; www.lezaky.cz) mark the site. Ležáky can be reached by taking the 37 southwards from Pardubice and turning onto the 337 around 7 miles south of Chrudim. It is south of the village of Miřetice.

Locations specifically associated with Roma suffering have historically not been well commemorated. An exception is the Museum of Romani Culture in Brno (Tue–Fri, 10.00–6.00; Sun, 10.00–5.00; 40 Kč; www. rommuz.cz), located east of the city centre at Bratislavská 67. The permanent exhibition addresses the Holocaust within the wider history of the Czech and Slovak Roma and Sinti. Brno's Jews, around 10,000 of whom were murdered, are commemorated by a simple memorial in the Jewish cemetery at Nezamyslova 27 in the city's east and a plaque at the site of the New Synagogue (destroyed by the Communists in the 1980s) at Ponávka 8 closer to the centre. The only surviving active synagogue (the only one in the entire country outside Prague) is a drab 1930s Modernist building at Skořepka 13.

In 2008, the government announced that a Roma Holocaust memorial and education centre will be created at the site of the Hodonín 'gypsy' camp which will be administered by the Museum of Romani Culture (check its website for updates). This was one of two such sites – the other at Lety – originally created as labour camps for 'asocial' elements but converted in October 1942 to hold Roma, most of whom (close to 1,500) were deported to Auschwitz. A further 500 died in typhoid epidemics which afflicted both camps. This history was ignored after the war: in a decision crass even by Communist standards, an industrial-scale pig farm was built at Lety in the 1970s; Hodonín remained a labour camp (for opponents of Communism) before becoming a children's recreation centre and then a tourist complex. Simple memorials were established close to both sites in the 1990s but attempts to further mark their history were resisted by nationalist and Communist politicians. Hodonín is on the 19/150 road, west of Kunštát (around 25 miles north of Brno), and not to be confused with the town of the same name on the Slovak border. The future of Lety is less clear although the government has hinted at the possibility of paying for relocation of the farm. It is around 40 miles south-west of Prague: take the 4 road south and turn onto the 19, passing through Lety village towards Orlík nad Vltavou – the memorial ('*Památnik*') is signposted.

CHAPTER 8

SLOVAKIA

Unlike its Czech neighbour, Slovakia was nominally independent during the war yet its collaborationist government was the first to willingly hand over its Jews to the Germans. As a result, approximately 80 per cent of Slovak Jews were murdered.

Jews lived in what became Slovakia as early as the Roman era but the level of settlement fluctuated until a period of steady growth commenced in the eighteenth and nineteenth centuries, accompanied by growing equality in civil rights. The 1930 census listed 135,918 Slovak Jews. Although the country, especially Bratislava, had a reputation for rigorous Orthodoxy, a sizeable assimilated community existed in which Hungarian language and culture were dominant. Orthodox Judaism itself was divided between the traditionalist mainstream and a powerful Hassidic movement in the east. Alongside these developments, anti-Semitism was an increasing factor in Slovak politics particularly amongst those nationalists who had hoped for an independent state when the Habsburg Empire collapsed. Jews were accused of being carriers of an alien Hungarian culture as well as, paradoxically, of being 'Prague-oriented'.

Anti-Semitism was, to a degree, constrained by Czechoslovakia's liberal democracy, but any equilibrium was destroyed by the events of 1938–39. Following the Munich agreement, Slovakia became an autonomous region yet also lost its eastern provinces to Hungary. Any disappointment felt by nationalists was soon outweighed by the creation of an independent Slovakia, for the first time in history, in March 1939 as a result of Hitler's final dismemberment of Czechoslovakia. The new one-party state, headed by the right-wing Catholic priest Jozef Tiso, was a puppet regime to some extent, yet its leaders needed little encouragement to pursue anti-Jewish policies. Even in the autumn of 1938, before independence, the SS-influenced Hlinka Guard paramilitaries carried out attacks on Jews, forcing many over the new border with Hungary. The 89,000 who lived in what remained of Slovakia were subjected to a series of laws which stripped them of their political and economic rights in the course of 1939 and 1940, a process clearly modelled on German policies. Indeed, following a meeting of Hitler and the Slovak leadership in July

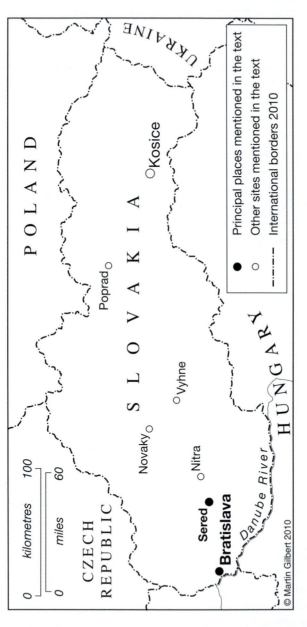

1940, it was decided to send a German advisor on Jewish affairs, Dieter Wisliceny, to Bratislava. In the following year, more than 10,000 Jewish businesses were forcibly closed. Slovakia's entry into the war against the USSR in 1941 saw a further radicalisation of policy, culminating in the promulgation of the *Židovský Kódex* (Jewish Code) in September, based on the German Nuremberg Laws. Jews were also expelled from certain urban areas, required to wear the yellow star and made liable for forced labour.

It is hardly surprising, therefore, that when the Nazis initiated the mass deportations, Slovakia was an eager participant. The first transport left in late March 1942 and in June the government even consented to pay the Germans a fee equivalent to $1.8 million to take its Jews on the promise that they would never return. Between March and October 1942, more than 58,000 were sent to Poland and 3,500 others interned in three labour camps (Sereď, Nováky and Vyhne) in Slovakia itself. The reaction of the Jewish leadership to these developments was unusual. The *Ústredňa Židov* (Jewish Centre) had been established in September 1940 as a Slovak equivalent of the Jewish Councils elsewhere; some of its members created the *Pracovná Skupina* (Working Group), a semi-underground organisation which attempted to prevent the deportations. Their methods included assisting escape to Hungary, expansion of the labour camps to show that Jewish labour was indispensable and, most controversially, large bribes to Wisliceny. The deportations did indeed cease in October 1942 although historians tend to see pressure on Tiso from sections of the government and the Catholic Church as the cause. However, the Jewish leadership felt sufficiently encouraged to launch the Europa Plan, an ambitious attempt to save remaining Jews in Slovakia and elsewhere by raising from Jews in the free world a $2–3 million ransom demanded by Wisliceny. Of course, this was illusory and Wisliceny's own motives are unclear. That said, some historians believe that the ongoing negotiations may have at least helped to prevent the resumption of deportations. However, the respite proved temporary, ironically as a result of the growing hostility to German rule. The Slovak National Uprising of August to October 1944 was the largest act of anti-Nazi resistance within central Europe – 2,000 Jews were amongst the tens of thousands who took part – but was ultimately defeated, enabling the Germans to directly occupy large areas of the country and to deport a further 13,500 Jews. Altogether, of the 89,000 Jews in Slovakia in late

1938, at least 70,000 died. In addition, most of the 46,000 who lived in the lost provinces fell victim to the Hungarian deportations of 1944. It is thus estimated that only 25,000 to 30,000 of the pre-war population of 135,000 survived. Faced with post-war pogroms, possibly initiated by the new Communist regime, most left the country in 1948–49.

Communist commemoration of the war tended to dwell on the National Uprising and certainly not on the Holocaust. Even today, Slovakia has fewer Holocaust memorials than its neighbours and the war remains a divisive topic, as highlighted by the international controversy in 2000 over plans to unveil a plaque to Tiso in Žilina. That said, the small Jewish community has revived since the fall of Communism, a number of Jewish properties have been restored and there has been public, often painful, scrutiny of Slovakia's unhappy role in the Holocaust.

BRATISLAVA

A Jewish presence in Bratislava was recorded as early as the tenth century, but the city really developed into a significant Jewish metropolis only in the seventeenth century during which time, as Pozsony, it was capital of Hungary. It became a leading centre of Orthodox Jewry in the early nineteenth century although it was later afflicted by the schism between Orthodox and Neolog communities that spread across Habsburg Hungary. However, Bratislava also acquired a reputation for anti-Semitism, particularly after its incorporation into Czechoslovakia when Slovaks tended to identify the Jews with the city's formerly dominant German and Hungarian elites. This intensified in the late 1930s and there were anti-Jewish riots in October 1938 in the aftermath of the Munich agreement and immediately upon Slovakia's independence in March 1939. Bratislava's Jewish population – which numbered 15,000 at the end of 1940 – endured growing persecution until it was dramatically reduced when the Tiso regime decided to clear Jews from certain districts in the autumn of 1941. By March 1942, 6,700 had been banished from their homes and forcibly resettled in the provinces or the newly created labour camps, their property looted by the state and given to Slovaks. Most of those who remained were deported, either in 1942 or following the German occupation in 1944. A further dimension to the Holocaust in Bratislava, as in nearby Vienna, was the arrival of thousands of Hungarian Jews in 1944 for use as slave labour on defensive fortifications. They were held in the Engerau camp until late March 1945 and then sent on a death march; those unable to walk were murdered in their barracks. Only a small number of Jews survived in Bratislava to welcome the Red Army on 4 April 1945. The horror did not end there, however, with a two-day anti-Semitic riot in 1946 being followed by more violence in 1948. Unsurprisingly, most Holocaust survivors left the country and Bratislava's Jewish population today is believed to be less than 1,000.

The historic Jewish quarter nestled under the castle until the 1960s when it was destroyed along with much of the rest of the Old Town by a typically insensitive Communist urban development programme which saw the construction of the enormous Nový Most over the Danube and of a connecting highway, Staromestská, through the heart of the city. Virtually all that survives of the Jewish quarter is a single street, Židovská, between the castle and Staromestská. The small but well-presented Museum of Jewish Culture at number 17 (Sun–Fri, 11.00–5.00; 200 Sk) includes a

Bratislava: Museum of Jewish Culture (Photograph by the author)

room dedicated to the Holocaust in Slovakia; a memorial wall lists the names of rabbis who died in the camps.

Zámocká, a left turn at the northern end of Židovská, has a simple memorial to Raoul Wallenberg uphill at a fork in the road. Bratislava's main Holocaust memorial is located in the square by St Martin's Cathedral at the end of Panská (from the museum, walk south along Židovská and through the underpass beneath elevated Staromestská). The 1996 memorial is constructed on the site of the former Rybné Square Synagogue, destroyed by the Communists in 1967. On the black wall of the underpass there is an outline of the Moorish-influenced building which forms a backdrop to a twisted metal sculpture, with imprints of hands and barbed wire, topped with a Star of David. The base is inscribed with the Slovak '*Pamätaj*' and Hebrew '*Zachor*' ('remember').

The only surviving synagogue in Bratislava is a rather intimidating Orthodox structure at Heydukova 11–13, north-east of the Old Town in the main commercial area. The main focus for Orthodox Jews, however, is the tomb of Chatam Sofer, located off Nábrežie armádneho generála Ludvika Svobodu, the main road which runs along the Danube's north bank west of the Nový Most (trams 4, 12 & 17, Chatam Sófer stop). The German-born Sofer was one of Europe's leading Jewish religious thinkers in the early nineteenth century, using his rabbinate and yeshiva in Bratislava as a platform from which to implacably oppose the Jewish Enlightenment. The site was originally a Jewish cemetery which was flattened by the Tiso regime in 1943. A small section, including Sofer's grave, was preserved beneath the new road; various reasons have been suggested for this decision, including bribery and fear of curses. The site was neglected under Communism but has recently undergone extensive restoration. It is entered through a striking thin black building by the tram tunnel under the castle hill; visits require advance arrangement (www. chatamsofer.com). On Žižkova, which runs behind the Sofer memorial, are two surviving Jewish cemeteries at numbers 36 and 50.

Across the Danube, the unlovely suburb of Petržalka was the location of the Engerau labour camp for Hungarian Jews in the last months of the war. Even with the intrusion of Communist urban planning, reminders of these events survive. Almost immediately east of the pedestrian exit of the Nový Most is the Leberfinger Inn, by a park on Viedenská cesta. The inn has existed since Napoleonic times but was requisitioned by the Nazis and some prisoners were held in the stables behind the main building. When Engerau was evacuated on 29 March 1945, 13 were killed in the courtyard. They are amongst the 497 Hungarian Jews buried in a mass grave in plot XII of the Petržalka cemetery much further to the south. A simple memorial stone with the names of 36 victims marks the site (to the right of the administration building at the back); there are also 13 individual named gravestones. The cemetery is served by the 180 bus but this operates only in the south of Petržalka. A more likely route is to take a train or trolleybus to Petržalka station from where it is a 15 minute walk: use the station's west exit, turn left onto Kopčianska, right onto Údernícka, left onto Gogoľova, right onto Dargovská and finally left to Nábrežná – the cemetery is at the end of the road. This route also skirts the large Matador industrial complex which contains the former Semperit factory which was the heart of the labour camp.

SEREĎ

Sereď was the best-known and ultimately most significant of the Slovak camps. It was established as a result of the 1941 Jewish Code; over the following winter a team of Jewish craftsmen converted what had been a military base into a forced labour camp. The initiative for this development came in part from the Jewish community leadership, as part of its strategy of using work as a means of preventing deportation. However, by the time the camp came into operation in the spring of 1942, the deportations had begun and Sereď, overseen by the Hlinka Guard, also became a transit camp. Around 4,500 Jews were sent on five transports to Poland in 1942, the last departing on Yom Kippur. Thereafter, conditions stabilised and around 1,000 Jews worked in the camp, their numbers rising to 1,300 in 1943. Indeed, Sereď was seen by the authorities as sufficiently productive for a Jewish Council under Alexander Pressburger to share in the camp's administration, with increased food rations, schooling for children and even temporary leave passes for privileged inmates. During the 1944 National Uprising, prisoners played an active role and many were able to escape. However, Sereď was recaptured by the Germans and became the principal transit camp for those areas of Slovakia still under Nazi control: 13,500 Jews were deported to Auschwitz, Theresienstadt and Sachsenhausen between October 1944 and March 1945. The Red Army liberated the camp on 1 April, a day after the last transport.

After the war, the camp reverted to its original function as an army base and remains under military control today. Its interior is naturally inaccessible, and for many years there was nothing to remind visitors or locals of its past. There is now a simple memorial, a concrete pillar by the gate with '*Zachor*' set in stone, although the monument's explanatory metal plaque has disappeared. That said, Sereď is a rather intriguing place to see, a former concentration camp that is still in use. The roadside buildings are post-war but the gateposts are original as are the barracks visible through the grille on the gate.

Sereď is 30 miles north-east of Bratislava and served by regular buses and trains, the latter requiring a change in Trnava or Galanta. The camp is on Kasárenská to the west of the town, almost directly opposite the train station but frustratingly on the other side of the tracks. From the station, it is necessary to walk south down Železničná and turn right onto Dionýza Štúra, the main road west out of town. Kasárenská is to the right, just after the road crosses the railway tracks, with the town's cemetery on the corner. The camp is a short walk from here, after Kasárenská turns to the left. Visitors coming by car must take the Sereď exit from the E571 and turn left into Kasárenská when the cemetery appears just before the bridge over the railway.

OTHER SITES

For an excellent database of sites, see www.slovak-jewish-heritage. org. Nitra, around 45 miles north-east of Bratislava off the E571, is the location of the only Holocaust memorial museum in Slovakia (Tue, Sat–Sun, 1.00–6.00; Wed–Thu, 9.00–12.00, 1.00–6.00; 10 Sk), in the women's gallery of its former synagogue at central Pri synagóge 3. The town's large Jewish cemetery (Thu, Sun, 8–2) is on Hviezdoslavova trieda, south-west of the centre.

Simple memorials of the type found at Sereď have been placed at three other key sites. Nováky labour camp is marked by a plaque on the outside wall of the town's railway station on Gašpara Košťála (the camp was actually located outside town but the site is inaccessible). Nováky is just south of the 50/E572, 35 miles north-east of Nitra. The camp at Vyhne, accessed by a minor road to the east of the 65/E571 at Bzenica, was looted and destroyed by locals at the end of the war and a recently opened water park stands on the site. There is, though, a memorial marker, similar to that at Sereď, in the centre of the village, easily missed by the side of the road. A plaque commemorates the first Slovak transport to Auschwitz (25 March 1942) at the train station in the northern city of Poprad, on Jiřího Wolkera. There is a further plaque on the wall of the former synagogue at Popradskej brigády 9, a little further east.

Up to 15,000 Jews from Košice and the surrounding area were sent to Auschwitz from May 1944 onwards during the Hungarian deportations. These events are commemorated by plaques at the synagogue at Puškinova 3, just east of the centre, where Jews were held prior to deportation. A former Hassidic prayer hall is around the corner at Krmanova 5, whilst a rare surviving example of an Orthodox Jewish compound of the type once common in this part of Europe is at Zvonárska 7. A short distance away, west of the centre, is another former synagogue at Moyzesova 66, notable for its remarkable dome. The dome was once topped by a large Star of David which now forms a Holocaust memorial in the main Jewish cemetery, accessed through the municipal Christian cemetery at Ratislavova 83, south of the centre.

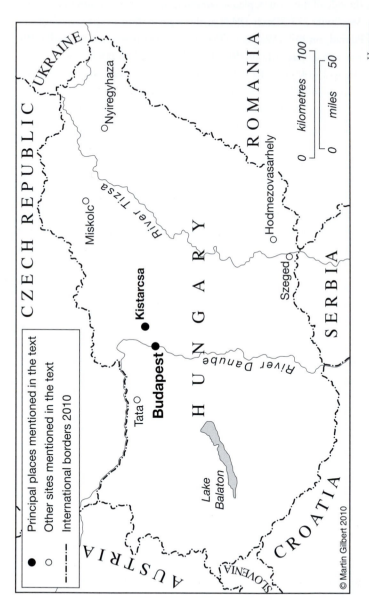

CZECH REPUBLIC

UKRAINE

○Nyiregyhaza

ROMANIA

Miskolc○

River Tisza

Kistarcsa

○Hodmezovasarhely

H U N G A R Y

Szeged○

SERBIA

Tata○

Budapest●

River Danube

Lake
Balaton

AUSTRIA

SLOVENIA

CROATIA

Principal places mentioned in the text
Other sites mentioned in the text
International borders 2010

●
○

kilometres   0   50   100
miles   0   50

Hungary

© Martin Gilbert 2010

CHAPTER 9

HUNGARY

A lthough the Holocaust came to Hungary later than to any other country, at a point when the Germans were clearly losing the war, the effects were so immediate and devastating that it suffered the highest Jewish losses of any nation other than Poland and the USSR. Indeed, the largest group of victims of Auschwitz-Birkenau were Hungarian Jews. Even after the weakening of Germany's military position and political changes inside Hungary had ended the deportations, the surviving Jews had to endure a brutal campaign of violence at the hands of home-grown Fascists which claimed further tens of thousands of lives.

Although Jews had lived in the region since Roman times – long before the Hungarians themselves – significant communities developed in the Middle Ages. They were subject to the same varying pattern of persecution and toleration as in neighbouring countries until Turkish rule in the sixteenth century brought greater stability and prosperity. However, Austrian conquests from the late seventeenth century engendered a resurgence of anti-Semitism which did not properly abate until the 1780s although this period also saw significant Jewish immigration. Religiously, Hungary's Jews were amongst the most diverse in Europe, the mainstream splitting in the 1860s into Orthodox, Neolog (Reform) and Status Quo (affiliated with neither). There were also significant Hassidic communities in the east of the country. That said, most Jews were united by a strong sense of Hungarian identity forged in the struggle for greater autonomy from Austria and tended to see themselves as a secure and integrated sector of society.

This was to change in the aftermath of the First World War when Hungary was stripped of two-thirds of its territories in the 1920 Treaty of Trianon. The sense of grievance thus created gave rise to an irredentist nationalist movement as fanatical as that in Germany. The feelings of loss and anger were generally shared by Jews, not least by those who now found themselves stranded in Czechoslovakia, Romania and Yugoslavia. Nonetheless, as in Germany, Hungarian nationalism rapidly acquired a strongly authoritarian streak augmented by a growing strain of anti-Semitism. The failed 1919 Communist revolution, a number of whose leaders were Jewish, was followed by pogroms. The emergence in 1920 of Admiral Miklós Horthy as regent (head of state) brought a weakening of democratic institutions although Parliament continued to exist. Anti-Semitism was not central to Horthy's brand of conservative nationalism but it was to the more radical elements in Parliament with the result that Hungary was the first inter-war state to pass an anti-Jewish law, introducing quotas for university enrolment in 1920. It was, however, Hungary's foreign policy objectives that were ultimately to prove fatal to its Jews. Although Horthy attempted to suppress the burgeoning Fascist movement led by Ferenc Szálasi, his desire to overturn Trianon led to an ever closer relationship with Germany. Hungary was rewarded with the return of territory from Slovakia and Romania in 1938 and 1940 respectively. It formally joined the Axis in October 1940, making further territorial gains by participating in the invasion of Yugoslavia in March 1941.

The price for these successes was increasingly paid by the Jewish population which had grown from somewhere less than 450,000 in Trianon Hungary to more than 725,000 (825,000, if Christians of Jewish origin are included) with the acquisitions. Laws in 1938 and 1939 introduced quotas for the professions and business, followed by a racial statute based on the Nuremberg Laws in 1941. Szálasi, imprisoned in 1938, was released in 1940 although his movement (organised into the Arrow Cross Party in 1939) was officially banned. Most dramatically, the outbreak of European war brought the institution of military-related labour conscription for Jewish men (they were forbidden to serve as soldiers). When Hungary consummated its commitment to the Axis by joining the invasion of the USSR, tens of thousands of Jews were sent to the Ukrainian front to serve as slave labour in construction projects; at least 27,000 died up to March 1944. A further 20,000 Jews who did not have Hungarian citizenship were deported at German request to Ukraine in August 1941. In theory, they too were sent as forced labourers but the vast majority – at least 15,000 – were murdered by the *Einsatzgruppen*. The Hungarians themselves committed a notorious massacre of Jews and Serbs in the annexed Yugoslav city of Novi Sad in January 1942.

Despite these atrocities, Horthy refused German requests to deport Hungarian Jews. As in Italy, it was the Axis's declining military performance that ironically changed this situation. Horthy, for whom the alliance had always been primarily a marriage of convenience, increasingly sought a way out of the war after Stalingrad; it was to forestall Hungarian withdrawal that Germany invaded the country on 19 March 1944. Although Horthy remained, a new government was installed which was committed to German objectives. A special SS team headed by Eichmann rapidly began its heinous work, with the yellow star introduced on 5 April. From 15 April, Jews living outside the capital were concentrated in major cities or towns which became temporary ghettos (none lasted more than six weeks). Systematic deportation began on 15 May: in less than two months, 434,351 people were transported on more than 145 trains, mainly to Auschwitz where most were killed on arrival. The fact that the Germans undertook such a complex logistical operation at a point when every train was needed for the war effort is a telling commentary on Nazi priorities.

By July, the only Jewish community left was that of Budapest, Eichmann's final target. However, Horthy stopped the deportations on 7 July. He still hoped to extricate Hungary from the war and was increasingly terrified of Allied retribution. Two Slovak Jews, Rudolf Vrba and Alfréd Wetzler had escaped from Auschwitz in April, aiming to inform both the West and the Hungarian Jews of its murderous activities. The latter's leadership chose not to make the report public, a cause of immense controversy ever since. The most commonly suggested reason is that they did not wish to antagonise the Germans at a time when they were engaged in secret negotiations with Eichmann to ransom Jews in return for goods from the Allies. As it transpired, the only positive outcome from the talks, which were almost certainly only ever a German ruse, was the departure of one train. However, the contents of the Vrba-Wetzler report were broadcast in the West in June and Roosevelt himself warned Horthy that he would be held responsible for the fate of Hungary's Jews. On the same day, a British diplomat sent a deliberately uncoded message suggesting that named government buildings in Budapest be bombed in retaliation. When the Americans indeed bombed the capital less than a week later, Horthy drew the obvious, though actually mistaken, conclusion. However, when he announced on 15 October that Hungary was making peace with the USSR, the Germans simply overthrew him and installed Szálasi as head of an Arrow Cross government. Tens of thousands of Jews were arrested and sent as forced labour to Austria whilst Arrow Cross members began a reign of terror in the capital. By the time the Red Army captured Budapest in January 1945, more than 500,000 Hungarian Jews had died since the occupation began 10 months earlier, almost 270,000 of them from within the Trianon borders. A further 63,000 had perished in the 1941–44 period. The modern community is estimated to number around 100,000 people.

Hungarian Jewry is commemorated by a large number of memorials across the country, mostly in cemeteries. Budapest, however, has more prominent memorials which are amongst the most impressive in Europe.

BUDAPEST

Budapest's Jewish community was the largest in Europe outside Poland. A significant presence had existed in the city (or rather cities – Buda and Pest were only officially united in 1873) since the twelfth century although Jews were expelled following the Austrian reconquest in the seventeenth century and forced to live on Buda's northern fringes until the 1780s. Both the city and its Jewish population grew dramatically in the nineteenth century; by the inter-war period, there were more than 200,000 Jews in Budapest, close to half of the entire community of Trianon Hungary. These numbers were further swelled by thousands of refugees from Germany and Austria and later from Poland and Slovakia. Although the Horthy regime's anti-Semitic laws caused great hardship, Budapest appeared an infinitely safer haven than any other central European city.

The German occupation brought immediate change: early measures included the closure of the city's 18,000 Jewish-owned shops and the confiscation of 1,500 apartments. There was no ghetto but, as the planned deportation drew near, Jews were restricted to designated buildings within the city, which became known as 'yellow star' houses. Eichmann had originally agreed to 2,639 such properties but this was reduced to 1,835 when the scheme was introduced in late June 1944. Tens of thousands of Jews found themselves having to vacate a total of 19,000 apartments and quickly relocate to the restricted blocks. The SS and the Hungarian police began combing the suburbs in early July, arresting 17,500 people who were then sent to Auschwitz. The rest of Budapest's Jews would have shared this fate had Horthy not intervened on 7 July. Eichmann still requested permission to deport them on 19 August (to begin the next day!) but was refused and his office was closed down five days later. The Red Cross was permitted

Budapest: shoe memorial (Photograph by the author)

to give assistance to Jews and the High Holidays were celebrated in a mood of some hope – the government even lifted the curfew on Jews for Yom Kippur (28 September).

Any optimism thus generated proved to be ill-founded. The Arrow Cross takeover in October was followed by attacks on Jewish neighbourhoods and the shooting of several hundred people. On 26 October, the new government agreed to deport Jews for forced labour in Austria: 35,000 were assembled within one week. They and others were marched westwards whilst yet others were dispatched by train to camps in the Reich. The Szálasi regime also established a ghetto in mid-November into which most Jews were concentrated by early December. A further 'international ghetto' emerged, consisting of properties owned or rented by neutral governments and thus considered extraterritorial. This accommodated 15,000 to 20,000 Jews who had been issued with protective documents by diplomats of neutral governments, the best known of whom was the

195

Swede Raoul Wallenberg. Their aim was to protect as many Jews as possible until the Red Army arrived through the distribution of papers claiming the bearer was a citizen of the appropriate country awaiting repatriation. Even before the international ghetto was created, Jews had been given sanctuary in diplomatically protected houses across the city as well as food and medical care.

The approach of Soviet forces created chaos in the last weeks of 1944 and whatever authority Szálasi had over the Arrow Cross melted away. Gangs had been raiding Jewish properties since 15 October but the violence intensified in mid-November. It was in this desperate situation that Wallenberg particularly showed his courage and tenacity. Contrary to popular belief, he did not issue the largest number of protective documents but he was perhaps the most tireless in seeking to frustrate the Nazis and Arrow Cross, halting German deportation trains and death marches to give passes to as many Jews as he could. When he learned on 12 January 1945 that the Arrow Cross planned to massacre all Jews in the ghetto, Wallenberg persuaded the German army to intervene and prevent the bloodbath. It is a tragic irony, therefore, that he lost his life at the hands of neither the Nazis nor the Arrow Cross but the Communists. On 17 January, the day before the ghetto was liberated, Wallenberg was seen in Budapest for the last time as he drove out to greet the Red Army. He was arrested for reasons that are still unknown and eventually sent to the Gulag. A Soviet statement in 1957 admitted Wallenberg's abduction but claimed that he had died of a heart attack in 1947. This is widely disbelieved; some witnesses claim to have seen him in the USSR as late as 1987.

Around 85,000 Budapest Jews were murdered during the Holocaust yet the efforts of men like Wallenberg prevented the figure from being even greater. The result is that more than 100,000 survived and Budapest is today the only central European city with a Jewish community of any great size, numbering 80,000 or more.

The ghetto

The location chosen by the Szálasi government for Budapest's ghetto in November 1944 was the city's traditional Jewish quarter in the seventh district. The physical survival of the area's buildings makes it a fascinating neighbourhood to explore, bearing witness not just to the horrors inflicted on it in 1944–45 but also to its prosperous pre-war Jewish culture. What

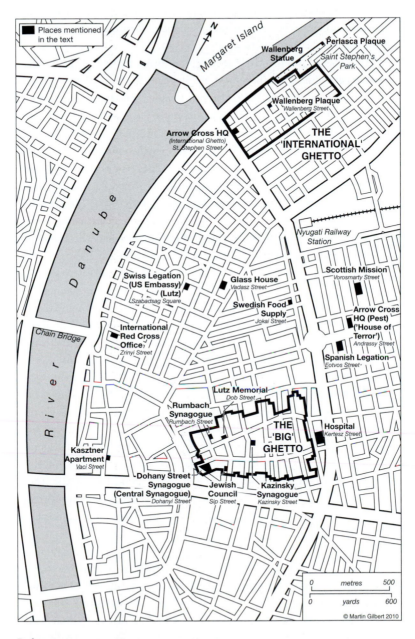

Budapest

makes Budapest's Jewish quarter unique amongst the cities of central and eastern Europe, however, is the endurance, albeit diminished, of this culture and of the community which created it.

The ghetto was centred around the main streets of Dob and Wesselényi, with its southernmost point being the Central Synagogue on Dohány utca. Built in 1859, the vast temple is the largest in Europe (Sun–Fri, 10.00–3.00; 1,400 Ft with museum). The magnificent Moorish exterior is matched by the ornate, cavernous interior – restored in the 1990s – which can seat up to 3,000 people. By the entrance there are a number of plaques to Holocaust victims as well as one to participants in the annual March of the Living to Auschwitz. The simple Jewish Museum (Sun–Thu, 10.00–5.00 (until 3.00, Nov–Feb); Fri, 10.00–2.00; www. bpjewmus.hu) is upstairs to the left of the synagogue in an annexe built in the 1920s on the site where Theodor Herzl was born. Three rooms contain a selection of ritual objects whilst a small fourth addresses the Holocaust with reproductions of wartime photographs and newspapers and a bust of Wallenberg. Stairs lead down to a tiny Holocaust memorial. Between the museum and synagogue, a passageway leads past the Heroes Synagogue, built as a memorial to Hungarian Jewish soldiers who died in the First World War, to the Wallenberg memorial garden at the rear. This is dominated by a giant sculpted metal weeping willow, its leaves inscribed with the names of victims, to the right of which is the memorial to Righteous Gentiles, a multi-coloured glass mosaic overlooking slabs listing the names of rescuers in Hungary. The most prominent, Wallenberg at their head, are listed on a large plaque on the floor, surrounded by hundreds of stones left by visitors. Beyond this is a symbolic mausoleum for named victims. At the back of the garden, a plaque honours Angelo Giuseppe Roncalli, better known as the future Pope John XXIII. The Papal Legate in Greece and Turkey, Roncalli played a prominent role in promoting Catholic rescue activities in Europe as a whole and in Hungary especially.

The garden looks onto Wesselényi. Easily missed on one of the supporting pillars of the outer wall of the Heroes Synagogue graveyard is a plaque marking the ghetto's liberation on 18 January 1945. This is opposite the site of one of the ghetto gates. Wesselényi 7 was the Goldmark Hall, a Jewish cultural centre closed by the occupation. Hit by a bomb in the Battle of Budapest, it was only rebuilt in the 1970s and now houses a Talmud Torah school. The next right off Wesselényi is Síp utca, a lovely street of crumbling, darkened buildings. Number 12 was the headquarters of the Jewish community council, as it remains today. It was here that the reaction to the Vrba-Wetzler report was debated and that Eichmann came to make his demands on the community. When the ghetto was sealed on 10 December 1944, a grenade was thrown at the building, killing several of those inside.

Back down Wesselényi, the street opposite the Wallenberg garden is Rumbach Sebestyén utca. The imposing Secessionist corner building at 6 housed a ghetto kitchen. Further along, the Rumbach Synagogue at number 11 was where Jews fatally deported to Kamenets Podolsky in Ukraine in August 1941 were held before their departure. Around the corner, at Dob 12, is a memorial to the Swiss diplomat Carl Lutz. As vice-consul, he worked with the Jewish Agency for Palestine to issue Swiss passes for emigration. Following the occupation, Lutz arranged with the Germans and Hungarians for a further 8,000 passes to be issued but deliberately chose to misinterpret this to mean 8,000 families rather than individuals. He also took the lead in coordinating the diplomats and was instrumental in the establishment of safe houses in the city. The memorial takes the form of a golden angel hanging from the wall and offering help to a prone bronze figure. Plaques in English and Hungarian quote from the Talmud but make no direct mention of the fact that Lutz saved Jews, apparently for fear of anti-Semitic defacement when the monument was created in 1991. The *Spinoza* coffee house at Dob 5 was a bakery in the ghetto. Opposite, by number 16, is the entrance to the Gozsdu udvar, a series of gently curving interlocking courtyards and apartments built in 1904 to accommodate Jewish artisans, which stretches through to parallel Király. Long neglected, this was for decades one of the most atmospheric streets in central Europe but is currently closed whilst it undergoes restoration into luxury shops and flats. A block further on, Dob intersects with Kazinczy whose synagogue (at 29–31) is the third point (with the other two synagogues) of the 'Jewish triangle', the core of the quarter.

Just beyond the north-eastern fringe of the ghetto, Wesselényi 44 (by the crossroads with Kertész) was designated as a hospital for Jews in June 1944. On 15 October 1944, Arrow Cross men celebrated their takeover by shooting into the building. It was hit by a shell on 20 January 1945 – a day before the full liberation – and many staff and patients were killed. There is now a memorial plaque on the wall.

Central Pest

One of Europe's most effective Holocaust memorials is located on the Danube embankment, the site of the horrific scenes in the winter of 1944–45. From 23 November, hundreds of Jews were seized each day by Arrow Cross thugs, brought to the river and shot – it is estimated that between 10,000 and 20,000 were murdered. These events are recalled through life-size iron casts of dozens of shoes, loosely arranged in a row by the water. The idea, the work of sculptor Gyula Pauer and poet Can Togay, is beautifully simple yet its effect is powerful. The memorial is south of the Parliament building, opposite Zoltán utca above. The only difficulty is reaching it which requires either crossing very busy Pesti Alsó rakpart or walking some distance along the embankment to the nearest pedestrian crossings.

The American Embassy at Szabadság tér 12 was the site of Lutz's bureau where Swiss protective documents were issued. The building is unsurprisingly surrounded by heavy security. A more substantial reminder of Lutz's efforts is the 'Glass House', two blocks away at Vadász 29. The modernist building was a Swiss-protected house from late July 1944; it is estimated that around 3,000 Jews were able to find shelter here. An Arrow Cross raid on 31 December 1944 seized 600 people but the owner of the property, Arthur Weiss, persuaded the police to step in although this was too late to save three residents. Weiss was murdered by the enraged Arrow Cross on the following day. On the exterior of the building are memorial plaques to Lutz, Weiss and the three victims of 31 December together with a further three killed on 6 January. Through the metal door (there is a buzzer if it is locked) and to the right of the courtyard is the Lutz Memorial Room (daily, 1.00–4.00; donation requested), a small exhibition space with testimony from survivors and reproductions of documents (an English language guide is available for a donation).

Further east, the House of Terror (Tue–Fri, 10.00–6.00; Sat–Sun, 10.00–7.30; 1500 Ft; www.terrorhaza.hu) is located in a building at Andrássy út 60 (Oktogon Metro) which housed the Arrow Cross party headquarters in 1937–45 and then the ÁVO (Communist secret police) from 1945 to 1956. This makes it an eminently appropriate site for a museum dedicated to totalitarianism but it is easy to see why the high-profile exhibition has been controversial. Although it claims to address the two dictatorships, virtually the whole exhibition focuses on Communist crimes – even the concluding Hall of Tears is dedicated to those 'murdered 1945–67'. There is also something of a theme park feel to some displays, risking trivialisation of the horror of Stalinism. One gets the impression that the museum, reasonably enough perhaps, is targeting the young.

On nearby Vörösmarty utca, the grand Collegium Josephinum at 34A was a hiding place for Jews. More famously, St Columba's Scottish Mission at 49–51 is associated with Jane Haining. This Scottish woman came to Budapest in 1932 to work in the school here, looking after young Jewish girls. Although the mission's aim was conversion, many of its charges were orphans who might otherwise have had nowhere to go. When the Germans invaded, Haining ignored the order to return to Scotland and was arrested by the Gestapo in April 1944. In addition to the predictable charge of espionage for the British, she was also accused of the unusual offence of weeping – at the sight of her girls sewing yellow stars into their clothes. She was sent to Auschwitz in May and died there in July. The mission building was later used as a protective home, under the aegis of the Swedish Red Cross, for around 70 Jewish children and 40 parents in November and December 1944.

Heading back down Andrássy, one passes the Spanish Embassy at Eötvös 11B. This was where Giorgio Perlasca, the most remarkable diplomatic rescuer, issued visas. A disillusioned former Fascist, Perlasca was working for the Italian government in Hungary when the Germans invaded. He took refuge in the embassy and became a Spanish citizen due to his Civil War service. He worked with the chargé d'affaires, Ángel Sanz Briz, to provide protective documents. Even after Sanz Briz was withdrawn in November 1944, Perlasca audaciously continued, pretending to be the replacement. On one occasion, he pulled two Jewish boys from a train at Józsefváros station, only later learning from Wallenberg that the officer he had confronted was Eichmann himself. When Perlasca returned to Italy, he told no one of his heroism, apparently not even his family, until tracked down by a group of survivors in 1987.

Jókai tér, further down Andrássy on its northern side, leads to Jókai utca. The building at number 1 was the Swedish Embassy food supply where hundreds of Jews were hidden. On 8 January 1945, at the height of the terror, the Arrow Cross seized and killed 266 of them. A plaque commemorates the victims. Around the corner at Andrássy 36, a plaque honours Wallenberg's driver Vilmos Langfelder who lived here and shared in the diplomat's fate.

There are a few places of note south of Parliament and west of the ghetto. The modern Intercontinental hotel, between Apáczai Csere János and Belgrád rakpart just south of Roosevelt tér, stands on the site of the Ritz which was the final location of the Portuguese Embassy in 1944. An unobtrusive pair of plaques in Hungarian and Portuguese on the river side pay tribute to Ambassador Sampaio Garrido and Consul Carlos Branquinho who issued 600 passports although the beneficiaries are referred to only as 'Hungarians persecuted for racist and political motives'. Nearby Váci 12 was the apartment of the controversial and ultimately tragic figure of Rezső Kasztner, marked by a wall plaque. Kasztner was the activist whose negotiations with Eichmann in the summer of 1944 led to almost 1,700 Jews being allowed to leave Hungary on a special train in exchange for a ransom of money, gold and diamonds. The transport left on 30 June 1944 and carried its cargo to Bergen-Belsen, breaking Eichmann's promise that the Jews would be taken to Switzerland. Nonetheless, almost all were able to eventually proceed to the original destination by the end of the year. Kasztner's defenders argue that he thus saved more Jewish lives than anyone else in the Holocaust. Kasztner himself believed that the negotiations were part of a wider effort to save all Hungarian Jews although in this he was being deceived by the Nazis. Critics accuse him of collaboration, especially of failing to warn the mass of the Jewish population of the fate that awaited them in order to safeguard the negotiations for the train. These issues came to a head in an infamous 1955 trial when the Israeli government, on Kasztner's behalf, sued one of his critics for libel, an action that backfired when the judge ruled that he had 'sold his soul to the German Satan'. Although the verdict was overturned on appeal in 1958, this came too late for Kasztner who had been assassinated in Israel a year earlier. Opposite Kasztner's building, number 11B was one of the 'yellow star' houses to which Jews were restricted from June 1944.

The 'international ghetto'

The 'international ghetto', also known as the little ghetto, was established in November 1944 for Jews holding protective documents. It consisted of a small group of streets north of the Margaret Bridge most of whose houses were placed under the authority of the neutral powers. More than 15,000 Jews were relocated here to apartments that had previously housed less than 4,000. In addition to the hardship caused by the over-crowding, the ghetto was not an entirely safe haven as Arrow Cross raids increasingly ignored the diplomatic protection given to the houses. As a result, many Jews were transferred to the main ghetto, not that this necessarily proved to be more secure. Even so, the international ghetto undoubtedly contributed to the salvation of many thousands of lives.

The area, a mixture of grand Secessionist buildings and modest apartment blocks, is a kilometre north of the shoes memorial and close to Nyugati Metro. The largest concentrations of protected houses were on Tátra and Pozsonyi along with intersecting Katona József. Most offer no indication of their history but the odd memorial exists. A plaque at Pozsonyi 1 (a Swedish-protected house) honours the Hungarian Jewish poet Miklós Radnóti. He had been amongst the Jews conscripted into the labour battalions in Ukraine; his group was later assigned to copper mines in Serbia. He was shot in the Hungarian village of Abda in November 1944. The elegant six-storey building at nearby Katona József 21 was raided by the Arrow Cross on 30 December 1944. The 170 residents were taken to the party HQ (now the House of Terror), stripped to their underwear and forced to march barefoot to the river where 50 of them were shot. Around the corner, Tátra 6 was Wallenberg's main office, where protective documents, along with food and medical treatment, were organised. This is not marked but the Swede's efforts are memorialised elsewhere by Raoul Wallenberg utca to the north. At its junction with Pozsonyi, there is a memorial plaque, incorporating a sculpture, on the north-east corner wall. Three of the four buildings at this crossroads were Swedish houses. The next street to the north is named after Radnóti. Turning left into it from Pozsonyi, numbers 40, 43 and 45 were Swiss-protected houses whilst 41 was for Jews nominated by Horthy. There is a bust of Radnóti on the wall of 45. A little further north, to the west of Pozsonyi, is Szent István park, which houses another monument to Wallenberg, in the not entirely appropriate form of a sculpture of a heroic nude St George (the other statues are unrelated). Opposite the northern exit to the park, on the wall of Szent István park 35, is a plaque to Perlasca.

Eastern Pest

The Holocaust Memorial Centre (Tue–Sun, 10.00–6.00; 1000 Ft; www.hdke.hu) is south-east of the city centre at Páva 39 in the ninth district (Ferenc körút Metro then a short walk east along Üllői út). When it opened in 2004, the choice of location caused some controversy given its distance from the ghetto area. However, the site is historically appropriate, the complex being built around a former synagogue which was used as an internment camp in 1944. A lot of government money was put into the centre and it shows in a well-arranged and thoughtful exhibition. Throughout, the main narrative is interspersed with personal stories whilst care is also taken to address the fate of Hungary's Roma community. The main displays are in a series of rooms based around the theme of deprivation – of rights, property, freedom, dignity – culminating in deprivation of life. The aim is to show how the systematic erosion of liberties by the Hungarian authorities as well as the Nazis paved the way for genocide. A particularly powerful exhibit in room 6 has five television screens showing the famous photographs of the Jews of Beregszász (now Bereghovo in Ukraine), taken in Birkenau on 26 May 1944. A clock in the top corner gives the time of each stage of their last moments, starting with the convoy's arrival at 9.14 a.m.; the whole process took less than six hours. Stairs lead up from the exhibition to the synagogue whose beautiful interior has been lovingly restored.

The now abandoned Józsefváros station was used for deportations in late 1944. Even Szálasi was trying to limit transports by this stage but his members were out of control, working with Eichmann to round up Jews. From 21 November, thousands were sent to Mauthausen and Ravensbrück. Wallenberg came to the station with protective documents on four occasions. In the case of the last train, on 24 December, he managed to stop it after it had left the platform and retrieve passengers. These efforts are marked by a memorial plaque along with another to the deportees on the wall of the station building which is set back from the road on the eastern side of Fiumei út (take bus 9 or tram 28 to Orczy tér and walk north or tram 37 to Fiumei út and walk south).

At the next junction to the north, Magdolna (off Fiumei út to the left) leads into a once strongly Jewish neighbourhood. At the corner of Magdolna and Dobozi there was fighting on 15 and 16 October 1944 as local Jews tried to resist the Arrow Cross takeover. Nearby Teleki tér was home to a legendary pre-war Jewish flea market (there is still a market at the site) which was raided by the Arrow Cross on 16 November 1944. Back at the Fiumei út junction, Salgótarjáni to the east leads to the Jewish section of the massive Kerepesi cemetery, accessed by a separate entrance at the end of the road (tram 37, MÁV, X. kapu stop). There are many grand graves but some sections, including those at the rear where some victims of the ghetto are buried, are so overgrown as to be inaccessible.

A happier state of affairs prevails at the Rákoskeresztúr cemetery (tram 37 to its Izraelita Temető terminus). This is the largest Jewish cemetery in Hungary and home to an especially striking Holocaust memorial behind the ceremonial hall to the left. A long L-shaped roof is supported by columns on which are inscribed the names of Holocaust victims. Touchingly, relatives have added thousands of other names, making the memorial more complete and personal. Close to the end of the long part of the L, there is a symbolic urn with ashes from Auschwitz-Birkenau, set in a black marble monument.

Buda

Castle Hill, from where Horthy ruled Hungary, was also the site of the Vatican Legation headed by Nuncio Angelo Rotta. Although less famous than Wallenberg or Lutz, he actually issued the highest number of protective passes to Jews, at least 15,000. Rotta's unique position enabled him to also provide fake baptismal certificates. His memory is honoured, rather unobtrusively, by a slightly faded plaque on the wall of the yellowish building at numbers 4–5 on Dísz tér, the castle's main square. The Lutheran church at Táncsics Mihály 28 in the north of the compound was served by pastor Gábor Sztehlo who worked with the Calvinist Good Shepherd movement to shelter Jewish children in late 1944. To this end, Sztehlo organised 32 refuges, in homes of friends and family in Buda together with church properties in Pest, giving shelter to 1,540 children and carers, all of whom survived. After the war, he created an orphanage for the hundreds of his charges left without parents which he oversaw until nationalisation by the Communists in 1951. He later ran hospices for children with disabilities and the elderly and was justly the first Hungarian to be recognised by Yad Vashem as Righteous Among the Nations. On the wall behind the tower, there is a memorial plaque depicting Sztehlo and the olive tree planted in his honour in Jerusalem. Number 26 next door was found to contain the remains of a medieval synagogue during restoration work in the 1960s (May–Oct: Tue–Fri, 10.00–5.00; 300 Ft) whilst 23 opposite was the site of the original Great Synagogue, burned down during the Austrian reconquest from the Turks.

A number of sites to the west of Castle Hill are accessible from the transport hub of Moszkva tér (Metro line 2; if walking from Castle Hill, take the northern exit down Várfok utca). Three blocks south-west of the square, Csaba utca intersects with Maros. Maros 16 was a Jewish hospital raided by the Arrow Cross on 12 January 1945; 92 patients and staff were killed in the garden. Csaba's next junction is with Városmajor whose western section has a number of significant buildings. Numbers 52 and 54 were amongst the Good Shepherd houses: 18 Jewish children and eight mothers were sheltered here. Less fortunate were the 90 residents of the Jewish old people's home at 62 on the corner with Alma who were murdered by the Arrow Cross on 19 January 1945, two days before liberation. On the other side of the crossroads, the former Jewish hospital at Városmajor 64–66 was raided on 14 January; the Arrow Cross killed 130 patients and 24 staff. There is a 2007 memorial plaque on the wall of 64. The most striking site in the area is another Wallenberg memorial. Erected in 1987, a statue of the Swede stands between two large stone slabs in a small park on Szilágyi Erzsébet, opposite house number 101 (bus 56 from Moszkva tér to Nagyajtai utca).

Further north, up a hill west of the Margaret Bridge, the elegant villa at Apostol 13b was Eichmann's residence. In its grounds, he beat to death a Jewish boy who was his gardener, the only one of the millions of murders for which he was convicted at his trial that he committed personally. The mansion's Jewish former owner Lipó Aschner was sent to Mauthausen but survived.

Bécsi 134–136 in Obuda was the site of a brickworks where the 35,000 Jews arrested in late 1944 were held before being sent onto Austria to work on defensive fortifications. The complex was destroyed in the 1990s.

KISTARCSA

Kistarcsa is the best known of the Hungarian transit camps, the holding centre for tens of thousands of Jews from the Budapest suburbs and surrounding region. Had the deportations not ceased in July 1944, it would have achieved greater infamy by performing the same role for the capital itself. The buildings were originally constructed to house local factory workers before being requisitioned by the Interior Ministry in the 1930s for use as an internment camp for political opponents. Even before the German occupation, Jews resided here, some as political prisoners, others as refugees. Kistarcsa was then earmarked by Eichmann as the principal assembly point for deportees from Budapest and central

Hungary; the camp was under SS control although largely administered by Hungarians. A transport of 1,800 people on 29 April was the first of 19 sent to Auschwitz before Horthy's intervention in July. This was not, however, the final act. Eichmann attempted to send another convoy on 14 July, over a week after the Regent's order, which was only stopped when the Hungarian commandant Vasdenyei – regarded by inmates as a relatively decent figure – and Budapest Jewish leaders tipped off Horthy, enabling the train to be turned back before the border. Undeterred, Eichmann engineered a further deportation of 1,220 people (mostly members of the abortive transport) on 19 July, using the ruse of summoning the Jewish leaders to a meeting in Budapest whilst the trains were loaded so that knowledge of the departure would arrive too late to prevent a reversal. These actions were highlighted at Eichmann's trial as evidence of his obsessive determination to destroy Europe's Jews at any cost. Following this final transport, roughly 1,000 Jews remained in Kistarcsa until 27 September 1944 when they were sent to labour camps.

As was so often the case in the Soviet bloc, Kistarcsa's dark history was destined not to end with the war. It was used as a concentration camp until Stalin's death and then as a prison camp for revolutionaries following the crushing of the 1956 Uprising. It later became a police-training centre and ultimately an internment centre for alleged illegal immigrants. Allegations of maltreatment of this last group of inmates led to the Hungarian government finally closing Kistarcsa in 1995 after significant EU pressure. The site now stands mostly deserted, the barracks slowly rotting behind a wire fence. The only memorial in the vicinity is to the victims of 1956, a rather disgraceful state of affairs given the camp's role not just in the deportations but also under Stalin and, indeed, in the pre-war era. As such there is little to see – there are gaps in the fence but it may not be prudent to wander in – but it is unusual to find a former camp which is intact but unused. This will probably change with time but for the moment it is a rather fascinating sight.

Kistarcsa can be easily reached on frequent local HÉV train services from Budapest's Örs Vezér tere station. Exit Kistarcsa station eastwards; after a few metres, opposite the railway bridge, there is a memorial wall to victims of 1956 on Október 23-a tér. Turn left past the wall, passing a statue seemingly of a medieval knight but actually of a local opera singer, and follow the road until it becomes a path: the barracks are ahead, separated from the modern housing by the fence. It is possible to see more of the camp by taking the right turn before the barracks and then going left onto Batthyányi. The building with the tower housed the camp administration.

OTHER SITES

Many communities affected by the Holocaust have been memorialised, often using the same device of a list of names so powerfully employed in Budapest's cemetery. The following are a handful of the more notable. For information on other specific communities (including contact details), see www.zsido.hu/guide/english.htm (under the link to 'community', then 'Jewish life in Hungary').

Miskolc, around 90 miles north-east of Budapest, had the largest pre-war Jewish population after the capital, numbering around 15,000. The hilltop Jewish cemetery, on Mendikás dűlő south-west of the centre, contains several Holocaust memorials listing victims from different communities in the region. The city's large synagogue, at Kazinczy 7, also has memorial plaques. There is a further plaque on Arany János around the corner, marking the short-lived ghetto.

Remnants of a destroyed Status Quo synagogue are incorporated into a very impressive arched memorial wall, again listing names, in the Jewish cemetery of Nyíregyháza to the east. It is located at Kótaji út 5–7, north of the centre. The surviving Orthodox synagogue stands at the end of Síp, overlooking central Mártírok tere.

Hódmezővásárhely is home to a permanent Holocaust exhibition – a rarity in provincial central Europe – in a former Jewish school at Szent István tér 2 (Fri, Sun, 1.00–5.00; free), next to the synagogue. The magnificent New Synagogue of nearby Szeged, often described as the most beautiful in the world, contains memorial plaques listing victims. It is on the corner of Gutenberg and Jósika, rather eclipsing the Old Synagogue behind it at Hajnóczy 12. The Jewish cemetery is at Fónógyari út 9, north-west of the centre.

Tata, 35 miles north-west of Budapest, unveiled a dramatic new memorial to 650 murdered local Jews in 2004 by the former synagogue (now a museum) on Hősök tér. It consists of a row of chained figures, each engulfed by a progressively larger block of black stone, an indication of how even relatively small communities can be effectively commemorated.

POLAND

P oland was the epicentre of the Holocaust. Home to Europe's largest Jewish population, it was the country chosen by the Nazis for the murder of Jews from across the continent, becoming the location of the principal extermination camps.

It has sometimes been suggested that this choice was the result of an innate Polish anti-Semitism but this is to overlook the admittedly complex but often glorious history of Polish Jewry. Indeed, Jews first migrated east in large numbers in the Middle Ages (often at the invitation of local rulers) as a result of anti-Semitism in western Europe, and they were generally protected by successive Polish kings from the hostility of the Church and sections of the wider population. By the time of Poland's formal union with Lithuania in 1569, it was home to the largest Jewish population in the world. The partitions of the late eighteenth century saw the southern province of Galicia taken by the comparatively tolerant Austria but the majority of Polish Jews found themselves ruled by the Russian tsars whose anti-Semitic policies generated mass emigration. Even so, Polish Jewry retained its vitality through developments as diverse as the spread of Hassidism and the emergence of new secular ideologies such as Zionism and socialism. The latter was represented by the Bund, a specifically Jewish socialist party which became a major force in both the Russian Empire and inter-war Poland.

The restoration of Poland's independence after the First World War brought mixed fortunes for its Jews. Their rights, together with those of other minorities, were supposedly guaranteed by the peace settlements and an active cultural and political life flourished. However, resurgent Polish nationalism increasingly acquired an anti-Semitic hue, especially after the death of dictator Józef Piłsudski in 1935, expressed in restrictions on Jewish economic activity and higher education. The government even gave serious thought to the insane proposal to deport thousands of Jews to Madagascar, a curious obsession of anti-Semites since the late nineteenth century which was to be resurrected by the Nazis.

Jews living in the western provinces of modern Poland were the first to suffer Nazi persecution, falling as they did within Germany's pre-war boundaries. Yet their experiences thus far were to pale in comparison

with the measures inflicted on the territories occupied in September 1939. For Hitler and Himmler, Poland represented a tabula rasa on which to impose their racist fantasies: the elimination in some form or another of the Jewish presence and of the Polish intelligentsia, and the enslavement of the remaining Poles to serve German settlers who would eventually colonise the east. Following Poland's defeat, which was accomplished within a month, the country was essentially divided into three. Under the terms of the Nazi-Soviet Pact, the eastern portion (with a Jewish population of 1.2 million) was taken over by the USSR and, with two exceptions (Poland's modern north-east around Białystok and a small enclave in the south-east), remained under Soviet rule after the war (see chapters 11, 14 and 15). The western section (around 600,000 Jews) was incorporated directly into the Reich, mostly as part of the *Warthegau*, a newly created administrative unit headed by Arthur Greiser, a fanatical proponent of Germanisation. The historic heart of Poland, with a Jewish population of 1.5 million, formed the so-called *Generalgouvernement* ruled by Hans Frank. In both latter regions, Jews were immediately subjected to random violence. However, the Nazis aimed for a far more radical 'solution' even at this early stage. In the early months of the occupation, the SS was fixated on the Nisko Plan, a scheme to deport Jews to the Lublin region which would form a Jewish 'reservation'. Several thousand were sent on transports from the Reich whilst Greiser energetically expelled Jews (and Poles) from his domain. However, the plan was abandoned in early 1940 due to its logistical impracticality and disquiet from Frank, supported by Göring. Frank's unease was certainly not the result of sympathy for the victims but rather the opposite: he did not wish his territory to become a dumping ground for racial 'undesirables'. In fact, he had already introduced anti-Jewish measures in the autumn of 1939, including expropriation of wealth and property, liability to forced labour and the imposition of a Jewish badge, in this case a white armband with a blue Star of David (similar policies were also imposed in the *Warthegau*). An even more sinister innovation was the creation of ghettos, beginning with Piotrków Trybunalski in October 1939. This was not a consistent policy at first – Kraków and Lublin did not have ghettos until 1941 and some towns even later – but the intention of the Nazis was clearly to concentrate Jewish populations in easily controlled locations prior to future 'resettlement' to an unspecified location. The Germans seriously considered Madagascar for this purpose in 1940, impractical though the plan was (the pre-war Polish government had considered 40,000 settlers to be too many). In the meantime, the unsanitary and impoverished conditions of the ghettos condemned tens of thousands of those imprisoned in them to death.

Having decided to murder most Soviet Jews (including those living in Poland's former eastern territories) in the summer of 1941, the Nazis made Polish Jews their next target. The first extermination camp was established in December at Chełmno for the communities of the *Warthegau* whilst the systematic destruction of those of the *Generalgouvernement* was carried out at three camps in *Aktion Reinhard* (1942–43). Auschwitz-Birkenau, meanwhile, became the principal site for the murder of Jews from the rest of Europe. A few hundred thousand Polish Jews were initially kept alive in the ghettos as slave labour but from late 1942 onwards, on Himmler's orders, they began to be relocated to labour camps. These later deportations were increasingly met with resistance by Jewish underground organisations, notably in Warsaw and Białystok, although the effectiveness of the uprisings would always be limited (as their leaders realised) given the superior military power of the Germans. Jewish resistance was also undermined by ambiguous attitudes on the part of the Polish underground, including the Home Army (AK) which had the support of the London-based government-in-exile. Although the AK provided weapons and shelter in some places (including Warsaw), its units could be as dangerous for Jews as the Germans in conservative eastern Poland. Even so, Jewish resistance shocked the Nazis, especially uprisings at Treblinka and Sobibór, prompting Himmler to order the elimination of almost all Jews remaining in the camps of the *Generalgouvernement*: on 3–4 November 1943, over 40,000 people in the Lublin region were murdered in an operation cynically dubbed *Erntefest* (Harvest Festival). The last remaining Jewish community of any size was the Łódź ghetto; it too was destroyed in the summer of 1944.

It is estimated that only around 300,000 of the 3.3 million Jews who lived within Poland's pre-war borders survived the Holocaust. Many intended to stay in the country but a number of post-war pogroms prompted most to leave. The majority of the remainder departed in 1968 when openly anti-Semitic persecution followed the Six Day War: less than 10,000 Jews live in Poland today. That said, Poland was unique in the Communist bloc in establishing prominent memorials at locations associated with the Holocaust. Far more progress has been made since

1989 with a renewal of interest in and a more honest approach to the country's multi-ethnic heritage. There are, of course, considerable variations but Poland has begun to embrace its Jewish past and to properly mourn the community which was so integral to its history for so long.

WARSAW

Poland's capital was, by the twentieth century, Europe's greatest Jewish metropolis. Although a presence was first established in the fourteenth century, Jews were forbidden to live in the city between 1527 and 1768. Warsaw's rise to pre-eminence was thus rapid, its Jewish population growing from barely 10,000 at the start of the nineteenth century to more than 300,000 a hundred years later largely as a result of migration from other areas of the Russian Empire. By the early twentieth century, there were around 300 synagogues and prayer houses in the city. Warsaw also became the leading centre of secular Jewish culture, the home of writers such as I.L. Peretz and Isaac Bashevis Singer and the heartland of the Bund. Only New York had a larger Jewish population and probably only New York exceeded the diversity and vitality of Jewish life.

Even though the Germans began their assault on the city on 8 September 1939, it held out for three weeks before capitulating. The Jewish population was immediately subjected to attacks and acts of humiliation by the occupiers. As in every major Polish city, a *Judenrat* was established; its leader was Adam Czerniaków, an assimilated Jew who had previously been a member of the city council and the Polish Senate. Although Czerniaków was later to be criticised by many ghetto inhabitants, not least for his background and poor command of Yiddish, his diaries reveal a man of transparent good faith placed in an impossible situation. His sense of duty led him to refuse offers to flee in the early months of the occupation, unlike some of his colleagues, and he was to pay a heavy price for his responsibilities.

The Nazis had first discussed establishing a ghetto as early as November 1939 but tensions within the administration had stalled the plan; the order was finally issued in October 1940 (on Yom Kippur) and the ghetto sealed in November. Although most Jews already lived in the area, the ghetto's creation entailed an enormous population transfer involving tens of thousands of Jews and Poles. By March 1941, the ghetto contained 445,000 people, the city's pre-war population having been swelled by voluntary or often forced migration of Jews from the provinces, the *Warthegau* especially. This intense overcrowding was to be a constant in the ghetto's history with inevitable consequences for food supplies and disease; monthly mortality rates reached 5,000 by the summer of 1941 and rarely fell below 4,000 thereafter. The fall in the population did little to ease the congestion, however, as the ghetto was subject to periodic reductions by the Germans. That is not to say that all suffered equally: perhaps more than any other major city, Warsaw saw the emergence of a 'ghetto aristocracy', especially smugglers, who patronised the restaurants and cabarets that emerged. Their existence illustrated the moral ambiguities of ghetto life. Although they were widely resented, not least for the pre-war criminal background of many, smuggling was essential for the ghetto's survival.

Deportations to Treblinka began on 23 July 1942. When the Germans demanded that the *Judenrat* supply 6,000 people a day, Czerniaków committed suicide. Although most victims had to be brought to the *Umschlagplatz* (the cordoned off assembly point from where the trains departed) by force, thousands of starving inhabitants were enticed by the widely publicised promise of bread and marmalade for volunteers. In the two months of the *Aktion,* the Germans deported between 254,000 and 270,000 people to their deaths in Treblinka and perhaps 10,000 more to other camps whilst an estimated 10,300 died in the ghetto. Most of the remaining 60,000 Jews had few illusions regarding the fate that awaited them, facilitating the development of the largest and most effective Jewish underground movement in Poland, the Jewish Fighting Organisation (ŻOB), commanded from November by Mordechai Anielewicz. The ŻOB had been created during the summer deportations but had been too weak to prevent them. However, the hiatus gave it time to organise and recruit so when a second wave of round-ups began in January 1943 it was able to offer resistance, believing that the liquidation of the ghetto had begun. When the deportations (which encompassed 6,000 people) stopped after less than a week, this was seen as a victory for the underground. The SS had, in fact, only intended a relatively small-scale *Aktion* but this perception was important in increasing support for and faith in the ŻOB. Thus, when the final liquidation began on 19 April 1943, the Germans encountered massive and unexpected resistance. There was never much likelihood that they would be defeated, of course, but the uprising defied the Nazis for a month and inflicted heavy losses. The uprising's greatest significance is often seen to be symbolic and moral, representing the first large-scale act of Jewish resistance (as well as encouraging Jews elsewhere). What is less well known is that it was actually the first large-scale act of resistance by *any* civilian population in occupied Europe.

Around 7,000 of the Jews seized during and after the uprising were sent to Treblinka, the remainder (more than 40,000) to the camps of the Lublin region where most were murdered in the *Erntefest*. Most of the ghetto territory was completely destroyed (photographs of the area in 1944–45 could be mistaken for Hiroshima); the same fate befell much of the rest of the city following the crushing of the equally heroic but doomed Polish uprising in the summer of 1944. Modern Warsaw, therefore, bears scant resemblance to the city it once was (at most, a few thousand Jews live there today) but the memory of the war remains

Warsaw: ulica Próżna (Photograph by the author)

tangible, expressed in memorials on almost every street and historic fragments whose scarcity makes them seem all the more precious.

The ghetto

The huge area of the ghetto harbours a few traces of its history, the most evocative of which is ulica Próżna whose redbrick tenements are one of the few examples of surviving original buildings. Long neglected, they are now awaiting restoration in advance of which, in a beautiful touch, the concreted windows have been covered with large pre-war photographs of Warsaw Jews. Próżna opens onto plac Grzybowski, the northern side of which is the heart of the modern Jewish community, illustrated by kosher restaurants and the Kamińska Jewish Theatre at 12/16. Slightly hidden in a courtyard behind the latter is the Nożyk Synagogue (Mon–Fri, 9.00–5.00; Sun, 11.00–4.00; 6 zł) at Twarda 6. It owed its survival to its use as a warehouse and stables by the Germans although it was badly damaged and only restored in the 1970s. On the southern side of plac Grzybowski, All Saints Church at 3/5 carries a plaque to Polish rescuers of Jews on its side wall.

South across Świętokrzyska, the park in front of the towering Stalinist Palace of Culture contains a memorial to Janusz Korczak, just to the west of the fountain. This roughly occupies the site of Śliska 9, the final location of the Jewish orphanage which Korczak (real name Henryk Goldszmit) had originally established before the First World War. A brilliant pedagogue and children's author, Korczak was – and still is – beloved to Jewish and Christian Poles for his work with his charges and his novel *King Matt the First*, often described as a Polish *Alice in Wonderland*. His reputation meant that there was no shortage of offers from the underground to smuggle him out but he chose to stay with the children to the very end. One of the most tragic scenes in the ghetto's history was the sight of Korczak leading them to the *Umschlagplatz* from where all were sent to Treblinka in August 1942.

A block to the west, Mariańska 1 (on the corner with Pańska) housed a nursing school relocated to the ghetto; a plaque honours its director Luba Blum who was later awarded the Florence Nightingale Medal by the International Red Cross. Continuing west, one can cross post-war Jana Pawla II at the large Rondo ONZ roundabout. A few blocks to the south are the main surviving fragments of the ghetto wall, accessible through the entrance to Złota 62: a sign marked '*Miejsce pamięci*' in the second

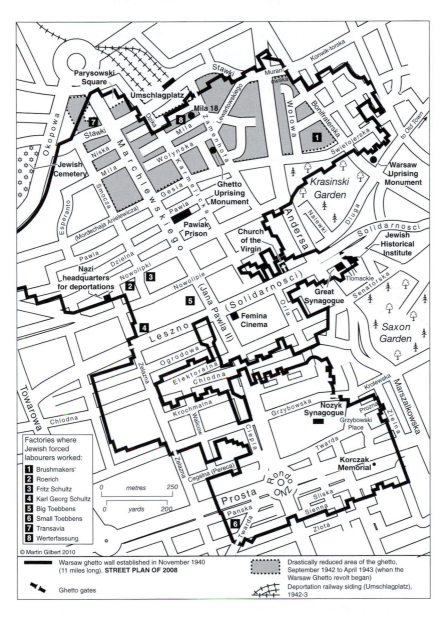

Warsaw

courtyard points the way (elderly residents are often on hand to do the same). To the right is a corner section adorned with memorial plaques and a map of the ghetto. A row of bricks on the floor marks the path taken by the wall towards another fragment to the left of the entrance. From here one can follow the arrow to a third fragment in the next courtyard. It is possible to exit from here through the archway of Sienna 55 by pressing the buzzer. This brings one into the street nicknamed 'the Champs-Élysées of the ghetto' due to the high concentration of middle class residents not to mention the new aristocracy of ghetto traders. It bears little resemblance to Paris today, mainly containing post-war apartment blocks, but the former Berson's and Bauman's Children's Hospital remains at number 60. Although built for Jews, it treated children regardless of ethnicity or religion and Korczak was one of its paediatricians before he opened the orphanage. It continued its mission during the war until closure in August 1942 when this section of the ghetto was cleared. On the rear of the building there is a plaque to its director Anna Braude-Hellerowa who was killed in a bunker with some of her patients during the ghetto uprising.

Back at the Rondo ONZ, the former mansion of the Jewish merchant Leo Osnos, technically Twarda 28, is on its north-west corner. Following the curve of the building northwards leads to I.L. Pereca, named after the great Yiddish writer who lived at number 1 (now a construction site). A turn into Walicόw reveals more fragments of the ghetto. The brick exterior of the building at 9/11 formed a part of the wall whilst the ruined tenement at 14 was the home of Władysław Szlengel, one of the ghetto's most popular poets; he died fighting during the uprising. There is another section of the wall on the north-west corner of the junction of Żelazna and Grzybowska whilst two further buildings survive at Żelazna's intersection with Krochmalna.

Żelazna's next junction is with Chłodna, arguably the ghetto's most famous street. The initial ghetto location of Korczak's orphanage was the no longer existing 33 to the west whilst the eastern side of the crossroads was the site of the famous bridge, created in 1942 when the western block was removed and the ghetto cut in two. The impressive white building at 20 was the home of Czerniakόw and other *Judenrat* members. Another surviving building is large Ogrodowa 10/26, a block to the north. Amongst its residents was Jόzef Lewartowski, a Communist leader of the underground who was murdered by the Gestapo in 1942;

there is a memorial plaque. Parallel Solidarności is a much widened equivalent of wartime Leszno whose cafés were the heart of the ghetto's social and cultural life. The most famous, the *Sztuka* (Art), was where Władysław Szpilman played piano and Szlengel read his poems. The only trace now is the *Femina* cinema at 115. The original cinema of the same name on the site was converted into a ghetto theatre; a plaque in the foyer commemorates murdered actors and musicians. Further east, on Solidarności's northern side, is the Church of the Virgin whose priest, Seweryn Popławski, smuggled Jewish children out through the basement.

Off the south-east corner of the next junction is Tłomackie, site of Warsaw's Great Synagogue. It was used for services until the ghetto was reduced in March 1942 at which point it became a store for plundered furniture. The Germans destroyed it on 16 May 1943, as a symbol of victory over the uprising. A dull building now occupies the site although there is a memorial plaque on its eastern side which faces the Jewish Historical Institute at Tłomackie 3/5 (Mon–Wed, Fri, 9.00–4.00; Thu, 9.00–6.00; 10 zł; www.jewishinstitute.org.pl). The institute, occupying the former synagogue library and home of the ghetto's Mutual Aid Society, serves as a museum and research centre, its most important possession being the Ringelblum Archives. Historian Emanuel Ringelblum led a team which compiled a comprehensive collection of documents of ghetto life encompassing private diaries, newspapers, public notices, advertisements, eyewitness accounts, scientific studies and a great deal more. The project, codenamed *Oneg Shabbat*, aimed to preserve these records for future historians and is indeed the most important source for scholars of the ghetto. The archives were buried in milk churns and metal boxes in 1943 on the eve of the uprising; some, but not all, were discovered after the war. The Institute's main exhibit on the first floor makes use of Ringelblum's work to relate the history of the ghetto. Upstairs is a gallery of Jewish art.

The ghetto's northern streets were particularly devastated during the uprising and its aftermath and virtually nothing remains. One exception is the few surviving remnants of Pawiak prison, preserved as a museum and memorial site, on the corner of Jana Pawła II and Dzielna (trams 16, 17, 19 and 33, Nowolipki). The largest prison in Poland, Pawiak was built by the tsars to house political opponents and performed the same function under the Nazis. More than 100,000 people passed through it during the war; an estimated 37,000 were shot and most of the remainder sent to concentration camps. The complex was largely destroyed after the Polish uprising but a section of the gate remains at the entrance, next to a bronze cast of an elm tree covered in plaques. The original tree somehow survived the destruction, thereby becoming a focus for remembrance, but later died hence the 2004 cast. More memorials line the courtyard walls. The museum (Wed, Fri, 9.00–5.00; Thu, Sat, 9.00–4.00; Sun, 10.00–6.00; free; www.muzeumniepodleglosci.art.pl) includes preserved cells; its well-presented main exhibition covers both Pawiak and the wider German persecution of Poles and Jews. One particularly shocking exhibit shows statistics compiled by the Polish underground on comparative food rations in German-occupied Europe. From Pawiak one can see the tall spire of St Augustine's Church on Nowolipki. This was the only building left standing in the vicinity. Just below the western end of Nowolipki, Żelazna 103 housed the SS command which organised the round-ups of 1942–43; a Gestapo prison was located in its basement.

Anielewicza, a block north of Pawiak and named after the ŻOB leader, was wartime Gęsia. Plac Bohaterów Getta (Ghetto Heroes' Square) by the junction with Zamenhofa is located in the area which was at the heart of the uprising and close to the sites of the *Judenrat* and ghetto prison which both stood on Gęsia. The principal memorial, unmistakeably Communist in origin but impressive nonetheless, was where West German chancellor Willy Brandt knelt in an apparent gesture of penance in 1971, an action which was widely criticised in Germany. Often overlooked is a small 1946 monument, reminiscent of a manhole cover, on the western edge of the square which is sometimes mistaken for a memorial to the Polish uprising. A nearby stone honours *Żegota*, an organisation established by the Polish underground in December 1942 which provided hiding places and aid for Jews. The park opposite the square is to be the site of the ambitious Museum of the History of Polish Jews (www.jewishmuseum.org.pl) which will open in 2011. Ghetto Heroes' Square contains a further four memorials which mark the start of the Path of Remembrance, a trail of granite blocks which leads to the *Umschlagplatz*: each stone commemorates an event, individual or group associated with the ghetto. Those in the square are dedicated to the ghetto victims, the uprising and Ringelblum. Most of the remaining stones along Zamenhofa commemorate ŻOB leaders and activists. An exception, on the right hand side, honours Szmul Zygielbojm, the Bund's representative in the Polish government-in-exile who committed suicide

Warsaw: Ghetto Heroes memorial (Photograph by the author)

in London in May 1943 in protest at the perceived Allied indifference to the Holocaust. The wall behind features ghostly figures and a quotation from Zygielbojm's last letter. Ahead on the left is the site of Miła 18, the ŻOB command bunker. After a three-week siege, it was surrounded on 8 May 1943; those inside died fighting the Germans or by their own hand. The site is marked by a mound of earth (which represents the height of the rubble left by the destruction of the ghetto) topped with a memorial stone. Below the mound, a triangular stone lists the 51 known names of the more than one hundred people who perished in the bunker.

On the corner of Dubois and Stawki, a stone honours Korczak whilst the dramatist and poet Itzhak Katzenelson is commemorated around the corner on the southern side of Stawki. Having survived the uprising, Katzenelson and his son Zvi were supplied with Honduran passports which led to them being sent to a camp for prisoners of Allied and neutral countries in Vittel in France. This was not enough to save them, however: they were deported to Auschwitz in 1944. Stawki 5/7 (now a school) served as headquarters for the SS unit supervising the *Umschlagplatz* and barracks for the Lithuanian and Latvian auxiliaries who guarded the deportees. The *Umschlagplatz* complex itself was opposite. The only remnant is Stawki 10 (wartime 6/8) which had previously served as a school and Jewish hospital. It was converted in 1942 into a detention area in which hundreds of thousands of people were held before being taken to the waiting cattle trucks – there were train platforms directly behind the building. This history is recalled by a plaque whilst two others relate the liberation of 50 Jewish prisoners from the building by an AK unit during the 1944 Polish uprising. To the left is the *Umschlagplatz* monument, erected in 1988, on whose walls are inscribed 448 Jewish first names, intended to represent the more than 300,000 people deported to Treblinka and other camps. East of here, one of several plaques to the Polish underground on the wall of St John's Church at Bonifraterska 12 commemorates three AK fighters who died whilst breaching the ghetto wall on 19 April 1943 in an attempt to aid the uprising. The church can be reached by taking tram 35 from the Dzika stop by the *Umschlagplatz* to Muranowska and then walking, passing an impressive monument to Poles (Jews amongst them) sent to the Gulag by Stalin. Incidentally, there is a striking memorial to the Polish uprising on plac Krasińskich at the bottom of Bonifraterska.

Warsaw's vast Jewish cemetery at Okopowa 49/51 (Mon–Thu, 10.00–5.00; Fri, 9.00–1.00; Sun, 11.00–4.00; 8 zł; trams 1, 22 and 27, Cmentarz

Żydowski) was initially included in the ghetto but then separated in December 1941 although some burials still took place. A touching memorial to the million Jewish children murdered by the Nazis is to the right of the gate, close to a statue of Korczak and the orphans. There are further symbolic graves of Holocaust victims in plot 9 behind plot 10 where Adam Czerniaków lies, rather incongruously buried next to Ludwig Zamenhof (the founder of Esperanto). A sign outside the gate points to Gibalskiego 21, built on the site of the pre-war *Skra* sports club whose playing field was used as a burial ground for bodies collected on the ghetto streets. It was later an execution site during the Polish uprising. To the left of the building (which houses the cemetery administration) is a rather abstract memorial to the Jews and Poles buried here, stairs sloping into a pit marked by a stone column. There are a couple of plaques in the car park of the administration building marking the sites of mass graves (some of the victims were relocated after the war to the Warsaw Uprising cemetery – see below). On the other side of Ogrodowa from the cemetery, a plaque on the tower block at Anielewicza 34 recalls that this was the site of the Gęsiowka concentration camp. The camp was established by the Nazis after the destruction of the ghetto and contained 5,000 foreign Jews brought from Auschwitz to clear the rubble. Most were evacuated on 29 July 1944 but around 400 were left behind to destroy the camp. The plaque celebrates the rescue of 348 of these prisoners by the AK during the Polish uprising; many of the freed Jews joined the Polish forces and subsequently fell in battle.

Elsewhere

A short tram ride from the Jewish cemetery at Grzybowska 79 (entry on Przyokopowa), the large Warsaw Rising Museum (Muzeum Powstania Warszawskiego; Fri–Mon, Wed, 8.00–6.00; Thu, 8.00–8.00; 4 zł (free on Sun); www.1944.pl) was established in 2004 to mark the sixtieth anniversary of the Polish uprising. The multimedia exposition will not be to everybody's taste but the rebellion is covered in exhaustive detail.

The original site of Korczak's orphanage is a block north at Jaktorowska 6, still performing the same function today and now named after its founder. It also houses the Korczakianum, a documentation and research centre dedicated to preserving the memory of his work. The garden is dominated by a bust of Korczak whilst there is a sculpture on the balcony near two plaques, one to Korczak, the other to his co-director Stefania Wilczynska who also shared the children's fate. There is a further memorial, immediately to the left of the gate, to the orphanage's Polish janitor Piotr Zalewski, shot here in August 1944. He was left to care for the building, having been badly beaten by the Gestapo in November 1940 when he wished to accompany Korczak and the orphans to the ghetto; as a non-Jew, this was forbidden. In happier times, the two men would get drunk on Zalewski's name day each year and seek to outdo each other in swearing competitions.

Further west, the Warsaw Uprising cemetery (Cmentarz Powstańców Warszawy; trams 8, 10, 26 and 27 to Sowińskiego) at Wolska 174/176 contains the remains of 6,588 Jews who died in the ghetto, transferred here after the war from the *Skra* field on Gibalskiego. Their mass grave is marked by a 1988 memorial stone which is the only one with a curved rather than flat top in the group of stones behind the hedge by the main memorial.

South-west of the centre, Grójecka 77 (in an alley between 75 and 79) is built on the site of a shelter for around 40 escapees from the ghetto, including Emanuel Ringelblum, who were hidden by gardener Mieczysław Wolski and his family. The location was betrayed in March 1944; all of the Jews together with Wolski and his nephew Janusz Wysocki were executed. There is now a plaque (trams 1, 7, 9, 14, 25 and 35 to Bitwy Warszawskiej 1920).

A more successful act of rescue is recalled in the city centre at Kopernika 4, an apartment building two blocks east of Nowy Świat, by a plaque from survivors Leon and Anna Joselzon commemorating their specially built hiding place.

South of the centre, the Education Ministry building at Aleja Szucha 25 rivalled Pawiak as the most feared address in wartime Warsaw as the headquarters of the Gestapo. The basement cells where Poles and Jews were interned and tortured were preserved at the war's end and now form the sobering Museum of Battle and Martyrdom (Wed, 9.00–5.00; Thu & Sat, 9.00–4.00; Fri, 10.00–5.00; Sun, 10.00–4.00; free; www.muzeumniepodleglosci.art.pl).

The Praga district on the east bank of the Vistula was an area of significant Jewish settlement. Although post-war apartment blocks and modern constructions intrude, much of the area retains an interesting mixture of Secessionist mansions and redbrick tenements, some still bearing visible scars from the Red Army's battle for Praga in the summer of 1944. Overt reminders of the Jewish past are less common although the grand building at Jagiellońska 28, which housed a school and a nursery, still carries the plaque identifying it as the Michał Bergson educational building (Bergson was the community's president at the time of its erection in the 1910s). Around the corner at Kłopotowskiego 31, a redbrick former *mikvah* (which also housed a school) survives from what was once a large Jewish community complex. Targowa, which runs parallel to Jagiellońska, is especially evocative of old Warsaw. Some of its courtyards sheltered prayer houses but they have either been demolished or are now inaccessible.

Warsaw Zoo, to the north of Praga, served as a hiding place for Jews thanks to its director Dr Jan Żabiński and his wife Antonina. Most of the cages had been emptied during the September 1939 bombardment and the Germans removed further animals to Berlin. The Żabińskis, therefore, used the cages as well as their own villa in the grounds as temporary shelters until more permanent hideouts could be found elsewhere in the city – it is estimated that several hundred people passed through. Żabiński, an active member of the Polish underground, was himself interned in a POW camp following the 1944 uprising but Antonina and their young son Ryszard continued to protect their charges. The family were recognised as Righteous Gentiles in 1965.

North-east of the zoo is the former Brodno Jewish cemetery on św. Wincentego by the Rondo Żaba roundabout (buses 127, 162, 169, 326, 406, 500 and 527, Rondo Żaba). The walls were destroyed during the war and stones used for paving (with others destroyed under Communism). The site is now surrounded by a fence which was erected at private initiative in the 1980s. There are a small number of standing stones amidst the trees but most are laid in huge piles suggestive of Max Ernst's visions of ruined cities, not far removed, perhaps, from what they represent.

TREBLINKA

Although it existed for little more than a year, Treblinka was the deadliest of the *Aktion Reinhard* camps. It was constructed in late spring 1942 in readiness for the planned destruction of Warsaw Jewry, the location chosen being close to a branch line of the main Warsaw to Białystok railway. The dense forest which surrounded the site further suited the Nazis' purposes as did the fact that there was already a labour camp for political prisoners (and Jews) nearby, known as Treblinka I. It was these prisoners, together with Jews from surrounding communities, who were forced to build the extermination camp which was designated Treblinka II. The first transports arrived on 23 July 1942; amongst the victims were the first of hundreds of thousands of Warsaw Jews. Even by the standards of the death camps, Treblinka was a site of the utmost horror in its earliest weeks. Commandant Irmfried Eberl, previously chief physician at Brandenburg and Bernburg T4 centres, aiming to advance his career by establishing Treblinka as the most murderous extermination site, accepted far more transports than the three gas chambers could cope with. Thousands of people were kept in cattle cars queued up outside the camp and the SS resorted to shooting huge numbers whilst rotting corpses piled up waiting to be thrown into mass graves. Eberl was sacked in late August and replaced by Franz Stangl, hitherto commandant of Sobibór. A new killing block with 10 gas chambers was constructed whilst, over the winter of 1942–43, a system of burning corpses was introduced. After a visit by Himmler in March 1943, it was also decided to exhume and cremate bodies from the existing mass graves to destroy the evidence. This horrific work was carried out, as at all of the death camps, by members of the *Sonderkommando*. By this stage, the extermination process was already winding down and there were few transports after April 1943. The Jewish prisoners left in the camp realised that they too would be murdered once the cremations were completed so made plans for revolt. On 2 August 1943, they seized weapons from the armoury and set fire to much of the camp (although the gas chambers were not destroyed). Of the roughly 1,000 prisoners, around 200 were able to break out although only a few dozen survived the war.

Historians generally believe the death toll to have been at least 800,000 and possibly more than 900,000. Most victims were from Poland; others came from Slovakia, Greece and Theresienstadt. A few prisoners were kept in Treblinka after the rebellion and cessation of transports (the last – from Białystok – arrived on 21 August 1943) to carry out the dismantling of the camp; when this was completed, they were deported to Sobibór in October 1943 and murdered. All of the buildings were demolished and trees planted on the site whilst a Ukrainian guard was settled in a cottage to create the impression that it was a farm and to prevent any intrusions. After he fled, local peasants thronged to the site to dig for 'Jewish gold'; they found decomposing human remains. So effectively did the Nazis destroy the camp that next to nothing remained and it was left rather deserted until its transformation into a memorial site in the 1960s.

Treblinka (Photograph by the author)

The information kiosk in the car park sells plans of the modern site and tickets for the new small museum (daily, 9.00–7.00; 2 zł). Reached by a path to the left, the museum's two rooms respectively cover the labour and extermination camps. The latter room displays items found at the site including a charred torah fragment, barbed wire, spoons and razors. A path to the right of the information kiosk leads to the area of the death camp, home to arguably the finest Communist Holocaust memorial which incorporates Jewish funerary traditions and symbolic representations of the camp. Beyond the gateway marked '*Obóz zagłady*' ('extermination camp'), standing stones represent the perimeter whilst concrete sleepers replicate the route of the railway line along which trains were famously pushed rather than pulled into Treblinka. They lead to the ramp where the transports were unloaded. In late 1942, Stangl ordered the construction of a fake station here, complete with fictitious timetables, signage and even a ticket window. Victims were thus led to believe that they had arrived at a transit station named Obermajdan from where they would be dispatched to labour camps further east after bathing. The building, actually a storage barrack for plundered items, was located on and to the right of the path that leads from the ramp to the main memorial; stones here list the countries from which Treblinka's victims originated. The area to the left of the path, largely in the trees, housed the 'reception camp' where victims were undressed and stripped of their possessions and the women shaved. They were then rushed through the '*Schlauch*' ('tube') or '*Schleuse*' ('sluice'), a 90 metre-long pathway enclosed by high barbed-wire fences, into the 'death camp' section of the complex. The path curved sharply close to the gas chambers in order to conceal the victims' destination until the last moment. The area of the 'death camp' roughly corresponds to the clearing in which the memorials now stand. The 'living camp', which housed the SS, Ukrainians and (in a separate section) the Jewish prisoners, was in the area to the clearing's left which is now covered by trees.

The large central stone monument stands roughly on the site of the later gas chambers. The shape of a menorah is incorporated on its rear side. Indeed, one of the reasons why the Treblinka memorial is so powerful is that it was almost unique amongst Communist structures in referring to the Jewishness of the victims. The monument is surrounded by three fields of roughly hewn stones, numbering some 17,000 in total, which stand on concrete bases; the earth underneath contains human ashes. Inscribed on 216 of the larger stones are the names of Jewish communities destroyed at Treblinka, Warsaw prominent amongst them near the front. This group of stones roughly covers the area of the earliest mass graves which were hastily dug during the chaotic Eberl era. Close to the monument, towards the left of this group, is the only stone dedicated to an individual: to Korczak along with the children ('*dzieci*'). The group of stones to the right of the monument stretches from the site of more mass graves eastwards to the site of *Sonderkommando* barracks. The biggest group is behind the monument on the site of the largest collection of mass graves. The cremation pyres in 1943 were located between this group and the monument, now marked symbolically by a mass of charred material. Bodies were burned on rails which had originally formed a short narrow-gauge railway from the gas chambers to the mass graves; corpses had been pushed on trolleys by the *Sonderkommando*.

A mile or so south of the extermination camp is the site of Treblinka I labour camp. For the first part of the journey, the road runs parallel to the former railway track which continued from the death camp to Treblinka I's quarry. Shortly before reaching the camp, a clearing to the left of the road is the site of a small surviving SS bunker beyond which one can overlook the large overgrown gravel pit and, to the left, the surviving ramp. Arrival at the site of Treblinka I is marked by a plan of the camp. It too was destroyed (in 1944) and only occasional foundations survive in forest clearings although panels mark the locations of the different buildings. A few hundred metres further along the road is Treblinka I's execution site, its mass graves now honoured by crosses and a memorial wall.

The memorial site is on a side road, signposted off the 627 between Małkinia Górna and Kosów-Lacki and closer to Poniatowo than Treblinka village. However, the narrow bridge over the river Bug just south of Małkinia which previously handled virtually all traffic to the camp was closed indefinitely in 2008; locals anticipate a long wait for a replacement. Travellers by car from Warsaw should, therefore, cross the Bug at Brok, turning from the 694 south onto the 50 and then eastwards on the country road through Prostyn to join the southbound 627. Those using public transport have little choice but to take a taxi from Małkinia station (cars wait for incoming trains), although the once short journey now involves a large detour to the same Brok crossing. It is sensible to ask the driver to wait at the camp.

BIAŁYSTOK

Białystok, at the heart of the most ethnically diverse region of Poland, was one of the country's great Jewish cities albeit one which developed comparatively late. It was little more than a village until the Industrial Revolution when its population increased from less than 1,000 to more than 60,000 in the century before the First World War. Jews formed more than two-thirds of the city's population at this time and owned over 80 per cent of its factories although the majority of the community consisted of poor workers who laboured in the same factories. Even after inter-war Polonisation policies, Jews remained a majority in 1939.

The city fell to the Germans on 15 September 1939 but, in line with the revised provisions of the Nazi-Soviet Pact, was handed over to Stalin a week later. It was thus only in 1941 that Białystok was exposed to the full ferocity of German policy, its position near the USSR's border meaning that it was quickly captured. On 27 June, the day of the Nazis' arrival, 2,000 Jews lost their lives, the largest proportion burned to death in the Great Synagogue. *Einstazgruppe B* carried out further massacres of thousands of prominent Jews in early July. In August 1941, 50,000 Jews – those remaining in the city along with others brought from surrounding towns – were confined in a ghetto located in the north of the centre. In contrast to many of the other newly occupied cities, this was not a prelude to another immediate wave of mass violence although 4,500 unskilled or sick Jews were transferred to the ghetto of Pružany (in modern Belarus) in the autumn from where most were deported to Auschwitz in 1943. Thereafter, the ghetto seemed to acquire a stability of sorts with most inhabitants engaged in the factories which covered much of its territory. Conditions were inevitably poor but the *Judenrat* was able to maintain an extensive social infrastructure of soup kitchens, hospitals and schools whilst the Germans largely left the ghetto unmolested through 1942. This did not fool everyone and a ghetto underground coalesced during the course of the same year. It was unprepared, however, for the first great ghetto *Aktion* which took place in February 1943. Around 10,000 people were sent to Treblinka whilst a further 2,000 were murdered in the ghetto itself. Even after this event, *Judenrat* chair Efraim Barasz believed that the remaining Jews could be saved through labour, a belief encouraged by senior figures in the German administration. This assumption led him to break with the underground, which he had previously supported with funds and facilities, in the summer of 1943. Barasz was, of course, proven to be mistaken and the liquidation of the ghetto was carried out that August. The underground resisted the Germans for five days before succumbing. Several hundred fighters lost their lives either in battle or by suicide; 7,600 ghetto inhabitants were deported straight to Treblinka and the remaining adults to Majdanek where, after another selection, they were sent either to Poniatowa or Auschwitz as labourers or to Majdanek's gas chambers. A transport of 1,260 children was sent to Theresienstadt from where they were deported to Birkenau in October (see chapter 7). Only around 2,000 people, mostly prominent figures such as Barasz, remained in the Białystok ghetto but they too were deported to Majdanek in early September. All of those sent to the Lublin camps were murdered in the *Erntefest* so it is believed that less than 500 Białystok Jews survived the war. Today, hardly any live in a city which was once the largest in Poland to have a majority Jewish population.

Much of Białystok was destroyed in the war. Most of the ghetto, which was roughly bounded by modern Lipowa, Sienkiewicza and Poleska, is now covered with apartment blocks but some remnants survive, notably on the southern section of Waryńskiego (wartime Polna) which runs between Lipowa and Piłsudskiego. A block north of the latter, opposite Żabia 14, a small park occupies the site of the ghetto cemetery (established in 1941). A central obelisk commemorates the 1943 uprising; a wall behind, by Proletariacka, carries a memorial to the 3,500 people who were buried here. Their bodies and the gravestones were removed by the Communists in the 1970s. Taking Proletariacka east leads to an intersection with Czysta, another street with surviving buildings; one of the ghetto gates was located at its northern end. South along Czysta, the next western turning is named Bohaterów Getta whilst at the end of Żytnia to the east one can see a surviving ghetto factory on the other side of the Biała River. The area beyond the river was where most workshops were located and where the uprising was concentrated. That part of the ghetto is now covered in post-war architecture (one exception is a yellow mansion at Jurowiecka 26 which adjoins the area where deportees were assembled in August 1943). Back off Czysta, Waryńskiego 24 is the former Cytron prayer house, now an art gallery – a rare plaque notes its history (this section of Waryńskiego is not continuous with that below Piłsudskiego).

Back on the other side of Piłsudskiego, Malmeda (originally Kupiecka) housed the *Judenrat* headquarters. During the February 1943 *Aktion*, a young man, Icchok Malmed, threw a jar of acid in the face of a German who, blinded, shot a colleague. In retaliation, the Germans murdered 100 Jews and threatened to destroy the entire ghetto unless Malmed surrendered himself which he promptly did; he was hanged in this street. There is a memorial to him on the wall of number 10. An elegant surviving building at Nowy Świat 9 to the west is close to the site where the killing of the 100 took place. Zamenhofa, parallel to Malmeda, is named after the Jewish creator of Esperanto who was born on the site of modern number 26. A mural depicts Zamenhof staring out from a balcony; beneath him are the Jewish intellectuals Jacob Shapiro and Abraham Zbar. Shapiro, founder of the Esperanto Society, was amongst those shot outside the city in July 1941. Towards the bottom of Malmeda there is a bust of Zamenhof in a small park.

Białystok's Great Synagogue, which was burned down on the night of 27 June 1941 with at least 600 people inside, was south of the ghetto, between Suraska and Legionowa. There is a striking 1995 memorial – a twisted metal frame (representing the burning dome) set on a paved

Star of David – hidden in a courtyard accessed from a path by Legionowa 14/16. A memorial pillar carries an image of the synagogue. Continuing through the yard past the BGŻ Bank building and adjacent car park leads to a modest 1958 plaque on the side of an unnumbered building on the corner with Suraska. Two former synagogues survive in part. The partially rebuilt Piaskower Synagogue at Piękna 3 (further west off Legionowa) houses the Zamenhof Foundation whilst the heavily remodelled Szmuela Synagogue at Branickiego 3, east of the centre, bears a plaque testifying to its past.

The surviving Jewish cemetery on Wschodnia (take bus 9, 27 or 100 to the Raginisa stop on Wysockiego, head back down the road and take the second left for a couple of hundred metres) to the north-east has a considerable number of stones. Many are in a bad way but the site is at least tended to. The most prominent memorial is a tall black monument to the victims of a 1906 pogrom. Some ghetto victims are buried here although the tombs are generally hard to decipher because of erosion.

Pietrasze forest was the site of the *Einsatzgruppen* massacres in July 1941. Around 5,000 Jews, including Communists, other political leaders and intellectuals, were murdered along with 100 Poles and a single Belarusian. The site is now a memorial cemetery, the mass graves flanking a central obelisk. Unfortunately, the large number of tracks crossing the forest make it easy to get lost. Take Aleja Tysiąclecia Państwa Polskiego north out of town and cross Andersa. A few hundred metres past the junction, after the electricity pylons and before the bridge, a small sign points to a picnic spot down a dirt track to the right. There is a gate pole ahead; the car park and the picnic area are to the right. In theory, one should park here although tyre tracks suggest that many visitors take the bumpy ride around the gate. Whether walking or driving, continue along the dirt track for a little over a kilometre where a distinctive Polish memorial marker points to the cemetery.

LUBLIN

Lublin, home to one of the oldest and most celebrated Jewish communities in Poland, was arguably the most important city in the history of the Holocaust. Jewish settlement was first recorded in the fourteenth century and Lublin was soon renowned as a centre of learning, nicknamed the 'Jewish Oxford' or the 'Polish Jerusalem'. It was also one of the principal bases of the Council of the Four Lands, the governing body of the Polish-Lithuanian Commonwealth's Jewish communities. Like most of southern Poland, the city was affected by the rise of Hassidism in the eighteenth century and became one of the movement's leading centres outside Ukraine whilst, as elsewhere, industrialisation in the late nineteenth century brought a significant increase in the Jewish population. Lublin's reputation as one of the great Jewish cities of eastern Europe was illustrated by the opening of what is believed to have been the world's largest yeshiva in 1930.

The Germans took Lublin on 18 September 1939. The original Nazi-Soviet Pact had allocated it to the USSR but the amended version exchanged the Lublin district for Soviet control over Lithuania. This proved to be a fateful development as for the next four years the region became central to Nazi plans. Thus, in addition to the harassment that Jews across German-occupied Poland suffered, the autumn of 1939 brought the Nisko Plan, the hare-brained scheme to turn the Lublin region into a 'reservation' to which Jews from across the Reich and the rest of Poland would be deported. The plan was abandoned in early 1940 but the idea that the most remote area of the *Generalgouvernement* could be important in 'solving' the 'Jewish Question' was to be resurrected with appalling consequences. In this context, the arrival of Odilo Globocnik as head of the SS and police in the Lublin district in November 1939 was to be of great significance.

1940 saw an escalation of persecution with thousands of Jews sent to labour camps in the city and surrounding region. More than 10,000 others were expelled to smaller communities in early 1941 in advance of the creation of the Lublin ghetto into which 34,000 people were officially corralled in March (the illegal return of expellees meant that the number was probably closer to 40,000). The ghetto barely lasted a year: more than two-thirds of its inhabitants were deported in March to April 1942 and the few thousand survivors relocated to a new ghetto in Majdan Tatarski, south-east of the centre.

The deportees were sent to the newly established Bełżec extermination camp as its first official victims. This reflected the fact that Lublin had become the heart of the murder operation as the headquarters of *Aktion Reinhard* under the command of Globocnik. Even after the failure of the Nisko Plan, Globocnik had been ambitious to give the region a central role in Jewish policy; he also promoted it as an area for German

Lublin: *Aktion Reinhard* headquarters (Photograph by the author)

colonisation, in due course overseeing the ethnic cleansing of Poles around Zamość. Himmler's faith in him as the man to administer these policies was a result not only of their friendship and shared anti-Semitism but also of the fact that the *Reichsführer* had saved Globocnik's career after he was sacked as *Gauleiter* of Vienna in 1939 for corruption, thus ensuring his loyalty. At some point in 1941, Globocnik was, therefore, given responsibility for what was to become the largest murder operation in human history. Although the locations he chose for the three camps were all some distance from Lublin, the city was the administrative centre of the programme. In addition to establishing the camps, selecting their personnel and overseeing their inhuman activities, Globocnik assembled a large bureaucratic apparatus in Lublin to organise the practicalities and to orchestrate the other key function of *Aktion Reinhard*: the massive plunder of Jewish property. The final account submitted to Himmler came to 178,745,960 Reichsmarks, roughly equivalent to $800 million in modern terms, although this naturally does not include the significant sums stolen by *Aktion Reinhard* staff themselves. From Lublin, Globocnik was also responsible for the large Majdanek concentration camp on the edge of the city, the Trawniki camp where the Ukrainian guards were trained, and a series of forced labour camps. It was only in late 1943, with the cessation of *Aktion Reinhard* and the murder of the Jews in these other camps, that Globocnik and most of his key personnel were transferred to his home town of Trieste and Lublin's unwonted pre-eminent role in the Holocaust ended (Globocnik committed suicide in May 1945 after being captured by British troops in Austria).

By this time, only a few hundred Jews remained alive in the city. Those who had been dispatched to the Majdan Tatarski ghetto in April 1942 were sent on to Majdanek or the forced labour camps either at that time or in the final liquidation of the ghetto in November of the same year. In Majdanek they were subjected to selections, only some surviving until November 1943 when almost all of the Jews in the Lublin district camps were murdered. The last few hundred prisoners were killed in July 1944. It is believed that less than 300 of the 1939 population of 40,000 survived in hiding or in the camps; perhaps 1,000 more had survived as partisans or in the USSR.

Lublin was the first significant Polish city to be liberated so it initially became a focus for the attempts to revive Jewish life. However, post-war anti-Semitism was particularly strong in eastern Poland and even those Jews who stayed in the country largely drifted to Warsaw; there are believed to be less than 100 Jews in the city today. Although memorials exist, commemoration of the Holocaust and Lublin's Jewish past is less prominent than in Warsaw, Łódź or Kraków.

The ghetto and around

The ghetto cut through a section of Lublin's beautiful Old Town and extended northwards to the historic Jewish quarter which nestled around the castle. Jewish settlement had historically been forbidden in the Old Town but by the twentieth century a number of individuals and institutions resided there. One example is Bramova 6, north of the Kraków gate, which housed a department of the *Bikur Holim* hospital. The ghetto's southern boundary began at the north of the Rynek and curved around the northern side of Rybna and Noworybna. On the southern side of the junction of these two streets, Rybna 8, marked by a plaque, served as the post-war headquarters of the Central Jewish Committee

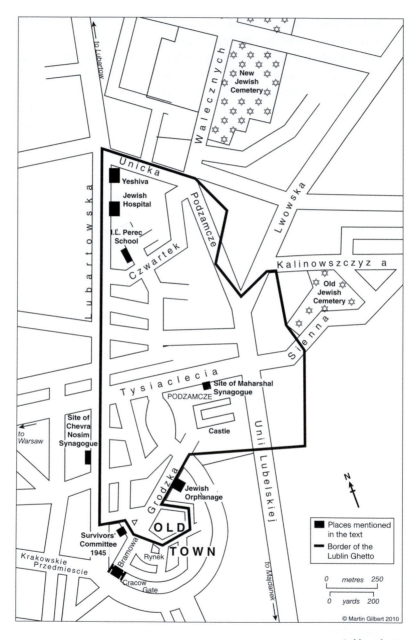

Lublin: ghetto

of Poland until relocation to Warsaw in 1949. This was where survivors congregated and recorded their experiences. Noworybna exits onto Lubartowska which formed the ghetto's western boundary. The rather tatty square between Lubartowska and Świętoduska is plac Ofiara Getta (Ghetto Victims' Square): Lublin's main Holocaust memorial was erected here in 1962 but has recently been moved. Down the hill, Lubartowska 10 housed the only surviving prayer room in the city but this too has been relocated.

North of the Rynek, Grodzka 11 was the site of a Jewish orphanage, a home for the aged and various communal offices. On 24 March 1942, the children were murdered at the airfield camp in Majdan Tatarski. The building also housed the *Judenrat* during the ghetto's brief existence. This history is recorded on two plaques. Out of the Old Town, through the Grodzka gate, a bridge leads to the castle which was used as a Gestapo prison (June–Aug: Tue–Sun, 10.00–5.00 (until 6.00, Sun); Sept–May: Tue–Sun, 9.00–4.00 (until 5.00, Wed & Sun); 6.50 zł; zamek-lublin.pl). A few hundred Jews held here as forced labourers were the last in the city to be murdered, on 21 and 22 July 1944, hours before the liberation. It is hard now to imagine the warren of streets and small houses which surrounded the castle but a plaque on plac Zamkowy, at the foot of its steps, carries a plan of the old Jewish quarter. This area was swept away by the Communists to construct the large Tysiąclecia highway to the castle's north. This runs through the site of Lublin's 1567 Great Synagogue, which anchored a complex that included two other prayer houses and one of Europe's greatest yeshivas. The synagogue was used as the assembly point during the deportations to Bełżec and then destroyed in 1942. It is preserved only as an image on a memorial plaque which stands on a verge above the path on the southern side of Tysiąclecia, opposite the bus station. The latter is the incongruous site of a little-noticed relic of the area's Jewish past. Near the point where the buses exit onto Ruska, a small, square, tower-like brick structure housed a well which served the community: even in the 1930s, most of the district's houses lacked proper water supplies and sanitation.

West of the bus station, the tall building at Probostwo 4 was a mill in which 150 Jews were employed as slave labour outside the ghetto. Some original buildings survive on the eastern side of Lubartowska (the ghetto's boundary) and on Czwartek, a turning to the right further up the street. Off the latter, Skolna 16 (set back from the road) was the

Lublin: new Jewish cemetery (Photograph by the author)

I.L. Perec Cultural Centre. Named after the writer, the complex was due to open on 1 September 1939. After the war, it initially served as a meeting-place for Holocaust survivors and a Jewish primary school. Lubartowska 81 is the former Jewish hospital (it is still a hospital today); its staff and patients were murdered on 27 March 1942. Next door, by the corner with Unicka which marked the northern point of the ghetto, is the grand Lublin Yeshiva, constructed in 1930 and intended to be a global centre for Jewish learning. It was forcibly closed by the Germans in 1940 and its property, including a famed library, stolen. After the war, it was used by the university's medical school but has been returned to the Jewish community whose headquarters are now based here. The community is gradually restoring the building, as shown by the now gleaming facade, and it can be visited for a mandatory donation (12.50 zł or $5). This enables one to see the wonderfully refurbished synagogue on the first floor and a small exhibition on the yeshiva's history.

The new Jewish cemetery on the eastern side of Walecznych was just beyond the ghetto borders. Opened in 1829, it was badly damaged by the Nazis who also used it as an execution site, including for severely ill patients from the hospital. Its modern wall is formed by twisted metal in the shape of menorahs and concrete stones many of which bear plaques commemorating Holocaust victims. There are a number of memorials within the grounds, including a mass grave of 190 Jews murdered at Majdan Tatarski in 1942 (in the rear section through the gate behind the unusual ceremonial hall). There is a further section north of Andersa but this is not enclosed and essentially functions as a park. The memorial structure in its centre is very badly cared for. The old cemetery, overgrown and partially ruined, is located to the south-east on Kalinowszczyzna (ring 0602 47 3118 for access). It too was used for executions, of both Jews and Poles, and for artillery positions in 1944. On the corner with Floriańska are two memorials to the Poles killed at the cemetery on 23 December 1939.

The SS city

The modern city centre to the west of the Old Town was the domain of the Germans. These were the buildings where the *Schreibtischtätern* (desk-bound murderers) of Globocnik's staff and associated institutions planned and administered the business of genocide. Despite the importance of these locations to the Holocaust, they are not marked although the quarter does contain the recently moved Holocaust memorial, a large black *matzeva*-like sculpture, at the corner of Radziwiłłowska and Niecała, behind the Europa Hotel (wartime centre of German propaganda operations) and plac Litewski (renamed Adolf Hitler Platz). There had been talk of relocating the monument from plac Ofiara Getta for some time but to a more appropriate site such as the yeshiva; quite why it has ended up here is a mystery. Around the corner, dilapidated Niecała 3 housed Ukrainian SS auxiliaries. During recent renovation work, a human skull was found embedded in the balcony above the door. Further down the same street, in a side turning to the left, the rather lurid green building at 14 was the Lublin headquarters of the Ostbahn (known as '*Gedob*'). This was where the deportation trains to the death camps were timetabled alongside civilian and military traffic. Across 3 Maja, the grand building at Chmielna 1 was an SS garrison. Its basement contained the *Aktion Reinhard* treasury where cash and valuables were sorted. At the back of the main building was a bench where Globocnik interviewed Franz Stangl for the post of commandant of Sobibór. Behind the smaller building to the right was a furnace where a group of Jewish prisoners melted down gold.

The Kredyt Bank building on the north-west corner of the crossroads of 3 Maja and Krakowskie Przedmieście was a wartime branch of the Reichsbank. The money and gold plundered in *Aktion Reinhard* was deposited here and taken to Berlin by a special courier. The Grand Hotel opposite served as the Deutsche Haus, the headquarters of the German civil administration. During the T4 murders of the disabled, the families of German Jewish victims received death certificates supposedly issued by the registry office in Chełm; the documents were, in fact, fabricated in Berlin and brought to Lublin where they were posted from the large main post office at Krakowskie Przedmieście 50 just to the east of the crossroads.

The next crossroads to the west, with Ewangelicka to the right and Chopina to the left, takes one to the heart of the Nazi city. The large building at Chopina 27–29 was the main depot for confiscated Jewish property, both from the death camps and from Lublin itself. On parallel Lipowa, a forced labour camp for Jews was established in 1939: thousands passed through before the last 2,500 were sent to Majdanek in November 1943. Thereafter, the camp housed non-Jews until its final liquidation in July 1944. A few fragments remained after the war but these were

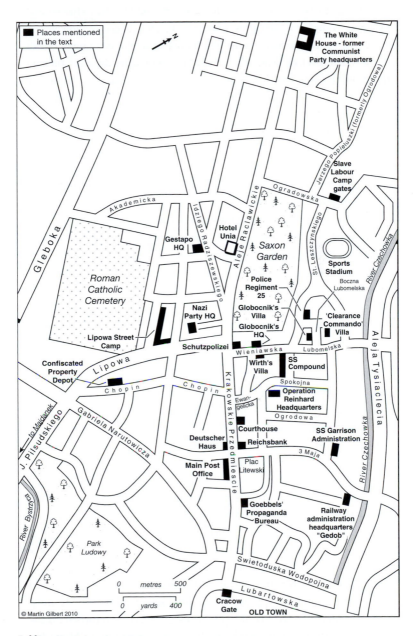

Lublin: city centre

recently destroyed to make way for the new Lublin Plaza cinema and shopping complex which now occupies the site. There is, however, a memorial on its southern wall, just across from the cemetery. North of the Plaza, after crossing Marii-Skłodowskiej-Curie, the next turning on the left leads to Zwirki i Wigury. The colonnaded building at number 1 was the Nazi Party HQ in Lublin. A couple of blocks to the west, at the junction of Radziszewskiego and Uniwersytecka, the building with the circular facade and rooftop clock was the home of the Gestapo, the only German building to be memorialised. On the Uniwersytecka side, a plaque stands over the entrance to the small museum (Wed–Sat, 9.00–4.00; Sun, 9.00–5.00; free) in the former cells, one of which contains preserved graffiti left by prisoners.

The most important sites in the extermination apparatus were located to the north of Krakowskie Przedmieście. Taking the Ewangelicka turn brings one to an elegant building which now houses the university's law college at Spokojna 1. Nothing indicates that this was the headquarters of *Aktion Reinhard*, the place where the deaths of close to 2 million people were orchestrated: the municipality refused requests for a memorial plaque to be placed on the recently renovated building. On the opposite side of the street are a group of free-standing buildings in an elevated area between Partyzancka and Tramecourta (previously Czugaly): they formed the SS recreational compound which included a restaurant, a casino, a bar and a brothel. The imposing building next up Spokojna was the headquarters of Ernst Zorner, governor of the Lublin district. One can walk through the SS compound to Wieniawska where the small villa at number 7 housed Christian Wirth in the second half of 1942 when he was brought to Lublin from Bełżec to become inspector of the *Aktion Reinhard* camps (he later moved to a residence in the airfield camp). Along with Globocnik, Wirth was the most important figure in the destruction of the Jews of Poland. An astonishingly unpleasant man even by the standards of his peers, he had served in three of the T4 centres before being appointed as a roving inspector of all of them. His new position in Lublin gave him similar control over the *Reinhard* camps. He is thus commonly seen as the individual directly responsible for the deaths of the largest number of people in the Holocaust. Transferred, like most of the Lublin staff, to Trieste in 1943 (although he briefly returned for the November massacres), he was killed by Yugoslav partisans in May 1944 and buried with full military honours.

On the opposite side of the street, the large block at Wieniawska 6/8 was Globocnik's headquarters in his capacity as SS and Police Leader as opposed to head of *Aktion Reinhard*. The building at number 4 on the other side of the alley was the headquarters of the *Schutzpolizei*, the ordinary uniformed German police force. Other significant buildings are to be found on Boczna Lobomelskiej, a left turn off Wienawska's northern continuation Lubomelska. The 1930s block at 4/6 was Globconik's personal villa whilst the house hidden behind trees at 3 opposite accommodated his secretaries and, during the liquidation of the Lublin ghetto in spring 1942, the leaders of the 'Clearance Commando', Globocnik's team of 'specialists' who organised deportations. Boczna Lubomelskiej then turns to the left; the large grey building on its corner with Leszczyńskiego was the barracks of Police Regiment 125, Globocnik's SS bodyguard.

Following Leszczyńskiego west eventually leads one uphill to the site of the Sportsplatz forced labour camp in Wieniawa, a suburb with a predominantly Jewish pre-war population. Following the relocation of the Jews to the ghetto, the area was earmarked by Globocnik for recreational facilities for the SS and the wider German population. Wieniawa's Jewish cemetery was destroyed and a sports stadium built on the site using Jewish labour, beginning in 1941. The Sportsplatz camp was established in 1942 as a sub-camp of Majdanek; its inmates were put to work in the construction of the stadium or in sorting medicines and cosmetics taken from victims of the death camps. Of the prisoners who were sent to the Sportsplatz (probably a few hundred), only one survived its liquidation in November 1943. Whereas the stadium is still in use on the north side of Leszczyńskiego, the camp buildings were largely destroyed. However, the original gates survive at Długosza 12, a right turn at the end of Leszczyńskiego. From there, one can see a hangar where goods were stored on the other side of Poniatowskiego.

Airfield camp and Majdan Tatarski

Most visitors heading to Majdanek from the centre of Lublin do not realise that they are passing the site of another camp. Lublin's pre-war airfield was converted into a labour camp in 1940 in which a variety of workshops existed. It acquired new significance during *Aktion Reinhard* when the aircraft hangars were used for storage and sorting of goods stolen from victims of the death camps. The connection was further emphasised by the appointment of Wirth as commandant in late 1942. The camp was liquidated in November 1943 when its inmates were taken to Majdanek and murdered in the *Erntefest*.

The camp was located to the north of modern Droga Męczenników Majdanka (wartime Chełmska) and east of the railway lines. Just beyond the railway bridge and up steps is Wirth's villa and headquarters as inspector of the *Aktion Reinhard* camps at number 2. The lopsided building even had its own restaurant which was regarded as the finest in Lublin; Himmler dined there three times. Bizarrely, the men who were overseeing the annihilation of Polish Jewry were served by beautiful young Jewish women. Walking around number 2, one comes to large number 4 which housed the SS. A path leads from here through the overgrown ruins of the camp; the crumbling building on the left was a tar paper factory. The path curves rightwards to connect with Wrońska: as it straightens at the approach to this junction, the brick building on the right was an SS mess which contained a canteen and a bar – one can see its almost square front behind the wall on Wrońska. Almost next to it, in the yard behind the wall, stood a gas chamber which was initially used to disinfect clothing but later to murder inmates. Heading south along Wrońska, the last of the hangars used to store the *Aktion Reinhard* plunder survive on the right. The camp actually extended much further on the eastern side of Wrońska but that area is now occupied by modern factories.

The Majdan Tatarski ghetto, into which the last surviving Lublin Jews were forced in 1942, was just north of the camp. The area is now occupied by post-war housing: Majdan Tatarski, a turning at the northern end of Wrońska, was the ghetto's main street.

The site can be easily reached by taking buses 7, 14, 16, 23, 28, 55, 153, 156, 158 or 502 to the Park Bronowice stop on Droga Męczenników Majdanka. The railway bridge is just ahead, the steps to Wirth's villa past the bridge on the other side of the road.

MAJDANEK

Majdanek, now surrounded by Lublin's post-war suburbs, was the largest camp in the *Generalgouvernement* and the first major Nazi camp to be liberated. Construction began in the autumn of 1941 under the command of Globocnik thus linking it to *Aktion Reinhard*. Until the spring of 1943 it was designated as a POW camp (it did indeed house thousands of Red Army soldiers) but this rather hid its true nature which reflected Himmler's demographic fantasies. Inmates were to become a massive pool of slaves (plans approved in March 1942 envisaged a camp population of 250,000) who would build SS complexes in Poland and the USSR around which permanent German communities would eventually develop. Although military realities rather limited these ambitions, Majdanek was a large site even before it was officially declared a concentration camp. After the early transports of Soviet POWs, most of those sent there were Jews and Poles. The Jews were generally skilled workers who had been at least temporarily spared during *Aktion Reinhard*; their numbers were swelled in 1943 with the final liquidation of the ghettos. Majdanek also handled plundered Jewish property from the death camps.

Majdanek is often listed as an extermination camp itself. It did indeed have gas chambers from late 1942 in which an unknown number of inmates were murdered, some on arrival, more often, it seems, when they were too weak to continue working (as was the case in many concentration camps). However, it perhaps had more in common with Janowska in L'viv or the Croat camp at Jasenovac than with Birkenau or Treblinka: the main methods of murder appear to have been starvation, overwork and execution. This should serve as a reminder of the complexity and scale of the Holocaust (something which the rather prurient focus on gas chambers sometimes obscures) and of the very simple fact that the Nazis killed Jews by whatever means they could find. Thousands died in the appalling conditions and others were shot. The largest latter such action took place in the *Erntefest* on 3 November 1943, when around 18,000 Jews were murdered, one of the largest single massacres of the Holocaust. Thereafter, the camp's population was predominantly ethnic Polish until its liberation in July 1944.

The USSR captured Majdanek before the Germans had had the chance to destroy the evidence, meaning that its horrors were apparent to the whole world (less well known was the fact that the NKVD then took over a section of the camp for internment of members of the Polish underground). It was decided in November 1944 to turn part of the complex into a museum, making it the first Holocaust site to be memorialised. However, one legacy of Communism, as at Auschwitz, was distortion of the camp's history with the USSR claiming that more than a million people had been murdered there (mostly Poles and Russians), a figure no serious scholar has ever accepted. The exact numbers of prisoners and victims has long been uncertain with around 300,000 dead often suggested. However, recent research suggests that the total number of inmates was around 120,000, three quarters of them Jewish. The current accepted figure for the death toll, now given in the camp museum, is 78,000 of whom 59,000 were Jewish – still a frightening figure. These numbers do not include other camps such as Poniatowa and Trawniki which were eventually incorporated into the Majdanek system.

The most immediately striking thing about the site (Tue–Sun, 8.00–4.00; free; www.majdanek.pl) is its huge size but what the modern visitor sees is, in fact, only part of the wartime Majdanek complex which stretched much further both east and west. The roadside entrance to the camp grounds is marked by an enormous 1960s abstract concrete sculpture which some believe to be suggestive of a menorah although that is frankly stretching things. Further east along the main road is the museum's visitors' centre which houses a cinema. From the monument, a path leads diagonally through the SS section of the camp, little of which survives: there are a few SS women's barracks on the edge of the prisoners' camp whilst the white doctor's house is to the right of the path. Beyond here, one passes through the gate which marks the entry to the prison camp.

Perhaps the most shocking feature of Majdanek is the presence of gas chambers almost next to the entrance in a converted bathhouse on the right. They were constructed in late 1942 and initially apparently intended only for disinfection purposes before a change of plan led to their adaptation for mass murder. Inadequate documentation and a lack of survivors means that knowledge of what exactly happened here is limited: it is not known for certain whether two (as suggested by the labelling) or three of the rooms in the block were gas chambers or, indeed, whether the first of the two rooms was used for killing or only for disinfection. This reflects continuing doubt over the precise nature of the extermination process in the camp with the gas chambers generally believed to have been subsidiary to mass shootings and starvation.

The wooden barracks beyond the bathhouse were used for storage of goods awaiting shipment to Germany; some are now given over to the exhibits of the museum. Blocks 43 to 45 cover the history of the camp whilst Block 52 contains the massive pile of shoes discovered at liberation. To the left of the path are the large 'Fields' (fenced off groups of barracks) into which the camp was divided although only Field III now contains huts. This was partly because of poor preservation by the Red Army units stationed here after the war but mainly due to local people taking wood for fuel. The barracks in the other fields were demolished in 1949 and their remains used to fully reconstruct the blocks in Field III which had survived in better condition. The other fields were then planted with trees but, when these threatened to engulf the site, they were felled in the 1960s. The area between Fields I and II housed the camp laundry and the old crematorium which is the surviving building in this area; this also contained two gas chambers. A path leads into Field II where a small shed contains a concrete sculpture of a castle constructed by prisoners; as in so many camps, such diversions gave inmates a sense of focus and escape, however fleeting. In this, they were encouraged by the original commandant Karl Koch who considered himself a man of culture; he was arrested in August 1942 for corruption. The main path curves towards Field III at the end of the store barracks; one can see the foundations of the SS garage which housed a gas van, apparently brought from Bełżec, just beyond this turning.

Field III mainly contained Polish political prisoners along with some Jews from Warsaw and Białystok. Blocks 14 and 15 are open, with reconstructions of bunks conveying a sense of the overcrowded conditions in which inmates were held. Rather surprisingly, Block 19 is not highlighted. This was the 'death block' where sick prisoners were simply dumped; every few days, a cart arrived to collect the bodies and transport them to the crematorium. At the eastern end of the field is another concrete sculpture, a pillar topped by three eagles. The SS actually allowed this work to be erected assuming the eagles represented Germany when, of course, they were also the symbol of Poland. Less well known is the fact that prisoners buried human ashes under the pillar in a further act of symbolic protest.

The route then heads south along what seems to be the camp's eastern perimeter but what was actually intended to become its central road in a planned 1944 extension. Most of the area to the east is now occupied by an incongruously located Catholic cemetery. The road leads to a brooding domed mausoleum which contains a vast mound of ashes collected from the earth in and around the camp in 1947 and relocated to this structure in 1969. To its right is the new crematorium which was built in the autumn of 1943 although much is reconstructed after the fleeing Nazis burned it down. Some guides tell visitors that there were

Majdanek (Photograph by the author)

gas chambers in this building but there is no evidence for this (by the time the crematorium went into operation, most of Majdanek's Jews had already been murdered) although people were undoubtedly executed here. A sarcophagus contains bones and ashes. Behind the crematorium and mausoleum are the *Erntefest* execution pits which were the real site of the largest mass murder of Jews in the camp but are missed by many visitors. A simple stone stands alongside, relatively recently amended to acknowledge that the victims were Jewish.

The camp is easily reached from the centre of Lublin on buses 23, 28, 47, 153, 156, 158 or 502 (Pomnik-Majdanek stop).

PONIATOWA

Poniatowa was one of the most appalling sites of mass murder in occupied Poland on two separate occasions. Developed as a factory complex for the Polish military just before the war, it was turned into a German army base

248

before becoming a POW camp in September 1941. Over the next three months, close to 24,000 Red Army soldiers were interned in completely ill-suited factory buildings. With starvation and typhus outbreaks adding to extreme cold, the death toll reached the scarcely believable figure of almost 1,000 per day in early 1942: by the spring, only around 500 were still left alive.

The site was transferred to the control of the SS in the summer of 1942 and turned into a forced labour camp for Jews. The largest contingent came from Warsaw, mainly employees of the Toebbens Company (the ghetto's largest employer), who began to arrive in February 1943 although most were forcibly brought to the camp after the uprising. Veterans of the Warsaw underground organised escapes but struggled to create a wider resistance movement, partly because of what appeared to be a relatively liberal regime. Even though Gottlieb Hering (previously commandant of Bełżec) took over at Poniatowa at the time of their arrival, the 10,000 Toebbens Jews had comparatively reasonable working conditions and food supplies, in line with the policy of encouraging skilled workers to believe that they could survive. Such notions were to prove short-lived, however: the camp was liquidated in *Aktion Erntefest* on 4 November 1943 when around 14,000 inmates were shot. Members of the underground who attempted to fight back were burned alive in their barrack. Only two people are known to have survived the massacre.

The camp returned to industrial use and was expanded after the war whilst Poniatowa village became a model Communist town as the workforce increased. Although the Jewish barracks have gone, the site otherwise remains largely intact. The buildings cluster around Przemysłowa (formerly the main camp road), a turning off Fabryczna, south of the town. A parking space opposite Przemysłowa stands on the site of a mass grave of *Erntefest* victims. A small signpost (*'Miejsce pamięci narodowej'*) points to the only memorial within the site of the camp, a simple stone which fails to mention that the victims were Jews, a few yards along Przemysłowa on the right. Ahead is a gateway formed by the post-war EDA factory, through which a road to the right leads past grey brick buildings which were the SS barracks. Through the fence one can see a small sports field; this stands on the location of the main *Erntefest* massacre and largest of the mass graves.

Continuing down Przemysłowa, the Jewish barracks were to the left of the road. The single-storey beige building to the right served as the

SS telephone exchange. The first surviving factory is on the left with a distinctive ridged roof, now occupied by Wentworth Tech. At the end of this building, one can see sections of the train ramp on both sides of the road: the stretch on the right leads to two more, now deserted, factories. Further along Przemysłowa on the right is another original ridged-roof building whilst the road to the left, past a single-storey brick building occupied by Art Plast, leads to more ruined workshops and warehouses both to the north and south. At the bottom of the camp, by its south-eastern corner, is the original brick power station, still in use.

Somewhere beyond the power station are the mass graves of the Soviet POWs. The exact location is unknown but there is a Communist era memorial, a large trapezoidal structure, by the camp's south-eastern corner. This is accessed by returning out of the camp and heading up Fabryczna. Just beyond the blue fence of the hospital, a signposted dirt track through the forest runs alongside the original camp fence. The memorial is to the right of the path in a clearing for electricity pylons after about a kilometre.

There is a further memorial in the town itself, on the north-west side of the junction of Fabryczna and its continuation Nałęczowksa with Modrzewiowa and 11 Listopada. The latter street was the site of a camp for privileged prisoners who were housed in the former Polish army barracks which line it. The Centrum Kultury to the south-east of the junction housed Ukrainian SS auxiliaries.

Poniatowa is around 20 miles west of Lublin on the 832. Turn south onto Fabryczna (marked by signposts for the hospital and the many enterprises occupying the site) for the main camp (the other memorial is north of the same junction). As the road curves to the left one can see some of the original fence on its southern side; continue to the signposts for Przemysłowa and the memorial. There are extremely frequent minibuses from Lublin (departing from the small bus park behind the main bus station) which terminate in Poniatowa at central Plac Konstytucji: walk southwards along Nałęczowska to the arched memorial. The main camp is more than a kilometre further south, following Fabryczna as it crosses the 832.

TRAWNIKI

Trawniki was a unique dual-purpose camp whose role in the Holocaust was of great significance yet its name is little known beyond academic specialists and war crimes lawyers. It was originally established in July 1941 in the grounds of an abandoned sugar factory as a detention facility for special categories of Soviet POW: those considered either especially dangerous or potential collaborators. It then became a training facility for SS auxiliaries from the territories of the USSR (primarily Ukrainians) in September. They were initially drawn from the captured Soviet conscripts but later included a substantial number of volunteers. The 'Trawnikis', known to the Germans as *Hiwis* (from *Hilfswillige*, volunteers), became notorious for their role as guards in the *Aktion Reinhard* camps. They were also deployed in camps such as Poniatowa and Janowska and used in ghetto clearance operations in major cities. Trawniki was thus crucial in supplying the SS with the manpower it required to implement the Holocaust.

Trawniki also played a more direct role in the murder, becoming a transit camp in spring 1942 for Jews from nearby Piaski (many of them deportees from the Reich) who were destined for Bełżec. Several hundred never reached the death camp, dying of suffocation in the overcrowded block where they were held or being used for 'training' of the Ukrainians. From the summer of 1942, a more permanent Jewish presence was established in the form of a forced labour camp based around the industrial facilities next to the training camp. Inmates were initially put to work sorting the clothing of those murdered in the *Aktion Reinhard* camps. In the following months, as part of Himmler's policy of transferring enterprises from ghettos, Jewish workers were relocated to Trawniki, most notably from the Warsaw ghetto's Schultz fur factory after the suppression of the 1943 uprising. Thereafter, the Jewish population numbered close to 6,000 and new barracks were built in the summer, suggesting apparent stability, an impression further enhanced by the arrival of Jews from Minsk in September. However, Trawniki was included in the *Erntefest*: it is believed that around 6,000 were murdered on 3 November 1943. The few remaining Jews were transferred to Majdanek in May 1944 although the training camp functioned until the arrival of the Red Army in July. The fate of the Ukrainians captured by the Soviets can be imagined but most fled westwards, presenting themselves to the British and Americans as refugees from Communism. Their subsequent lives and careers remain a source of controversy to this day.

Sections of the camp survive, incorporated into the modern village. The main elements can be seen by following the unnamed roads which skirt the former camp perimeter with the easiest point of orientation being the train station. Standing in its forecourt, facing the village, the building on the right was the villa of Franz Bartetzko, the camp's deputy commandant. Turning right here, one joins the road which marked the camp's boundary. A short distance along, opposite the bus car park, a side road turns sharply back to the left. The large building at this junction, facing recycling bins, housed the camp command. Its basement contained cells for errant Ukrainians; during recent work, residents discovered skulls which had been hidden for 60 years. Heading along this side road, which runs back roughly parallel to the main road, one comes to the entrance to the sugar factory, now the Trawena works. The buildings are wartime except for the distinctive tall chimney – the metal original, an easy sighting point for Soviet planes, was destroyed. There was a gas chamber on the other side of the factory although most of those murdered at Trawniki were shot.

Rejoining the main road at the command building, there is a car park on the next corner. This occupies the site of a mass grave which was until very recently left as a field. There is at least a simple monument, albeit incorrectly dated 1939–44, with a later addition highlighting the Jewish victims of the *Erntefest* massacre. Turning left here, one passes the building behind the car park: it was built on another mass grave and residents recall human remains being excavated during its construction in the Communist era. The next group of buildings, set back from the road behind the grass and trees, were SS living quarters. Turn left at the next crossroads; a section of the original camp wall stretches for a couple of hundred metres on the left-hand side of the road. Little else remains beyond this point but one can continue along this road past the factory to the next junction on the left which is with the former *Lagerstraße* that separated the industrial area from the Jewish camp to the north-west. The latter is now covered in fields with a few modern houses. Following the *Lagerstraße* back down to the main part of the village, one turns left again at its end to head back towards the station.

Trawniki is signposted off the 12/E373, 22 miles south-east of Lublin from where there are regular trains and minibuses (the latter stopping opposite the command building).

SOBIBÓR

Construction of the second *Aktion Reinhard* camp began in March 1942 in an area of dense forest near the Bug River. After experimental gassings of

Jews from nearby labour camps in April, Sobibór officially commenced its murderous work in May under the command of T4 veteran Franz Stangl. In the first stage of operations, from early May to late July, close to 100,000 people were murdered; most were from the Lublin region but there were also large-scale arrivals from the Reich. There was then a temporary cessation whilst the railway line was repaired although more than 3,000 Jews from nearby communities were still murdered in August. The hiatus was used to increase the camp's killing capacity, the original three gas chambers being replaced by a new block with six chambers. In the same period, Stangl was transferred to Treblinka and replaced by Franz Reichleitner. Large-scale transports resumed in October 1942 and, as the number of Jews in the *Generalgouvernement* dwindled, Himmler ordered in early 1943 that Sobibór should also receive deportations from France and the Netherlands to relieve pressure on Birkenau. In fact, the latter formed the only group for which more or less precise figures exist such was the efficiency of the Dutch bureaucracy: 34,313 people were brought to Sobibór from Westerbork and Vught; 18 survived. Unlike the Polish Jews, who not infrequently resisted on the 'route to heaven', the westerners generally went peacefully to the gas chambers, believing the welcoming speech from an SS man (often dressed as a doctor to enhance the effect) that they were to be bathed and quarantined before being sent to work in Ukraine; some even applauded. The total number of victims of Sobibór is generally believed to have been around 250,000.

The last large transports were from liquidated ghettos in the Soviet Union, including Vilnius and Minsk, in September 1943. The camp would doubtless have continued its murderous work for longer – construction of a new munitions supply area (Camp IV) was underway in the autumn of 1943 – were it not for the justly celebrated revolt by Jewish prisoners in October of the same year. Around 200 were held in Camp III (the extermination area), isolated from the other prisoners, where they were forced to remove the bodies from the gas chambers and bury them. Several hundred more were engaged in forced labour for the SS in Camp I to the south. There were escape attempts throughout Sobibór's history: for example, five prisoners were able to exploit the German festivities on 25 December 1942 and flee. Any attempt was met with collective reprisals (i.e., executions of other prisoners) but this was not always a deterrent, such was the desperate situation. In late July 1943, eight members of a group working in the forests were able to escape after

Sobibór (Photograph by the author)

getting their guard drunk and killing him. Their success had a significant psychological effect on other inmates and an organised underground developed in the camp in the late summer. This was boosted by the arrival of Jewish former Red Army soldiers from Minsk, one of whom, Alexander Pechersky, provided the conspiracy with effective leadership and experience. The uprising, on 14 October 1943, involved luring SS men individually to barracks in Camp I with the promise of new clothes and the like from the workshops, killing them and forcing a way out of the camp with the captured weapons. Twenty Germans and Ukrainians were killed and around 300 of the 700 prisoners were able to escape into the forests (many others were shot within the camp itself). Most lost their lives in the SS manhunt or in the minefields which surrounded the camp but more than 50 were able to survive, a remarkable act of successful defiance against the odds.

The rebellion prompted the SS to abandon plans to turn Sobibór into a regular concentration camp and it was decided instead to close it: the murder facilities were dismantled and trees planted on the site. Unlike the other two *Reinhard* camps, however, Sobibór was not completely destroyed immediately: its central section accommodated SS men involved in constructing anti-aircraft positions in 1944. The barracks were also used to hold Ukrainians from the Lublin region during the post-war population exchange before demolition in 1947. The site was then neglected until the 1960s when simple memorials were erected. The modesty of these memorials and the apparently innocuous surroundings rather contrast with Treblinka and Bełżec but Sobibór is perhaps all the more affecting as a result.

The entry to the car park is marked by a wall bearing memorial plaques in several languages. Both the car park and the small football field to the south are within the area of the Ukrainian barracks. On the other side of the road, the long platform by the railway is post-war although a stretch of the track that ran into the camp is original. Across the rails is the wartime Sobibór station, a small yellowish building. The only original structure in the buildings on the camp side of the road is the two-storey commandant's building (next to the yellow road sign) which was nicknamed 'The Merry Flea' for reasons that are unclear.

The wooden building by the car park houses the camp museum (May–Oct: daily, 9.00–2.00 (by arrangement at other times); 3 zł; www. muzeum.wlodawa.metronet.pl – the memorial area is free and accessible at all times). The small exhibition in Polish covers the history of *Aktion Reinhard* and the camp, also focussing on the survivors and the fate of the perpetrators. Differing plans of Sobibór produced by some of these individuals illustrate the difficulties confronting historians in attempting to determine the exact topography of the death camps although archaeological operations, supplemented by aerial photography, have enabled a more accurate understanding of the site which is now reflected in the museum and memorials. A path behind the museum leads past the site of Camp I although this area is now overgrown and thus difficult to explore. During the uprising, the escapees fled to the south into the thick forest and surrounding swamps. An original watchtower which stood by the path collapsed in 2003.

Just north of the car park, a paved road leads to the memorials. Around 250 metres along, a turning to the left marks the shockingly short 'route to heaven' taken by the victims. Where once the sides of the path were lined with high barbed-wire fences, there are now stones bearing the names of the murdered, the result of a joint memorial project involving Polish, German and Dutch organisations. The path runs first through the site of Camp II where the incoming prisoners were robbed of their clothes and possessions. Initially, they had to undress in an open square but a special barrack was created after a few weeks. In the same square were tables with stationery on which the unsuspecting western Jews were encouraged to write reassuring postcards to friends and relatives; many examples of these cards survive in the Netherlands. The path then curves to the north. To the right at this point was the barrack where the women's hair was cut off. The path terminates by a new memorial stone, standing where the gas chambers are now believed to have been located.

To the right of the new stone are two 1960s memorials, a brick block and an anguished sculpture, built on what was then thought to be the site of the gas chambers. In the field beyond, blue flags mark the sites where remains were found during recent excavations. The field is dominated by a large pyramidal structure usually referred to as the mound of ashes. This pile of earth was landscaped during the construction of the memorial in a section of the field believed to hold cremated remains although later research has suggested that this was only true of part of the area of the mound. The largest mass grave appears to have been to its right, running virtually the entire length of the clearing.

Sobibór is the most inaccessible of the death camps, located close to the borders with Belarus and Ukraine. Most visitors come from Lublin which involves taking the 82 to Włodawa and then heading south on the 812 to Chełm. On the way, the road passes the lakeside resort of Okuninka where the SS men spent holidays with their families. The Sobibór turning is signposted to the left about 5 miles south of Włodawa; the road leads through the forest to the camp which is some distance south-west of Sobibór village. The site cannot really be accessed by public transport, rail services having ceased in the 1990s, although it is possible to take a bus to Włodawa and get a taxi there.

IZBICA

Izbica was an almost entirely Jewish town which became a transit ghetto for around 26,000 Jews during *Aktion Reinhard*. In the spring of 1942, more than 10,000 were sent from the Reich and Slovakia to await onward deportation to Bełżec and Sobibór. The town's 4,000 Jews along with 2,500 deported there from the *Warthegau* in 1939 were sent to Bełżec in March to free space but there was nonetheless immense overcrowding, bringing mass deaths from disease, starvation and Nazi executions. Thousands of Polish Jews were also relocated to Izbica in the autumn of 1942, increasing the population density to such an extent that people were camping in the streets. Mass deportations took place in October and November; those who could not be accommodated on the transports were shot in the Jewish cemetery.

The main area of the transit camp was in the field which stands opposite the post-war train station although there is nothing to suggest its horrendous history. There is, though, fitting commemoration at the cemetery which is significantly further up the main 17 road, accessed by an uphill path from a small yard at the corner with Fabryczna. The cemetery's recent restoration is a model of Holocaust memorialisation, a joint initiative of the Foundation for the Preservation of Jewish Heritage in Poland and the German Embassy, working closely with the staff and children of the local school. A new monument commemorates the Izbica Jewish community and signs point to the mass graves, themselves marked by monuments. The project has also seen the return of gravestones which were seized by the Nazis; some have now been used to cover the *ohel* of Mordechai Josef Leiner (1814–78), founder of the Izhbitzer-Radziner

Hassidic dynasty. Underneath the cemetery, the small house at Fabryczna 5 was the pre-war home of Sobibór survivor Tom Blatt. After the uprising in the death camp, he and two fellow escapees returned and took refuge with a local farmer who eventually betrayed them: Blatt was left for dead after being shot in the jaw (the bullet remains there today) and his companions were murdered. The gravestones stolen from the cemetery were used by the Germans to build a prison next to the regional Gestapo headquarters. The latter, now the town police station, is at Gminna 8 to the west of the main road.

Izbica is 40 miles south-east of Lublin on the 17/E372. There are occasional trains from Lublin and Zamość; buses run much more frequently.

BEŁŻEC

Bełżec, the first *Aktion Reinhard* camp, was the template for those that followed. There is some uncertainty about when exactly the decision to create the camp was taken – the most common belief is that Himmler gave the order to Globocnik in October 1941 – but construction began in November. The location reflected Bełżec's position on the main Lublin to L'viv railway (unlike Sobibór and Treblinka, the site was not isolated). The village had also been the site of labour camps for Jews and Roma in 1940 (by some estimates, the largest complex of such camps in the *Generalgouvernement* at the time) but they were abandoned in October of that year and were not related to the death camp either in location or personnel. Instead, Bełżec established what were to become the key features of *Aktion Reinhard*. The SS men were T4 veterans, most notably Christian Wirth, who commanded the camp until his promotion to inspector of *Aktion Reinhard* camps in August 1942, and Gottlieb Hering, his replacement. The relatively small number of SS were supported by Ukrainian 'Trawnikis' as guards whilst groups of selected Jewish prisoners were forced to work, forever at risk of being killed themselves. It also established the basic layout of the death camps – the ramp, the undressing areas, the 'tube' to the extermination facilities in a separate area – although modifications were later made at both Bełżec and the other camps.

Following experimental gassings on Jewish prisoners in February 1942, the camp officially commenced operations in mid-March, its first victims a

Bełżec (Photograph by the author)

transport from Lublin. Tens of thousands of people were murdered in the first month before a temporary hiatus when Wirth went to Berlin to receive orders to expand the camp. Although the murders resumed in mid-May, transports were again halted after a month to allow implementation of Wirth's new instructions. The three original wooden gas chambers were replaced by a larger six-room structure in which hundreds of thousands lost their lives from July 1942 onwards. The last major transports were in December, there being few Jews left to kill in southern and eastern Poland. By this stage, the decision had been taken to destroy the traces of the crime by exhuming and cremating the bodies buried in mass graves all over the camp although recent archaeological evidence shows that this was never completed. The camp was dismantled and trees planted in spring 1943. The last Jewish prisoners who had carried out this work were sent to Sobibór and murdered in the summer. The total number of victims of Bełżec is estimated to have been around 500,000. From one point of view, it was the most lethal camp in that only two inmates are known to have escaped and survived the war. Rudolf Reder managed to slip away in November 1942 when he was taken to L'viv to collect sheet metal and his guard fell asleep whilst Chaim Hirszman escaped from the last train out of the camp to Sobibór. Hirszman was murdered in Lublin in March 1946, a day after giving evidence of his experiences in Bełżec.

A low-key memorial site was created at Bełżec in the 1960s, rather resembling a slightly neglected country park. This changed dramatically with the creation of a new museum and memorial in 2004 (Apr–Oct: daily, 9.00–6.00 (museum until 5.00); Nov–Mar: daily, 8.00–4.00 (museum from 9.00); free; www.belzec.org.pl) which has completely transformed the site. The entrance, marked by a quotation from the Book of Job, is across the main railway line at the site of the unloading ramp. To the left of the gate, a pile of rails represents the siding which ran into the camp; the rails are actually from Treblinka as insufficient surviving material was found at Bełżec. The excellent new museum to the right includes items discovered around the site, most recently from archaeological excavations in 1997–99, which have significantly increased knowledge of the camp – for example, it is now clear that its boundaries extended beyond those of the memorial area both to the north-west and to the south-east. Amongst the items on display are one of the pipes which fed the carbon monoxide into the gas chambers (found in the 1950s) and the plaque which greeted new transports with instructions for undressing and the handover of valuables (found by a resident immediately after the war). More personal artefacts include keys, coins, shoes and Star of David armbands. Most intriguing are numbered concrete discs found in considerable numbers in the excavations. One theory is that they were given to victims as tokens for their money and documents which were handed over at a special window – this would have heightened the illusion that they were about to enter a bathhouse.

The territory of the camp itself has become the memorial, a rising field now covered in industrial slag; its perimeter is marked by twisted metal and walls lined with the names of exterminated communities, arranged alphabetically by date of deportation. The site is thus intended to serve as a symbolic cemetery, its design suggestive of a field of ashes from afar. The 33 mass graves discovered during the archaeological research are covered with a blue-grey slag to distinguish them. The hill is cut through with a path, like a crack in the earth, which approximately marks the route to the gas chambers. This ran straight at Bełżec; the sharp bends in the 'tubes' at Sobibór and Treblinka were a response to this 'flaw' in design which failed to fully hide the destination from the victims (although the later gas chamber building was located behind a small copse). The path passes through ever higher walls, which generate unnerving acoustics, before halting at a high stone wall inscribed with biblical quotations; Jewish first names are written on the opposite wall. Steps on either side lead back up to the surface of the camp, near to one of the main mass grave sites (the largest concentration of mass graves was along the north-western side of the memorial). Perhaps the greatest surprise is how high this section of the camp was, as shown by the sharp drop in the trees behind and the view back down over the memorial and the village. This inevitably meant that some of what occurred in the camp was visible; indeed, some local residents claim to have watched the murders from the top floors of their houses. The overall effect of the memorial is powerful although not without its critics, not least because the few remaining fragments of the camp have been removed (only the trees on the south-eastern side survive) and the possibility of further archaeological research at the site is now precluded.

To the north-west of the camp is a redbrick locomotive shed in which the clothes of victims were stored next to the tall water tower which fed the deportation trains. These buildings can be reached by taking the dirt track which runs parallel to the train lines on the camp side of the railway although they have become a hangout for local drunks. Almost a quarter of a mile north-west up the main road from the memorial are a pair of two-storey houses with roughly triangular upper floors which jut out from the roof. The first, with a tiled roof and a single upper-floor roadside window, was Wirth's home and office as commandant. The next building along, with a corrugated iron roof and two roadside upper-storey windows, housed other SS personnel: unlike at Sobibór and Treblinka, the SS at Bełżec lived outside the camp.

The forced labour camp of 1940 consisted of a series of locations in the village and surrounding area. Traces of the main site still exist and can be reached by heading further north up the main road, over the level crossing, and taking the 865 road to the left, signposted for Jarosław. After a little over a kilometre along this road, a sign marked '*Pomnik Przyrody*' points down a dirt track to the left. This track was actually the route through the centre of the camp: Roma were held to the east (left), Jews to the west. An original partially whitewashed barrack stands in the latter field. In the copse across the railway track behind the Roma camp is a mass grave. Back on the 865, there is a turning to the right (north) just ahead which passes a pond. Hermann Dolp, the commander of the labour camp who was famed for both his cruelty and his corruption, would force Jewish prisoners to submerge themselves in the pond. If they surfaced before he told them to, they would be shot. Dolp himself lived in the house at number 77, back down the road towards the centre of the village.

Bełżec is on the 17/E72 road just north of the Ukrainian border. The site of the camp is signposted in the south of the village. The rail service has been steadily reduced in recent years and there is currently one train a day to and from Zamość. In summer, and at certain other times, there is also a daily train to and from Warsaw and Lublin which bizarrely terminates at Bełżec. If coming from Lublin, a more flexible option may be to take a bus to Tomaszów Lubelski and catch a connecting bus from there.

KRAKÓW

Poland's ancient capital was chosen by the Germans to perform the same function for the *Generalgouvernement*, leaving one of the oldest and largest Jewish communities in the country especially vulnerable. Jews had first settled in Kraków in the thirteenth century, both within the royal city and in Kazimierz to the south, but rising Christian anti-Semitism culminated in their expulsion from the former in 1495. This, however, enabled the development of Kazimierz as a predominantly Jewish town which became a centre of learning and trade largely protected by the Polish kings. The city was a relatively benign environment for Jews during the partition era, especially as the semi-independent Free City of Kraków which existed for three decades after 1815. Thereafter, it was under Austrian rule, meaning that equal rights were achieved in the 1860s at which time Kazimierz officially became part Kraków. The Jewish population rapidly increased, growing to around 60,000 by 1939.

The Germans entered Kraków on 6 September and Frank's administration was established in October. This proximity to the heart of Nazi power in Poland had inevitably disastrous consequences. In addition to suffering the measures introduced across Frank's domain (including the creation of a *Judenrat* in November), Kraków's Jews were the first in the *Generalgouvernement* to be subjected to large-scale resettlement, the governor intending his capital to be the exemplar of the new Poland. Deportations to outlying towns and villages, and to the Lublin region, began in May 1940 and continued until March 1941 by which time an estimated 41,000 people had been expelled from the city. At this point, the 15,000 or so remaining Jews were forced into a ghetto. Perversely, in light of the expulsions, around 6,000 Jews from surrounding villages were added to its population in October 1941. After months of harassment, the first great *Aktion* took place in late May and early June 1942: 6,000 people were deported to Bełżec and several hundred murdered in the ghetto. Following a similar *Aktion* in October, the ghetto was finally liquidated in March 1943, the workers relocated to the newly established Płaszów camp south of the city, the remainder sent in trucks to Auschwitz. Kraków was officially *Judenfrei*.

A few thousand of the city's Jews survived the war although the modern community numbers only hundreds. However, the fall of Communism and the subsequent renewal of interest in Poland's Jewish past – helped by the global impact of *Schindler's List* – have brought a transformation of sorts. Kraków now vies with Prague as the leading destination for Jewish heritage travel in Europe, attracting Jews and Gentiles to its restored synagogues and cemeteries. It is thus slightly surprising that there are few prominent Holocaust memorials but Kraków does at least preserve and, indeed, celebrate traces of its Jewish history.

The ghetto

The ghetto was located in Podgórze on the south bank of the Vistula. Although many Jews lived here, the majority did not: the film footage of their doleful procession across the river has become one of the iconic images of the Holocaust. One of the most striking features of the ghetto is how small it was, only a fraction of the size of those in Warsaw, Łódź or even Białystok. Of course, it had a much smaller population as a result of the mass expulsions but, even so, 15,000 people were confined in an area which had previously accommodated little more than 3,000.

The northern ghetto gate was located on plac Bohaterów Getta (trams 9, 13, 24 and 34 to the stop of the same name) which, as plac Zgody, was the assembly point during the deportations. It is now dominated by a 2005 memorial consisting of 33 large sculpted chairs; further smaller chairs are set around the square. The intention is to represent, literally

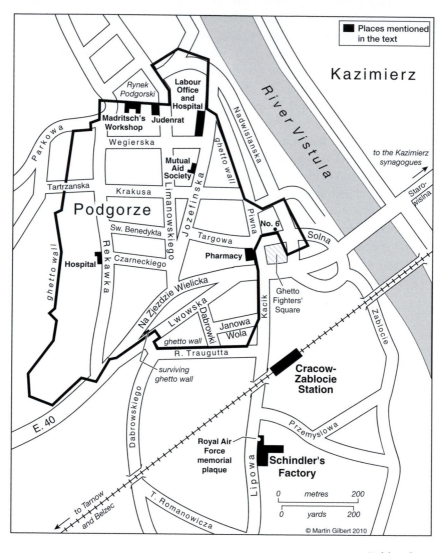

Kraków: ghetto

and metaphorically, furniture thrown out during the deportations. However, although the sculptures are impressive when illuminated at night, their meaning would be opaque without any prior knowledge. At the northern end of the square, a small pavilion bearing the dates 1941 and 1943 is intended to be a place for leaving candles although local drunks have clearly put it to other uses. A more concrete reminder of the square's history is a plaque at number 6 on the western side, marking the headquarters of the ŻOB, the ghetto underground. Unlike its Warsaw namesake, the resistance lacked the numbers and support to effectively resist in the ghetto but instead carried the attack to the Germans with raids in the 'Aryan' side of the city. On the south-western corner at number 18 is the former *Apteka pod Orłem* (Under the Eagle Pharmacy). Its owner Tadeusz Pankiewicz was the only Gentile living within the ghetto and his was the only pharmacy. He was awarded the title of Righteous by Yad Vashem for his efforts to assist the population, which included hiding prospective deportees, smuggling in food and, naturally, providing medications, often free of charge. Even apparently mundane products could mean the difference between life and death: in his memoirs, Pankiewicz recalled how people used hair dyes to disguise their identities. The pharmacy is now a small museum (Apr–Oct: Mon, 10.00–2.00; Tue–Sun, 9.30–5.00; Nov–Mar: Mon, 10.00–2.00; Tue–Thu & Sat, 9.00–4.00; Fri, 10.00–5.00; 5 zł; www.mhk.pl) addressing the history of the Holocaust in Kraków.

Józefińska, a block to the south, was the site of many of the ghetto's most important buildings. The rather grand number 18 housed the Jewish Mutual Aid Society, which provided essential charitable help to the population, whilst the salmon-coloured building at 14 was a hospital. Next door, 10/12 was occupied by the ghetto orphanage and the German-run Labour Office which determined the fate of inhabitants. Limanowskiego, the next street to the south, leads to Rynek Podgórski, the ghetto's western edge (the main gate was located at this junction). The large building stretching around this corner (Rynek Podgórski 1) was the headquarters of the *Judenrat*. Further along the square, number 3 housed a factory owned by the Viennese industrialist Julius Madritsch. Although less famous than his friend Oskar Schindler, Madritsch also contributed to saving lives by employing as many Jews as possible in his workshops which were designated as armaments factories and thus relatively protected. On the southern edge of the ghetto, Rękawka 26/30 (facing Czarnieckiego) housed the hospital for infectious diseases. Following Rękawka eastwards leads to a modern school (Gymnasium 35) at Limanowskiego 62. A section of the curiously aesthetic ghetto wall stands in the playground to the left. The other surviving piece of the wall is a short walk away at Lwówska 25/29.

North-east of the wall (up Traugutta, and then a right turn under the bridge at Zabłocie train station), Lipowa 4 is better known as Schindler's *Emalia* factory. By 1943, it was employing close to 1,000 Jews but the liquidation of the ghetto meant that they were relocated to Płaszów from where they had to march to the factory each day. Well aware of the dangers of the camp, not least of his supposed friend Amon Goeth, Schindler had them transferred to the comparative safety of barracks erected on Lipowa at his personal expense. It was the closure of the factory (ordered in August 1944) that prompted the famous list. After most of his workers were returned to Płaszów, Schindler found new premises in the Sudetenland and was able to get permission for many of them (and Madritsch's workers) to be sent to join him rather than to their intended destinations of Gross-Rosen and Auschwitz. Within days of the order to abandon the factory, a British Lancaster bomber crashed by it; a memorial plaque recalls the three members of the crew who died. After decades of continued industrial use, accompanied by creeping dilapidation, the factory itself is being converted into a museum, part of which will be devoted to Schindler (including his office and the staircase which featured so prominently in Spielberg's film). More controversially, much of the complex will become a museum of contemporary art and host cultural events. The project was due to open in late 2009.

Kazimierz

The location of the ghetto in Podgórze rather than the traditional Jewish quarter of Kazimierz reflected Hans Frank's desire that the historic city north of the Vistula not be 'contaminated' by the presence of Jews. This was rather ironic given that the same racist logic had made Kazimierz Jewish in the first place when Jews were expelled from the royal city four and half centuries earlier. Even after emancipation, Kazimierz remained the centre of community life. It largely survived the war unscathed, at least physically, making it the best preserved former Jewish quarter of any major city in central and eastern Europe. Neglected under Communism,

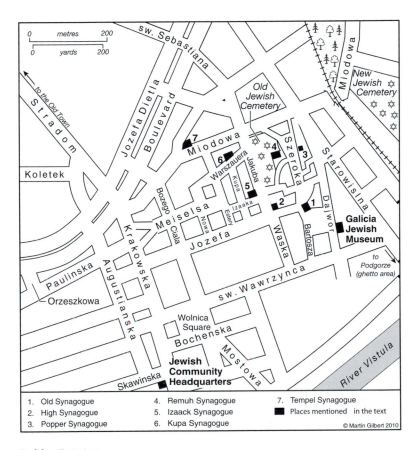

1. Old Synagogue	4. Remuh Synagogue	7. Tempel Synagogue
2. High Synagogue	5. Izaack Synagogue	■ Places mentioned in the text
3. Popper Synagogue	6. Kupa Synagogue	© Martin Gilbert 2010

Kraków: Kazimierz

Kazimierz has, since 1989, been revitalised both as a magnet for Kraków's bohemians and as a showcase of the Jewish culture which so graced the city until the Holocaust. Indeed, it is now one of Poland's major tourist attractions. This has not entirely been to everyone's taste, not least because it is essentially a Jewish quarter largely without Jews. Even so, Kazimierz is one of the few places in this part of Europe that manages to evoke some sense of its Jewish past, not least through its annual summer Festival of Jewish Culture (www.jewishfestival.pl).

The heart of the district is Szeroka, nominally a street but essentially a square, which is lined with 'Jewish-style' restaurants along with three synagogues. The Old Synagogue on the south of the square at number 24 is the oldest preserved such building in Poland, founded in the fifteenth century and remodelled in the sixteenth. It now houses the Judaica branch of the city museum (Apr–Oct: Mon, 10.00–2.00; Tue–Sun, 9.00–5.00; Nov–Mar: Mon, 10.00–2.00; Wed–Thu & Sat–Sun, 9.00–4.00; Fri, 10.00–5.00; 8 zł (free on Mon); www.mhk.pl). A memorial stone outside commemorates 30 Poles killed at the site in October 1943. The former Popper Synagogue at 16 is now an art gallery whilst the tiny Remuh Synagogue (Mon–Fri, 9.00–6.00; 5 zł) is on the western side at 40. The adjacent old cemetery contains a striking 'wailing wall' Holocaust memorial of the type popular in Poland, made of fragments of tombstones damaged by the Nazis. There is a further memorial at the southern end of the garden (itself enclosed by a fence whose rails are shaped as menorahs) at the top of Szeroka.

From the north-eastern corner of the square, past a former *mikvah* at Szeroka 6, one can walk along Miodowa under the railway bridge to the new cemetery, opened in 1800. To the right of its entrance is an unusual Holocaust memorial, a squat marble block covered in plaques and fragments of tombstones which commemorate individuals as well as the community. Located two blocks to the south, recently renovated Przemyska 3 was a former Jewish student hall of residence, attested to by the Polish and Hebrew lettering above its doorway; the Germans turned it into an army brothel. Back across Starowiślna, Dajwór 18 is home to the Galicia Jewish Museum (summer: daily, 9.00–7.00; winter: daily, 10.00–6.00; 12 zł; www.galiciajewishmuseum.org). Opened in 2004, it is not an orthodox museum of Jewish history but rather an exhibition of photographs by its late British founder Chris Schwarz of Jewish and Holocaust sites in Polish Galicia.

Back by the Old Synagogue, Józefa runs west of Szeroka through the centre of Kazimierz. A former prayer house at 42 is marked by Stars of David and Hebrew lettering whilst number 38 is the former Wysoka (High) Synagogue, so named because the prayer room was upstairs, a result of the building's proximity to the Christian quarter of Kazimierz when it was constructed in the sixteenth century. Badly damaged in the war, it was renovated as an art restoration workshop in the 1960s, in the process altering the interior. It is now open for temporary exhibitions, traces of original frescoes surviving on the walls (daily, 9.00–7.00; 9 zł), and also houses an excellent bookshop. Fragments of wall decorations also survive in the Izaak Synagogue (Sun–Fri, 9.00–7.00; donation) at Kupa 18. Another restored synagogue, the Kupa, is up the road at Warszauera 8 although entered from the other side (Miodowa 27; Sun–Fri, 9.00–6.00; free).

The Tempel Synagogue at Miodowa 24 has a magnificently restored gilded interior (Sun–Fri, 9.00–6.00; 5 zł). Podbrzezie around the corner was a street of schools, two of which are marked by plaques: at number 6 (honouring Zygmunt Aleksandrowicz, founder of the crafts school for Jewish orphans which occupied the building) and on the corner with Brzozowa (to a former Hebrew secondary school). There is a former prayer house in the yard of Brzozowa 6, usually accessible through the front door (there is also a plaque on the exterior wall). Within the vicinity, Dietla 64 was the home of the Jewish Orphans' Institute whilst a relief plaque at Joselwicza 5 honours Mordechai Gebirtig, a famed Yiddish poet and songwriter murdered in the ghetto *Aktion* of June 1942.

From the Tempel Synagogue, Estery leads to plac Nowy, dominated by its central rotunda which was a ritual slaughterhouse. Estery 12 on the square's eastern side was a Hassidic prayer house. Another former prayer house on the western side, at Meiselsa 17, is now the Jewish Cultural Centre, a venue for exhibitions and performances (there is also an antique shop in its basement). Meiselsa 18, on the next corner, was also a prayer house as was Bocheńska 4 three blocks to the south. Bocheńska 7 was a Jewish theatre.

The area west of Krakowska was less Jewish but the corner building at Krakowska 41/Skawińska 2 was and still is the community headquarters. A plaque on the latter side pays tribute to the ŻOB and its commander Aharon Liebeskind (codenamed Dolek) who was killed in the fighting which followed the raid on the *Cyganeria* café (see below). Skawińska

8 was a Jewish hospital whilst św. Stanisława 10 to the north-west was the Beth Jacob Seminary where girls from Orthodox families studied the Torah, marked by a large plaque. Immediately after the invasion, the school accommodated Jewish refugees.

Elsewhere

The Wawel castle complex, former home of the Polish kings, was the seat of Hans Frank and the *Generalgouvernement*. Close to the northern foot of the hill, the 1920s apartment block at Straszewskiego 7 was Schindler's home.

North of the Rynek, Szpitalna 38 housed the *Cyganeria* café which was popular with Wehrmacht and SS officers. It was attacked by a ŻOB unit on the night of 22 December 1942, killing seven Germans although the reprisals on the group were severe. There is a memorial plaque on the wall whose reference to the Communist *Armia Ludowa* as co-conspirators betrays its origins (the date is also wrong). Szpitalna 24 was home to a prayer house, now an Orthodox church.

PŁASZÓW

Płaszów was a forced labour camp established in Kraków's southern suburbs in 1942 on the site of two Jewish cemeteries which were flattened by workers brought from the ghetto. The camp was originally intended to accommodate up to 4,000 mainly Jewish prisoners but rapidly expanded with the arrival of around 8,000 Jews after the liquidation of the Kraków ghetto in March 1943. A separate section was designated for Polish prisoners in July of the same year and the camp also held Roma. The Polish contingent increased to around 10,000 following the 1944 Warsaw uprising whilst the Jewish numbers were swelled by transports from smaller ghettos and from Hungary; at its peak in 1944, by which time Płaszów had been designated a concentration camp, it held close to 25,000 inmates. Conditions were brutal, especially under Amon Goeth (February 1943 to September 1944), its most notorious commandant, whose reign of indiscriminate beatings and shootings was depicted in *Schindler's List*. In addition, 1,400 inmates were deported to Auschwitz in May 1944 and gassed on arrival. Construction actually began on gas chambers within Płaszów itself but the proximity of Auschwitz led to it being deemed unnecessary. Nonetheless, the camp became a site of

Płaszów (Photograph by the author)

mass shootings of Jews and Poles. Remaining prisoners were evacuated to Auschwitz and camps in the Reich over the winter of 1944–45, the last 180 departing on 14 January 1945, one day before the liberation. Goeth was executed after being convicted by a Polish court in 1946.

Virtually nothing of the camp survives and most of its area is overgrown and notoriously difficult to navigate. It is criss-crossed by unsignposted paths making it easy to get lost. The routes suggested here involve some doubling back but are hopefully the easiest to follow. The site is skirted on its eastern side by Jerozolimska and its continuation Heltmana which run through what was the SS area of the camp; indeed this street was called SS-Straße. Although most of the buildings have been replaced by post-war blocks, two serve as points of orientation. Goeth's squat villa is at Heltmana 22 whilst down the hill at the junction of Jerozolimska and Abrahama (the latter in reality no more than an unmarked dirt track which becomes a path) is the more imposing 'Grey House' which housed other SS officers and had a torture chamber in its basement. A sign opposite advises visitors that they are entering the territory of the camp (meaning the prisoners' section) and exhorts them to show respect. Abrahama roughly follows the route of the main camp road from the Grey House. On the right is a 1984 memorial to 13 Poles murdered in September 1939. A paved path behind leads to a new memorial stone in Hebrew, beyond which lies a large pile of rubble, remnants of the new Jewish cemetery's monumental pre-burial hall, part of which was used as a morgue in the camp. The building was partially destroyed by the Germans and the remainder demolished after the war. A few fragments of tombs survive further up the hill. These can be reached by following a path which runs diagonally uphill from the Hebrew memorial. A more circuitous but perhaps easier to understand alternative is to return to Jerozolimska and head north to the point where the road curves to the right. At this exact point, there is a path on the left of the road next to another sign and a board with a map of the camp (a curious location for the only such information panel in the whole of Płaszów). Following this path through the undergrowth, past more ruins of the pre-burial hall in a small clearing on the left, and then uphill for a couple of hundred metres, one reaches a junction with the path from the Hebrew memorial. Turn right and the bases of tombs will soon appear on the left. There is only one surviving stone (Chaim Jacob Abrahamer, died 25 May 1932), about 65 metres after the junction, to the left of the path.

Abrahama continues westward from the Polish and Hebrew memorials through the centre of the camp, past limestone quarries on the left and the site of the *Appellplatz* on the right. It is possible to reach the main memorial area from here but one is far less likely to get lost by returning to the Grey House and then going up the hill past Goeth's villa. By Heltmana 40B is a signposted and paved turning to the memorial area. This passes a mass grave, marked by a cross, before reaching Hujowa Gorka, the remnants of an old Austrian fortification on the western edge of the camp where mass executions took place (around 8,000 in total); the bodies were exhumed and burnt in 1944. The site is dominated by a striking Communist memorial on the ridge of the fortifications. More modest are the two specifically Jewish memorials on the approach to the ridge, dedicated to all Polish and Hungarian Jews who passed through Płaszów and to Hungarian Jewish women held here in 1944 before being sent onto Auschwitz.

The easiest way to get to the camp without getting lost is to take trams 3, 6, 9, 13, 23, 24 or 34 to the Dworcowa stop. Turn right into the road which runs uphill between McDonald's and the Shell garage and head up the steps between Wielicka 81 and 83. Goeth's villa is a couple of houses to the left on the opposite side of the road.

AUSCHWITZ-BIRKENAU

The innocuous origins of Auschwitz offered no hint of the infamy to which it has justly been condemned. Shortly before the First World War, the Austrian authorities began building barracks on the edge of the Silesian town of Oświęcim as accommodation for seasonal workers migrating to Germany. However, construction was only completed in 1918 meaning that the complex passed into the hands of the newly independent Poland which converted it into an army base (it also temporarily housed Polish refugees from territory granted to Czechoslovakia). On Himmler's orders, the site was adapted for use as a concentration camp in the late spring of 1940 with Rudolf Höss as its commandant. For the first year of Auschwitz's existence, almost all of its inmates were Polish political prisoners, Jews amongst them. In this sense, it differed little from the concentration camps in Germany (the Auschwitz region was, in fact, technically within the Reich during the occupation) although the fact that the prisoners were Poles meant that their treatment was even more atrocious.

273

It was only in 1941 that Auschwitz began to acquire a distinctive character and even then Jewish policy was not the initial driving force. Following an inspection in March, Himmler decreed an expansion of the existing camp accompanied by two further developments. Auschwitz would supply slave labour to the I.G. Farben company to enable the construction of a massive synthetic rubber (Buna) plant whilst an enormous new camp, capable of accommodating 100,000 people, would be created in the village of Brzezinka (Birkenau in German). This latter site, Auschwitz II, would hold Soviet prisoners of war in the coming conflict. In fact, construction of Birkenau did not begin until October, by which time the war in the east was well underway. Indeed, the building was largely carried out by 15,000 POWs who had already been placed in the main camp (now Auschwitz I); most did not survive the winter. Work on the Buna complex began earlier, in April 1941, and was never completed, such was the scale of the project. Those who laboured there were accommodated in another camp (Auschwitz III) in the abandoned village of Monowice from late 1942. By this stage, the whole Polish population of Oświęcim and the surrounding area, designated the camp's 'development zone', had been expelled to make way for the growth of the Auschwitz empire.

It is not entirely clear when the decision was taken to make Auschwitz part of the Nazi extermination machinery but the first experiments with Zyklon B were conducted in late summer 1941, primarily on Soviet POWs. The first gas chamber was created in the main camp in the autumn, before the establishment of Chełmno or the *Aktion Reinhard* camps. However, Auschwitz's role in the murder of the Polish Jews was peripheral at this stage – around 300,000 were sent there but mainly in 1943–44 when the other death camps had already closed or were being wound down. Instead, it was the expansion of the Holocaust to seek the murder of all European Jews that was to give Auschwitz its pre-eminent notoriety, a reflection of its size and position at the heart of the continent's rail network. On 15 February 1942, Jews from Bytom (then Beuthen in Germany) became the first transport to be gassed. This took place in the main camp but the construction of two gas chambers in the forest near Birkenau meant that most subsequent murders occurred there. In addition to Jews from the Reich, those from Slovakia, France, Belgium and the Netherlands were deported to their deaths in 1942. Spring 1943 saw the creation of four large crematoria, each containing bigger gas chambers, which replaced the existing killing facilities. This was part of a wider expansion of Auschwitz II which reflected its dual nature. Unlike the other death camps, where all but a handful of deportees were murdered on arrival, Birkenau was also a slave labour camp. Selections were performed for each new transport with those the SS considered fit for work inducted into the camp although few survived beyond six months. As a result, both the camp population and the number murdered were greater in 1943 when Birkenau received transports from Greece and Italy (both continuing into 1944) as well as from the countries previously mentioned. However, the most horrendous operation in the camp's history was the destruction of the Jews of Hungary when more than 400,000 people were murdered in two months in the late spring and early summer of 1944.

Plans for even further expansion of the complex were suspended as a result of the advance of the Red Army in the summer of 1944. This development had also brought the capture of Majdanek, the revelation of whose horrors had destroyed whatever international reputation Germany still had. Not wishing for a repeat, the SS began eliminating the evidence of their crimes. Realising that their days were numbered, members of the *Sonderkommando* revolted in October 1944, setting Crematorium IV on fire and killing two SS men in Crematorium II. Some were able to escape to the woods but only one of the rebels survived; he later died in Ebensee. The remaining crematoria were dismantled in November and December, their technical installations sent to Gross-Rosen and their brick structures blown up. During the autumn, prisoners had begun to be sent to camps such as Gross-Rosen and Bergen-Belsen by rail. This was merely a prelude to horrendous death marches: most of the 58,000 prisoners forced westward in January 1945 are believed to have died. When the Red Army arrived on 27 January 1945 (now the UN's International Holocaust Remembrance Day), 7,650 prisoners whom the SS had not had the time to kill were liberated. The haste of the Germans' departure also meant that much of the camp system remained physically intact.

Like Majdanek, Auschwitz was used by the Soviets immediately after the war but in 1947 it was decided to turn it into a museum. Almost nowhere else, however, has memorialisation of the Holocaust been more controversial. This was for decades partly a question of numbers. A Soviet investigation inflated the number who died – as if it needed inflating – to produce a figure of 4 million people. This sum was displayed prominently around the site (some references have only been removed in the last five years) and is still sometimes encountered in public discourse. The real figure will never truly be known – not least because the Gestapo destroyed many records in the summer of 1944 – but that used by the modern museum authorities and generally accepted by historians is somewhat above 1.1 million: around 1 million Jews, 75,000 non-Jewish Poles, 21,000 Sinti and Roma and 15,000 Soviet POWs. Although the early Communist investigators seem to have reached the 4 million total in good faith (making calculations based on the capacity of the crematoria), it clearly came to serve a political agenda. There has never been much doubt that between 1 and 1.5 million Jews died at Auschwitz so the Communist figure clearly implied that the majority of victims were Poles and Russians, thereby minimising the specificity of Jewish suffering and lending legitimacy to the Communists as the saviours of the Slavic peoples from the Fascist butchers. This was also the tone of the museum displays which paid little heed to the Jewish experience before the collapse of Communism. Even since 1989, Auschwitz has had the power to divide, being the supreme symbol for both Jews and Poles of their respective wartime agonies. This dichotomy was reflected in a series of unfortunate controversies dating back to John Paul II's visit to the site in 1979 which periodically saw Catholic nationalists planting crosses both near to the main camp and at Birkenau. These disputes have abated in recent years, enabling a more honest and suitably respectful approach to the tragedy of Auschwitz.

Auschwitz main camp

When the memorial was created in 1947, the decision was taken to concentrate it in the main camp which is now the most visited museum in Poland (daily: Dec–Feb, 8.00–3.00; Mar, Nov, 8.00–4.00; Apr, Oct, 8.00–5.00; May, Sept, 8.00–6.00; June–Aug, 8.00–7.00; free; www. auschwitz.org.pl). The exhibits are certainly powerful and moving although some visitors depart with mixed feelings. This is largely because the camp is such a major tourist attraction that it is often hardly a place of contemplation. In an effort to improve the situation, a system was introduced in 2008 whereby members of tour groups listen to their guides on headphones thus reducing the noise.

The museum's Communist origins were long a further cause of unease. Along with the inflated figure of 4 million dead, the most pernicious

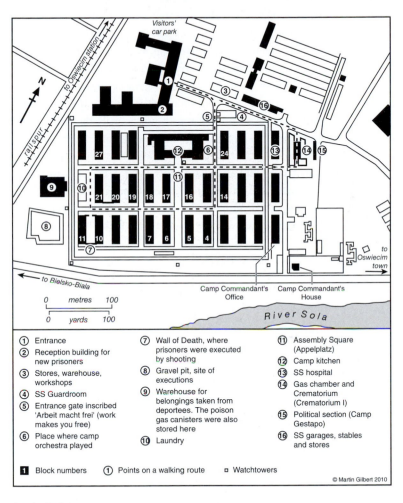

Visitors' car park

to Oswiecim station

rail spur

N

to Bielsko-Biala

Camp Commandant's Office

Camp Commandant's House

to Oswiecim town

River Sola

| 0 | metres | 100 |
| 0 | yards | 100 |

① Entrance

② Reception building for new prisoners

③ Stores, warehouse, workshops

④ SS Guardroom

⑤ Entrance gate inscribed 'Arbeit macht frei' (work makes you free)

⑥ Place where camp orchestra played

⑦ Wall of Death, where prisoners were executed by shooting

⑧ Gravel pit, site of executions

⑨ Warehouse for belongings taken from deportees. The poison gas canisters were also stored here

⑩ Laundry

⑪ Assembly Square (Appelplatz)

⑫ Camp kitchen

⑬ SS hospital

⑭ Gas chamber and Crematorium (Crematorium I)

⑮ Political section (Camp Gestapo)

⑯ SS garages, stables and stores

1 Block numbers　　① Points on a walking route　　▫ Watchtowers

© Martin Gilbert 2010

Auschwitz I

element was the establishment of exhibitions for different nationalities, mostly from the Eastern Bloc, relegating Jews to the status of one of many groups who suffered in Auschwitz. Thankfully, these old displays have mostly been swept away since the late 1990s to be replaced by often excellent new exhibitions. However, one legacy of the Communist museum concept which remains is the fact that only a section of the camp is included within the memorial area. Heading, as most visitors do, down Leszczyńskiej from the station, there are SS barracks constructed in the 1942–44 expansion (now used as housing and army barracks) to the left, a block before the car park; no mention of this is made in the museum. The unremarkable entrance to the car park was actually the site of the main camp gate from 1942 onwards whilst the visitors' centre, often assumed to be post-war, was the reception area for new prisoners. Thus, when visitors exit this building, passing surviving SS barracks to their left (which are marked as such), and reach the infamous '*Arbeit macht frei*' gate, they are not, as most assume, at the entrance to the camp. To be fair, it did have this role in Auschwitz's early history but the Holocaust-era expansion relegated it to an inner barrier whilst, of course, very few of the Jews sent to Birkenau ever saw it.

The main route from the gate passes the point where the camp orchestra played, setting a tempo for the prisoners as they departed for work, and leads down to the easternmost group of barracks. These blocks form the principal exhibition, intended to give an overview of the camp's history, beginning with Block 4 (which has a little-noticed plaque to Austrian victims to its left). The block's theme (*Extermination*) is self-explanatory and has been updated to give more prominence to the fact that most of those murdered were Jewish. The display that leaves the greatest impact on most visitors is that of the masses of human hair shaved from female prisoners in room 5, the liberation preventing it from joining the huge amounts already shipped to the Reich for use in mattresses and clothing. Chemical analysis by Kraków University found traces of prussic acid, the core element of Zyklon B, in the hair; during the murder of the Hungarian Jews, it appears that victims were shaved after they were killed. The theme continues in Block 5 whose rooms contain similarly enormous collections of artefacts stolen from the dead, including glasses, prayer shawls, suitcases, shoes and even prosthetic limbs.

Block 6 covers the everyday life and suffering of inmates, the focus very much on political prisoners. The photographs lining the walls are mostly of Poles – the Germans had little need to photograph the majority of Jews arriving in Birkenau. The experiences of the politicals are vividly portrayed in sketches by Mieczysław Kościelnak in room 5. Block 7 provides more material evidence of living conditions, with examples (some reconstructions) of bunks, toilets and washrooms. Perhaps the most revealing is the relative comfort of a *kapo*'s cell.

Block 10 (closed) was the centre of medical experiments. In addition to Mengele's horrific work on twins, the block also hosted the appalling Carl Clauberg who performed mass sterilisation on Jewish and Roma women, often by injecting acid into their wombs. The 'death yard' between Blocks 10 and 11 was the site of executions (mainly of Poles), now marked by memorials. Block 11, the 'death block' where prisoners were held prior to execution, now houses exhibitions devoted to their fate. The basement of the building was where the fateful first experiments with Zyklon B were conducted in August and September 1941 on 600 Soviet POWs and 250 sick prisoners, mostly Polish Jews. The rooms upstairs cover resistance in the camp, including the revolt of the Birkenau *Sonderkommando*.

The next row of blocks, sadly bypassed by many visitors, are those dedicated to different nations along with Block 27 (*Jews*), a former clothes storehouse, at the start of the opposite row. The exhibit here was created in 1968 and revamped a decade later, leaving it as a rare relic of the Communist era. The display is almost entirely visual, made up of photographs of the Holocaust from across Europe and of Jewish partisans. Whilst this is striking to some, the rather dated and wordless presentation contrasts unfavourably with the new exhibitions created in the other blocks. The old displays, with their mendacious references to 'victims of Fascism' and excessive preoccupation with Communist prisoners, were something of a disgrace but their replacements are historically appropriate both in the countries covered and in the fact that the main focus is Jewish suffering. Although the ground floor section on Italy in Block 21 (a former hospital barrack) is rather disappointing, that on the Netherlands upstairs is a beautifully presented portrayal of the fate of Dutch Jews. Similarly honoured are the Jews of France and Belgium (Block 20 – also a hospital barrack), Hungary (18) and the Czech and Slovak Republics (16). In fact, the only unchanged display apart from Block 27 is that in Block 17 for Austria, significantly a non-Communist country (the Yugoslav section that occupied its top floor has now closed).

In the light of the intellectual honesty that the alterations have given to the site, it is surprising that there are still some omissions, perhaps most obviously of Polish Jews; Block 15 is mainly a general history of Poland in World War II with little on the fate of either Jewish or Gentile Poles in Auschwitz. Another obvious absence, for the moment at least, is that of Soviet POWs: the original USSR exhibit in Block 14 is currently being replaced. One very glaring oversight in the original museum has been rectified by the outstanding *Extermination of European Roma* in Block 13, created by Heidelberg's Sinti and Roma Documentation Centre.

The route then leads out of the main prisoner area, past the SS hospital on the left, to the site of the Gestapo HQ, now occupied by the gallows from which Höss was hanged in 1947. Next to it is the first crematorium and gas chamber, in the former mortuary which was converted in late 1941. This is significantly reconstructed, the Germans having destroyed the original ovens, chimney and some of the walls. In the original museum concept, this represented the symbolic ending of the route and some visitors still leave believing this is 'where the Holocaust happened'. Appalling though what occurred here was – and this small gas chamber remained in use until mid-1943 – that grim appellation belongs, insofar as it can belong to any one place, two miles away.

Almost all visitors except those on tour buses come via Oświęcim train station from where buses 2 and 3 run to the camp (Muzeum stop). There are also always rather rapacious taxi drivers.

Birkenau

The extermination camp receives only a fraction of the visitors to Auschwitz I yet almost all who make the journey find it a far more powerful experience (same hours as the main camp). This is due not only to the absence of crowds or even to the knowledge of what happened here; the sheer size and desolation of the place, mostly forests of chimneys (the only brick elements of most barracks), are overwhelming. With one exception, there are no exhibitions, just the odd information board, often bearing the famous photographs of the transport from Beregszász in Hungary in May 1944 taken by an SS man for unknown reasons. On arrival, it is worth ascending the stairs to the top of the gate tower to truly appreciate the scale of Birkenau, a striking contrast to the small *Aktion Reinhard* camps and seemingly more appropriate for the enormity of the crime.

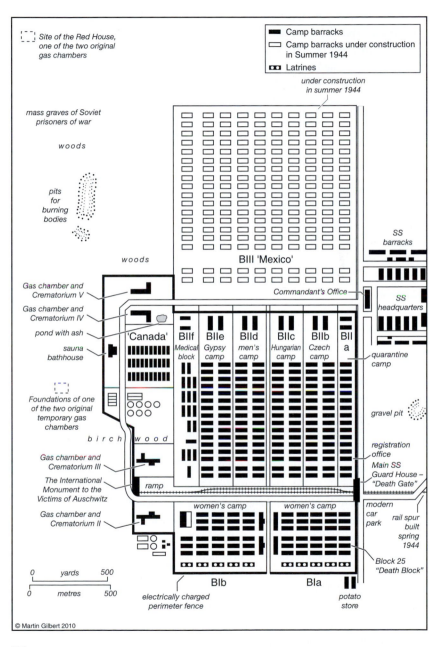

Site of the Red House, one of the two original gas chambers

■ Camp barracks
□ Camp barracks under construction in Summer 1944
▭ Latrines

under construction in summer 1944

mass graves of Soviet prisoners of war

woods

pits for burning bodies

woods

BIII 'Mexico'

SS barracks

Gas chamber and Crematorium V

Gas chamber and Crematorium IV

pond with ash

sauna bathhouse

Foundations of one of the two original temporary gas chambers

b i r c h   w o o d

Gas chamber and Crematorium III

The International Monument to the Victims of Auschwitz

Gas chamber and Crematorium II

Commandant's Office

'Canada'

BIIf
Medical block

BIIe
Gypsy camp

BIId
men's camp

BIIc
Hungarian camp

BIIb
Czech camp

BII a

SS headquarters

quarantine camp

gravel pit

registration office
Main SS Guard House – "Death Gate"

ramp

women's camp

women's camp

modern car park

rail spur built spring 1944

Block 25 "Death Block"

BIb

BIa

0   yards   500
0   metres   500

electrically charged perimeter fence

potato store

© Martin Gilbert 2010

Birkenau

The railway spur runs through the gate to the selection ramp where the tracks separate. This is the iconic image of the Holocaust but for most of Birkenau's history Jews were actually unloaded a kilometre away and driven to the camp on foot (this earlier ramp, reconstructed in the 1990s, can be reached by heading back up the approach road to Birkenau and taking the first path to the right). The spur into the camp was constructed in early 1944 in readiness for the arrival of the Hungarians: the new ramp then became the site of scenes of the utmost horror as the disorientated Jews found themselves pulled off the trains and at the mercy of Mengele. To the right of the railway are the ruins of Birkenau II (BII), the massive 1942–43 extension to the camp, which principally housed male prisoners. The barracks in the row nearest the gate (BIIa) survive, several of them open; this was the quarantine zone where new prisoners were held. The only other surviving barrack of BII is in the next field (BIIb) which became the 'family camp' in 1943–44 for 10,000 Jews brought from Theresienstadt. Its name derived from the fact that, although men and women were held in separate barracks, the sexes were allowed to mix freely. They were also not assigned to labour and allowed to communicate with relatives still in Terezín. All of this was a ruse, of course, lest the Red Cross decide to inspect Birkenau as well as the Czech ghetto. When it became clear that this would not happen, everyone in the family camp was murdered.

Opposite the ramp is the entrance to the original camp (BI) which became the women's camp after the expansion. Most of the barracks on the southern side of each section are intact whilst the washrooms and toilet blocks run along the southernmost edge. In the eastern section (BIa) there is a weathered memorial to 'French patriots' next to the remains of Block 9. Block 25 near the fence was the 'death block' where exhausted or sick female prisoners who had failed the regular selections were held before being led to the gas chambers. Alongside are the remains of Block 31 where more than 200 Jewish children used in Mengele's 'experiments' were held in 1944. In section BIb, Block 1 housed the penal company – those prisoners who had broken camp rules and were thus selected for the hardest work – in the days when this was the men's camp. At that same time, Block 6 was the isolation barrack for sick prisoners prior to being sent to the gas chambers. When it was full, new arrivals were dumped in the yard outside.

From BIb, a path leads past one of the camp's two large sewage plants (another reflection of Birkenau's growth) to the looming presence of

Birkenau (Photograph by the author)

ruined Crematorium II, much as the Germans left it in 1945. As at all four of the crematoria, an information panel provides a detailed plan of the extermination facilities. Stones in Polish, English, Hebrew and Yiddish mark the pond alongside (one of the places where ashes were thrown), as they do at the other crematoria. Crematorium III, a mirror image of II, stands on the other side of the International Monument to the Victims of Auschwitz (previously to the Victims of Fascism), a piece of Communist abstraction. At least the panels at its base now give a more correct death toll and acknowledge that most victims were Jews.

Beyond the other sewage plant, the path passes the foundations of 'Canada' where the possessions of the murdered and the new prisoners were sorted for dispatch to Germany (the nickname derived from the perception of Canada as a rich country). A small glass canopy over the ruins of Block 5 covers a pile of cutlery and other items. Opposite is the 'sauna' where new arrivals who passed the selection were brought. This has now been turned into the only exhibition building in Birkenau. There was some unease when the project was first announced but the result is sensitive and effective. Glass flooring traces the path taken by prisoners, from the reception room, along the corridor past the chambers where clothes were disinfected with steam, to the rooms where they were shaved, showered and then made to wait (often for hours). The final room, where they received their uniform and clogs, houses a beautiful display of photographs of Jewish families, mostly from the cities of Będzin and Sosnowiec.

Behind the sauna, a path leads through the fence to the site of one of Birkenau's original two gas chambers created in 1942 (this can also be reached from Crematorium III by continuing through the trees after the sewage plant rather than turning to the sauna). Although it was replaced by the new crematoria in 1943, the building remained standing and was put back into use in 1944 during the Hungarian deportations. Only its foundations survive now, opposite those of the undressing barracks. Ashes were buried in the field behind, again marked by memorial stones.

The path from the front of the sauna leads to Crematoria IV and V, again mirror images but with a different design to II and III. Little survives of IV which was badly damaged in the *Sonderkommando* revolt and subsequently dismantled. By V are three photographs of the open-air cremation of bodies at this precise spot, secretly taken by a member of the *Sonderkommando* in August 1944. In the birch trees beyond the large pond by IV (where ashes were thrown), heartbreaking photographs show members of the Beregszász transport waiting whilst the gas chambers were readied, the huts of Canada clearly visible behind them.

From here one can walk the road alongside BII back towards the camp's eastern perimeter. On the opposite side of the ditch, fence posts are all that remain of 'Mexico' (BIII), a planned extension of Birkenau which would have effectively doubled its size. Construction began in the summer of 1944 but was never completed due to the Soviet advance. The former command building is at the top of the road with former SS barracks behind it.

There are further elements of Birkenau beyond the main complex although they are more difficult to get to and seldom visited. The mass grave of Soviet POWs who lost their lives in 1941–42 is marked by simple memorials in a large fenced field. In the woods behind, pyres cremated the bodies of Jews murdered in Birkenau's first gas chamber. The nearby 'Red House' was a converted peasant's cottage which operated until early 1943 at which point it was completely demolished – not even the foundations survive. Its site is now a field, located slightly further east along the road from the mass grave, holding three memorial stones. The quickest way to reach these locations from within the camp is to continue along the path by the other temporary gas chamber, rather than returning to the sauna, through the gate out of the camp complex. Turn right and follow the road alongside the fence. After a few minutes, it skirts a separately fenced off field – this is the mass grave. Continue to the end of the field where the memorials are visible and accessible through a rather difficult to open gate next to the padlocked main gate. The Red House is slightly further along the road on the left, marked by a large information board. From here one can walk back to the sauna or continue along the road, skirting Mexico, to the command building.

There are hourly shuttle buses between the two camps; one can otherwise take the ubiquitous taxis either from the main camp or the train station.

Oświęcim

Until the war, Auschwitz/Oświęcim was better known by its Yiddish name Oshpitsin, a reflection of the fact that it was a largely Jewish town. This history is recalled in the Auschwitz Jewish Centre (Sun–Fri, 8.30–8.00 (until 6.00, Nov–Feb); free; www.ajcf.org), a museum and education centre on plac Ks. Jana Skarbka. The square, used in round-ups in 1941, is named after the local priest Jan Skarbek who was seen as a friend of the Jewish community and was himself imprisoned by the Gestapo. In 1945, he helped to care for liberated Auschwitz inmates in the local Red Cross hospital. The Centre adjoins the sole surviving synagogue. On the other side of Dąbrowskiego, Berka Joselewicza was pre-war Żydowska (Jewish Street), some of whose old buildings survive. An information board stands on the site of the Great Synagogue, destroyed by the Nazis in November 1939. Excavations in 2004 uncovered ritual items which are now on display in the Jewish Centre. Both sites are a short walk from the Miasto stop, served by several buses from the train station. Further along Dąbrowskiego, by its junction with Wysokie Brzegi, is the town's Jewish cemetery (Cmentarz stop, many bus services).

Significantly further to the east, a huge area is given over to the Synthos chemical company in Monowice, which occupies the site of the I.G. Farben Buna plant and its related facilities. Access is restricted although the massive factory chimneys are visible from miles around. Auschwitz III, whose inmates included Primo Levi and Elie Wiesel, was to the south-east, roughly covering the area now skirted by Bartosza Głowackiego, south of Fabryczna, but nothing survives.

ŁÓDŹ

Poland's second largest city was home to its second largest Jewish community and what proved to be the longest lasting and most controversial of all of the ghettos established by the Nazis. Łódź was essentially a product of the Industrial Revolution, its population growing from less than 3,000 in the 1820s to 665,000 by 1939. The rise of the 'Polish Manchester' was greatly facilitated by Jewish capital and labour with the result that Jews formed a third of the population with some 223,000 people on the eve of the war.

The Germans captured the city on 8 September 1939 and, after some initial hesitation, included it in the *Warthegau* in November. Even before this official incorporation into the Reich, the Jewish population had been subjected to violence and theft but the terror intensified from November, the most immediate expression being the destruction of synagogues. In the longer term, the Nazi authorities aimed for the complete expulsion of Jews from the city and some 60,000 people did indeed leave by spring 1940, some by choice, most involuntarily deported to the *Generalgouvernement* (as also were tens of thousands of Poles in line with Greiser's aim of rapid Germanisation). It was in this context that a secret memorandum in December 1939 provided for the creation of a ghetto as a holding centre during the deportations which were intended to be completed by October 1940 (ironically, Łódź was to be the last rather than first Polish city to become *Judenfrei*). The public order for the creation of a 'Jewish quarter' was issued in February 1940, forcing tens of thousands of people to relocate to a working class suburb north of the city centre. The area was sealed off at the end of April with approximately 164,000 people crammed into what was now officially the Litzmannstadt Ghetto, the city having been renamed after a First World War general a few weeks earlier.

Although the Germans naturally had the ultimate control, a considerable degree of authority, more so than in any other ghetto, was delegated to Chaim Rumkowski, the most controversial Jewish figure of the Holocaust. 'King Chaim' was a former businessman, orphanage director and Zionist activist chosen by the Germans, for reasons which are less than clear, as the chair of the *Ältestenrat* in October 1939. All of its members apart from Rumkowski were then arrested a month later (most were murdered); their replacements naturally proved reluctant to defy either the Germans or the chairman who officially became the Eldest of the Jews even before the ghetto was created. To his enemies, who included a significant section of the ghetto population, he was a Jewish quisling; to his defenders, many of them survivors, he saved Jewish lives however flawed his methods might have been. Rumkowski's basic philosophy – that a productive ghetto would become indispensable to the Germans – was little different from that of many other ghetto leaders whilst he deserves credit for the extensive system of social and economic regulation which ensured that Łódź largely avoided the extremes of wealth and poverty that characterised Warsaw. More contentious, however, was his increasingly autocratic style which saw him interfere in all areas of public life and even enlist the Germans against his enemies. When leftist parties organised strikes against both cuts in food rations and his leadership in 1940–41, Rumkowski brought in the German police to assist his Jewish forces in the brutal suppression of the unrest. There is also evidence that he deliberately selected known opponents for deportation. This relates to the most contentious issue of all: Rumkowski's cooperation with the Nazi *Aktionen*. He came to believe that the only way to save the ghetto as a whole was to give in to German demands in the short term; he was thus prepared to draw up deportation lists and to allow the Jewish police to be used in the round-ups. His hope appears to have been that the remainder of the ghetto would either be left alone or would at least survive until the arrival of the Red Army.

Although more than 7,000 men had been sent to forced labour projects from December 1940, the first really major population transfer in the ghetto was actually inwards: in October 1941, transports began to arrive which would eventually bring almost 20,000 Jews from the Reich. A further 18,500 came from smaller communities in the *Warthegau*, beginning in December 1941 on the very day that the Chełmno extermination camp commenced operations. The influx thus presaged the start of the deportations, the first victims being 5,000 Roma from Burgenland in Austria who had been brought to a specially isolated section of the ghetto in November 1941 and were sent to

Chełmno in January 1942. They were immediately followed by Jews with three waves of transports in January, February–March and May, the latter almost entirely consisting of the Reich Jews. By mid-May 1942, 57,064 Jews from the ghetto had been murdered at the death camp. Worse was to come in September during the *Gehsperre* (curfew): in this *Aktion*, the Germans entered the ghetto and combed it for those less fit to work. They had already told Rumkowski that all people over 65 and all children under 10 must be deported. When his appeal to parents to hand over their children unsurprisingly went unheeded, the Germans carried out the selections themselves. According to the official figures, 15,681 people were sent to Chełmno during this week whilst 600 were shot in the ghetto. The following period appeared to offer some vindication for Rumkowski as there were no more major deportations for 20 months even though every other ghetto in Poland was destroyed in 1943. It seemed that the tens of thousands of Jews engaged in the ghetto factories were too valuable for the Germans to lose. Himmler, however, had different priorities and in May 1944 he ordered the final liquidation of the ghetto (which now contained approximately 77,000 people). Transports were resumed to Chełmno, itself reactivated for the purpose, in late June but the death camp was considered too inefficient (7,200 murdered in three weeks). The remaining almost 70,000 inhabitants, Rumkowski amongst them, were instead sent to Auschwitz in August. Most were gassed on arrival although around 5,000 survived, mostly by being transferred to other camps for work. The only other survivors came from two small groups which had been kept in the ghetto: around 600 who were sent to Germany in October 1944 and a group of almost 850 who remained in the city and who managed to live to see the liberation in January 1945.

In the immediate post-war period, many Holocaust survivors congregated in Łódź (38,000 by the end of 1945) but almost all migrated either abroad or to Warsaw. Only a few hundred Jews still live in the city today. Needless to say, next to nothing was done under Communism to highlight Łódź's Jewish past and there was no immediate change thereafter. However, the sixtieth anniversary of the ghetto's destruction in 2004 provided the impetus for the city to properly confront its history with a vigorous lead provided by Mayor Jerzy Kropiwnicki. This was achieved to such an extent that there is now arguably no city in Europe that has so effectively commemorated the Holocaust.

The ghetto

Like its Warsaw equivalent, the Łódź ghetto occupied a huge area of the city. Unlike the capital, a large number of buildings survive – especially around the ghetto's two main squares to the west. The city's tourist office produces an excellent free leaflet, *The Trail of the Litzmannstadt Ghetto* (also available at en.cityoflodz.com/_plik.php?id=71), which follows a route through some of the more significant structures and highlights others. Many of these buildings have had explanatory plaques attached, labelled in Polish, English, Yiddish and Hebrew.

Bałucki Rynek, previously the site of a major street market, became the heart of both the German and the Jewish ghetto administration, much of the latter concentrated in wooden huts in the middle of the square. This area was separated from the rest of the ghetto and was only accessible with a permit. The huts were destroyed after the liquidation and the square is now again covered in market stalls. However, buildings of significance remain around it, notably Łagiewnicka 25 on the eastern side, which housed several administrative offices. In November 1942, on German orders, a clock was placed on its roof to provide a standard time for the ghetto. Around the corner, Organizacji WiN (previously Dworksa) 1 was also home to a number of departments including the Presidium Secretariat, which prepared and issued Rumkowski's orders, identity cards and food coupons. A couple of blocks further east, Organizacji WiN intersects with Młynarska: number 32 to the north on the latter was the site of the main communal soup kitchen whilst 25 to the south housed Jews from Hamburg for six months from November 1941 until their deportation to Chełmno.

North of Bałucki, Łagiewnicka 34/36 was Hospital No. 1 until its patients were deported in the *Gehsperre*; during this time, it served as the main assembly point in the east of the ghetto. Rumkowski also lived in an apartment here prior to the deportations. After the hospital's closure, the building housed tailors' workshops and, in the last days of the ghetto, the 600 Jews who were earmarked for labour in Germany rather than deportation to Auschwitz. The large structure, one of the ghetto's most striking relics, is now dilapidated. Number 37 opposite was the site of the paediatric hospital whilst Hospital No. 4 was around the corner at Tokarska 7. Ceglana, which runs parallel to Łagiewnicka, is today essentially an overspill of the market. The three-storey building at

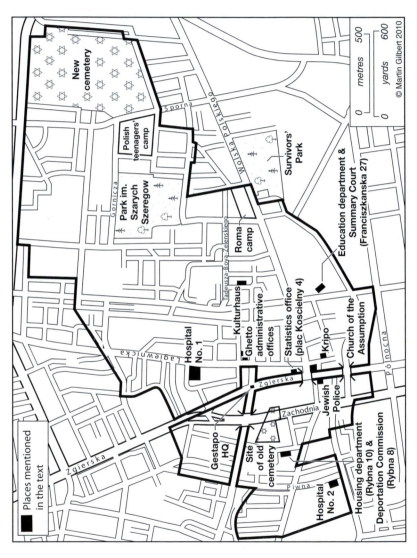

Łódź

© Martin Gilbert 2010

Places mentioned in the text

New cemetery

Polish teenagers' camp

Park im. Szarych Szeregow

Roma camp

Survivors' Park

Education department & Summary Court (Franciszkanska 27)

Kulturhaus

Ghetto administrative offices

Statistics office (plac Koscielny 4)

Kripo

Church of the Assumption

Hospital No. 1

Jewish Police

Gestapo HQ

Site of old cemetery

Housing department (Rybna 10) & Deportation Commission (Rybna 8)

Hospital No. 2

Sporna

Wolska Polskiego

Gornicza

Tadeusza-Boya-Zelenskiego

Lagiewnicka

Zgierska

Zachodnia

Piwna

Pólnocna

Zgierska

number 7 was the main storehouse for the goods of Jews from provincial ghettos who had been murdered at Chełmno.

Zgierska, on the western side of Bałucki, was a major north-south thoroughfare through the city. Therefore, although the houses on either side fell within the ghetto, the street itself did not. The same was also true for Limanowskiego which ran west from the square. The ghetto was thus split into three sections connected only by bridges. In the traffic island formed at the intersection of these streets, Limanowskiego 1, now a pharmacy, was the Gestapo HQ. There is a 1984 memorial plaque to the victims of the ghetto, the only Communist acknowledgement of the Jews of Łódź. Following Zgierska northwards from here, number 56 was a metal factory, 68 a dry cleaning shop and 70 accommodation for Jews from Frankfurt (until their murder, when it housed the ghetto's clothing department). The only bridge connecting this north-western sector with the rest of the ghetto was on Limanowskiego at the site of the junction with post-war Zachodnia. There are a couple of notable locations further west. Ciesielska 7 was the site of a special bank which purchased valuables such as jewels, foreign currency, fur coats and even art from residents who were paid in the ghetto's own currency (known as '*chaimki*' after the Eldest). Especially brisk business was done when the transports of Reich Jews arrived. A modern police station stands on the site but there is a plaque. Urzędnicza 11 housed Jews from Berlin; it became a brush factory when they were deported in May 1942.

One of the most significant streets in the ghetto was Rybna, which runs south from Limanowskiego, opposite Ciesielska. Just before number 15, an alley leads past a small basketball court to a grassy square carrying a memorial stone to the old Jewish cemetery which spread eastwards from here. The story related by the plaque is familiar: partially damaged by the Nazis, the cemetery was destroyed by the Communists, in this case to make way for the construction of Zachodnia. Rybna 15 was successively an elementary school, housing for Düsseldorf Jews and a shoe workshop. On the other side of the street, number 10 became the base of the housing department whilst several important departments were located in number 8, including those dealing with food coupons and displaced persons (new arrivals in the ghetto from the provinces or abroad). More ominously, from May 1942, it housed the Deportation Commission which prepared the lists of Reich Jews to be sent to Chełmno. Six blocks to the west, Gnieźnieńska 20/22 housed the ghetto's public prosecutor and court as well as a pharmacy; 28 on the same street was a home for the aged until all of its residents were sent to Chełmno in September 1942. At the south-western edge of the ghetto, Drewnowska 75, its grand facade partially hidden behind high walls, was Hospital No. 2 until the *Gehsperre* when it served as the principal assembly point for the west of the ghetto; it was later a clothing workshop.

A couple of blocks to the east of Rybna (following Lutomierska), plac Piastowski (wartime plac Bazarowy) was the site of public executions. The first victim was Maks Hertz from Cologne who was hanged on 21 February 1942 for trying to escape; he had been caught at the train station when his Star of David armband had fallen out of his pocket. Modern apartments at Lutomierska 13 stand on the site of the ghetto's juvenile court and fire brigade. However, one element of the complex survives, accessible through the courtyard of number 15; in front of this remaining building (Zachodnia 14), Rumkowski delivered his public speeches to the crowds in the so-called fire brigade's square. The most notorious was his anguished 'Give me your children' appeal during the *Gehsperre* on 4 September 1942 in which he begged parents to hand over their offspring to the Germans in order, he believed, to save the rest of the ghetto. Even the official chroniclers recorded the mood of hostility and despair in the crowd. Despite the parents' resistance, the deportations were carried out by the Jewish and German police (most of the 600 people killed in the ghetto during the *Gehsperre* were those trying to protect their children).

Lutomierska leads to plac Kościelny, the other major ghetto square. This is dominated by the redbrick Church of the Assumption which was used in 1942 as a warehouse for the property of Jews murdered in Chełmno; it later housed a workshop for the sorting of feathers. The corner building at Lutomierska 1 was the headquarters of the Order Service (Jewish police) established by Rumkowski in April 1940. In due course, the police grew to such an extent that there were five district stations spread across the ghetto. Almost opposite on the other side of Lutomierska, a green space holds a large memorial stone to Hamburg Jews deported to Łódź. The building next door to the police HQ, at Zgierska 24, housed the offices of price control and sanitation. This was also the location of one of the three ghetto bridges, crossing Zgierska by the southern side of the building and descending into the street on the northern side of the square; the bridge, with its views of the free city to the south, was an especially common site for suicides. Opposite Zgierska

24, plac Kościelny 4 housed a number of important institutions including the ghetto post office, rabbinical college and statistics office. It is most celebrated, however, as the place where the staff of the latter department compiled the Ghetto Chronicle. The initiative for the Chronicle came from Rumkowski and from January 1941 to July 1944 it recorded daily life, from the terror of the deportations to mundane details such as the weather – a unique record of a community living through unimaginable circumstances. In the north-eastern corner of the square, Łagiewnicka 1 had been a thriving pre-war Jewish market, known as Jojne Pilcer square; in 1941, it became the ghetto's main vegetable depot as well as housing one of the many soup kitchens – in this case, for doctors. Wartime cobbles and tramlines survive on the Łagiewnicka side of the building. The stretch of Wojska Polskiego (wartime Brzezińska) east of here is especially evocative. Number 10 was occupied by a printing house which produced official announcements, ration coupons and posters advertising cultural activities; it also contained a milk kitchen for babies. Number 24 was described by the Chronicle as the 'Eldorado for smokers', the site of the ghetto's tobacco department, established as a monopoly by Rumkowski in late 1941. Back on plac Kościelny, the brick building at Kościelna 8 (known as the 'Red House') was the base of the Kripo, the German criminal police. Its agents, typically Łódź Germans, were responsible for tackling smuggling and confiscating Jewish property. In time, the building's basement became a place of torture and murder.

The final ghetto bridge was south of plac Kościelny, at the crossroads of Zgierska and Podrzeczna. To the east of here, on Wolborska, was Łódź's Old Synagogue which was destroyed in November 1939. Near its site, in Park Staromiejski opposite Wolborska 7, is a statue of Moses erected in 1995 by the Foundation for the Commemoration of the Presence of the Jews in Poland. Nearby Jakuba 10 accommodated Jews from Vienna and Prague and later housed the tailoring department. A labour camp on the same street accommodated the last 600 survivors of the ghetto in 1944 (soon joined by 230 Jews found in hiding) who were kept behind to prepare deportees' possessions for transport to Germany. When they realised that they too were about to be murdered – pits had been dug at the cemetery – the Jews escaped in January 1945 and survived to see the liberation a few days later. At its eastern end, Wolborska comes to a junction with Franciszkańska, the longest street in the ghetto. Franciszkańska 13/15 successively housed a school, Prague

Jews and a linen and garment factory. Number 27, hidden by a fence next to a church, served as a Jewish police HQ and the home of the education department. It was also the location of the Summary Court, established by Rumkowski, which dealt with serious offences without lawyers being present. Number 29 was originally a primary school before being given over to arrivals from Prague and then a tailors' workshop whilst 31A, a pre-war cinema, became accommodation for Jews from Hamburg and then a Reform prayer house; it is now a supermarket. Number 30 opposite also housed Hamburg Jews.

The streets north and east of the junction of Franciszkańska and Wojska Polskiego preserve fewer traces of the ghetto although the low, long building at Krawiecka 3 was the *Kulturhaus*, heart of the ghetto's active cultural life. The former cinema officially opened for this purpose in March 1941 and staged theatre (including children's performances), musical concerts and the inevitable Rumkowski speeches. The arrival of the Reich Jews brought noted performers such as the Prague opera singer Rudolf Bandler. Such events became less frequent after the *Gehsperre* and the building was converted into the blanket department. Other key buildings in this area such as the central prison at Czarnickiego 14 and the assembly point at Szklana 7 no longer exist. It is sensible, therefore, to take a tram from the Franciszkańska/Wojska Polskiego junction to Głowackiego, the eastern corner of the short-lived 'gypsy camp'. Around 5,000 Austrian Roma were held in a single block (also bounded by Wojska Polskiego, Obrońców Westerplatte and Sikawska) from early November 1941. In the few weeks of their incarceration, 719 people died before the remainder were sent to Chełmno on 16 January 1942 – the first deportation from Łódź to the death camp. There is a plaque in Polish, English and Romani on the wall of Wojska Polskiego 84 commemorating them. After their murder, the tenement at number 90 became a workshop for the manufacture of straw shoes for German troops on the Eastern Front – nearly 7,000 people, half of them children, were employed there. Opposite the Głowackiego tram stop (outside the ghetto territory), is Park Ocalałych (Survivors' Park), another product of the 2004 commemorations, in which ghetto survivors and their relatives have planted trees. The park also contains a monument to Polish Righteous, topped by an eagle, next to a garden whose hedges form a Star of David.

Around the corner from the Roma camp, Organizacji WiN 74 was a home for the elderly until the *Gehsperre*; it then became a hospital for contagious diseases. Amongst those treated there were inmates of a camp for Polish teenagers established in December 1942 near the Jewish cemetery. In theory, this camp was for juvenile criminals but many of its residents were the children of Poles murdered or imprisoned for their political activities. By January 1945, more than 1,500 had passed through it. In contrast to the Jews, they were commemorated by the Communists through a disturbing sculpture of an emaciated child hollowed out of a circular stone at the eastern entrance of Park im. Szarych Szeregów on Bracka. It is flanked by curved tomb-like stones bearing the names of places of murder in Poland. The camp itself was bounded by Bracka, Emilii Plater, Górnicza and Zagajnikowa. The only surviving element is the administration building at Przemysłowa 34. Slightly further north, Okopowa 119 was the site of a Jewish orphanage and an assembly point during the deportations.

Bracka continues past the south of the Jewish cemetery but it is a long walk to its entrance on Zmienna (the main gate at the corner of Bracka is closed). An alternative is to take trams 1 or 6 to their terminus, continue up Strykowska and take the south-west path at the junction with Inflancka. The entrance is behind an unobtrusive door marked with a Star of David (Sun–Fri: summer, 9.00–5.00; winter, 9.00–3.00; 4 zł; cmentarz.mm.com.pl). The largest Jewish cemetery in Europe is then properly entered through a grand gate taken from the old cemetery. Just before, to the right of the gate, is a simple Holocaust memorial behind which lies a field of stones to victims. There is a plaque to Czech Jews on the gate wall whilst there are many more to individuals and families on the other side. Most of the cemetery's tombs are modest but there are exceptions, none more so than the incredible mausoleum of the industrialist Izrael Poznański in plot I. A striking contrast is provided by taking a left turn at the gate and continuing until the tombstones give way to a vast overgrown open space. This is the 'ghetto field' in which 43,527 people – those who succumbed to illness or starvation or were executed – are buried. Most plots are unmarked although section LV has been cleared and each person given a small plaque by the Israeli Defence Force. A few other individuals have modern stones, notably Wilhelm Caspari, a famed professor of medicine from Berlin who died in the ghetto in January 1944 (in PIV at the junction of aleja 6 and ulica 4). His field and neighbouring PV contain many unmarked graves, amongst them those of the Roma who died over the winter of 1941–42.

Łódź: Radegast station memorial (Photograph by the author)

Whilst the cemetery bears witness to the tragedy of ghetto life, the most prominent memorial in Łódź is to be found to its north-west just outside the ghetto. The former Radegast (Radogoszcz in Polish) station was the point of arrival for the Reich Jews and Austrian Roma and the point of departure for the close to 150,000 people deported to Chełmno and Auschwitz. Long neglected, it was transformed into a memorial site during the 2004 anniversary and officially opened in 2005. The first thing the visitor sees is the Hall of Towns topped by a chimney suggestive of both the factories which made Łódź and the crematoria in which so many of its citizens perished. Inside are the names of the home towns of victims of the ghetto; panels bear the deportation lists. Each of the years 1939 to 1945 is inscribed on the long exterior wall in heavy Germanic lettering, a motif repeated throughout the memorial. Beyond lies the wooden station building, to the left of which is a Reichsbahn train and wagon donated from Germany. To the right, a memorial wall carries various plaques, that from the city of Vienna 'in mourning and in shame'. Behind the station building are six large *matzevot* inscribed with the names of the two death camps, together with the four concentration camps – Stutthof, Ravensbrück, Sachsenhausen and Gross-Rosen – in which those who survived Auschwitz found themselves. The memorial is located on aleja Pamięci Ofiar Litzmannstadt Getto, opposite Zagajnikowa on the northern side of Inflancka. It can be walked from the cemetery although this is over a kilometre. The Inflancka bus stop on Zagajnikowa is far closer; buses 57, 81 and 87 run from the Sporna tram stop or the Górnicza bus stop (near the teenagers' camp).

Marysińska 100 (bus 57 to Inflancka stop on Marysińska) was a Jewish orphanage. The children were relocated when this neighbourhood was removed from the ghetto in early 1941 but it was restored in the autumn whereupon the building housed a shoemaking workshop. It is again an orphanage today.

Elsewhere

The diversity of Jewish life in Łódź is illustrated by the city centre's decayed tenements and spectacular mansions. The most astonishing of the latter is the home of Izrael Poznański (whose mausoleum so dominates the cemetery) on the corner of Ogrodowa and Zachodnia which now houses the city museum. Poznański's huge factory complex, one of the best preserved examples of industrial architecture in Europe, stands alongside on Ogrodowa.

Several relics of the Jewish past can be found around the magnificent main street Piotrkowska. Just east of plac Wolności, Pomorska 18 is the headquarters of the small modern community; in 1939, before the creation of the ghetto, it was transformed by the Germans into the Jewish Labour Office. On parallel Rewolucji 1905 roku, Łódź's tiny surviving pre-war synagogue is hidden in the second courtyard of number 28; during the war, it was used as a salt warehouse. Along the street, faded Yiddish lettering survives over the archway of 19. Across Piotrkowska, Zachodnia 70 – now occupied by an office building and car park – was the site of the Wilker Shul, destroyed in 1940 but not before it was used for scenes in *Der Ewige Jude,* the most notorious Nazi propaganda film. At the corner of the next junction, Więckowskiego 13 was a post-war Jewish school until the persecution of 1968, marked by a plaque. Crumbling Więckowskiego 32 was the pre-war Jewish People's Library.

In between, Wólczańska 6 was the site of another destroyed synagogue. Back on Zachodnia, passing the site of former community offices and a prayer house at 78, the Great Synagogue stood on the south-eastern corner of the crossroads with Zielona and Zachodnia's continuation Kościuszki until its destruction in 1939. The taxi rank and kiosks which occupy the site have been joined by a memorial stone (inscribed with an image of the synagogue) on the corner and a huge picture posted on the wall behind. Much further down Piotrkowska, an elegant former prayer house is located in a courtyard accessible from both 114 and 116.

The former Radogoszcz prison, north of the ghetto at Zgierska 147 (trams 4, 11, 11A and 46, plac Pamięci Narodowej), was a pre-war factory converted into a camp for Polish men in 1940; around half of the 40,000 who passed through lost their lives. The remnants of the complex have been turned into an engaging museum (Tue, Thu: 10.00–6.00; Wed, Fri, 10.00–4.00; Sat–Sun, 10.00–3.00; 2 zł; www.muzeumtradycji.pl/muzeum_tnr) which addresses Łódź's wartime history. After exhibits outlining the occupation and German ambitions for the city – from the mundane (altered street signs) to the tragic (photos of blonde Polish children destined for 'Germanisation') – there is a section on the ghetto before the focus turns to the prison itself. There are horrific photographs from the night of 17 January 1945 when 1,500 inmates were burned or shot; 30 survived.

CHEŁMNO

Chełmno (Kulmhof in German) was the first extermination camp, created in late 1941 to murder the Jews of the *Warthegau*. There is some debate amongst historians as to whether this was a result of pressure by local Nazi authorities or planned from Berlin but its establishment, soon followed by the beginning of *Aktion Reinhard*, clearly marked a decisive escalation in German policy. That said, Chełmno differed from the other Polish death camps in that it was not a single site with fixed gas chambers. Instead, in the first phase of operations from December 1941 to April 1943, victims were mainly held in an abandoned manor house (known as the palace or *Schloßlager*) in Chełmno village, having been brought from Koło (the nearest town of any size). They were then herded through a corridor into gas vans. The killing generally took place whilst the vans were stationary within the grounds of the palace; the bodies were then driven to the *Waldlager*, a camp in the Rzuchów forest around three miles to the north, where they were buried in large mass graves by a prisoner *Sonderkommando*. The murder operation began with the Jews of the Koło region before expanding in 1942 to encompass the Łódź ghetto. Transports were temporarily suspended in the summer to allow for the exhumation and cremation of the thousands of bodies in mass graves but it was not until the spring of 1943 that the killing ceased: the palace was blown up as were the mobile crematoria in the forest. Chełmno was then reactivated in 1944 for the final liquidation of the Łódź ghetto. With the palace destroyed, operations were largely concentrated in the *Waldlager* (although victims were held in the village overnight). Taken in lorries to the forest, they were directed into newly constructed barracks intended to give the appearance of a labour camp. They then filed through an enclosed passage, modelled on the 'tubes' at the *Aktion Reinhard* camps, to a ramp which led into the rear of waiting gas vans. New fixed crematoria disposed of the bodies. Ten transports brought 7,200 Jews from Łódź in June and July 1944 before the operation was switched to Birkenau. The forest camp was again dismantled in September and a *Sonderkommando* of 47 or 48 Jewish prisoners disposed of the remaining corpses. As the Red Army approached in January 1945, they were shot in groups of five. The waiting men revolted and killed two guards, enabling two of the inmates, Mordechaj Żurawski and Szymon Srebnik, to escape. Along with Michał Podchlebnik (who escaped in 1942), they were the only inmates of Chełmno to survive the war. An initial post-war Polish investigation produced a figure of 350,000 people murdered; modern estimates suggest a minimum of between 160,000 and 170,000.

Although a memorial was created in the forest in the early 1960s, the village was largely ignored. The grounds of the palace were taken over by an agricultural cooperative (the Polish equivalent of a collective farm) which did considerable damage to the site. However, archaeological research began there in 1997 and the whole site was purchased by the Polish government and transferred to the Konin District Museum (which administers the forest site) in the following year, enabling it to be opened to visitors in summer (June–Sept: Mon–Fri, 8.00–6.00; free; www.muzeum.com.pl/en/chelmno.htm). A sign points the way down a track just north of the church; the building on the right side of this track housed the drivers. A boulder to the right of the gate bears plaques in German and Polish relating the history of the site: this is one of several such stones erected by the German-Jewish Association of Hamburg at key locations associated with the camp. Straight ahead is a single-room museum in a surviving building of the cooperative. It displays items recovered from the excavations at the palace and in the forest, including such everyday objects as toothbrushes, dentures and money. Amongst them is a tattered child's shoe. In 1998, researchers found human remains buried near the palace; it is thought that they may belong to prisoners who were blown up with the building in 1943 and reburied in 1944. A small memorial stone in Polish and Yiddish to the left of the museum, which was erected in 1957 by the Jewish communities of Łódź and Włocławek, was for four decades the only form of commemoration at the site. To the right of the museum are the excavated remnants of the palace, the floor plan evident. Further right is the granary building which housed the *Sonderkommando* in 1944–45, beyond which two excavation pits have been left uncovered.

Opposite the track to the palace site is a turning off the main road, signposted Umień. The single-storey grey building on the right side of this road housed the fire brigade and the camp's garages. The church, back down the main road, played a prominent role in Chełmno's history. This was where Łódź Jews were interned in the summer of 1944 before being driven to the forest whilst in 1942 it held victims' clothes and luggage, as testified by another memorial boulder outside. Further down the road, two houses flank the bus stop on the southern side. The grey easternmost building housed the camp commandant. A little further along on the northern side (beyond the other bus stop), the two-storey building set back from the road was accommodation for SS men.

The *Waldlager* is a short car/bus ride from the village. A small memorial stone in the car park (next to a mast insensitively placed by the Communists) bears the figure of 360,000 dead. The museum to the right (Apr–Sept: daily, 10.00–6.00; Oct–Mar: daily, 8.00–2.00; free; same website as above) tells the story of the camp and the Łódź ghetto and displays a small selection of objects retrieved from the ghettos of the *Warthegau*. The path from the car park leads past the mass grave of Polish hostages murdered in September 1939, marked by a memorial and a cross. A white pillar to the side commemorates Stanisław Kaszyński, secretary of Chełmno village council who was shot by the Germans in February 1942 for attempting to pass on information to the underground about the camp. The large, jagged concrete memorial-mausoleum ahead, supported on pyramidal stilts, is very much of its time but nonetheless imposing. To its left is the Lapidarium, a collection of tombstones retrieved from the destroyed Jewish cemetery of nearby Turek and placed here in 1994 by Israeli descendants of the town as a tribute to their ancestors; some find the presence of pre-war gravestones at a death camp rather inappropriate.

A Hamburg memorial stone marks the start of a path which leads south-west from the main memorial to a symbolic grave for the children of the Czech village of Lidice who were murdered at Chełmno in 1942; this actually stands in the area where the first Jewish victims were murdered in December 1941. The first of four large mass graves is south of the path in a forest clearing. Visitors familiar with Chełmno from the opening scenes of Claude Lanzmann's *Shoah* may be surprised by the recent tendency to leave the fields unmown, causing the graves to be covered with long grass. This is also true of the larger field, reached via the main path which passes a smaller grave to the right. The extensive clearing contains three parallel mass graves, marked by simple memorials, although excavations have revealed that they do not exactly correspond to the concrete boundaries laid in the 1960s. Past the graves, the 'path of remembrance' leads through the field. To its right, excavations (which are still ongoing) have discovered the sites of an estimated five mobile field crematoria used in 1942. The intention of the path is to allow memorials to be erected for different communities – Łódź is amongst those honoured – but the dependence on private initiative means that this is inevitably selective, a contrast to the inclusive memorials at Treblinka and Bełżec. The surviving foundations of one of two fixed crematoria which are believed to have operated in 1944 are at the end of the path. The wall of remembrance behind is for plaques to individuals and families.

At the peak of the deportations in the summer of 1942, the mill in the village of Zawadka to the north was used as an overnight holding centre. There is no trace of the mill today but there is another Hamburg memorial stone marking the site of the station in Powiercie to which victims were brought by narrow-gauge railway from Koło before being marched the mile to the mill. Taking the signposted western turn for Zawadka in Powiercie, one can reach the stone, which is hidden behind a wire fence and sheltered by trees, a couple of properties along on the left. There is another memorial stone in Koło, in front of the train station where the transports arrived before being sent on to the mill or the palace. The station is located on Ks. Opałki in the north of the town.

All of the principal sites – the village, the forest, Powiercie – are located along the 473 between Dąbie and Koło. The forest camp is signposted from both directions just before the car park whilst the village church, at a turn in the road, is an unmistakeable landmark. It is possible to reach the sites by taking a train to Koło and then an onward bus. However, a simpler route from Łódź is to take a direct bus from the main bus station next to Fabryczna train station (ensuring that the destination is this Chełmno not the town near Gdańsk). Local buses which run between Dąbie and Koło roughly every 60 to 90 minutes can be used to travel between the sites.

STUTTHOF

Stutthof was originally established at the beginning of September 1939 as a civilian prison camp for Poles from the Danzig/Gdańsk region and thus initially had a purely localised function. It developed, however, into a site of great importance in the history of the Holocaust. Stutthof was designated as a concentration camp in January 1942 at which time it held less than 4,000 inmates. Its new status brought massive expansion with prisoners arriving from the USSR, Norway and Denmark. They were put to work in a variety of factories as well as in clearing the forests around the camp for further development. Conditions with regards to discipline, rations and disease (there were typhus epidemics in 1942 and 1944) are generally regarded as having been amongst the worse in the Nazi system with some historians arguing that Stutthof deserves to be seen as a death camp.

There were very few Jewish inmates before 1944 but this changed dramatically due to the German retreats elsewhere. It is estimated that 50,000 Jews passed through the camp in two main waves: Lithuanian and Latvian Jews evacuated from Kaiserwald and the Estonian camps in late summer 1944; Hungarian, Czech and Greek Jews, especially women, brought from Auschwitz as the year progressed. Facilities were completely inadequate for this influx and thousands died from disease or in the camp's gas chamber. More lost their lives in the death marches which began in January 1945; cut off by the Soviet advance, the Germans then forced the survivors back to the camp prior to evacuation by sea in April. Some groups of prisoners were simply taken to the Baltic and murdered. It is believed that around 25,000 people (half of all prisoners in the Stutthof network at the time) lost their lives in this period. Similarly, over the whole existence of the camp, an estimated 65,000 out of 115,000 inmates died. Stutthof was the very last camp to be liberated, on 9 May 1945; the Red Army discovered around 100 prisoners in hiding.

Although most of the camp was destroyed, a reasonable number of elements survive (daily, 8.00–3.00 (until 6.00, May–Sept); free; stutthof. beep.pl/en/main.htm). The short access road passes the commandant's villa (now a private residence) and the SS dog kennels on the right. The complex eventually stretched for over a mile to the west of the access road but that area is now forested over. The entry to the camp is via a path to the right by a small brick former guardhouse which serves as an information building; the car park is a little further along on the left. The first major structure along the path to the camp is the large command building which now houses the museum administration, a cinema and a collection of artwork. The single-storey block to its right was the SS garage. The wooden gate is just beyond the command building, flanked by two wooden barracks. That to the left contains piles of shoes, only a fraction of the huge mound discovered at liberation as illustrated by photographs.

The area through the gate was the original camp and then the women's camp after the 1943 enlargement. The exhibition proper begins in Block 8 to the right (past the foundations of the camp kitchen) which was converted into a quarantine block in 1943. The display outlines the history of the site with plans illustrating Stutthof's dramatic expansion. The barrack opposite continues by focussing on the prisoners and their experiences. A series of rooms reconstruct different facets of camp life – bunks, a dining room, medical equipment, a washroom – but the most personal elements are a pillar still inscribed with original graffiti and examples of drawings and greetings cards which prisoners made for each other.

The crematorium lies at the end of the original camp, next to a small gas chamber marked by a large cross and a Star of David; originally constructed for disinfection of clothes, it was used from June 1944 to murder inmates considered too sick to work. The crematorium contains many memorials along with a continuation of the exhibition covering the extermination process and the chaotic evacuation in 1944–45. It also addresses post-war justice or, as so often, the absence of it: for example, Otto Knott, who poured the Zyklon B into the gas chamber, was found not guilty at his trial in West Germany in 1964. Behind the crematorium stand gallows and a train on a stretch of the railway which led into the camp.

To the north is a large concrete Communist monument whose abstract reliefs are suggestive of human figures. The path then leads back west parallel to the old camp. To its right, beyond the monument and slightly hidden by trees and a barbed-wire fence, are the large workshops which made up Stutthof's factory complex. Further along on the right, a large field contained the new camp where men were imprisoned from 1943 – small walls indicate the end of each barrack. To the left of the path is the camp's vegetable garden, its greenhouse still intact.

The path turns right at the car park, passing the western edge of the new camp. On the left is the new kitchen, constructed in 1943–44 but never completed; it was converted into temporary accommodation for Jewish women during the mass arrivals from Estonia and Latvia in the summer of 1944. The site of the Jewish camp is in the trees beyond the new camp, marked by a single barrack wall, a Star of David and a menorah. From here one can follow the signs marked '*Stos*' through the forest to reach the site of the pyres on which corpses were burned, now marked by a ring of stones.

The camp is west of Sztutowo village on the 501. To reach it by car, take the 7/E77 from Gdańsk and turn onto the 502 at Nowy Dwór Gdański and then onto the 501 at Stegna. There are regular buses from Gdańsk's main bus station. The bus stop is just past a large concrete marker.

GROSS-ROSEN

The territory of Gross-Rosen camp in Lower Silesia lies in Poland today but was, until 1945, in Germany. It was thus part of the network of Reich concentration camps, having been established as a satellite of Sachsenhausen in 1940 and become an independent camp in May 1941. The majority of early prisoners laboured in an adjacent granite quarry although other enterprises were added with time. These inmates were predominantly Polish and German political prisoners but several hundred Jews were sent to what was still a fairly small camp before being deported to Auschwitz in late 1942. For the next year, there were no Jewish inmates but 57,000 (almost half of them women) entered Gross-Rosen or its sub-camps between October 1943 and January 1945. This was a result of the relocation of skilled Jewish workers following the final liquidation of the Polish ghettos and the large-scale transfer of prisoners during the dissolution of Auschwitz. Gross-Rosen was itself evacuated in February 1945. Although prisoners were transported by train, many still died from lack of food whilst inmates of several satellites were sent on death marches. It is estimated that of the 125,000 who passed through Gross-Rosen and its sub-camps, around 40,000 died.

Very little of the camp survives (daily, 8.00–7.00 (until 4.00, Oct–Apr); free; www.gross-rosen.pl). This is evident in the car park, just inside the SS camp, where a small information kiosk adjoins the exposed foundations of the guardhouse; those of an SS barrack stand on the other side of the road. The only significant remnant of the SS camp is the former canteen (which housed the kitchen, mess and casino) on the right although only the arcaded lower level is original. The upper floor was reconstructed in the 1970s and hosts a small exhibition on the camp's history in Polish. Just past this building, to the left of the camp road, are the foundations of the SS hospital.

The surviving granite gatehouse was constructed by inmates in 1944, replacing the wooden original. A memorial and a wagon of the type prisoners had to push stand near the steps up to the enormous quarry, its current size a testament to the fact that it remained in use long after the war. Through the gate, the foundations to the left are those of the reception building to which inmates were brought on their arrival. To the right is the *Appellplatz* with reconstructed gallows. The main extant building is the brick kitchen behind the square although even this is only the lower level of the original. Facing the kitchen is a reconstruction of the camp's bell tower, the 1944 original having been destroyed by a storm in 2002. The other main preserved element is the bathhouse, on the opposite side of the road near the trees. Otherwise, only remnants survive. Amongst the more notable on the uphill right-hand side are Block 19, which housed the penal company, and Block 22, site of the Convict Labour Camp. This latter institution, relocated from Wrocław in December 1943, inflicted 8 weeks of punishment work on foreign forced labourers who had broken the law. Blocks 17 and 14, closer to the camp road, were Siemens workshops.

Behind this row of barracks is the main memorial area, marked by a mausoleum containing retrieved ashes. A mass grave for 81 inmates whose remains were discovered buried in the grounds lies in front of it by the road. The site of the execution area and crematorium (which were separated from the rest of the camp by barbed wire) is behind the mausoleum. There are many memorial plaques, including to Jews and Poles brought to Gross-Rosen after the suppression of the two Warsaw uprisings. The crematorium oven stands exposed amidst foundations, the building having been destroyed during the retreat. This fixed facility went into use in January 1943, replacing a smaller mobile crematorium. Down the steps behind is the pit where ashes were dumped.

A memorial to the prisoners at the rear of the camp is now topped by a cross dedicated to Władysław Błądziński, a priest who died in Gross-Rosen and was later beatified by John Paul II. One can just discern from here the vestiges of the 'Auschwitz camp', built in late 1944 to accommodate the influx from the death camp; very little remains in the largely forested area beyond the fence. Returning back through the barracks on the other side of the camp road, one comes to Block 9 which was the only one in the main camp to have the same two-level design as the 'Auschwitz' barracks: its lower floor survives and contains a reconstructed dormitory. The remains of the Blaupunkt workshop where prisoners produced capacitors are in the basement of one of the hospital barracks in the next row of buildings.

The camp is about 2 kilometres south of Rogoźnica, a village on the 374 between Jawor and Strzegom: turn onto ulica Gross-Rosen (signposted for Godzieszówek and Kostrza) in the centre of the village. There is a memorial stone to camp victims by the fire station at number 15. Infrequent buses and trains run to Rogoźnica from Legnica. Buses stop by the turning for ulica Gross-Rosen from where the camp is a roughly 25 minute walk. The train station (which has a memorial plaque on its trackside wall) is north of the village: turn left at the end of its access road and continue until the church; turn left onto the 374 to see ulica Gross-Rosen on the right.

OTHER SITES

Given that virtually anywhere in Poland can be considered a Holocaust site, the following list is inevitably highly selective. Visitors interested in other specific locations are advised to contact the Jewish Historical Institute in Warsaw (www.jewishinstitute.org.pl) or to consult polin.org.

pl (maintained by the Foundation for the Preservation of Jewish Heritage in Poland).

Jedwabne, north-east of Łomża on the 668, was the site of a pogrom in July 1941 in which sections of the local Polish population forced most of the village's Jews into a barn and set it alight. The massacre was blamed on the Germans and the truth only came to widespread notice as a result of Jan T. Gross's 2000 book *Neighbours*. The original Communist memorial at the site of the barn was replaced in 2001 although the new text simply states that Jews were murdered without identifying the perpetrators, a reflection of the passions aroused by the book. It is located on the edge of the village: take the road east from the church, turn left and then right down a track which leads to the site.

A beautifully renovated synagogue at Czerwonego Krzyża 7 in Włodawa serves as a Jewish museum (Mon–Fri, 10.00–3.00; Sat–Sun, 10.00–2.00; 5 zł; www.muzeum.wlodawa.metronet.pl). This institution also administers the Sobibór memorial. Chełm, due south of Włodawa and Sobibór, occupies a legendary place in Jewish folklore as the archetypal 'town of fools'. Only a memorial in the Jewish cemetery on Starościńska commemorates the community (the former synagogue at Kopernika 8 houses a bar!). However, there are memorials in the Borek (or Borki) forest, on a hill south-east of the city off Wojsławicka, to the more than 30,000 Soviet and Italian POWs executed in the so-called *Patelnia* (frying-pan); Jewish prisoners were brought from Majdanek to burn the bodies in the winter of 1943–44.

A very effective Holocaust memorial is located at the site of the former Jewish cemetery in Kazimierz Dolny, 35 miles west of Lublin. On a small hill, fragments of gravestones form a 'wailing wall' monument which is cut with a jagged gap leading through to a darkened forest where a few remaining stones stand. This is south-east of the town on Czerniawy, which runs off Nadrzeczna. The former synagogue, recently returned to the Jewish community, is on Mały Rynek, behind the main square.

Most of the Jews of Zamość (renamed Himmlerstadt) were killed at Bełżec in 1942–43 whilst more than 100,000 Poles from the region were expelled to make way for ethnic Germans (around 10,000 were simply murdered). The Renaissance synagogue at Zamenhofa 9–11 is to become a museum of local Jewish history. A memorial by the Old Lublin Gate on Akademicka commemorates the Polish 'children of Zamość' who fell victim to Nazi ethnic cleansing – more than 30,000 were taken from their parents. The main Holocaust memorial, made from remnants of gravestones, is in the surviving section of the Jewish cemetery at the end of Prosta, north-east of the centre. The former Rotunda fortress, south of the centre, houses a museum dedicated to the thousands of Jews and Poles murdered there and to the wider Nazi genocide in the region; it also addresses Soviet repression.

Tarnów is the most impressively commemorated of Polish Galicia's Jewish communities. A plaque on the corner of the Rynek and Żydowska marks the first major *Aktion* of June 1942 whilst, further along Żydowska, only the *bimah* survives as a memorial from the Old Synagogue (destroyed in November 1939). Nearby plac Bohaterów Getta leads to plac Więźniów Oświęcimia where a monument commemorates the Jews and Poles who were the first to be sent to Auschwitz in June 1940. They were held overnight in the Moorish *mikvah* on the square. On the corner of Nowa and Waryńskiego, there is a memorial plaque to the destroyed New Synagogue, a surviving pillar of which is incorporated into a Holocaust memorial in the cemetery on Słoneczna to the north. Tarnów's Ethnographic Museum at Krakowska 10 (Tue, Thu 10.00–5.00; Wed, Fri, 9.00–3.00; Sat–Sun, 10.00–2.00; 4 zł; www.muzeum.tarnow.pl) has exhibits focussing on the history of the Roma in Poland. Ninety-three Roma were murdered in the village cemetery of Szczurowa (north-west of Tarnów at the junction of the 768 and 964 roads) in the summer of 1943. Local residents erected a memorial in 1956 which is now the focus of the annual Caravan of Memory in July which departs from Tarnów and passes through other murder sites before reaching the village.

Around 20,000 Jews from Kielce were murdered in Treblinka. This is recalled by a monument in the former Jewish cemetery (itself the site of executions), south-west of the centre on Janusza Kusocińskiego (off Pakosz). This has recently been supplemented by a memorial to the ghetto, a sculpted menorah rising from the pavement, on Aleja IX Wieków Kielc. However, Kielce is most infamous as the location of the worst of the post-war pogroms when 42 Holocaust survivors were murdered in July 1946. This is commemorated by a rather abstract 2006 memorial opposite the menorah, on the junction of Aleja IX Wieków Kielc and Piotrkowska, and a plaque around the corner at Planty 7/9, the Jewish refuge which was the main focus of the attack. A remodelled former synagogue, now an archive building, stands in a traffic island further east on Aleja IX Wieków

Kielc (by the junction with Warszawska); a memorial to Polish Righteous and another to Holocaust victims are to its rear.

Poznań's Seventh Fort (a couple of miles west of the centre on Polska) was the site of the first Nazi experiments with gas in October 1939 when around 400 psychiatric patients were murdered. The complex, which later served as a Gestapo prison and labour camp, is now a museum (Tue–Sun, 9.00–5.00 (until 4.00, Oct–Mar); free; www.muzeumniepodleglosci. poznan.pl).

Wrocław was, as Breslau, home to pre-war Germany's third largest Jewish population. The imposing New Synagogue, destroyed on *Kristallnacht*, is commemorated at Łąkowa 8 on the south-western edge of the centre. The surviving White Stork Synagogue is reasonably nearby at Włodkowica 7. The restored cemetery is further south at Ślężna 37–39. It is a telling comment on the effects of the Holocaust that Wrocław's current Jewish community of perhaps a thousand people is the second largest in Poland.

Lithuania

CHAPTER 11

LITHUANIA

In proportional terms, Lithuania suffered the heaviest losses of any nation in the Holocaust with perhaps 95 per cent of one of Europe's most celebrated Jewish communities wiped out. The tragedy was made all the more distressing by its speed and the identity of the killers, many of whom were Lithuanian.

Jews had first come to Lithuania in significant numbers in the fourteenth century during the great wave of Ashkenazi migration to the east. However, it was Lithuania's growing ties with Poland, formalised in the 1569 Union of Lublin, that made it such a stronghold of Jewish culture with both Jews and Poles settling in major cities and towns. Nonetheless, Lithuanian Jews – known as Litvaks – developed an identity and culture which separated them from those of Poland, reflected in a distinctive Yiddish dialect and, stereotypically, a more intellectual and rigorous devotion to the precepts of Orthodox Judaism. Vilna (Vilnius) and Kovno (Kaunas) became two of the greatest cities of the Diaspora, but the world of the Litvaks was primarily that of the *shtetlach* with Jews often the majority of the population of small towns across the country. Following the Polish partitions, Lithuania spent over a century under the rule of the tsars whose oppressive policies engendered large-scale emigration. Nonetheless, Lithuanian Jewry continued to enhance its reputation in this period with the foundation of famed yeshivas and a growing engagement with the new movements of Zionism and socialism.

Lithuanian independence after the First World War offered the promise of civil equality but Antanas Smetona's nationalist dictatorship, which emerged in 1926, promoted ethnic Lithuanian interests. That said, Smetona himself cultivated a pro-Jewish image and a degree of communal autonomy was maintained, including state sponsorship of Jewish schools. Of more immediate impact on Jewish life was the Polish conquest of Vilnius and its hinterland in 1920: a closed border thereafter divided the Litvaks until the USSR intervened. The Nazi-Soviet Pact had originally placed Lithuania within the German sphere of influence but, following Stalin's concessions on Poland, it was transferred to the Soviet zone. Vilnius was thus conquered during the Red Army's occupation of eastern Poland in September 1939. Stalin returned the city to Lithuania

311

at the end of October, in return for consent to a Soviet military presence, thus using it as bait to facilitate annexation of the whole country in mid-1940. Communist rule initially seemed to offer some benefits for Jews, ostensibly including freedom from discrimination and the prospect of protection from Nazi aggression – an especially important factor for the thousands of refugees from German-occupied Poland. As a result, a minority of mainly younger Jews openly welcomed the invasion. For the majority, however, Stalinism brought nationalisation of businesses, destruction of communal institutions and the arrest of around 7,000 Jews in June 1941. Nonetheless, extreme Lithuanian nationalist organisations, encouraged by émigré groups based in and funded by Berlin, claimed that the Jews were responsible for the Communist takeover, even though they formed a disproportionate number of the victims of the Soviet terror.

It was in this climate that Lithuania fell to the Nazis within days of the invasion of the USSR in late June 1941. Pogroms were inflicted on the Jewish populations of many towns, often before the Germans had arrived. The virulence of this anti-Semitism was intensified by the widespread Lithuanian perception of the invaders as liberators who would restore the country's independence even though the Nazis had no intention of doing so. Systematic destruction came with the arrival of *Einsatzgruppe A* which began its campaign of mass murder in July 1941. The earliest victims were typically men but the killings rapidly escalated to the elimination of entire populations. Lithuania's Jews were thus the first in Europe to be subjected to the Nazi policy of complete extermination. It is estimated that only 40,000 of the 220,000 Jews in Lithuania at the time of the invasion were still alive by the end of 1941. The scale of annihilation was assisted by the collaboration of Lithuanian nationalists who were formed into auxiliary police battalions which often carried out the shootings (so effectively that they were later sent to kill Jews in Belarus and Poland). The remaining Jews were concentrated in ghettos and labour camps, marking the beginning of a period of relative calm until 1943 when the ghettos were liquidated or turned into concentration camps. The approach of the Red Army saw the final destruction of the latter in the summer of 1944. In total, more than 200,000 Lithuanian Jews were murdered. A significant proportion of the few thousand who survived consisted of young people smuggled out to join the partisans by the resistance groups which had existed in both major ghettos.

Many survivors chose not to stay in Lithuania after the war; with further emigration from the Gorbachev era onwards, there are only around 4,000 Jews left in the country today, most in the capital. A number of memorials were created under Communism but they were usually remote and inevitably failed to identify the victims. The situation has improved considerably since independence although commemoration is less visible than in Poland.

VILNIUS

As Vilna, the capital occupied an iconic position within the Jewish world as the 'Jerusalem of Lithuania', a reflection of the city's reputation as the pre-eminent centre of Orthodox Jewish learning in Europe. Jews were first invited to settle in 1326 and the community grew steadily over the next few centuries. However, it was in the eighteenth century that Vilnius began to acquire its eminence throughout the Diaspora when the Vilna Gaon achieved international fame as a teacher and scholar. This reputation was cemented in the decades following his death (there were over 100 synagogues and prayer houses by 1900) whilst industrialisation swelled the population: the first tsarist census of 1897 recorded 63,831 Jews in the city, the largest single ethnic group. Secular currents also took hold: the Bund was founded in Vilna in 1897 whilst it also became a major Zionist centre, giving an ecstatic welcome to Herzl in 1903.

The city was the focus of the poisonous dispute between Poland and Lithuania from 1918 onwards. As Vilnius, it was the historic Lithuanian capital, but most non-Jewish residents were Poles for whom it was Wilno. The struggle was resolved by superior Polish force of arms in 1920 but a lingering sense of bitterness remained which prevented any effective cooperation between Poland and Lithuania in the inter-war period and which was exploited by Stalin in 1939–1940. The Soviet occupation coincided with a dramatic increase in the Jewish population with the pre-war community of around 58,000 augmented by an influx of thousands of refugees from German-occupied Poland in late 1939. However, emigration, Communist terror (5,000 or more were deported in June 1941) and flight into the interior of the USSR meant that around 57,000 Jews were in Vilna when the Germans arrived.

The city fell on 26 June 1941 and *Einsatzgruppe A* swiftly followed. Shootings began on 4 July and an execution site was created at Paneriai

Vilnius: Žemaitijos gatvė (Photograph by Elizabeth Burns)

forest (Ponar in Yiddish), south-west of the city. In the space of just 16 days, 5,000 Jews were murdered whilst a further *Aktion* at the beginning of September killed another 8,000. This was a prelude to the establishment of two ghettos in the heart of the city on 6 September 1941: 29,000 were incarcerated in the larger ghetto which was earmarked for workers with permits, 11,000 in the other. The true purpose of the separation was revealed in October 1941 when the small ghetto's inhabitants were murdered at Ponar in a series of *Aktionen* starting on Yom Kippur: this ghetto survived for less than two months. Throughout this time, Jews from the large ghetto also continued to be killed.

The large ghetto was then left in relative peace for the next 18 months with a legal population of 12,000 and perhaps as many as 8,000 more living in hiding. The dominant figure was Jacob Gens, arguably the most controversial of all ghetto leaders after Rumkowski in Łódź. Originally head of the Jewish police, Gens was appointed *Judenrat* chairman in July

1942. Like Rumkowski, Gens had an authoritarian style which, together with his willingness to participate in selections, inevitably made him enemies. Most notoriously, the Vilna ghetto police themselves carried out an *Aktion* in the small town of Oshmyany (now Ašmjany in Belarus) in October 1942 although in the process they succeeded in reducing the German demand for 1,500 Jews to 406 elderly people. To his defenders, Gens's readiness to collaborate and his philosophy of 'work for life' offered the only hope of survival, however unsuccessful he might ultimately have been. One area where Gens's contribution is generally seen more positively is in assisting the remarkable efforts of the ghetto's inhabitants to maintain some semblance of civic life with a hospital, an orphanage, a home for the elderly, schools, a library and three synagogues. Most striking was the continuation of cultural activity, notably through the ghetto theatre which staged plays and concerts. This attempt to retain some sense of normality has been seen by some as spiritual resistance. More direct resistance came from the FPO (United Partisans Organisation), formed in January 1942 by Communists and Zionists. Some members were able to escape in 1943 to join Soviet partisans in the forests. However, the FPO's attempts to rouse the ghetto through propaganda met with little success and were largely opposed by Gens; most inhabitants still believed that through work they could save themselves. It was not until 1 September 1943 that there was open armed resistance in the ghetto when FPO fighters skirmished with the Nazis but the rising fizzled out.

By this stage, the decision to liquidate the ghetto had already been taken. Those Jews still considered fit to work were sent to slave labour camps in Estonia and Latvia, chiefly Klooga and Kaiserwald; the remainder were dispatched to Ponar or Sobibór. Six centuries of one of the Diaspora's greatest civilisations were effectively terminated with the final liquidation of the ghetto on 23 September 1943. When the Red Army reached Vilnius in July 1944, only 200 Jews remained in hiding in the city. In total, between 2,000 and 3,000 of the city's 1941 population survived. Even after the return of additional refugees from central Asia, the community was merely a shell of its former existence.

Most survivors left after the war, mainly for the USA or Israel. According to the 2001 census, there are only 2,700 Jews in modern Vilnius (0.5 per cent of the population), mostly survivors from other parts of Lithuania and their descendants. To compound matters, the Communists destroyed much of the city's Jewish heritage. The situation

315

has improved since 1991 with memorial plaques appearing in the former ghetto areas. Yet despite the growing number of Jewish visitors to the city, relatively few Lithuanians seem interested in it, perhaps a reflection of the fact that the current population has virtually no connection to the Jews and Poles who dominated Vilnius for the best part of half a millennium.

The ghettos

The few streets which made up the small ghetto were the heart of Jewish Vilna, centred around the Great Synagogue on Jewish Street (Żydowska – *Yidishe gas* to its inhabitants), now known by its Lithuanian equivalent Żydų gatvė. The synagogue, originally constructed in the sixteenth century and rebuilt in the seventeenth, was an enormous structure capable of accommodating 3,000 people and anchored a complex which also included smaller prayer houses and the renowned Strashun Library, one of the world's leading collections of Judaica. The buildings were badly damaged during the war but not irretrievably so; nonetheless, the entire complex was demolished in the 1950s by the Communists. An unappealing building housing a kindergarten was erected on the site but it too now stands in some disrepair. In 2005, a large information board explaining the history of the synagogue and the quarter was erected opposite it. To the side of the kindergarten, on the wall of Żydų 3, is a 1997 plaque dedicated to the Vilna Gaon on the bicentenary of his death; this roughly marks the site of his prayer house which was in the synagogue courtyard. He is also commemorated by a rather unflattering bust.

Virtually the whole of the small ghetto area east of the Great Synagogue survives, including the remainder of Żydų which curves gracefully to the intersection of the main streets. Most of the buildings have been restored since 1991, now housing restaurants and upmarket craft shops. Żydų crosses Stiklių (Szklanna in the time of the ghetto) and becomes Gaono. The Austrian Embassy (Gaono 6) carries a plaque testifying that the sixteenth-century building served as a prayer house for 80 years prior to 1941. On the other side of the street, at number 5, two wall plaques mark the site of the ghetto gate. The main plaque consists of a map of the two ghettos; the other briefly explains the small ghetto's history.

Before returning in the direction of the large ghetto, it is worth continuing along Gaono as it becomes Universiteto. The university, at

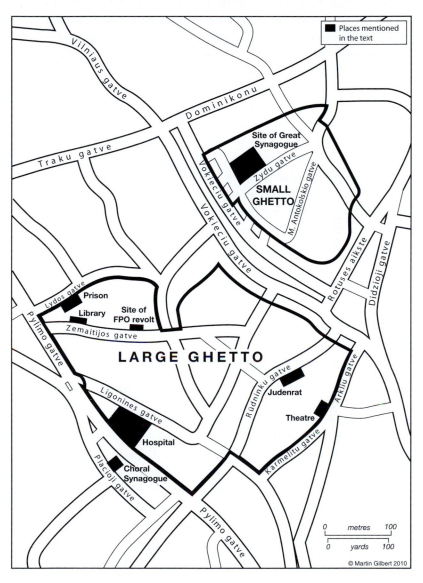

Vilnius

number 7, is home to the Vilnius Yiddish Institute which runs annual summer schools. By the entrance to the Yiddish Institute, in the courtyard to the left of the gate, there is a memorial plaque to the Lithuanian Righteous Ona Šimaitė. A university librarian, she regularly entered the large ghetto on the pretext of recovering books from former students, using the opportunity to smuggle in food and other supplies and to smuggle out invaluable Yiddish and Hebrew books, lest they fall into the hands of the Nazis. She was captured in 1944 and sent to Dachau but survived the war, dying in France in 1970.

Heading back down Gaono to the crossroads, a left turn into the southern section of Stiklių and then an immediate right brings one to M. Antokolskio, named after the Jewish sculptor Mark Antokolski, born in this street in 1840. Before and during the war, this was the northern section of Jatkowa (Butchers' Street), the longest street in the Jewish quarter which continued through the length of what became the large ghetto. An arch between the buildings is the only surviving example of the several which once lined Jatkowa. It is now used to advertise the adjacent restaurant; the arches performed a similar role even in the nineteenth century. Only a short section of the street survives before it opens out into a grassy area which separates M. Antokolskio from the site of the Great Synagogue. Until the war, this area was a warren of small alleyways and interlocking courtyards where many of the poorest Jews lived, beautifully recalled in Chaim Grade's memoir *My Mother's Sabbath Days*. This lost world extended beyond the Communist apartment blocks to the west.

The ghettos were separated by Niemiecka, now Vokiečių, both names meaning German Street. This was the main pre-war commercial thoroughfare of the Jewish quarter, lined with shops, offices and newsstands selling papers in a bewildering multiplicity of languages. It is now a wide street, a pair of roads divided by a grassy promenade, but only the western side, today mainly occupied by bars and restaurants, is original. Niemiecka's other side was actually the western edge of the promenade. A little reminder of the past is a cobbled section of the promenade which marks the course of Jatkowa/Antokolskio as it proceeded across Niemiecka/Vokiečių. Crossing the western section of the latter here brings one to the southern part of Jatkowa, still known as Butcher's Street in its Lithuanian form, Mėsinių. This too is cobbled, part of an attempt by the city authorities to preserve and restore traces of the Jewish past. At the first junction, there is a small car park which contains an unobtrusive memorial stone to the 'martyrs and fighters' of the Vilna ghetto.

Beyond the next crossroads is grassy Geto aukų aikštė (Ghetto Victims' Square) which stands on the site of buildings destroyed after the war. On the Mėsinių/Dysnos corner, there is a recently erected statue of Dr Tsemakh Shebad, a pre-war physician and community leader who, amongst other achievements, set up free soup kitchens during the First World War, was active in the establishment of YIVO and was elected to the Vilnius City Council and Polish Parliament. Shebad died in 1935 but the memorial is dedicated both to him and to the lost Jewish community.

On the square's eastern side, Rūdninkų 8 (a pre-war Jewish school) was the *Judenrat* headquarters. A plaque commemorates an *Aktion* on 3 November 1941 when 1,200 were selected for Ponar in the courtyard. The ghetto's only gate was located further down the street by number 18, marked, as in the small ghetto, by a pair of plaques. One of the most dramatic incidents in the ghetto's history took place on this street on 15 July 1943. After arresting leading Communists in the city, the Germans had learned of Communist activist Yitzhak Witenberg and demanded that he be handed over; they did not know that he was also the leader of the FPO. The Jewish police, assisted by Lithuanians, arrested Witenberg during a meeting in the *Judenrat* between Gens and the FPO and began dragging him towards the gate. A group of FPO fighters ambushed the party and secreted Witenberg away. However, when the Germans implied that there would be reprisals against the whole ghetto if he were not surrendered, the FPO leadership and ultimately Witenberg himself agreed that he should be handed over. On 16 July, he was delivered to the Gestapo – the next morning he was found dead in his cell, having taken cyanide given to him by Gens.

From January 1942 onward, the ghetto's theatre was located in Arklių 5 – actually the rear of the same complex as housed the *Judenrat* – which is now home to the Vilnius Puppet Theatre. Gens's decision to create the theatre a month earlier was controversial, with critics arguing, 'you don't make theatre in a graveyard'. However, the success of the early performances won over most opponents and it is generally agreed that cultural activity helped to sustain morale. There is a memorial plaque on the exterior wall of the theatre. In the courtyard it shared with the *Judenrat* is a further memorial, a curving metal sculpture known as the *Flame of*

Hope, dedicated to the murdered Jews of Lithuania. Unfortunately, it is rather difficult to access. Walk down Arklių, following the curve to Karmelitų, and enter the archway headed '*Teatro Kolonos kavine*'. Go through the wooden door in the far right corner (i.e., diagonally across from the entrance) which takes one into another, smaller courtyard. Cross this to the glass and wooden door where the caretaker should let visitors through the corridor to see the monument. Incidentally, further down Karmelitų, number 5 carries a plaque to the Yiddish poet Moshe Kalbach, a former resident.

Just south of Rūdninkų, beyond the confines of the ghetto across Pylimo, Gėlių hides more traces of the pre-Holocaust civilisation. In the courtyard of number 3, facing the entrance archway, is a former prayer house; the original window arches of the women's gallery are on the upper floor of this now dilapidated residential building. The former Zavel Synagogue is at Gėlių 6, in an even worse state. The only temple still in use is the Choral Synagogue, at Pylimo 39 (Mon–Fri, 8.00–2.00, 7.30–8.00; Sat, 10.00–2.00; Sun, 8.45–2.00, 7.30–8.00). The synagogue was built in 1903 and had a reputation as the *shul* of the intellectuals and middle classes. However, as its name suggests, large numbers would attend to hear its famed cantors. Opposite the synagogue, Pylimo 38 became the ghetto hospital in 1941, the building having performed the same role for the city's poorest Jews since 1794. In the war, it was entered from Szpitalna (now Ligoninės); its courtyard can now be accessed from Pylimo although there is no trace of its history.

Returning to Ghetto Victims' Square, Šiaulių leads from the end of Mėsinių to a junction with Žemaitijos gatvė, perhaps the most evocative of all of the streets in the former Jewish quarter. Before the war, this was Strashuna, named after the Jewish scholar and bibliophile Mattiyahu Strashun whose collection of books was the basis of the library which adjoined the Great Synagogue. The modern building at 8A is built on the site of Strashuna 12, the scene of the FPO's ill-fated uprising in September 1943, marked by a memorial plaque. On the southern side, 7 and 9 carry Yiddish shop inscriptions, discovered and retained during restoration work. Number 4, the pre-war library of the Association to Spread Enlightenment, served as the ghetto library under the auspices of the diarist and Bundist Herman Kruk. The library, as much as the theatre, played a vital role in sustaining cultural life in the ghetto and within a little over a year it circulated 100,000 books. Early meetings of the

FPO took place here: on 31 December 1941, the writer and emergent partisan Abba Kovner read a manifesto calling on Vilna's Jews to 'not be led like sheep to the slaughter'. Franz Murer, the sadistic deputy head of the Nazi administration, regularly sat on a bench outside this building and harassed passing young women. In its courtyard, one can see the ghetto's prison, marked with a number 3 on the wall. An open space opposite the library serves as a car park for residents: on the exposed brick wall on the western side there is the imprint of a *Magen David*, a ghostly reminder of the site's past. Žemaitijos 2, at the corner with Pylimo, has a small plaque in Lithuanian testifying to the street's former name and paying tribute to Strashun. When the ghetto was created on 6 September 1941, the numbers streaming in here were larger than expected and huge crowds developed by the afternoon. The Nazis drove 2,000 people into parallel Lydos instead from where they were marched overnight to Lukiszki prison; most were executed at Ponar on 10 and 11 September. A memorial plaque at Lydos 3 recalls the event; this is actually on the exterior wall of the ghetto prison.

The streets north of Lydos were outside the ghetto but are still redolent of Jewish Vilna, nowhere more so than inside a group of atmospheric interlocking courtyards between Prančiskonų and Vokiečių, accessed through a crumbling archway on the former.

The Jewish Museum and around

The Vilna Gaon Jewish State Museum is located in three buildings north and west of the large ghetto. This is actually the third Jewish museum in the city's history, the first (founded in 1913) unsurprisingly destroyed by the Nazis, the second (1944) closed by Stalin after just five years. It was to be another 40 years before the current institution was permitted in the twilight of the Soviet era.

The building closest to the ghetto is also the newest – the impressive Tolerance Centre (Mon–Thu, 10.00–6.00; Sun, 10.00–4.00; 4 Lt for whole museum; www.jmuseum.lt), opened in 2001 in a building which had served as a pre-war Jewish theatre at Naugarduko 10. Its permanent exhibition on the top floor outlines the history of the Litvaks through a range of ritual objects and artwork, including a reproduction of a Chagall painting of the Great Synagogue. There are also examples of ghetto art, including the remarkable paintings of Samuel Bak – now an internationally recognised artist – who had his first exhibition in the ghetto at the age of nine. Other floors host temporary exhibits whilst the auditorium is regularly used for conferences and cultural events. Just around the corner at Aguonų 5 is another former Jewish school; a small former prayer house is in its courtyard.

The oldest section of the museum is in the former Tarbut Gymnasium (Mon–Thu, 10.00–2.00, Sun, 10.00–2.00) at Pylimo 4 which also houses the headquarters of the national and city Jewish community. Permanent exhibits include a room dedicated to Jewish resistance and the spartan but moving Gallery of the Righteous upstairs. A plaque in the courtyard of the nearby Benedictine nunnery at Šv. Ignoto 5 commemorates priest Juozas Stakauskas, teacher Vladas Žemaitis and nun Marija Mikulska who hid and cared for 12 Jews in the nunnery's archive. The building on the corner of Šv. Ignoto and Benediktinių, marked by a plaque, was where Theodor Herzl met Jewish community leaders on his 1903 visit.

The third museum branch is the Green House (Mon–Thu, 9.00–5.00; Sun, 10.00–4.00; ring bell), a small wooden building up a slight hill at Pamėnkalnio 12 (west of the top of Pylimo). The exhibition's title, *Catastrophe*, is self-explanatory. Most of the exhibits are labelled in Lithuanian and Russian but one can pick up an English information booklet at the entrance which should be returned on leaving. Refurbishment of the rather old-fashioned displays will occur in the coming years but they nonetheless show the development of the Holocaust in Vilna and Lithuania clearly. It should also be borne in mind that this was the first institution in the Soviet Union to openly address the Holocaust. Outside the building is a rather abstract monument honouring the Japanese diplomat Chiune Sugihara (see Kaunas) and another around the corner dedicated to his Dutch collaborator Jan Zwartendijk.

Elsewhere

West of the ghetto, at the intersection of T. Ševčenkos and Švitrigalios, the 'Kailis' fur factory was a labour camp which employed around 1,000 Jews in the premises of a pre-war radio factory. The camp survived the liquidation of the ghetto but not two *Aktionen* in 1944. On 27 March, families were told to take their children to a nearby camp for anti-typhoid injections; they were snatched by the Germans and sent to Poland. As the Red Army approached in July 1944, the remaining inmates were taken to Ponar. The factory is on the south-western corner of the junction at Ševčenkos 16. The wartime buildings are most visible from the courtyard entered further along the street. The Jewish prisoners were housed in two buildings, one of which was the brick building on the north-eastern corner (Ševčenkos 15/Švitrigalios 14); the other was destroyed. The site is a relatively short walk from the Tolerance Centre; it can also be reached by taking buses 2, 6 and 73 or trolleybuses 10, 13 and 17 to the T. Ševčenkos stop.

Nearby A. Vivulskio 18 was the site of the headquarters of YIVO (Yiddish Scientific Institute), the global centre for the study of Yiddish language, history and culture. As something of a backwater in Poland's eastern borderlands, Wilno rather declined in the inter-war period; however, the choice of the city ahead of New York and Warsaw (the world's two largest Jewish cities at the time) as the base of YIVO in 1925 was an indication of its continued prestige. The institute amassed an enormous archive of Yiddish books, periodicals and research. Under the occupation, much of the material was taken as waste paper but a team of Jewish intellectuals, including Herman Kruk and the poet Abraham Sutzkever, was employed to sift through the collection to preserve significant documents on behalf of the representatives of Alfred Rosenberg, Nazi ideologue and Minister for the Eastern Territories. Rosenberg's agents scoured the great Jewish libraries of Europe seeking artefacts for his collection in Frankfurt supposedly to form the basis of an institute for the study of 'an extinct race'. In fact, the Jewish workers smuggled out notable items which were then hidden, many brought out of the ghetto by Ona Šimaitė. The documents sent to Frankfurt were discovered after the war and transferred to YIVO's new base in New York. The site is currently a large open space as the post-war bathhouse which stood here is itself being replaced.

North of here, off Vilnius's main street Gedimino prospektas, the forbidding building at Aukų 2 is home to the Museum of Genocide Victims (Tue–Sat, 10.00–5.00; Sun, 10.00–3.00; 4 Lt; www.Muziejai. lt/Vilnius/genocido_auku_muziejus.en.htm). This was the NKVD/KGB headquarters in 1940–41 and 1944–91 and was unsurprisingly employed by the Gestapo in between. Contrary to the impression given by the museum's name, its focus is only Soviet terror. That said, it is a sobering place to visit, especially the preserved prison cells; it also stages temporary exhibitions on other cases of genocide, including the Holocaust.

On the other side of Gedimino and Lukiškių aikštė, the still functioning Lukiszki Prison (Lukiškės in Lithuanian) is located on Lukiškių skersgatvis off Lukiškių gatvė. The prison was often an antechamber to Ponar, especially in the early months of the occupation when gangs of Lithuanian 'snatchers' roamed the city looking for Jews. Many of those imprisoned here never even made it to Ponar, dying of hunger or beatings in their cells.

Across the river (via footbridge at the top of Tumo-Vaižganto) and on the other side of Upės gatvė, another memorial to Sugihara is incongruously located next to a casino in a grass park. The memorial and the surrounding cherry trees are gifts of his alma mater Waseda University.

Rather further east along the Neris's north bank, on Olimpiečių, is the site of Vilnius's first Jewish cemetery whose origins may date back to the fifteenth century and which closed in 1830. As so often in the USSR, it was destroyed by the Communists rather than the Nazis. The site is now occupied by the concrete Palace of Sports but there is a simple memorial near the road. The nearest bus stop is Žvejų (bus 33) from where Olimpiečių runs east. The city's other old Jewish cemetery, which opened in the nineteenth century, was located uphill in the eastern suburb of Užupis but was also destroyed by the Communists – the stones were used in construction projects. A striking 2004 memorial, funded by the US Commission for the Preservation of America's Heritage Abroad, consists of retrieved *mazzevot* arranged to form a sloping wall along with a symbolic gatepost. There are a few remnants of stones on the hill behind. It stands on the eastern side of Olandų, technically number 22. It can be reached by taking buses 27, 34, 37 or 44 to the Krivių stop. It is also accessible on foot from the Old Town, through Užupis along Užupio and Krivių although this is a far more comfortable walk returning downhill. Užupis itself, now home to Vilnius's bohemians, was once an area of major Jewish settlement though there is little obvious trace of this today.

Shortly before the ghetto's liquidation, around 1,250 people were resettled to work in the German military garages (*Heereskraftfahrpark*) which became the HKP labour camp. This was located south of Užupis in apartment blocks built to house poor Jews by the ubiquitous Austrian Jewish entrepreneur and philanthropist Baron Hirsch. Although the camp was liquidated in July 1944, around 250 inmates survived – the head of the garage, Major Karl Plagge, warned them of the coming *Aktion*, giving them time to find hiding places. The buildings which housed the prisoners still stand at Subačiaus 47 and 49 (buses 4, 4A, 10, 13, 34 and 74 to Subačiaus). Plaques on the wall of 47 explain the history whilst a symbolic gravestone and a large monument stand between the buildings.

The only surviving Jewish cemetery is in the northern Šeškinė suburb at Sudervės 28 (buses 43 and 46 to Buivydiškių). The land was purchased by the community before the war, meaning that the first people to be interred were those who died in the ghetto. The first stone on the left is a symbolic grave for Witenberg along with FPO messenger Sonia Madejsker who was murdered by the Gestapo. Behind are further memorials to other leaders of the organisation. Slightly further ahead on the left is a memorial to victims of the ghetto (*'Geto Aukos'*) alongside the graves of prisoners who were murdered during the liquidation in September 1943. In the front corner of this group, a book design on a grave indicates a memorial to ghetto teachers. Behind is the Vilna Gaon's mausoleum, relocated from the original Jewish cemetery.

PANERIAI

Paneriai forest was a popular pre-war recreation spot for citizens of Vilnius, conveniently located next to a major railway junction. The site was requisitioned during the Soviet occupation and six large pits intended for fuel storage were dug. These pits, together with Paneriai's proximity to the city and its transport connections, made it an obvious choice for one of the largest killing operations in the USSR. To keep prying eyes away, the forest was surrounded with barbed wire and notices warning of dire consequences.

Executions began a little over a week after the Germans arrived and escalated through the course of 1941 as victims were brought in their thousands, sometimes on foot, sometimes by train or truck. The first rumours of what was occurring reached the Jewish leadership in Vilnius as early as 10 July but, as in so many other places, there was an unwillingness to believe them. Even after six wounded women escaped from the pits on 3–4 September, most Jews in the newly created ghettos were not aware of what was transpiring until it was too late. The mass *Aktionen* in the following two months began to dispel illusions but the fact that the incipient FPO leadership issued a manifesto on 31 December calling on Jews to realise that 'all roads lead to Ponar' is an indication that there were still people unaware of the truth even after most Vilna Jews were already dead: at least 33,500 had been murdered by the end of 1941. Further killings continued through the remainder of the occupation, encompassing Jews from Vilnius and other communities in Lithuania and Belarus. The most notorious example of the latter came in April 1943 when trains carrying people from small Belarusian ghettos supposedly to Kaunas were sent to the forest. Amongst the more than 4,000 killed were several hundred from the Vilna ghetto enticed by German notices inviting them to join relatives in Kaunas. Paneriai was also used for the murder of Soviet POWs, Polish intellectuals and resistance fighters and other enemies of the Nazis; it is estimated that between 70,000 and 100,000 people were killed there. In a typically gruesome postscript, the Germans then tried to hide the evidence of their crimes by forcing a team of 80 Jews and Russian POWs to exhume and burn the bodies of 68,000 people between September 1943 and April 1944. The unfortunate prisoners were kept chained together in a pit yet still endeavoured to escape by digging a tunnel. Although the majority were caught and murdered, 11 were able to flee on 15 April 1944 and join the partisans

Jewish survivors erected a memorial with a Yiddish inscription at the site shortly after the war but this was torn down in 1952 at the height of Stalin's anti-Semitic campaign. The small community then raised funds for a new memorial during the reawakening of Jewish civil society under Khrushchev only to be rewarded with a bland granite structure in Lithuanian and Russian which acknowledged the murders and even referred to 'local accomplices' but made no reference to who the victims were. A central stone was added in 1990 pointing out that 70,000 Jewish men, women and children were murdered. This is still the first thing that visitors encounter at the site, located in the parking area which is actually where the terrified crowds were made to wait in line before proceeding to the pits below. A path to the right of the car park leads to a memorial to Poles killed at Paneriai, marked by a cross next to the railway. On the other side of the tracks, a boulder commemorates Lithuanian underground printers killed on 23 August 1941.

The main path from the car park leads down into the woods, passing three newer memorials to the left, two dedicated to Lithuanians and the third, a more low-key stone, to the 7,514 Red Army soldiers murdered in 1941. The peace of the forest is regularly disturbed by the clanking sound of passing trains which adds to its eerie atmosphere as does the not infrequent sight of locals wandering through the trees in search of strawberries. The main memorial area lies at the foot of the hill, faced by a small building housing a branch of the Vilna Gaon Museum which displays personal items recovered at the site. Unfortunately, it often fails to observe the published opening hours (Mon–Thu, 10.00–6.00; Sun, 10.00–4.00). Opposite is the specifically Jewish memorial, erected in 1991. The large stone has a menorah at its base etched with images of people being led through the ghetto to the forest. There are further Jewish memorials behind, including a stone to the inmates of the Kailis and HKP camps. A tall obelisk erected in the 1980s was designed to resemble the original Yiddish monument but was predictably still dedicated to 'victims of Fascism'.

Paths lead to the large pits which were landscaped and given memorial plaques in Soviet times. There are two behind the museum: that to the left contained the bodies of up to 3,000 Red Army officers, the other was used by the Germans to store valuables stolen from the victims which were then sold to locals. Following the main path clockwise from the principal memorial leads to two facing pits. The excavated pit to the left was where the corpse burners were held whilst that to the right was the principal execution site for the Vilna Jews murdered in 1941. At the back of the complex are two more pits which were used for executions in 1942–43, one of which is enormous.

Paneriai is a short ride from Vilnius on frequent trains, although it is worth checking return times before departure as there can be long gaps in the afternoon. Exit the station to the right and follow the road which runs parallel to the railway into the woods. The walk takes about 10 minutes.

KAUNAS

The name Kovno was almost as celebrated as that of Vilna. There are records of a Jewish presence from the fifteenth century but for four centuries this was largely confined to the Slobodka suburb, separated from the main city by the river Neris. Jews who settled in the centre were subject to periodic expulsion until the final lifting of residence restrictions in the mid-nineteenth century. Thereafter, Jewish life flourished, its most famous symbol being the Slobodka yeshiva, established in the 1860s. Like Vilnius, the city became a major centre of both religious and secular culture with 40 synagogues, a renowned schooling system and a strong Zionist movement. Although the tsarist government ordered mass expulsions during the First World War, Kaunas's position as inter-war capital of independent Lithuania prompted further growth. It is believed that the Jewish population in 1939 was close to 40,000, having long since spread beyond the bounds of Slobodka.

The first blow came with the Soviet occupation in 1940 when Kaunas was especially hard hit as the location of national institutions which were almost entirely abolished. Hundreds of Jews were ensnared in mass arrests on 14 June 1941, including a large proportion of the independence-era communal leadership and intelligentsia. This did not prevent local nationalists from blaming Jews for the evils of Communism, creating a climate receptive to the Germans who occupied the city on 24 June 1941. Indeed, Kaunas was to achieve infamy for the horrific pogroms which swept the city even before the Germans had arrived. Vigilante gangs murdered hundreds in Slobodka whilst around 60 Jews were taken to the Lietūkis garage in the city centre and clubbed to death as German soldiers looked on. *Einsatzgruppe A* arrived in early July and launched a more systematic killing campaign: it is estimated that 10,000 Jews were murdered by Germans and Lithuanians in June and July 1941. The main killing sites were a series of forts around the city which had been created by the tsarist regime from the late nineteenth century. Eight had been constructed in Kaunas itself and several were used by the Germans. However, it was the Ninth Fort, outside the city, which eventually became the principal murder site.

An order was issued in July 1941 giving Jews one month to relocate to a ghetto in Slobodka, or rather two adjoining ghettos separated by barbed-wire fences. When they were sealed on 15 August 1941, they contained almost 30,000 people. The small ghetto was destroyed on 4 October, its inmates sent to the Ninth Fort, and on 29 October the 'Great *Aktion*' saw the same fate befalling close to 10,000 Jews from the large ghetto. That was the last of the major *Aktionen* for some time, leaving around 17,500 alive. However, the area of the ghetto itself was subject to reductions in 1942 and 1943 which naturally increased the overcrowding and distress. Reich Jews were transported to Kaunas from late 1941 but they were usually sent straight to the Ninth Fort.

Ghetto inmates were engaged in forced labour across the city. In addition, the *Ältestenrat* established workshops in Slobodka which eventually provided work for almost 6,500. Kovno's Council differed in a number of respects from Vilna's *Judenrat*, partly a reflection of the fact that most members had been chosen through election by the community. Its chair, Dr Elhanan Elkes, was a popular and respected physician who contrasted with the abrasive Gens. As in Vilna, the council sponsored cultural life and social welfare, illicitly maintaining education and religious observance even after they had been banned by the Germans in 1942. More strikingly, it actively supported the underground movements which united in 1943 to form the General Jewish Fighting Organisation; a significant proportion of the Jewish police were members. The council thus pursued a twin-track strategy of seeking salvation through work, as in so many other ghettos, whilst also covertly encouraging resistance. In time, around 300 members of the underground were able to escape and join the partisans.

Unlike Vilna, the Kovno ghetto was not destroyed in the autumn of 1943 but was instead converted into a concentration camp, known by its German name Kauen, meaning that the SS took over direct control. More than 3,500 Jews were sent to sites outside the city whilst a further 2,700 were deported in late October, the adults to Estonia, the children and elderly to Auschwitz. A major *Aktion* in March 1944 saw the murder of 1,800 people. As the Red Army approached in July 1944, the ghetto, much reduced from its 1941 borders, was evacuated with most remaining inmates sent to Dachau or Stutthof. Many sought to hide in specially prepared underground bunkers but were forced out by German grenades and firebombs: around 2,000 died in the ensuing carnage and virtually the whole ghetto territory was burned down. When the Soviets arrived on 1 August 1944, only around 90 Jews had survived in bunkers and a few hundred more in the forests with the partisans. A further 2,000 emerged alive from the concentration camps. As a result of emigration, the modern community is only a few hundred strong whilst remnants of the city's Jewish history are generally less evident than in Vilnius.

The Slobodka ghetto

Slobodka, now known as Vilijampolė, is accessed from the Old Town by the bridge of the same name which leads to Jubarko gatvė. This street had originally been designated as part of the small ghetto but was cleared, along with Raudondvario and Tilžes to the west, on 15 August 1941, the day the ghettos were sealed. Jubarko was the main focus of the Lithuanian pogrom in June 1941. The private house at number 16 next to the Jubarko bus stop was the site of one of the most horrific incidents when Rabbi Zalman Osovsky was tied to his chair, his head laid on an open Gemara and then sawn off.

The large ghetto stretched from Veliuonos (the street immediately north of Jubarko) for two kilometres to the north. The destruction of 1944 means that the area is largely covered by post-war buildings although some original wooden structures survive, primarily in the streets around Jubarko, Veliuonos and the southern end of Linkuvos. At the latter's junction with Kriščiukaičio, an unobtrusive memorial stone marks the site of one of the gates. There is otherwise little to indicate the history of the area. The small ghetto was located in the streets to the west of the lower section of Panerių. The only visible recollection of its existence is a memorial plaque at Goštautų 4 which marks the site of its hospital which was burned down on 4 October 1941 with patients and staff still inside.

The most touching reminder of the Jewish presence in Slobodka lies outside the ghetto area in the former cemetery. Overgrown and barely accessible for many years, the site has been cleaned up and is signposted ('*Senosios žydų kapinės*') off Tilžes, just after the turning for Kėdainių. Now a meadow rolling gently uphill, it contains a memorial stone stating that this is the former Jewish cemetery. The only other standing stone in the field, back to the left, is dedicated to the victims of the June pogrom, many of whom were buried here. In parts, one can just discern original graves under the grass.

Elsewhere

Visitors seeking tangible traces of Jewish Kovno are more likely to find them near the Old Town although they still tend to be fairly well hidden. The only active synagogue is the Choral Synagogue, east of the Old Town at Ožeškienės 13. In theory, it is open only for services (Sun–Fri, 5.45–6.30; Sat, 10.00–12.00) but it is worth ringing the buzzer – foreigners are usually given the chance to admire the lovely interior. In the yard behind is a memorial sculpture for children killed in the Holocaust. A short walk south-west of the synagogue are a few remnants of pre-war civic and religious life. At Gruodžio 25, on the corner with Smalininkų, the tall redbrick building with a large inscription in Russian and almost entirely faded Yiddish was once a Jewish orphanage. Located on Smalininkų's next junction, Poškos 21 was a home for the Jewish elderly. Nearby Puodžiu 1 is a partially remodelled former synagogue, now occupied by a car repair business. Another former synagogue is two blocks to the west at Zamenhofo 7.

An affluent hilltop district east of the New Town was Kaunas's diplomatic quarter during its tenure as capital. Amongst those who resided here was the Japanese consul Chiune Sugihara. When the USSR occupied Lithuania, most diplomats were withdrawn but Sugihara and Jan Zwartendijk, the representative of the Dutch government-in-exile, remained for over a month more. They were able to use this period to assist Polish Jews who had fled to Lithuania and who were seeking a way out of Europe. A plan was concocted whereby Zwartendijk issued certificates for passage to the Dutch colony of Curaçao. However, the Soviet authorities would allow passage only to those with valid visas for the next onward destination. Therefore Sugihara, acting on his own initiative in defiance of orders from Tokyo, issued hand-written Japanese transit visas, even to Jews who did not necessarily have the Dutch passes. It is believed that at least 6,000 people thus benefited; witnesses recall Sugihara still writing out visas and throwing them from the train window as he left in September 1940. Not all of the Jews survived – some failed to leave Lithuania before June 1941 – but thousands were able to make their way eastwards to Japan. Most eventually found themselves in Shanghai where the Japanese refused their ally's request to hand over or kill them. After other diplomatic postings, Sugihara was asked to resign in 1947. The Foreign Ministry later claimed that this was due to cost-cutting measures but his family has always maintained that he was punished for his actions in Kaunas. The house that he rented at Vaižganto 30 is now the Sugihara House Museum (Mon–Fri, 10.00–5.00; Sat–Sun, 10.00–4.00; donation; www.geocities.jp/lithuaniasugiharahouse). It is not accessible by public transport but can be reached from Bažnyčios gatvė which turns off Vytauto prospektas by the main bus station. At the end of the street, steep steps lead up to Fryko which runs parallel to Vaižganto.

Another former Jewish cemetery is north-east of the Sugihara House on Radvilėnu plentas, close to Kaunas zoo. There are a significant number of surviving gravestones and a new memorial has been placed by the entrance but the cemetery is overgrown away from the entrance and has become a hangout for local teenagers. It is probably best to visit in the morning. The easiest way to get there from the centre is to take buses

2, 10, 20, 21 or 37 to the stop for the zoo and turn northwards into Radvilėnų for a few hundred metres.

Around a mile north-west of the cemetery, the Seventh Fort was the site of the murder of 3,000 Jews by the SS's Lithuanian auxiliaries in the first week of July 1941. There is a simple memorial stone located within the run-down grounds but entry is forbidden – the fort is owned by the military. It is possible to see the exterior of the complex at the end of Archyvo, just north of the bus stop of the same name on Tvirtovės alėja (buses 17, 27, 36 and 41 and trolleybuses 8 and 9). The First, Fourth and Sixth Forts were also used as murder sites but are similarly unwelcoming. The Sixth Fort, north-east of the train station at the end of Baršausko, does have an astonishing memorial outside in the form of a field of crosses which commemorates Lithuanians murdered by the Soviet secret police. The Kaunas tourist office (visit.kaunas.lt) offers tours of the grounds of some of the forts but the focus is on their tsarist military history.

Kaunas's modern Jewish cemetery is south of the river Nemunas, hidden between army barracks and a wooded hill off Minkovskių. At one end is a memorial stone to those killed in the destruction of the ghetto in July 1944. It can be reached by taking bus 35 to the Elevatorius stop. Look for the large factory complex on the right hand side; just after it are the white army barracks. On exiting the bus, walk to the entrance to the barracks and follow the road through to a gateway at the end; the cemetery is straight ahead across the railway tracks.

THE NINTH FORT

Although most of the Kaunas forts were employed as murder sites, the Ninth Fort (just outside the city limits) is the most infamous. It was constructed between 1902 and 1913, the only one of a planned series of 12 new forts to be completed. Its more advanced defensive capacities and greater distance from the city made it a site of considerable potential utility, a point not lost on the successive rulers of Lithuania even after its original raison d'être had disappeared with Russia's defeat in the First World War. It was thus converted into a prison in 1924, a role it maintained during the Soviet occupation of 1940–41when several thousand people were detained there before their deportation to the Gulag. Unsurprisingly, the Nazis put the fortress to similar uses; in the early days of the occupation, it mainly held Communists – most of whom were shot. Executions initially took place in the fort's courtyard but 600 Soviet POWs were forced to begin digging large pits in July 1941. The major *Aktionen* against Kovno Jews took place on 4 and 29 October 1941 at the fort; on the latter occasion, according to the German records, 9,200 people were murdered, almost half of them children. Killings of foreign Jews began in November: the victims would ultimately include Jews from the Reich, Poland and France. It is estimated that at least 50,000 people perished there, more than 30,000 of them Jewish. The Germans began destroying the evidence in the autumn of 1943, employing a team of 72 Jews and Soviet POWs. Remarkably, nearly all were able to escape at Christmas 1943, exploiting the drunkenness of the guards.

In the immediate post-war period, there was no question of any memorial at the Ninth Fort as, with leaden predictability, it was again taken over by the Soviet security forces; it later became a base for collective farm managers. It was only under Khrushchev that the site

The Ninth Fort (Photograph by Elizabeth Burns)

was converted into a museum with four cells given over to an exhibition on Nazi atrocities which naturally chose not to dwell on the identity of the victims. A far more ambitious development came in 1984 with the inauguration of a specially built museum, a bleak concrete building in front of the fort (Apr–Oct: Mon, Wed–Sun, 10.00–6.00; Nov–Mar: Wed–Sun, 10.00–4.00; 5 Lt; www.muziejai.lt/kaunas/forto_muziejus.en.htm). The exhibition has been completely redesigned since independence to cover both Nazi and Soviet repression. The theme of parallel dictatorships is developed with displays on Stutthof and Norilsk, one of the most notorious camps in Stalin's slave empire. The focus is very much on the suffering of Lithuania as a nation – the section of Stutthof examines the fate of a few dozen nationalist intellectuals sent there in 1943 – but any misgivings this may inspire should be set against the fact that specific Jewish agony is addressed in the fort itself, reached by a path behind the museum.

Before entering the fort proper, visitors pass seven bronze wall sculptures depicting scenes from the Holocaust created by the Lithuanian artist Arbit Blatas (also found in Paris and Venice) and cypress trees planted in honour of Sugihara. A mannequin of a guard in the corner watchtower is a questionable touch but the interior of the fort is undoubtedly sombre. The main exhibition is housed in converted cells, the most dramatic of which is to the right of the entrance. Its walls preserve the graffiti left by Jews sent to Kaunas on convoy 73 from Drancy, the only French transport not to be sent to Poland. Around a third of the party of 878 were sent onto Tallinn but most met their deaths in the Ninth Fort. Names and dates remain on the walls along with the haunting message 'Nous sommes 900 français'. The remarkable Eve Line Blum-Cherchevsky, whose father was amongst the victims, has spent years researching the history of the convoy and put together a multi-volume book at her own expense, containing names and biographies of the deportees (www.convoi73.org). Other cells address the history of the Kovno ghetto and the partisans, the concentration camps, Sugihara and Zwartendijk, the massacres in Lithuania and the fate of 1,000 Munich Jews deported to the fort and murdered in November 1941.

The area outside is dominated by a colossal group of sculptures created in the 1984 redevelopment and dedicated to 'victims of Fascism'. Despite their size, it is only at close range that one realises that the giant thrusting forms represent people. The path to the monuments passes a wall where shootings took place and the long channel where bodies were burned. Nearby are a series of more restrained memorials dedicated to Jewish victims. They include specific stones for convoy 73 and the Munich Jews, the latter, from Munich city council, beginning with the words 'In sorrow and shame – and appalled by the silence of the bystanders'.

The Ninth Fort is to the north-west of Kaunas, next to the junction of the A1 and A5 highways and signposted. Buses 23 and 35 make the journey from the centre and Slobodka to the 9-ojo forto muziejus stop on Vandžiogalos gatvė but this requires a walk back along the road under the A1 and then a rather perilous rush across the grass and the southbound slip road connecting the A1 to the A5. The car park is a short walk up the hill.

OTHER SITES

Many locations associated with the Holocaust have some form of memorial, albeit often an inexpressive Soviet monument. The enterprising Baltic Mass Graves Project, organised by Britain's Holocaust Educational Trust and the Lithuanian government, has placed stone markers at the sites and erected standardised road signs, but it is generally necessary to know roughly where to look when heading for a specific location. Equally, urban remnants of Jewish life are usually well hidden. The best advice is to contact, where possible, the nearest Jewish community – details of those that still exist can be found at www.litjews.org.

The most important Jewish community after those of Vilnius and Kaunas was in Šiauliai (Shavli). However, it is poorly commemorated although there is a memorial for one of the city's two ghettos on Trakų gatvė. As in Kaunas, the ghetto officially became a concentration camp in 1943 and thus continued to exist until 1944 at which point survivors were dispatched to camps in the Reich. However, most of Šiauliai's Jews had long since been murdered, chiefly in the Kužiai forest to the west of the city. It can be reached by taking the A11 out of Šiauliai and turning north at Kužiai village onto the road to Verbūnai (Gruzdžių gatvė).

The most active form of remembrance beyond the two main cities is to be found at Kėdainiai (Keidan), around 25 miles north of Kaunas, which had a Jewish population of around 3,000 in 1941. One of two adjoining former synagogues on the town's old market square (Senoji rinka 12) now houses the Kėdainiai Museum's Multicultural Centre

(Tue–Sat, 10.00–5.00; 4 Lt; www.kedainiumuziejus.lt) which includes an exhibition on local Jewish history and the Holocaust. The museum staff can assist in locating other local sites, notably the two former Jewish cemeteries to the west of the town (on Lakštingalų and just around the corner on A. Kanapinsko) and the memorial in the woods behind the Catholic cemetery at the end of Dotnuvos (across the Smilga creek from the Jewish cemeteries) where 2,000 Jews were murdered on 28 August 1941.

CHAPTER 12

LATVIA

The fate of Latvia's Jews was similar to that of those of Lithuania with most murdered by the end of 1941. In addition, thousands of Jews from the Reich met their deaths in the forests around Riga.

Jews had lived in Latvia from the sixteenth century but in relatively small numbers compared to those in Lithuania. The community grew considerably in the nineteenth century, and briefly reached 200,000 in the early twentieth century, but much of this population was transient. Emigration, as well as expulsions by the tsarist regime during the First World War, meant that there were 93,479 Jews by the time of the 1935 census. Latvia's independence had initially brought them equal rights in the 1920s but some erosion occurred after the emergence of Kārlis Ulmanis's nationalist dictatorship in 1934. In particular, their economic and educational freedoms were curtailed along with those of other minority groups including Russians and Latvia's sizeable ethnic German population. That said, the Ulmanis regime generally eschewed violence and clamped down on the country's emergent Fascist movements as much as on the parties of the left.

The outbreak of war left Latvia, like Lithuania, within the Soviet sphere of influence and it was no surprise when the country was occupied by Stalin in June 1940. Although some Jews undoubtedly welcomed the Communists – as the lesser evil compared to Nazism – the majority did not and, as in Lithuania, they were disproportionately targeted in the NKVD terror: around 5,000 were arrested in the year of the Soviet occupation, the largest number in massive round-ups barely days before the German invasion. Naturally, this did not stop the Latvian far right from concluding that the Jews were responsible for the country's misfortunes, creating fertile ground for the Germans to harvest.

With local nationalists carrying out pogroms, especially in Riga, anti-Semitic violence began before the Nazis gained control of the whole country on 10 July 1941. In due course, the most fanatical of these hooligans were organised by the Germans into auxiliary units, the most notorious being the Arājs Commando, which worked alongside *Einsatzgruppe A*. As in Lithuania, the killing squads began primarily with Jewish men but from late summer onward targeted entire communities.

337

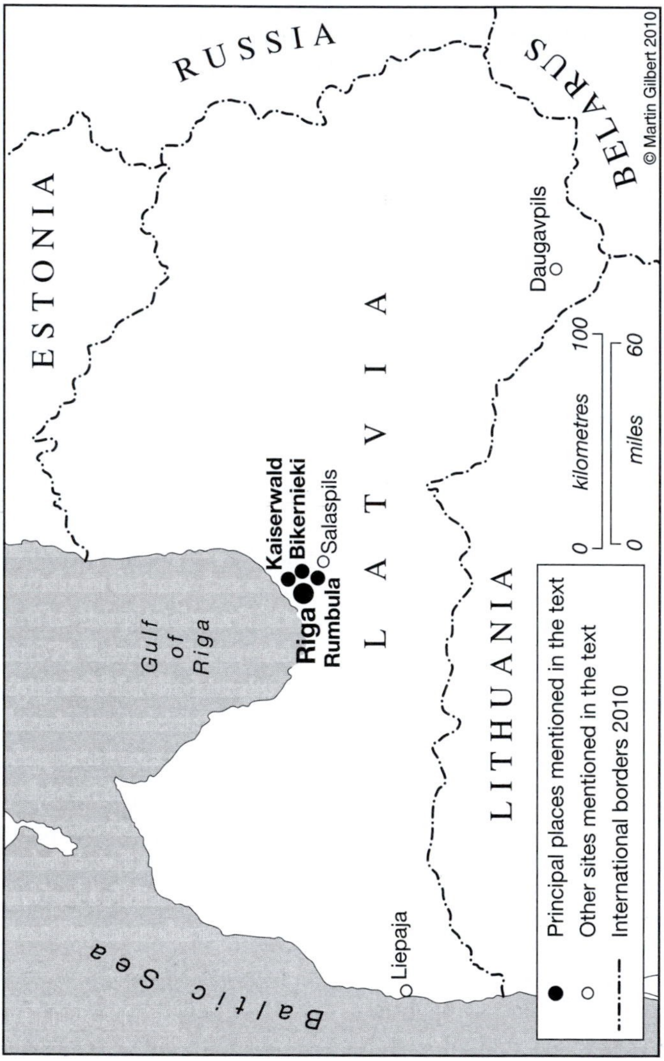
ESTONIA
RUSSIA
BELARUS
LATVIA
LITHUANIA
Gulf of Riga
Baltic Sea
Kaiserwald
Bikernieki
Salaspils
Riga
Rumbula
Liepaja
Daugavpils
0 kilometres 100
0 miles 60
Principal places mentioned in the text
Other sites mentioned in the text
International borders 2010
© Martin Gilbert 2010

Latvia

Almost half of the between 70,000 and 75,000 Jews in Latvia at the start of the occupation had been murdered by the time a ghetto was created in Riga in October 1941. The pace of extermination then quickened so that only a few thousand Jews survived to the end of the year: perhaps 4,000 in Riga and less than 1,000 each in Daugavpils and Liepāja. The largely emptied Riga ghetto was then used to accommodate thousands of Jews transported from the Reich from late November 1941 onwards. They too were murdered, mostly in the first half of 1942, with the result that a mere 5,000 Jews were still alive in the whole of Latvia by the start of 1943. The Kaiserwald concentration camp was created that year for this remnant which was subsequently evacuated to Stutthof in the summer of 1944 as the Red Army approached. After the ensuing death marches and massacres, approximately 3,000 survived to the end of the war. In addition, the Nazis and their local accomplices murdered around half of Latvia's pre-war Roma population of 4,000.

Jewish life in Latvia, or at least in Riga, was able to revive to some extent due to the return of thousands of exiles who had fled before the Germans arrived and later immigration from other parts of the USSR. This community was able to achieve a notable partial victory in the 1960s when its activists persuaded the Communists to erect a memorial with Yiddish text at the Rumbula murder site but commemoration of the Holocaust was otherwise constrained by the Party. This situation has changed dramatically since independence with some very striking memorials erected at most of the major sites. Although there have been questions about Latvia's willingness to fully confront the past, especially the vexed issue of collaboration, it is undoubtedly the former Soviet republic which has done the most to address the legacy of the Holocaust.

RIGA

Close to half of Latvia's Jews – some 43,000 at the time of the 1935 census – lived in the capital. A community had first been established in the seventeenth century but was expelled in 1742. They returned by the end of the eighteenth century and, despite Riga's position outside the tsarist Pale of Settlement (the area to which Jewish residence was restricted), the city developed into a Jewish centre of some significance over the following decades. It naturally acquired more prominence in the inter-war period, due not just to its status as capital of independent Latvia but also to its role as a major sanctuary for émigrés from the Soviet Union.

Riga fell to Hitler's forces on 1 July 1941 and its Jews were immediately subjected to horrific acts of violence, initially at the hands of locals rather than the Nazis. The city had a large and well-established German population but much of the initiative came from Latvian nationalists (in particular from members of the Fascist Thunder Cross), who arrested and beat large numbers of Jewish men from the very first day of the occupation, a pattern that continued throughout July. Thousands were executed in the Biķernieki forest on the edge of the city whilst all but one of Riga's synagogues were burned, many on the night of 4 July. This misery was accompanied by the familiar litany of Nazi laws over the course of the summer and early autumn, including the announcement in August that a ghetto was to be created. On 23 October 1941, the Germans ordered all Jews into the ghetto within two days. By the time it was sealed on 25 October, it is believed to have contained 29,602 people, over half of whom were adult women – the fact that only around 8,000 adult men were in the ghetto is an indication of the impact of the July murders. Jews with work permits (approximately 4,000) were separated from the others on 19 November as a prelude to the latter's destruction. The Germans cleared the whole of the ghetto's western half on 29–30 November when 10,000 people were marched south to the Rumbula forest and murdered. The 15,000 or more who remained without work permits suffered the same fate on 8–9 December.

The survivors were left in the 'small ghetto', the tiny corner to which they had been confined on 19 November. Part of the 'large ghetto' was settled by deportees from the Reich: the first transport had been dispatched straight to Rumbula but most of those who arrived thereafter were sent to the city, eventually exceeding 20,000 people. Indeed, although the murder of Riga's Jews would have happened anyway, the timing is generally believed to have been dictated by the decision to deport German Jews to the city. The two ghettos were separated by a fence and each had its own institutions until they were merged in November 1942. By this time, large numbers had died as a result of starvation, disease, exhaustion or the periodic *Aktionen* to which the ghetto was still subjected by the Germans – most of the Reich Jews were murdered in the forests in 1942 and 1943. In the course of 1943, the ghetto's population was gradually transferred to the newly created Kaiserwald concentration camp which became a base for labour projects across the city. The ghetto was finally destroyed at the end of that year: following a selection in November, those remaining Jews considered capable of work were sent to Kaiserwald; the 2,000 or more others were deported to Auschwitz-Birkenau.

The dissolution of the ghetto, and later of Kaiserwald, meant that there were around 150 Jews left alive in the city by the time the Red Army arrived in October 1944. Only a few hundred more were able to survive the camps and death marches. Remarkably, however, Riga Jewry underwent something of a renewal after the war so that from the 1950s through to the 1970s the population hovered around the 30,000 mark, not hugely less than in 1941. This was partly due to the return of Latvian Jews from the interior of the Soviet Union – those who had fled in 1941 and, occasionally under Khrushchev, survivors of the Gulag – but mainly a result of Soviet policy in the 1950s which encouraged the repopulation of Latvia through migration of citizens, Jews included, from other republics. As a result, Riga emerged as one of the leading Jewish centres in the USSR, rather eclipsing historically more significant cities such as Vilnius and L'viv. The population has subsequently fallen due to emigration but Riga remains one of the few former Soviet cities where a meaningful Jewish presence can still be said to exist.

The ghetto and around

The ghetto was located south-east of the centre in the Moscow Suburb, an area traditionally inhabited by poor Jews and Russians. It remains a rather run-down quarter today and there is still a very strong Russian presence. Much of it is post-war, especially on its northern edges where the small ghetto was, but there are still many pre-war buildings – faded Secessionist mansions and crumbling wooden cottages – especially on central Ludzas iela and the streets to its south.

The original 1941 ghetto gate was at the junction of Lāčplēša and Sadovņikova. On the southern corner of the junction, Lāčplēša 141, a grand building set in gardens, housed Riga's first Jewish secular school from 1887. In the autumn of 1941, it became the headquarters of the first Nazi-appointed Council of Elders for the ghetto, chaired by Michael Elyashov. The short-lived council vainly attempted to improve conditions in the ghetto but even most of its own members were murdered at Rumbula in November and December.

The main street running through the ghetto began as Sadovņikova before bending and becoming Ludzas, known to the Germans – Nazi and Jew alike – as Leipziger Straße. The whole area from Lāčplēša in the west to Ludzas between Daugavpils and Mazā Kalna was cleared on 29 and 30 November 1941 and thereafter ceased to be part of the ghetto. The fading beige building at Ludzas 25 was just on this side of the division. A pre-war gynaecological clinic, it was converted by the Council of Elders into the ghetto's hospital in 1941, only to be requisitioned as a medical centre for the SS following the murder of its patients and staff at Rumbula. East of here, Ludzas then formed the boundary between the small ghetto for the Latvian Jews to the north and the German ghetto to the south. Ludzas 41–43 (now a school), near the corner with Mazā Kalna, was the Refuge for Poor Jews, founded in the nineteenth century to provide shelter for orphans and the disabled. During a pogrom in the 1905 Russian Revolution, a crowd of hooligans burst in, killing two and injuring ten. Far worse was to follow on 30 November 1941 when children who were too sick to be taken to Rumbula were stabbed with bayonets and bludgeoned with rifle butts.

On the 'German' side of Ludzas, shortly after the junction with Mazā Kalna, the mansion at 56 was the principal administrative building within the ghetto. It housed the Nazi institutions – the ghetto command and police – alongside the German Jews' *Ältestenrat* and the Jewish police. The next crossroads, with Līksnas, was the location of the gates which separated the two ghettos. Most of the buildings in this area are modern but a left turn at the next junction into Viļānu leads to a once grand building at number 14 which was the main bathhouse and delousing centre for the small ghetto. The southern stretch of Viļānu on the other side of Ludzas leads to a small wooded park across Virsaišu which was the site of the Jewish cemetery. The victims of ghetto massacres were buried here including those who were too weak to be taken to Rumbula on 30 November 1941. All 40 of the ghetto's Jewish policemen were buried here on 31 October 1942: they were shot after the Germans captured the first group of would-be partisans who had managed to escape from the ghetto and discovered that most of the police were members of the emerging underground. The park, landscaped by the Communists, reveals nothing of this history beyond a simple stone bearing a large Star of David in its south east, near the junction of Ebreju and Līksnas. It is rather surprising, given the overall excellence of Holocaust memorials in

Latvia, that there are no other markers within the territory of the ghetto itself.

From the cemetery park, one can walk down Ebreju onto Maskavas and head back westwards. Although only a part of this street was in the ghetto, it is the most redolent of pre-war life. The ghetto boundary can be followed by taking Maskavas into Jersikas. Off the latter, the large building at Mazā Kalna 2 housed mainly Viennese Jews along with elderly Berliners. The first major selection of German Jews took place outside this building on 5 February 1942, the so-called *Dünamünde Aktion*. The SS officer who carried out the selection, Gerhard Maywald, informed those chosen for extermination that they were being sent to work at a fish cannery in a village called Dünamünde at the mouth of the Daugava River. At his trial in 1977, Maywald claimed that this story was invented to quieten the victims. More than 1,000 of the Berlin Jews and around 400 from Vienna were selected, apparently believing Maywald's fiction as they were dispatched to their deaths in the Biķernieki forest.

Returning to Maskavas, there are two further traces of pre-war Jewish life. The former *Bikur Holim* hospital, opened in 1924, is at 122–128; a plaque commemorates its chief surgeon, Professor Vladimir Mintz, who perished in Buchenwald in February 1945. Maksavas 57, close to the junction with Lāčplēša, was the site of the Old-New Synagogue which was burned down on the night of 4 July 1941. The building was reconstructed as a residential property by the Communists and has since been restored to Jewish ownership.

Riga's main Holocaust memorial is actually outside the territory of the ghetto, a short walk west at the junction of Gogoļa and Dzirnavu. This was the site of the Great Choral Synagogue, constructed over three years between 1868 and 1871 but destroyed in a few hours on 4 July 1941. The Latvian nationalist militias had spent the day rounding up Jews on the streets and driving them to the synagogue where they joined around 300 refugees from Lithuania who had taken shelter in its basement. All were burned alive. After the war, the Communists razed the synagogue remains and created a park around the site. The basement, still with charred bones inside, became a rubbish dump. It was only in 1988 that the site was properly cleaned up and a memorial erected in the form of another large stone with a Star of David. There is a plaque dedicated to all Jews killed in Latvia in what remains of the basement. Alongside is Riga's newest memorial, a collapsing wall held up by seven pillars which list the names of Latvians who saved Jewish lives. The third and largest pillar has an inscribed picture of Jānis Lipke, a former dock worker who used his position as a contractor with the Germans to smuggle around 40 to 50 Jews out of the ghetto to hiding places in the countryside.

The memorial and the ghetto area are accessible by trolleybus 15 and buses 18 and 18a which run down Gogoļa, stopping just after the memorial and continuing, making a number of stops, through the ghetto along Sadovņikova and Ludzas. Return services go along Kalna, the ghetto's northern boundary. Trams 3, 7 and 9 skirt the southern fringes, rumbling along Maskavas.

Elsewhere

Riga's only surviving synagogue is south of the Old Town at Peitavas iela 6–8. It escaped destruction because of the fear of fire spreading to neighbouring buildings in the narrow streets; instead, the Germans used it for storage. Nearby Peldu iela 15 was the house of Anna Alma Pole who hid seven Jews. They were discovered on 25 August 1944 by the police who had to call in SS help after the armed Jews fought back. Some were killed on the spot, the others, together with Pole, were shot in prison. There is a memorial plaque.

The Museum of the Occupation of Latvia (daily, 11.00–5.00 (until 6.00, May–Sept); free; www.omf.lv/eng/about_us/welcome.html), located in an ugly yet striking building which previously housed a museum dedicated to the pro-Bolshevik Latvian Riflemen, is a block north on Strēlnieku laukums. The exhibition covers Latvia's history from 1940 to 1991. The main focus is inevitably on the Soviet periods but it does address the Nazi occupation and the Holocaust. Local involvement in the latter is perhaps underplayed but the museum is a serious attempt to address the twin misfortunes which befell so many people in eastern and central Europe.

A pre-war Jewish theatre at Skolas 6 on the north-eastern edge of the centre now houses the Jewish community headquarters. Latvia's Jewish Museum (Sun–Thu, 12.00–5.00; donations) is upstairs. The exhibition is fairly small (three rooms) and clearly has limited funds but nonetheless does its job effectively with the Holocaust covered in the third room. There is a kosher café in the building's basement.

The city's well-maintained Jewish cemetery is five miles north-east of the centre at Lizuma 4. Opened in the 1920s, it was damaged by the Germans although some pre-war graves survive. To the left of the entrance are memorial stones to Jews from various German cities. Further ahead, on the right, is a memorial to Jānis Lipke paid for by the Jewish community in 1990. Some of the graves of Holocaust survivors list the names of other family members on the rear of the stone; the date of death is invariably 1941. The cemetery can be reached by taking trolleybus 4 to its terminus. Go back in the direction the bus came, cross the busy road, and take the first right turning into Lizuma. Walking up this road, across the railway tracks, the cemetery wall will appear on the right – do not take the first right marked 4a but instead continue to follow the walls as they curve around to the entrance.

KAISERWALD

Kaiserwald concentration camp was established in March 1943 in Mežaparks, a village on the edge of Riga. Its earliest inmates were German criminals but it soon became the major internment centre, along with the Estonian camps, for the surviving Jews of the Baltic states. The remnant of the Riga ghetto was transferred from June 1943 onwards and was joined by other Latvian Jews and women from the Vilna ghetto in November of the same year. A number of Jews from Hungary and Poland were also sent to the camp in 1944. By March 1944, Kaiserwald's population numbered 11,878 of whom only 95 were not Jewish. The prisoners were used as forced labour in Kaiserwald itself and in a number of sub-camps, mainly for German enterprises in the Riga region, notably the AEG electrical company. Other inmates were used for mine clearing at the front line. The approach of the Red Army triggered the evacuation of prisoners to Stutthof in August and September 1944, although not before the Germans first murdered all those considered unfit to work, ever convicted of any infringement of camp rules or simply outside the 18–30 age group. Kaiserwald was empty when the Soviets liberated it on 13 October.

Mežaparks has long since been swallowed by Riga and the site of the camp is now occupied by housing, a typical example of the failure of the Soviet authorities to properly commemorate locations associated with Jewish suffering. In fact, a memorial for Kaiserwald was created only in 2005. Sadly, it is less impressive than the other modern memorials in the Riga area – a small steel tower, set in a triangular pit, supports pieces of loosely arranged corrugated glass, as if the artist had been given the task of creating something out of found materials. Only the brief text at the base explains the context.

The memorial stands on Tilta iela, between the railway tracks to the west and Viestura prospekts to the east. The camp was bounded by these roads. It can be reached by taking trolleybus 3 to its terminus and then walking a further 250 metres or so along Tilta, across the railway lines. If taking a taxi, do not ask for 'Kaiserwald' or 'Mežaparks' as hardly anyone is aware of the monument's existence; they will associate the names with the forest and the beach a couple of miles to the east. Instead ask for the Russian Orthodox church near the corner of Tilta and Viestura which is next to the memorial.

BIĶERNIEKI

Biķernieki forest was the principal killing site for the Reich Jews sent to Riga. Its dark history dates from almost the moment of the occupation when it was the main location for the shooting of thousands of Jewish men captured by Latvian Fascists in July 1941. Although the mass killings at the end of that year took place at Rumbula, 1942 saw the resumption of murder operations. It is generally believed that up to 40,000 Jews were shot at Biķernieki between 1941 and 1944. The forest was also used for the murder of political prisoners as well as Soviet POWs, bringing the estimated total number of victims to 46,500.

The site was largely neglected after the war although the Communists did allow commemoration in 1962 in an unsuccessful attempt to divert attention from Jewish pressure for memorialisation of Rumbula (see next entry) – the fact that Biķernieki's victims also included Gentiles made it marginally more acceptable to Soviet orthodoxy. Mass graves were marked in the forests but there was no identification of victims aside from a plaque to members of the Komsomol (Communist Youth League) killed by the Nazis. This changed in 2001 with the creation of arguably the most impressive memorial in the former USSR, largely funded by German cities working with Riga city council. Its entrance is marked by two black commemorative stones and an angled archway. The centrepiece is a canopied altar-like black marble cube which quotes from the Book of Job, surrounded by fields of rocks, creating the impression of crowds of figures. Plaques by the rocks give the names of the mainly

German cities from which the victims came. Paths lead off to the mass graves in the woods which are marked by raised grass banks and stones. There is a further group of mass graves on the western edge of the forest (walk 630 metres along the main road from the memorial area and then another 700 metres northwards along a path through the woods – there is a map on a memorial stone by the entrance to the path).

The memorial site lies on Biķernieku iela, a lengthy road running through Riga's eastern suburbs. The relevant section is a stretch of forested road, approximately a mile long, between western Lielvārdes iela and eastern Strautu: the memorial is about halfway along on the southern side. Buses 15 and 16 stop near the entrance but are not practical if coming from the centre (although 15 does eventually go on to Rumbula). It is perhaps more straightforward to take trolleybuses 14 or 18 which stop at each end of the forest, necessitating a 10 minute walk from either direction. Probably the easiest way of ensuring the correct location is to

Biķernieki (Photograph by Elizabeth Burns)

stay on the bus through the forest, passing the memorial, and walk back to it from the next stop (by a grim Communist housing block). One can walk westwards from the memorial to the other mass graves and then to the stop after the junction of Biķernieku and Lielvārdes to catch a bus back to the centre.

RUMBULA

The site chosen for the destruction of Riga Jewry was a forest a few miles south of the city. At least 25,000 people were murdered at Rumbula on 30 November and 8–9 December 1941 by *Einstzgruppe A* and Latvian auxiliaries. Victims, exhausted by the march from the city, were forced to strip in sub-zero temperatures and lie in specially dug pits on top of the bodies of those already shot. It is believed that only three people out of the thousands sent to the forest returned alive. Additional hundreds of Jewish men were murdered at the site in the summer of 1944 during the gradual liquidation of Kaiserwald. The approach of the Red Army saw *Aktion 1005* operations at Rumbula, with several of the pits opened and bodies burned.

Soviet forces arrived in time to prevent complete destruction of the site but their leaders subsequently showed little interest in maintaining it. Rumbula was consciously ignored by the authorities as an embarrassing symbol of exclusively Jewish anguish – even to publish information about it was prohibited. This systematic neglect led a group of young Riga Jews to begin to clean up the site from 1961 and erect their own memorials which were then removed by the state. The Communists partially relented and allowed a small memorial to be placed there in 1964, albeit one which had to follow Party dogma, causing it to be nicknamed 'the Aryan Compromise'. A more appropriate memorial was inaugurated in 2002. A giant twisted metal sculpture, suggestive of the broken branch symbol used on Jewish gravestones, juts into the main road to indicate the turning. The encroachment of industry, another unhappy legacy of Communism, has largely destroyed the Rumbula forest but the wooded knoll where the murders occurred remains. The central memorial area, surrounded by mass graves, consists of a large menorah (again sculpted from twisted metal) encircled by jagged rocks arranged in the pattern of a Star of David. The rocks are engraved with the names of victims whilst the paving around them is inscribed with those of the streets of the Riga ghetto. The simple Aryan Compromise monument (dedicated to 'Victims of Fascism' in Latvian, Russian and Yiddish) is rather overshadowed alongside. Even so, the very fact of its existence – at a time when many other murder sites in the USSR such as Babi Yar were unmemorialised – is a testament to the dedication and courage of the Jewish activists. A path continues round the left of the hill to more mass graves, some of which are right next to the train line; steps lead down to the side of the railway.

Rumbula is easy to reach from Riga. To do so by car, take the main southbound A6/E22 from the city; the memorial is 7 miles south of the centre, the broken branch sculpture impossible to miss on the left-hand side of the road. This follows the route along which Riga's Jews were marched in 1941. The most direct means of public transport is the local train to the Rumbula halt. Disembark at the primitive platform and walk back alongside the tracks in the direction the train has come from. After about 200 metres, one will see steps to the left – this is

Rumbula (Photograph by Elizabeth Burns)

349

the entrance to the rear of the memorial site. On its way to Rumbula, the train passes through Šķirotava station which was the usual point of arrival for the Reich Jews. The first transport arrived from Berlin on 30 November 1941: its 942 passengers were immediately sent to Rumbula. It is estimated that around 2,000 elderly or weakened deportees were shot in the vicinity of Šķirotava in 1941–42 and buried in pits over which the Germans built a new railway line.

OTHER SITES

Salaspils 'work and education camp' was constructed in early 1942 by 1,500 German Jews, more than two-thirds of whom died in the process. There is evidence that it was originally meant for Reich Jews but it instead became a camp for mainly Latvian political prisoners, deserters, and forced labourers in transit to the Reich (there was also a separate POW camp nearby). Estimates of the number of inmates range from 6,000 to 20,000 (including children); several thousand died. It was decided shortly after the Rumbula controversy, for motives which are not hard to imagine, to make the site the principal memorial to victims of Nazi terror in Latvia. As if to emphasise the point, Soviet propaganda progressively inflated the death toll to 100,000 by the 1980s. The memorial site is extraordinary, a forest clearing dominated by massive concrete sculptures with names such as 'The Red Front' and 'Solidarity'. It is north of Salaspils town and less than four miles south-east of Rumbula along the E22. The nearest train station, around a mile from the site, is Dārziņi, the next halt after Rumbula.

Daugavpils (Dvinsk) was home to a pre-war Jewish population of more than 11,000, most of whom were murdered in the summer of 1941. Survivors were forced into a short-lived ghetto in the small fortress (now a prison) on the south-west side of the Daugava river, opposite the Citadel. The main surviving trace of Jewish life is the synagogue, at central Cietokšņa 38, which has recently been restored with financial assistance from the children of Dvinsk's most famous son, painter Mark Rothko. The principal murder site was Poguļanka forest, marked by a memorial off the northbound P67 out of town (located on the right shortly after Daugavas iela curves away from the river to become Rīgas šoseja). The easiest way to find it is to consult the local Jewish community (www.dvinsker.lv).

Liepāja (Libau) had a Jewish population of around 6,500 in June 1941. By the time a ghetto was established a year later, 832 remained alive (most of them were sent to Kaiserwald in 1943). Massacres had occurred around the city but most infamously on the Šķēde sand dunes where, between 15 and 17 December 1941, 2,749 people (mainly women and children) were forced to strip in the freezing winter and murdered by the Germans and their Latvian auxiliaries. Visitors to any Holocaust museum will have seen the notorious photographs of the naked women awaiting execution. A Soviet obelisk was erected after the war, supplemented in 2005 by an astonishing new memorial in the form of a group of connected curved walls which form the shape of a menorah. The memorials are close to the water treatment plant off Viestura iela, several miles north of the city proper. Another murder site was the fish-processing factory on the corner of Roņu and Zvejnieku, near the Olimpija stadium. Just off central Lielā iela, a plaque at Tirgoņu 22 marks the home of Roberts and Johanna Seduls, who saved 11 Jews by hiding them in their basement for two years. A memorial wall in the Jewish section of the Līvas cemetery on Cenkones iela to the south lists the names of 6,423 Liepāja Jews murdered by Hitler and Stalin.

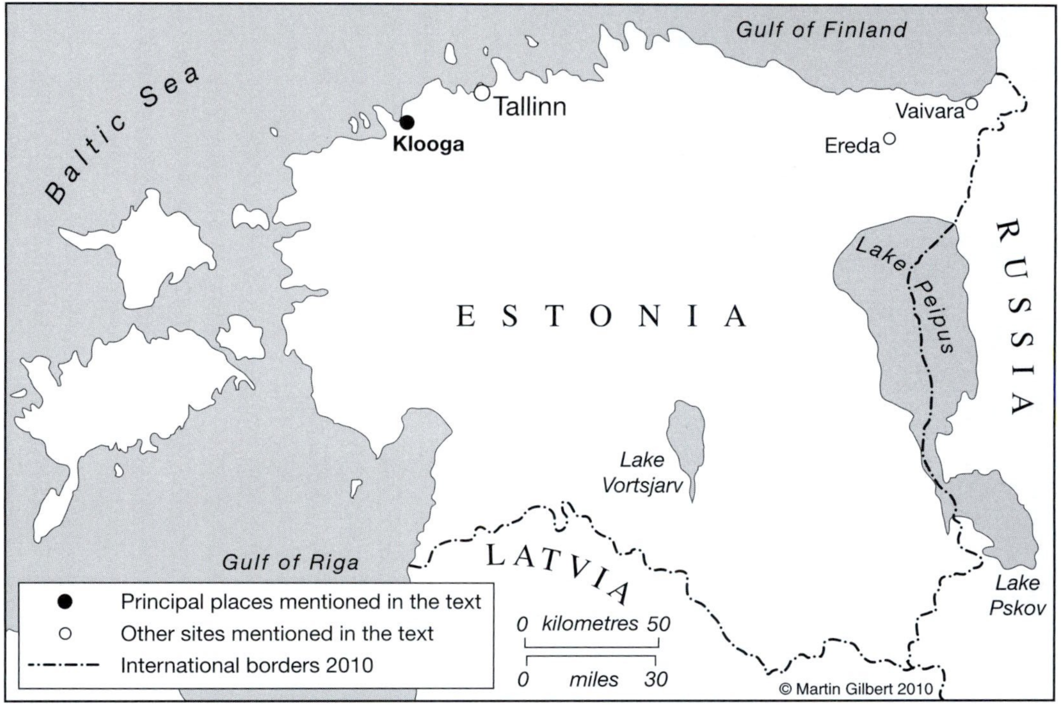
Gulf of Finland
Baltic Sea
Tallinn
Klooga
Vaivara
Ereda
ESTONIA
RUSSIA
Lake Peipus
Lake Vortsjarv
LATVIA
Gulf of Riga
Lake Pskov
Principal places mentioned in the text
Other sites mentioned in the text
International borders 2010
0 kilometres 50
0 miles 30
© Martin Gilbert 2010

Estonia

CHAPTER 13

ESTONIA

C ompared to its Baltic neighbours, Estonia had a tiny Jewish population yet it was destined to play a significant role in the Holocaust as the location of a network of notorious concentration camps which were especially important in the fate of the Lithuanian Jews. Jewish settlement in Estonia developed only in the nineteenth century and by the 1930s the population numbered less than 5,000. Jews were disproportionately targeted following the Soviet occupation in 1940: around 500 were amongst the 10,000 Estonians arrested and sent to the Gulag a little over a week before the German invasion. Most of the remaining Jews were able to flee into Russia so that only around 1,000 remained when the Germans arrived. Virtually all of this latter group were murdered: *Einsatzgruppe A* reported that 936 Jews had been killed in Estonia by January 1942 and that the country was now 'free of Jews'.

However, from autumn 1942, thousands of Jews were sent to Estonia, especially from the Lithuanian ghettos in 1943–44. The main camp was officially Vaivara in the east of the country but this served primarily as a transit facility, most inmates spending a short time there before being dispatched to larger camps of which the best known was Klooga near Tallinn. Prisoners were used for forced labour, mainly for military purposes, which inevitably took its toll on people who had already spent months or years in ghettos or other camps. As the Red Army approached in summer 1944, many were shipped across the Baltic to Stutthof; those who remained were murdered.

Even by Soviet standards there was little memorialisation of the Holocaust after the war, a pattern largely repeated in the post-independence era when the main focus was on Communist tyranny. However, the Estonian government, in partnership with the US Commission for the Preservation of America's Heritage Abroad and Britain's Holocaust Educational Trust, is now placing memorial markers at 22 sites representing camps and mass graves. The first five markers were erected in 2005 and the project is ongoing.

KLOOGA

Klooga is the best-known of the Estonian camps due to its size and to the horrific events that took place there in September 1944. It was created in the summer of 1943 and most inmates were survivors of the Vilna ghetto, sent via Vaivara in August and September of that year. They were housed in separate camps for men and women, each with a large two-storey building for the prisoners (around 100 Soviet POWs were also inmates of the men's camp). Men mainly worked in cement and brick factories or in sawmills in inevitably back-breaking conditions (300 were required to run from the factory to the railway station, each carrying a 50 kg sack of cement) whilst women laboured in quarries around the camp. Food rations were meagre with no evening meal; any prisoners who had managed to hide a small piece of food during the day were liable to fall victim to an SS guard nicknamed 'Six Legs' because he was accompanied by a large dog which was trained to pounce on them. Those who committed other minor infractions of camp rules were subject to corporal punishment during the roll call when luckless victims were tied to a curved bench and beaten with a birch rod and, bizarrely, a bull's penis reinforced with steel. The overwork and lack of food and water inevitably lead to severe illnesses which were dealt with by the camp's 'sanitation officer', Dr Bodman, who administered poison to those he considered incurable; no medical treatment was available in Klooga.

Given that the camp contained many survivors of the Vilna underground, there was a resistance movement which was able acquire weapons, but the high turnover of inmates meant that it was difficult to organise effectively whilst the knowledge that the Soviets were approaching persuaded many to bide their time. Prisoners were, therefore, taken by surprise when the liquidation of the camp began on 19 September 1944 following Germany's military collapse in Estonia. Surrounded by the SS, they were taken in groups into the forest and shot. The fact that the first group contained 300 of the healthiest men who were called to carry firewood created a false sense of security. As it transpired, the wood was used to stack the bodies in piles, ready for burning in an attempt to destroy the evidence. When the Red Army arrived on 28 September, they found three still smouldering bonfires and a fourth which the Germans had not had the time to light. Approximately

Klooga (Photograph by Elizabeth Burns)

2,500 people were slaughtered at Klooga, 2,400 Jews and the 100 Soviet soldiers. A mere 82 managed to survive by hiding in the camp or running into the woods.

Despite the haste of their exit, the SS were able to destroy most of the camp so that the site is now almost completely forest. It is, though, commemorated by three memorials. Approaching from the railway, the new memorial marker – a black marble diagonal stone with text in Hebrew, Estonian and English – is set back slightly from the path on the left. A little more than 100 metres further along the path, again on the left, is a raised bank of earth surrounded by a concrete wall. This is the mass grave of the victims, marked by a 1951 Soviet memorial, predictably dedicated to 'victims of Fascism'. However, new plaques have been added explaining explicitly that this is the burial site of around 2,000 Jews murdered by the Nazis on 19 September 1944. A few metres ahead, to the right of the path, a large meadow contains a specifically Jewish memorial, erected in 1994. This honours not just the Klooga victims but all Jews murdered in Estonia.

The simplest way to get to Klooga is to take the electric railway from Tallinn's main station to the Klooga Aedlinn halt (not Klooga). Cross the railway tracks to the north towards the forest. Take the right turn on the dirt track which then almost immediately bends round northwards to the left. After a 5 minute walk, the new memorial will appear on the left. To reach the site by car, take the 8 road from Tallinn to Paldiski. Immediately after the road crosses the railway near Klooga village there is a sign pointing to the memorials. As this is coming from the north, the route will be the reverse to that described above, so the first thing visible will be the Jewish memorial in a clearing to the left, about 2 kilometres along the forest road.

OTHER SITES

Tallinn's Patarei prison, north of the train station on Kalaranna, was the site of the execution of 207 Estonian Jewish men in 1941 as well as of French Jews in 1944. The latter were part of convoy 73 from Drancy which was sent to Kaunas and whose members left the '*Nous sommes 900 français*' graffiti in the Ninth Fort. A section of the former prison (which only closed in 2002) has been opened as a rather macabre tourist attraction (www.patarei.com) but the focus is on its role under the

KGB and the tone is not entirely sombre. There are memorial plaques on the south-eastern wall to the Estonian and French Jews as well as an additional memorial to victims of Communism but they are inaccessible. Follow Kalaranna eastwards from the main entrance until it swings to the left and becomes a cobbled driveway: ahead are two sets of gates and a watchtower. The memorials can be seen through the gates. Whilst in Tallinn it is worth visiting the small Jewish community's impressive new synagogue (2007), encased in a striking glass exterior, at Karu 16, east of the Old Town.

There is little trace of the concentration camps which are now often just patches of forest. The Holocaust marker project is changing this but it may be some time before all are memorialised. Vaivara is marked by a large boulder and one of the new memorials. The village is off the main Russia-bound E20 road, near Sillamäe. Heading south from the E20, the memorials are on the left by a cluster of trees shortly after the railway lines.

The only other camp to have a significant memorial is Ereda, also in the east of the country, where there is a rather interesting 1960s Soviet construction; one of the new markers has been placed in front. The memorials are accessed via a forest track to the west of the road that runs from Kohtla-Järve to Ereda, just after the village of Sompa. Alternatively, one can leave the E20 at Jõhvi and head west through Sompa.

Belarus

BELARUS

B elarus was home to one of Europe's largest Jewish populations and the destination of tens of thousands of deportees from the Reich. It also provided the most striking examples of prolonged and widespread Jewish resistance to the Nazis anywhere in the continent.

The territories that comprise modern Belarus were incorporated into Lithuania in the thirteenth century, engendering the emergence of significant Jewish communities. Following the partition of the Polish-Lithuanian Commonwealth in the late eighteenth century, the whole of the country came under Russian rule; in the following century, the Jewish population increased more than tenfold, exceeding 700,000 in the 1897 census. Nearly all major cities, including Minsk, had majority Jewish populations whilst most small towns were overwhelmingly Jewish; the world of these *shtetlach* is most famously evoked in the paintings of Marc Chagall (Moishe Shagal), born near Vitebsk in 1887. The Jews of Belarus were seen by others and generally saw themselves as Litvaks (Lithuanian Jews), sharing the Yiddish dialect and commitment to religious Orthodoxy (expressed in famed yeshivas, notably at Volozhin and Mir) of their neighbours although Hassidism made inroads in the south and east.

The absence of a specifically Belarusian Jewish identity was symptomatic of uncertainty over the extent to which Belarus existed as a distinct entity as was the historic competition for control of its territory between Russia and Poland which resurfaced after the First World War when the west was taken over by Poland and the east by the Soviet Union. Life in the former region continued much as before albeit subject to the growing anti-Semitism of Polish policy from the mid-1930s. Change in the Soviet zone was more dramatic. In theory, Jews had equal civil rights and, until the early 1930s, a degree of autonomy. However, religious life was attacked – nearly all synagogues and yeshivas were closed – and Jewish businesses, like all others, were nationalised. More generally, rapid industrialisation accelerated Russian and Belarusian influence in the cities, a process which had begun in the last years of tsarism. Although Stalinism had not yet become explicitly anti-Semitic, many thousands of Jews were victims of the Great Terror from the mid-1930s. Similar developments were to befall western Belarus when it was annexed in September 1939 under the terms of the Nazi-Soviet Pact. Even so, Stalinist rule was welcomed by many as a guarantee of security from Hitler.

This assumption was to prove tragically mistaken in June 1941. Lying in the route of the main German advance on Moscow, most of Belarus fell by the end of that month. On the eve of the invasion, more than 1 million Jews were residing in the country, close to two-thirds of them in the former Polish provinces. *Einsatzgruppen* mass killings began in July. The initial pace of executions was slower than in Lithuania, at least in the west of the country, but waves of murder at the end of that year and from the following spring meant that most Belarusian Jews were dead by the end of 1942. Killings generally took place in forests and fields outside urban centres but in late 1941 an extermination camp was established at Maly Trostenets near Minsk. This camp also played a significant role in the murder of the 55,000 or more Reich Jews who were sent to Belarus from November 1941 onwards. A small number of ghettos, including Minsk, survived into 1943 but they too were destroyed by the autumn of that year. Estimates of the death toll vary, not least because most of the victims lived in the western provinces and are thus often included in the figures for Poland, but at least 800,000 Jews were murdered on the territory of modern Belarus.

This figure would have been higher were it not for resistance offered by Jews themselves. In many ghettos, notably Minsk, underground groups arose which focused primarily on escaping to partisan units in the forests which cover so much of Belarus. The most extraordinary of these latter organisations was that led by the Bielski brothers in the Navahrudak region: a specifically Jewish partisan group which took in not just potential fighters but all Jews who could get to the forests – children, the elderly, the sick – and protected them for the duration of the occupation. In total, more than 1,200 people survived in the Bielski family camp until liberation in 1944, a significant proportion of the at least 25,000 Jews who reached the forests. It was partly as a result of these efforts, combined with the return of exiles from other republics, that Belarus was able to maintain a Jewish population of more than 100,000 for most of the post-war period. The modern community is probably less than 50,000.

Although a specifically Jewish memorial was created in Minsk shortly after the war, remembrance of the Holocaust was subject to the same constraints as in the rest of the USSR. What makes the country depressingly unique is the fact that this is still generally the case even today. Some explicitly Jewish monuments were erected in the brief flurry of liberalism in the early 1990s but since President Lukashenka's accession to power less progress has been made. The government has also continued the Communist policy of destroying historic Jewish properties to make way for public projects. As a result, outside of Minsk, Holocaust memorials and sites associated with Jewish heritage are generally neglected and hard to find even by the standards of the former USSR.

Although most citizens have Russian as their first language, all street signs and most maps are labelled in Belarusian; the latter language has therefore been used for place names in this chapter with the exception of Maly Trostenets given that virtually all historians use this Russian name.

MINSK

The Minsk ghetto was the largest in the Soviet Union. This is perhaps unsurprising as the city was once the biggest in the world to have a majority Jewish population. A Jewish presence was first recorded in the fifteenth century but it was in the nineteenth century that it mushroomed: in the first tsarist census of 1897, the Jewish community numbered 47,560 people (52 per cent of the population). The numbers continued to grow, but Jews ceased to be the majority due to the demographic changes which followed the Russian Revolution. The latter also had a more direct impact on Jewish life with the closure of all but one synagogue by the end of the 1920s (this sole survivor was demolished in the 1960s) although certain forms of cultural autonomy, such as Yiddish schools and theatre, were permitted. The Jewish population grew rapidly in the late 1930s: estimates for June 1941 put it between 80,000 and 90,000. This partly reflected the rapid pace of urbanisation under Stalin (the city's overall population was close to 300,000) but more specifically the flood of refugees from Poland in late 1939.

Minsk fell to the Germans on 28 June 1941. Killings began almost immediately and the order for the establishment of a ghetto was issued on 20 July 1941, earlier than in most other major Soviet cities. Unusually, the ghetto was sealed off by barbed wire rather than a wall, imprisoning around 100,000 people. Major *Aktionen* in August led to the murders of 5,000 Jews. Himmler himself visited the city during this period and was visibly shaken after witnessing a mass shooting, giving greater impetus to the SS's quest to find an easier method of killing. Further *Aktionen* in November killed

19,000 people in order to clear space for Reich Jews who were settled in the eastern section of the ghetto. Many of the newcomers – nicknamed 'Hamburgs' due to the origin of the first transport – were themselves sent straight to Maly Trostenets but several thousand were accommodated in Minsk, separated (partly voluntarily) from the rest of the ghetto. There were yet more mass killings in April and July 1942, most of the Reich Jews being amongst the 30,000 or so murdered on the latter occasion. A steady campaign of attrition was waged through the course of 1943 (less than 8,000 people were still alive by the summer) before the final liquidation in the autumn with transports to Sobibór and Maly Trostenets.

However, the Nazis were unable to completely eliminate Minsk Jewry because of the efforts of the ghetto underground which was established in August 1941, earlier than in virtually any other city. It enabled 10,000 people to escape to the forests although many of them failed to survive the war. The underground was assisted by the *Judenrat* which provided money, clothing, hiding places and forged papers. In fact, the Minsk *Judenrat* was relatively unusual in that it generally enjoyed the confidence of inhabitants, its members having apparently been chosen almost at random, generating sympathy for their unenviable burdens. This was especially true of the first chair Ilya Mushkin (selected, it was believed, only because he could speak German), an active supporter of the resistance and generally regarded as a good man doing his best in impossible circumstances; he was hanged in February 1942.

The Jewish community revived somewhat after the war, with a population in excess of 50,000, due partly to migration from smaller towns and other republics. The current community numbers less than half that figure but has undergone something of a revival since the collapse of Communism despite occasional difficulties created by the state. Minsk itself was almost completely rebuilt in a Stalinist style following the immense damage caused by the war but a few remnants of its Jewish past survive.

The ghetto

Although much of the ghetto's physical fabric survived the war (ironically, it was one of the few areas of Minsk where this was the case), little now remains, concrete tower blocks having long since occupied most of the district. A case in point is Jubiliejnaja ploshcha (Jubilee Square – easternmost exit of Frunzienskaja Metro) which was the heart of the

Minsk: *Yama* memorial (Photograph by the author)

ghetto. The sole hint of its past is a tiny memorial stone near the corner with Rakaúskaja (opposite the Belarusian Potash Company building).

A far more impressive memorial can be found by taking Miel'nikajte (wartime Ratomskaya) north from Jubilee Square to the crossroads with Zaslaúskaja where the *Yama* (pit) was the site of the most horrific massacre in the ghetto's history; 5,000 people were killed here on 2 March 1942 (Purim), amongst them the inmates of the orphanage which stood on Špaliernaja. Children were thrown into the pit and buried alive whilst the German administrator Wilhelm Kube threw in sweets. When the operation was completed, the German party, which included Eichmann, made their way to Jubilee Square for a prepared lunch. Later that day, many labourers returning from work were selected and shot to make up the numbers. Unusually for the USSR, this became a memorial site almost immediately after the war. Even more unusually, an obelisk was placed in the deep hollow which not only contained text in Yiddish but also mentioned that the victims were Jews. This has been supplemented by 1990s additions, most hauntingly a remarkable sculpted group of figures descending into the pit next to the stairs. Plaques on a stylised menorah list the sponsors of the project. To the side is the *Aleja Pravednikaú Susvetu* (Alley of the Righteous), a small row of trees planted to honour Belarusians who saved Jewish lives.

Another significant memorial is found in the former Jewish cemetery, which formed the ghetto's southern boundary and was another scene of mass killings. Rather predictably, it was destroyed by the Communists who turned a section into a park. The German-funded memorial, created in the early 1990s, stands just inside the park at the bottom of Suchaja (south from Jubilee Square). Three stones commemorate the murdered Jews of Bremen, Hamburg and Düsseldorf. Loosely arranged next to them are retrieved gravestones from the original cemetery.

The one section of the ghetto which survives physically is around Rakaúskaja (Rakovskaya in Russian, Ostrovskaya in the war) which runs east from Jubilee Square. The sturdy nineteenth-century buildings are especially in evidence at the crossroads with Vyzvaliennia and Vitebskaja; this was the area of the ghetto cleared in November 1941 to make way for the German Jews. The yellowish building on the north-west corner at Rakaúskaja 24, now a school, was once the Zalcman Synagogue although this had ceased to function in the 1920s. The redbrick building on the north-east corner contained a variety of Jewish institutions and was notable for a remarkable doorway on the Rakaúskaja side, its wooden frame carved to incorporate a large *mezuzah*. This was something of a tourist attraction for Jewish visitors to Minsk in the 1990s but the current owner had it removed – a section can be seen in the Jewish Museum. The Rokavskiy Brovar restaurant at Vitebskaja 10 occupies a former yeshiva whilst, a little east of the crossroads, Rakaúskaja 19 was a Jewish wedding house.

Elsewhere

Standing just across the Svislač River from the ghetto area, the Troitskoye Predmestie (Trinity Suburb) is a block of restored nineteenth-century buildings. Amongst them is the former Kitayevskaya Synagogue now occupied by the House of Nature at Maksima Bahdanoviča 9A. To get there from the ghetto, follow Niamiha (the ghetto's eastern boundary) northwards and cross the river; the Suburb is the group of houses to the left of the road, immediately north of the bridge. The synagogue nestles in a courtyard accessed by a path between numbers 9 and 11.

Minsk's only currently active synagogue is the nineteenth-century Main Synagogue, at Daúmana 13B (tram 5 to the first stop on Daúmana). The heart of modern community life, however, is the Minsk Jewish Campus (www.meod.by), located in a modern compound at Viery Charužaj 28, north-east of the synagogue and a reasonably short walk west from the Maksima Bahdanoviča stop for buses 29, 38, 44 and 59 and trolleybuses 12 and 22. This is the home of the Belarusian Museum of Jewish History and Culture (donations) which occupies only a single room but contains interesting exhibits. The museum receives relatively few visitors and there do not appear to be fixed opening hours so it is probably wise to arrange a visit in advance (jewish_museum@mail.ru) although a Westerner just turning up should be allowed through the security.

For a rather different approach to Belarus's history, one can visit the State Museum of the History of the Great Patriotic War (Tue–Sun, 10.00–5.00; 5000 BYR; Kastryčnickaja Metro), located in a dull concrete building on central Kastryčnickaja ploshcha (more widely known by its Russian equivalent Oktyabrskaya ploshchad). The extensive displays have no English labelling but the photographs and objects are usually understandable enough. There is a small section on the persecution of the Jews whilst Maly Trostenets is represented by a diorama and a collection of items retrieved from the site including a jar filled with earth and bones.

Valadarskaha 5, located further south and off the Stalinist showcase Niezaliežnasci, is the Maxim Gorky Theatre but was once the Choral Synagogue, widely regarded as the most beautiful in Minsk. Following the Revolution it was converted into a workers' club and then a cinema before becoming the Jewish Theatre in 1930. Wartime damage led to the creation of the current neoclassical facade but it initially continued to function as a specifically Jewish institution, with performances in Yiddish, until 1948. In fact, the theatre was itself to play an unwitting role in the emerging anti-Semitic persecution of the late 1940s: Solomon Mikhoels, the legendary actor-director and chair of the Jewish Anti-Fascist Committee, was murdered in Minsk in January 1948, having come from Moscow to watch a performance. Shortly thereafter, the theatre was Russified and renamed after Gorky.

These events reflected Stalin's adoption of an explicitly anti-Jewish policy in his last years, a policy which inevitably had ramifications for the memorialisation of the war and the Holocaust. A literally concrete example can be found on Kastryčnickaja vulica (a short walk from Pieršamajskaja

Metro). A wall plaque by the entrance to the yeast factory at number 16 commemorates three Communist partisans who were executed at the site in October 1941. This is one of the most celebrated incidents of the occupation and is given lavish attention at the Museum of the Great Patriotic War. As on the plaque, the martyrs are always listed as Kiril Trus, Volodia Shcherbatsevich and an 'unknown woman' – even though the whole of Minsk knows the woman's name: Masha Bruskina, a seventeen-year-old Jew who worked as a nurse and helped wounded Red Army soldiers to escape from hospital. Despite incontrovertible evidence of her identity and campaigns by the local Jewish community, the authorities have persisted for over six decades in the fiction that she remains unknown.

In the far north-west, a memorial park containing mass graves stands on the site of the Masiukoúščyna (Masiukovshchina) POW camp through which 80,000 Red Army soldiers passed. It is on the corner of Cimirazieva and Naračanskaja (buses 60, 73, 130, 555 and 576 to 2-ja Haradskaja Dzicjačaja Bal'nica). Šyrokaja (Shiroka) was an even more notorious camp on the street of the same name in Minsk's north: it held tens of thousands of Jews and POWs, but nothing survives.

MALY TROSTENETS

Of all of the Nazi extermination camps, the least is known about Maly Trostenets (Maly Trascianiec in Belarusian). The former Karl Marx collective farm was initially adapted into a labour camp in the autumn of 1941 but, although the exact timing is unclear, it soon became a death camp. Reich Jews were brought there to be murdered from May 1942 onwards but killings in the vicinity of Maly Trostenets began as early as November 1941 when most members of the Hamburg transport were shot. As at the other extermination camps, victims were brought by train with a small number chosen to form a *Sonderkommando* and the remainder dispatched straight to their deaths. As at Chełmno, gas vans were used rather than fixed killing facilities although shooting also remained a major method of murder. The shootings mainly took place in the Blagovshchina forest a few miles to the east until the autumn of 1943 when the Shashkova forest, on the edge of the camp, became a new killing site. The camp itself was the centre for the gassing operations (which seem to have begun in June 1942) and for the sorting of victims' belongings. The dead were buried in pits by members of the *Sonderkommando* (themselves subject to regular selections).

There is uncertainty about the exact number and identity of the victims of Maly Trostenets given that there were several killing sites in the vicinity of Minsk and that barely any eyewitnesses survived. It is clear that tens of thousands of Reich Jews were murdered there, mainly in 1942, whilst most of the victims of the later *Aktionen* in the Minsk ghetto (from July 1942 to October 1943) were killed en route in gas vans. Partisans and prisoners of war were also victims. Post-war official estimates put the figure above 200,000, based on 1944–45 investigations of the Blagovshchina and Shashkova forests. However, the number will never be truly known as the Germans largely destroyed the evidence in *Aktion 1005* operations from October 1943; 100 Jews who refused to carry out the order to exhume and burn the bodies were themselves gassed. Perhaps 100,000 corpses were burned at Blagovshchina whilst an execution pit at Shashkova was turned into a primitive crematorium where thousands more bodies were destroyed. On 28 June 1944, during a Soviet air attack, remaining inmates were forced into barracks which were then ignited by the Germans. The rest of the camp was burned down on 30 June including a barn (which had previously served as a temporary barrack in 1941) inside which were the bodies of several hundred prisoners brought from the camps and prisons of Minsk and shot there before the German retreat. When the Red Army arrived on 4 July 1944, the fires were still burning. Only around 20 Jews had been able to escape to the trees and hide out until this time; their reward was to be sent to the Gulag until 1946.

Only fragments of the camp survived the German fires and the Soviet authorities let the site go to ruin with the result that it is now a large meadow which gives no indication of its awful past. There are, though, two somewhat hidden memorials at either end of the former camp. The more prominent is located on the edge of the Shashkova woods near the site of the improvised crematorium. A simple stone, dedicated to 'Soviet citizens', stands between the trees behind a metal fence. It adjoins a small car park where an information board refers to the 206,000 victims who are believed to have died here. A path from the left of the car park skirts the edge of the woods and comes out into the meadow. Continuing ahead along the path, one passes some small brick remnants of buildings. The path eventually comes to a T-junction with another path. Taking a right turn towards the wooden cottage (number 58) leads to some more ruins although they are probably not from the camp. A left turn at the cottage leads to a path that almost immediately forks in two, the left-hand fork forming an avenue of poplars; the trees were planted by the prisoners and stretch, with some modern interruptions, to the main highway. Between the two paths, in the trees behind a small blue fence, is the other memorial: it commemorates the prisoners killed in the barn (which stood near here) in June 1944.

To reach the Shashkova memorial, take the number 9 bus from Mahiliouskaja (Mogilveskaya) Metro station. The bus exits the city, passing under the outer ring road, onto the Mogilev highway; after about 2½ kilometres, it turns right onto Sialickaha, passing Communist tower blocks on the right and a meadow (the site of the camp) on the left. When the road reaches a factory, it bends to the left; the Sasnovaja stop is a further 400 metres or so along the road, a short walk from the memorial's car park. To return, walk back to this bus stop or continue northwards along the avenue of poplars from the barn memorial – when this reaches the village cemetery one can follow the paths down to Sialickaha from whose Maly Trascianiec stop services 9, 21 and 93 return to Mahiliouskaja.

A memorial is located closer to Minsk in Bolshoy Trostenets (Vialiki Trascianiec), another execution site. This was the principal Soviet monument, a grand obelisk which naturally fails to mention that Jews were murdered, referring instead to 'peaceful citizens, partisans and prisoners of war'; a smaller memorial honours Red Army soldiers. A road leads to the memorials from the Vialiki Trascianiec stop for Minsk-bound buses from Maly Trostenets on the northern side of the highway. Alternatively, one can walk the same route (almost a mile): head north along Sialickaha, turn left onto the highway and continue to the bus stop where one can take the underpass to its northern side.

There is a further small memorial at the Blagovshchina forest although this is difficult to get to without private transport. It is reached via the turning for Sosny beyond the huge landfill mound on the northern side of the highway, more than a mile east from the turning for Maly Trostenets. The memorial is a few hundred metres along this road.

OTHER SITES

Sites specifically associated with the Holocaust generally have few memorials, usually unobtrusive stones in seldom visited locations. The most prominent exception is Navahrudak (Novogrudek). Over 10,000

Jews from the town and its surrounding area were murdered, mainly in four *Aktionen* between December 1941 and May 1943. However, the region was also the base of the Bielski partisans and hundreds fled from the ghetto to the forests. Most strikingly, the less than 250 remaining Jews were able to escape from the labour camp in which they were interned in September 1943 through a tunnel dug over the previous months. Although many were shot during the flight, around 100 reached the partisans. One of the escapees, Jack Kagan, who now lives in London, paid for the erection of memorials at the massacre sites in the 1990s and has since devoted his considerable energies to maintaining the memory of its Jewish past (see www.novogrudek.co.uk). He has been assisted in his endeavours by Tamara Vershitskaya, curator of the town's Museum of History and Regional Studies, who has established a permanent exhibition dedicated to Navahrudak's Jewish past, the Holocaust and the Jewish partisans. In July 2007, a further memorial, including the excavated entrance to the tunnel, was established on the site of the former labour camp (in the grounds of the courthouse east of the centre on Minskaja). The various memorial sites are rather spread around the town so it is best to visit the museum first to get directions; it is located off central ploshcha Lienina at Hrodnenskaja 2 by the St Nicholas Church.

Hrodna (Grodno), most of whose 25,000 Jews were deported to Treblinka and Auschwitz in 1942–43, has a 1991 memorial (a metal arch incorporating a menorah, alongside a wall plaque depicting Jews being led from the ghetto) at the entrance to one of its two ghettos on Zamkovaja, just off ploshcha Savietskaya. The large Great Synagogue, around the corner at Vialikaja Traetskaja 59A, was returned to the Jewish community in 1992. It is worth asking there for guidance on finding other traces of Jewish Hrodna. Alternatively, one can contact the local community in advance (www.fjc.ru/Communities/instIndex.asp?cid=84412).

For most other sites away from Minsk, it is sensible to hire a guide given that Holocaust memorials and remnants of Jewish culture are often well hidden and rarely signposted or marked on maps. The Minsk Jewish Campus (www.meod.by) may be able to recommend guides whilst two organisations which offer Jewish-related tours are the Minsk-based Jewish Heritage Research Group (www.jhrgbelarus.org) and the state travel agency Belintourist (www.belintourist.by).

Ukraine

RUSSIA

kilometres 0 200

miles 0 100

Drobitsky Yar

Kharkiv
(Kharkov)

River Dnieper

BELARUS

Dnepropetrovsk

Babi Yar
Kiev

U K R A I N E

Sea of
Azov

Zhovkva

POLAND

Janowska

L'viv (Lvov)

River Dniester

MOLDOVA

Odessa

Black
Sea

SLOVAKIA

HUNGARY

ROMANIA

● Principal places
mentioned in the text

○ Other sites mentioned
in the text

–··– International borders
2010

© Martin Gilbert 2010

CHAPTER 15

UKRAINE

N owhere other than Poland were more Jewish lives lost in the Holocaust than in Ukraine. Whilst the Germans were the principal perpetrators, significant roles were also played by Ukrainians and Romanians, the latter in possibly the most obscure aspect of the Holocaust.

Jews had lived in the territory of what became Ukraine since the Dark Ages. However, it was from the fourteenth century – when most of Ukraine fell under the control of Poland and Lithuania – that it became one of the major centres of European Jewry although life was often precarious. Polish rule was deeply unpopular and the perception of Jews as Polish agents reinforced traditional anti-Semitism. Most infamously, tens of thousands of Jews and Poles were massacred in the uprising led by Bohdan Khmelnytsky (Bogdan Chmielnicki in Polish) in the mid-seventeenth century. In the aftermath, the east of the country fell under Russian rule whilst the Polish-Lithuanian Commonwealth began its slow decline. It is sometimes suggested that the rise of mystical forms of Judaism in the eighteenth century, most obviously Hassidism which was born in Ukraine, was a reaction to this era of destruction. Following the Polish partitions, most of Ukraine was held by Russia but the west (where most Jews lived) was incorporated into the Austrian Empire, largely as the province of Eastern Galicia. Although anti-Semitism remained a central feature of tsarism until 1917, the relatively more liberal Habsburgs granted their Jews equal rights in the 1860s. Growing autonomy for Galicia also made it a centre of Polish nationalism whilst simultaneously fostering the development of a Ukrainian equivalent. These competing ideologies were to contribute to the misfortunes which befell Ukrainian Jews during and after the First World War. Cossack units of the tsar's army were the first to carry out pogroms but worse followed. During the Russian Civil War and its associated conflicts, competing Russian, Polish, Ukrainian and Romanian armies fought for control of Ukraine: nearly all massacred Jews, the forces of the short-lived Ukrainian government of Symon Petliura (1919) being considered particularly notorious. When a Ukrainian Jewish anarchist, Sholom Schwartzbard, assassinated Petliura in Paris in 1926, he was acquitted by a jury.

The Bolsheviks eventually re-established Russian control over most of the country and Jews shared in the appalling suffering caused by Communism in Ukraine. The former Austrian provinces were largely divided between Poland and Romania, both of which limited Ukrainian rights albeit less than Stalin. This was to engender what might seem a paradoxical outcome: western Ukraine – spared the famine and terror of Soviet Ukraine – became the home of the most aggressive nationalists precisely because a sense of grievance was combined with the relative freedom to express it. Although the Poles were seen as the main enemy, the increasingly strident movement still saw Jews (themselves subject to similar losses of rights) as Polish allies. This was as nothing, however, compared to the fury generated by Stalin's annexation of western Ukraine under the Nazi-Soviet Pact, the first time that the region had ever been under Russian rule. Although some Jews initially welcomed the invasion (a minority through ideological conviction, most through the pragmatic assessment that Hitler was even worse than Stalin), there was little basis to the view propagated in nationalist circles that they were collaborators. In fact, the waves of terror that swept western Ukraine in 1940–41 largely targeted Poles and Jews whilst Ukrainian culture and interests were increasingly promoted in an attempt to win over the majority. Nonetheless, Ukrainian sentiment remained overwhelmingly anti-Communist and increasingly focused on the Jews as scapegoats, a view encouraged by Berlin-based exiles.

The Germans were, therefore, widely welcomed as liberators. This would prove to be a mistaken assumption: when radical nationalists proclaimed an independent Ukraine, their leader Stepan Bandera was imprisoned. Nonetheless, Bandera's followers, including the Nightingale Battalion (a German-trained unit which accompanied the invasion), collaborated in appalling massacres of Jews and Poles in western Ukraine in the summer of 1941. Some nationalists went further still and volunteered for auxiliary units of the SS – almost every major extermination camp was guarded by Ukrainians. Such complicity was far less common in central and eastern Ukraine but this was the first region of the country to be subjected to the policy of killing all Jews: from September 1941 onwards, *Einsatzgruppe C* murdered entire Jewish communities in cities such as Kiev and Kharkiv. The process soon extended to southern Ukraine where *Einsatzgruppe D* often took a secondary role to the Romanians. Romania's participation in the invasion of the USSR had been rewarded by Hitler with control over Transnistria, a region encompassing Odessa and the hinterland to its north between the rivers Dniester and Bug. More than 100,000 Jews from Bessarabia (modern Moldova) and Bukovina (inter-war Romanian Ukraine) were deported to ramshackle labour camps and ghettos in northern Transnistria. Most died over the winter of 1941–42, initially from starvation and typhus, then in Romanian massacres; the same misfortunes befell tens of thousands of Jews from Odessa who were sent north in early 1942. By this stage, almost the only surviving Jews – apart from the several hundred thousand who had been able to flee from eastern Ukraine in the summer of 1941 – were those of the west. Former Eastern Galicia had been the site of the earliest mass killings but its incorporation into the *Generalgouvernement* meant that its Jews then shared the fate of those of Poland rather than the USSR. Deportations to Bełżec began in the spring of 1942 whilst those not sent to the extermination camp were largely murdered at Janowska in L'viv. These victims are often included in the death toll for Poland. However, they also form part of the probably more than 1.5 million Ukrainian Jews who were murdered by the Nazis and their accomplices. More than 100,000 Jews live in Ukraine today.

Post-war memorialisation was constrained by Soviet ideology and was further complicated by the evidence of Ukrainian collaboration which did not fit the Communist narrative of the war except when used to discredit Banderite rebels who continued to wage a guerrilla campaign in western Ukraine until the 1950s. The situation has improved since 1991 but still compares unfavourably with that of Poland or even Lithuania. That said, there are significant regional variations whilst *Yahad-In Unum*, an organisation for Catholic-Jewish understanding headed by the French priest Father Patrick Desbois, is undertaking a project to locate and document every mass grave site in Ukraine (www.yahadinunum.org).

KIEV

The history of the Holocaust in the Ukrainian capital was brutal and short. Although Jews had settled in Kiev by the ninth century at the latest, they were forbidden to live there for much of the tsarist period. It was only in the 1860s that wealthy Jews were allowed to reside in specified areas although others came to the city illegally. The population increased dramatically after 1917 to around 160,000 by the time of the invasion. It is believed that 100,000 were able to flee eastwards before the arrival of the Germans on 19 September 1941 but there was to be no escape for those that remained, mostly women, children and the elderly. On 24 September a series of bombs planted by NKVD agents destroyed much of the city centre; the Germans made this an excuse for annihilation. Within a week, more than half of the Jews still living in the city had been murdered at Babi Yar (Babyn Yar in Ukrainian) on the outskirts (see next entry). Most others were murdered in the following months. Astonishingly, the catastrophe did not destroy Kiev Jewry as the return of refugees and migration of survivors from other parts of Ukraine meant that up to 200,000 Jews lived in the city by the 1950s. Although less than half that number are still there, Kiev is the modern centre of Jewish life in the country.

There are no Holocaust memorials beyond Babi Yar but a number of sites associated with pre-war Jewish culture survive. The historic centre of Jewish life was Podil, the low-lying commercial district north of the hilltop city centre. The Podil Synagogue, still in use, is at Shchekavytska 29 (Kontraktova ploshcha Metro). On parallel Yaroslavska, number 55 was a *mikvah* and number 40 a day shelter for girls; the two buildings at 22 were prayer houses. The school at Kostyantynivska 37A to the south was originally founded in 1910 as a junior school for Jewish boys. Andriyivsky Uzviz, Kiev's most atmospheric street, connects Podil with the upper town. The lovely Museum of One Street at 2B (Tue–Sun, 12.00–6.00; 15 UAH) manages to say much about Jewish Kiev through its imaginative accounts of the street's residents.

The other major area of note is concentrated around the restored Central Synagogue at Shota Rustaveli 13 (near Palats Sportu Metro); the cinema at number 19 was previously also a synagogue. Across the crossroads from the Central Synagogue, a statue of the great Yiddish novelist Sholem Aleichem stands on Rognidynska. There is also a sculpted plaque at Saksagansky 27, a short walk south, where the writer once lived. A similar plaque commemorates Golda Meir's birthplace at Baseyna 5A to the north. Kiev's main street Khreshchatyk (whose destruction triggered the massacres) runs north from here. Parallel Volodymyrska (Zoloti Verota Metro) has associations with two figures more directly connected with the Holocaust: 47 was where Janusz Korczak worked in the First World War whilst 40/2 was once the home of prominent Soviet journalist Ilya Ehrenburg. Ehrenburg and fellow writer Vassily Grossman compiled *The Black Book*, the first detailed attempt to document the Holocaust in the

USSR. Embarrassed by the focus on Jewish suffering and the evidence of Ukrainian, Lithuanian and Latvian collaboration, the authorities refused to publish the book. Volodymyrska 15 was the courthouse where the Beilis case, the most notorious example of tsarist anti-Semitism, was tried in 1913. Further west at Zhilanska 97A, the former Galitsky Synagogue – closed by the Communists in 1930 and used as a factory canteen – is now a Jewish educational centre.

Kiev's Museum of the Great Patriotic War (Tue–Sun, 10.00–5.00; 5 UAH) is located under the towering *Rodyna Mat* (Mother of the Nation) statue at Sichnevoho Povstannya 44, south-east of the centre (bus 20). Although the Brezhnev-era museum addresses Babi Yar, there is predictably little focus on the Holocaust.

BABI YAR

Babi Yar (Grandmother's Ravine) on the edge of Kiev was the site of the most infamous massacre of the Holocaust. Following the explosions in Kiev, the Nazis put up notices ordering all Jews to assemble near the Jewish cemetery on 29 September 1941. The Germans had assumed that only around 6,000 people would appear but the actual number was more than five times greater, the victims believing they were to be relocated to labour camps. They were led in groups to the large ravine and shot by troops of *Einsatzgruppe C*. According to the German figures, 33,771 people were murdered in two days. In the following months, thousands more – Jews as well as Red Army soldiers, Russian and Ukrainian civilians and Roma – were similarly killed: it is estimated that the final death toll at Babi Yar may have been 100,000. In the summer of 1943, the site was excavated and the bodies cremated by inmates of the nearby Syrets concentration camp (of which no trace survives). Fifteen members of this *Sonderkommando* were able to escape on 29 September 1943.

After the war, Babi Yar was the most potent symbol of the USSR's failure to commemorate the Holocaust. Much of the ravine was filled whilst a dam constructed nearby caused a mudslide in 1961 which killed hundreds (though the Communist authorities never admitted it). That same year, Yevgeny Yevtushenko penned the poem *Babi Yar* – its opening line 'No monument stands over Babi Yar' – which was widely circulated in underground circles; these words were set to music in Shostakovich's 13th Symphony a year later. Although both works were long banned, the

Babi Yar (Photograph by Elizabeth Burns)

embarrassment caused to the Party helped to prompt the decision to create a memorial, which was finally unveiled in 1976 albeit with no mention that Jews were killed. Since 1991, a number of more appropriate memorials have appeared at the site which is now essentially a large park. The first that most visitors see is a disturbing statue of broken toys by the northern (right) exit to Dorohozhychi Metro station dedicated to the child victims of Babi Yar. The principal Jewish monument, erected in 1991, can be reached by taking the path north from here, turning right after about 400 metres and continuing uphill. However, an easier route is to head east down Melnykova from the station, passing the giant TV tower, until one comes to number 44 on the left – this was the administration building of the Jewish cemetery. Turn left after this building onto a paved path which leads directly to the memorial, a menorah with reliefs of human forms. An Orthodox cross nearby commemorates two priests murdered in November 1941. Behind the menorah is the main surviving stretch of the ravine, more or less the point where the September massacre took place. It is possible to descend into the ravine by taking the path which curves to the left of the menorah. Taking the straight path to the right of the menorah (as opposed to the curved path leading to the cross), one can find a remnant of the Jewish cemetery where the path forks after about 100 metres.

Returning to the Metro station and taking the underpass to the southern side of Melnykova, one reaches the park containing the Soviet memorial: its typically muscular figures perch on a concrete outcrop. By the path towards it, a cross is dedicated to 621 Ukrainian nationalists killed at Babi Yar whilst a small monument is supposedly the cornerstone of a planned Jewish heritage centre – the stone was laid in 2001 and nothing has happened since. There is a further memorial to Ukrainian forced labourers sent to Germany in the south eastern corner of the park. A memorial to the victims of the Syrets camp stands on the edge of another park a block to the west, at the south western corner of the junction of Dorohozhytska and Shamryla.

L'VIV

The many names by which L'viv has been known (Lwów to Poles, Lemberg to Germans and Austrians, Lvov to Russians and Jews) are a testament to its multi-ethnic past. The city was founded in the thirteenth century and conquered by the Poles a century later. They invited Jews to settle and thereby gave L'viv the character which was to shape its history until the war: a largely Polish and Jewish city surrounded by a predominantly Ukrainian countryside. The community mostly prospered until the partition of Poland when Jewish rights were curtailed. Even so, Austrian rule was preferable to Russian and full civil equality in the 1860s prompted further Jewish growth. L'viv also became a centre of both Polish and the newly emerging Ukrainian nationalism. The first fatal fruit of these developments was to be tasted at the end of the First World War when the city changed hands several times with both sides perpetrating pogroms.

Inter-war Lwów was home to the third largest Jewish population in Poland, numbering some 110,000 people by 1939. However, both Jews and Ukrainians were subjected to the government's Polonising policies, particularly with regard to access to higher education. In this context, the city increasingly became a focus for Ukrainian nationalist activism which primarily drew its strength from the rural hinterland (Ukrainians were less than 20 per cent of the urban population). It was in this context that the Red Army marched into L'viv on 22 September 1939. As elsewhere, Jews and especially Poles were the principal targets of Soviet terror but there was almost universal hostility to the new regime from Ukrainians. By contrast, some Jews had welcomed the USSR as the lesser of two evils whilst the community was swelled dramatically by a flood of refugees from western Poland; even after the mass arrests and further migration, there were around 160,000 Jews in L'viv in 1941.

The Germans (accompanied by the Nightingale Battalion) entered the city on 30 June 1941. The consequences were immediate: 4,000 Jews were killed in the first four days of the occupation in the 'Prison *Aktion*', so named because of the NKVD atrocities discovered after the Soviets' departure. The Nazis and their accomplices had little difficulty in convincing sections of the enraged populace that the Jews were to blame. Even after the *Aktion* supposedly ended on 3 July, random murders, beatings and arrests continued, culminating in the 'Petliura Days' in late July when a further 2,000 died, mostly at the hands of Ukrainians. By this stage, Jews had also been forced to wear the Star of David and form a *Judenrat*. Lower-level violence continued through the summer, with most of the city's synagogues destroyed in August and September. The noose tightened further with two developments in late 1941: the creation of the Janowska labour camp to the north-west of the city (see next entry) and the establishment of a 'Jewish quarter'. The latter was not yet a formal ghetto but its creation was accompanied by further mass killings and its territory was progressively reduced in the months that followed. In March 1942, it was subjected to the largest *Aktion* yet, marking the beginning of deportations to Bełżec: around 15,000 people were sent to the death camp whilst others were interned in Janowska which itself increasingly became a murder site. The 'Great *Aktion*' in August saw tens of thousands more dispatched to the two camps and the quarter officially became a ghetto, fenced off from the rest of the city. *Aktionen* occurred every few weeks, usually accompanied by further reductions in the area of the ghetto, until its small rump was converted into the *Julag*, an SS-administered work camp, in January 1943. The ghetto was finally liquidated in June 1943 with the remaining few thousand shot at Janowska or in forests outside the city. Following the murder of the last prisoners at Janowska in November, there were probably less than 300 Jews left in and around L'viv when the Red Army arrived in July 1944.

Modern L'viv is a beautiful city but one in a state of some amnesia regarding its history. A few memorials to the vanished Jewish community appeared in the early 1990s but they are now ill cared for and contrast with the flurry of new monuments dedicated to Ukrainian victims of Communism. In part, this reflects the dramatic transformation wrought by the twentieth century: with the Jews dead, the Poles were expelled after the war, the USSR thus ironically fulfilling the nationalists' dream of a Ukrainian L'viv. The contemporary population, therefore, has little sense of connection with the city's past. However, the not infrequent vandalism to which Jewish memorials are subjected suggests that, for some, old prejudices have not completely disappeared.

The ghetto and Jewish quarter

The Jewish quarter established in November 1941 initially occupied a large portion of the north of L'viv which was progressively reduced in the frequent *Aktionen*. Its core lay to the north of elevated railway tracks which formed a natural barrier with the rest of the city and it was this area that became the ghetto after the Great *Aktion* in August 1942. Thereafter, further reductions diminished the ghetto until it became the *Julag*, a small triangle of streets bounded by modern Zamarstynivska, Khimichna and the railway, in early 1943.

L'viv's Holocaust memorial is located at the junction of Chornovola (formerly Pełtewna) and Dolynskoho on the northern side of the railway. This was the site of the 'under the bridge *Aktion*' during the creation of the Jewish quarter in November and December 1941. German and Ukrainian policemen carried out selections on Jews coming from other parts of the city, using the bridge as, in their words, a 'sluice'. Between 5,000 and 10,000 people – mainly the elderly and women – were taken to other locations in the city and shot. The memorial takes the form of a small park in which a path lined with plaques leads from a menorah to a large sculpture of a contorted figure. Unfortunately, although the park is fenced, some locals treat it as a place to walk their dogs.

Most ghetto buildings were destroyed by the Germans but a few traces remain, mainly concentrated on Kushevycha and Lemkivska to the east of Chornovola. Kushevycha 9 was the site of the Jewish quarter's last hospital, liquidated in the Great *Aktion*. The Germans were afraid to enter the rooms due to their rather obsessive fear of infectious diseases so patients were shot at from the doors. After this *Aktion*, various *Judenrat*

379

offices were relocated to these streets. Little more than a week later, in September 1942, the buildings were raided. The *Judenrat* chair Dr Henryk Landsberg and randomly selected Jewish policemen were hanged from balconies on Łokietka, a no longer existing street that ran to the west opposite Teslenka; the *Judenrat* was billed for the rope.

The streets to the south of the railway were within the original designated Jewish quarter but were cleared before or during the Great *Aktion*. In contrast to the ghetto, the area is largely intact although few buildings are marked. In fact, the main memorial in the area is to Ukrainian victims of Communism by the former prison at Zamarstynivska 9 on the corner with Detka. Although it pays lip service to Poles and Jews, the memorial clearly promotes a nationalist agenda. As a new stone explains, the site is to become a museum dedicated to the 'Ukrainian Calvary', the 'torture' apparently inflicted on Ukraine by not just the Nazis and Communists but also the Poles and Austrian Habsburgs. No mention is made of the fact that Jews were tortured here during the war. Similarly, there is nothing to indicate that ploshcha Sviatoho Teodora (St Teodora's Square) to the south was the major assembly point for deportees in the Great *Aktion*. Until that time, the *Judenrat* was based at Muljarska 2A, to the east of the square. Vuhilna 3 on the southern side is a former Hassidic prayer house which now houses the Sholem Aleichem Cultural Centre. Just to the south, a rare plaque on a side wall by a small park marks the site of the Great Synagogue of the Suburbs (destroyed in August 1941) at the corner of Sianska and Vesela. The massive Reform Synagogue (destroyed July 1941) is similarly commemorated on Stary Rynok to the east.

There are other sites of note to the west although the only obviously visible hints of a Jewish past are a plaque to Sholem Aleichem on the corner of Kotliarska and Shpytalna and the Stars of David ringing the Moorish dome of the imposing former Jewish hospital on Rappoporta. The latter was confiscated by the Germans in November 1941 and handed over to the municipal administration even though it initially fell within the Jewish quarter. To the north of the hospital, encircled by Bazarna, Brovarna and Kleparivska, the Krakiwski market stands on the site of L'viv's old Jewish cemetery which existed from the Middle Ages and was largely destroyed by the Nazis and then flattened by the Communists. Sholem Aleichema 12, just to the south, was the pre-war headquarters of the Jewish community and housed a Jewish museum; it is now occupied by a Jewish cultural centre.

Aleichema borders Brygidki prison, one of the centres of the Prison *Aktion*. As elsewhere in the city, the retreating NKVD had murdered their prisoners and set fire to the buildings in an attempt to destroy the evidence but large numbers of bodies were found. Ukrainian nationalist mobs and the SS dragged Jewish men to the prison and forced them to bury the charred corpses, both following the fatuous reasoning that Jews and Communism were synonymous. Hundreds were murdered: the Germans threw grenades and fired randomly into the crowds; during intervals, Ukrainians were allowed to beat up the men. There is no indication today of any of the horrors committed at Brygidki in the war, whether by Communists, Nazis or Ukrainians; bizarrely, the only memorial on the front of the building (still a prison today) at Horodotska 20 is a plaque to Ukrainian nationalists executed by the Polish authorities in June 1939. The gate to the naturally inaccessible courtyard where the murders took place is around the corner on Danylyshyna.

Elsewhere

A short walk from Brygidki, Nalyvaika 13 preserves pre-war Polish and Yiddish shop signs on its wall although how long they will survive is uncertain; similar writing at number 11 was recently whitewashed over. An open space on Bankivska, a small street between Doroshenka and Kopernyka to the south, was the site of the Sikutski Synagogue which was destroyed in August 1941. Nearby Doroshenka 31 was the site of a workshop, most of whose 200 Jewish forced labourers were killed a year later.

The historic L'viv Jewish community had first settled in the centre of the city but there is little to suggest this beyond the street name Staroievreiska south of the Rynok. The famed sixteenth-century Golden Rose Synagogue stood past number 37 on this street until destroyed in 1942; it is believed that Ukrainians rather than Germans were the culprits. A few fragments carrying a memorial plaque survive but are currently hidden behind a corrugated iron fence. The space opposite where local drunks and teenagers congregate was the site of the Great City Synagogue, burned down in August 1941.

The militia building on the corner of Kopernyka and Bandery (named after the nationalist leader) was Lackiego prison, another site of atrocities in the Prison *Aktion* and frequently used thereafter as a holding centre for arrested Jews who were then taken to Janowska or shot in the forests. There are plaques and a large monument opposite dedicated to victims of the NKVD but none to victims of the Nazis. The hill to the east was the Cytadel, a former Habsburg fortress converted into a POW camp. It is estimated that more than 100,000 Red Army soldiers died there. Near the western end of Bandery, the sole surviving active synagogue is at Brativ Mikhnovskykh 4.

L'viv's new Jewish cemetery (opened in the 1850s) was badly damaged by the Nazis who used the tombstones for paving the Janowska camp. The cemetery still exists with a Holocaust memorial obelisk by the gate but its Jewish character has otherwise almost entirely disappeared, as indicated by the large number of Communist and, increasingly, Christian graves. The cemetery is on Yeroshenka, which runs north off Shevchenka, the main road north-west out of the city. The latter was to be the last street that most L'viv Jews saw. Two kilometres further up the road, after Shevchenka passes the junction with Vynnytsia and crosses the railway, is Klepariv station. This was the point of departure for transports to Bełżec from across Eastern Galicia, as attested by a memorial plaque on the eastern wall. However, not all Jews made it this far. Those not sent to Bełżec were subjected to a different but ultimately as lethal fate, between the cemetery and the station, in Janowska.

JANOWSKA

There were no gas chambers at Janowksa but it was nonetheless a death camp by any reasonable understanding of the phrase. In the autumn of 1941, the DAW (the SS-owned armaments company) took over a formerly Jewish-owned factory on Janowska Street (now Shevchenka) on the north-western edge of L'viv, prompting the SS to establish a camp for forced labourers to the west of the industrial area. Growing numbers of Jewish men (women's barracks were created in early 1943) were seized from the city's streets and brought to Janowska although not necessarily for work: even in the camp's early months, new arrivals were subjected to selections. Those considered unfit for work were taken to the Piaski (Sands) ravine to the north of the camp and shot. The same fate befell those inmates who fell sick or succumbed to exhaustion. This was only one manifestation of the barbarism which characterised Janowska and surpassed the brutality of other concentration camps. For example, 'death races' were organised in which prisoners were ordered to run around the camp with the slowest sent to the Sands; SS men would sometimes trip up the runners. Commandant

Gustav Wilhaus and his wife shot at inmates from the balcony of the camp office to amuse their nine-year-old daughter. All the while, the tortures were inflicted to the sounds of the camp's orchestra. This was allegedly created after Deputy Commandant Wilhelm Rokita, who had played in jazz groups in pre-war Poland, met a former bandmate (a Tarnów Jew named Kampf who was promptly named head *kapo*) and decided that the camp needed music; Rokita later murdered Kampf. From March 1942, Janowska also served as a transit camp for the deportations to Bełżec but even in this period executions continued at the Sands. Following the closure of Bełżec in early 1943, Janowska increasingly took on the role of an extermination camp itself. In June, a brigade of more than 100 prisoners was assigned to exhume and cremate the corpses of murdered Jews, first at the Sands and then at other killing sites around L'viv. Sensing that their days were numbered, the men escaped on 20 November 1943. Nearly all were captured and executed but those who did get away were amongst the very few survivors of Janowska which had been liquidated the previous day. It is estimated that between 100,000 and 200,000 people lost their lives in the camp in the two years of its existence, nearly all of them Jews (the few thousand Polish inmates were held in a separate section and not subjected to the same level of sadism).

After the war, the inmates' camp was taken over by the NKVD. It is still a prison today, hidden behind high walls and barbed wire on the corner of Shevchenka and Vynnytsia, although few of the original buildings remain. That said, some areas of the former camp territory are accessible. The disused tram terminal just before the prison was the site of the entrance and the track that runs from it (Tatarbunarska) essentially follows the course of the road which separated the inmates' and the SS camps. Shevchenka 152 housed German guards. The surviving DAW workshops are incorporated into a run-down industrial zone to the east of the prison, sections of which are visible from Tatarbunarska and Yavorivska, a dirt track off the former that runs parallel to Shevchenka. There is also a privately funded memorial near the Piaski ravine although its location is such that it is largely unnoticed: following Vynnytsia as it curves around the side of the prison, just past the end of the graffiti-covered concrete wall (the brick sections of the wall were built by the Germans), there is a turning to the right where one finds a memorial boulder accompanied by a large sign. The area through the gate beyond was a section of the killing grounds. There were so few survivors of Janowska that the exact topography is unclear whilst the German clear-up operation in 1943 substantially changed the nature of the site. Nonetheless, human remains are undoubtedly still buried in the large field – the Soviet investigating commission in 1944 found ashes and bones spread over an area of 2 square kilometres. The ruined barracks in the field were not part of the camp but rather erected by the Soviets when this site was used for the training of police dogs and pig breeding.

To reach both Janowska and Klepariv, the easiest option is to take a taxi although the driver may not have heard of the former – use the street names. Many *marshrutki* (minibuses) head up Shevchenka past both the prison and the station but neither is an official halt so one would need to use some Ukrainian to get the driver to stop.

ODESSA

Odessa was home to the largest Jewish population in the Soviet Union. Founded at the end of the eighteenth century, it was famed for a tolerance unique in the tsarist era, a result of the need to attract settlers to the new port. It was thus a magnet for persecuted groups, notably Jews who formed around a third of the population and did much to give the city its distinctive character despite occasional pogroms (most notoriously in 1905). Although there were dozens of synagogues and prayer houses, Odessa was particularly remarkable for its secular Jewish culture: to both its admirers and detractors, it was the worldliest city in the Russian Empire, home to artists, bankers, humorists and revolutionaries. It was a major centre of liberal and socialist opposition to the tsars and of Zionism (its port was nicknamed the 'Gateway to Zion'). The Communists did their best to squeeze the vitality out of the city but it was still home to 180,000 Jews in 1941.

Odessa was besieged by German and Romanian forces in early August 1941 and fell on 16 October. The delay enabled tens of thousands of Jews to flee but around half still remained when Axis troops entered the city. Several thousand Jews and Communists were immediately killed by *Einsatzgruppe D*, assisted by the Romanians. However, what makes the Holocaust in southern Ukraine unusual is the fact that the latter were the principal perpetrators, with Odessa becoming the capital of the Transnistria region. On 22 October 1941, a bomb planted at the Romanian military HQ killed more than 60 staff. In an echo of Babi Yar, appalling massacres of the Jewish population were carried out over the next few days on the orders of the Romanian dictator Antonescu; more than 40,000 people were murdered with some estimates putting the figure above 50,000. It is often written that the killings occurred at the port but there were, in fact, several sites in and around the city where victims were shot or burned alive. The remaining Jews – generally estimated at between 35,000 and 40,000 – were herded into a hastily created ghetto in the Slobodka district where thousands were left without housing and froze to death. In January and February 1942, 19,000 survivors were deported to the camps of Transnistria where they were murdered (mostly at Domanevka). Jews who remained in Odessa were largely killed in 1942–43. Although refugees returned after the war, later emigration has meant that around 30,000 Jews live in Odessa today.

The Jewish Museum of Odessa (Sun–Thu, 1.00–7.00; free; english. migdal.ru/museum) is hidden at the back of the courtyard of Nezhinskaya 66, just off central Preobrazhenskaya. The museum is small but does a decent job of evoking the breadth of pre-war Jewish life. The room devoted to the Holocaust sets out the grim figures and uses the story of survivor Leonid Dusman and his family to speak for thousands of others. More visible traces of the past exist in the city centre. The fortress-like former Brodsky Synagogue is a looming presence at Zhukovskogo 18 (corner with Pushkinskaya); number 15 across the road was a Tarbut school. Just to the west, at Rishelievskaya 17, a plaque commemorates Isaac Babel, the greatest literary chronicler of Jewish Odessa; he was murdered by the NKVD in Moscow in 1940. Yevreyskaya (Jewish Street) runs parallel to Zhukovskogo: at number 25 is the main Choral Synagogue, closed by the Communists in 1927 and recently restored. Further east down the street, 12 was a home for Jewish children orphaned in the Russian Civil War and 1 the house of Vladimir Jabotinsky, leader of the right-wing Zionist Revisionist party. Located two blocks south, at Osipova 21, the city's second active synagogue is the charming former tailors' prayer house, recently reactivated after closure in the 1920s. A plaque at Osipova 30 marks the former home of Meir Dizengoff, Tel Aviv's first mayor. The former prayer house of kosher butchers, set back from the road at Malaya Arnautskaya 46A to the south, now houses various Jewish communal organisations.

The principal Holocaust memorial is located on Prokhorovsky Square, an assembly point during the deportations, past the western

Odessa: Holocaust memorial (Photograph by Elizabeth Burns)

end of Bolshaya Arnautskaya. A contrast to the low-key memorials often found in Ukraine, its main element is a group of naked figures standing on a large concrete block surrounded by barbed wire. Rows of birch trees on either side honour citizens of Odessa who saved Jewish lives. At the southern corner of the small park, a memorial stone carries the names of the sites in Transnistria to which Jews were sent; one side also honours Roma victims. The memorial is on the edge of the Moldovanka district, the historic Jewish quarter celebrated in Babel's stories. A couple of relics remain around the corner on Miasoyedovskaya: a former prayer house at number 13 and a former Jewish hospital (still a hospital today) at 32 on the corner with Khmelnitskogo.

The other major site to have been memorialised is a former artillery depot over two miles south of the train station where up to 25,000 Jews were brought during the October 1941 massacres. The Romanians forced them into the buildings and set fire to them; the flames burned for days. A simple stone stands in the scruffy yard which occupies the site between Lustdorfskaya Doroga 46 and 47. Lustdorfskaya, the main street southwards out of the city, is extremely long and confusingly numbered – this section is after the street turns to the right at the Tolbukhina Ploshchad roundabout. It is easiest to take a tram (13, 26 or 31) to the Tolbukhina stop: the site is about 100 metres further along Lustdorfskaya on the left. This route passes the sites of Odessa's first two Jewish cemeteries, both destroyed by the Communists. All that remains of the original eighteenth-century cemetery is the derelict ceremonial hall at Vodoprovodnaya 11; the grounds, together with those of the adjacent Christian and Muslim cemeteries, were turned into a park in 1936. The second cemetery (destroyed in 1978) was at the top of Lustdorfskaya, opposite the Christian cemetery. It too is now a park although there is a reconstruction of the old gate by the road.

West of the centre, the territory of the short-lived Slobodka ghetto is covered in post-war housing but there is an easily missed memorial plaque to its victims on the wall of the naval academy at Malovskogo 10 (trams 22 or 30 to the Gradonachalnitskaya stop, walk north along Balkovskaya and turn left into Malovskogo – the memorial is uphill, past the railway bridge). Significantly further west is Odessa's third Jewish cemetery (opened 1916) at Khimicheskaya 1 (trolleybus 8 or *marshrutka* 208). This was badly damaged by the Romanians so most graves are post-war (there are also many Tatar graves at the rear). In the south-west corner, there is a large memorial to victims of the 1905 pogrom, relocated from the second cemetery.

OTHER SITES

There are naturally many sites associated with Jewish history and the Holocaust in Ukraine. However, the generally limited nature of memorialisation often makes it difficult for the visitor to locate them, a phenomenon exacerbated by the country's sheer size and lethargic transport system. It is, therefore, advisable to contact the local Jewish community (where one exists) for information on particular places: a list can be found at www.fjc.ru/communities.

In general, the most honest and public approaches to the Holocaust are to be found in eastern Ukraine. A particularly admirable institution is the Tkuma All-Ukrainian Centre for Holocaust Studies in Dnepropetrovsk (tkuma.dp.ua) which has played an active role in Holocaust education. It is in the process of establishing a national Holocaust museum which will adjoin the city's restored Golden Rose Synagogue at Sholom Aleichem 4, the pride of one of Ukraine's most vibrant Jewish communities (djc. com.ua).

A small Holocaust museum already exists in Kharkiv at Petrovskogo 28 (holocaustmuseum.pochta.org – Russian only) whilst a memorial wall at the corner of Moskovsky Prospect and 12-go Aprelya commemorates the short-lived ghetto. East of the city is the Drobitsky Yar massacre site where an estimated 30,000 people, mainly Jews, were murdered. The largest such killing took place on 15 December 1941 when more than 15,000 were shot. A large new memorial complex has been built at the site which lies north of the E40 (the continuation of Moskovsky Prospekt), a few hundred metres beyond the ring road.

As the case of L'viv suggests, memorialisation is more problematic in western Ukraine. Memorials, if they exist at all, are generally in obscure locations and often poorly cared for, whilst remnants of Jewish culture have been allowed to rot. A more positive development may arise in Zhovkva to the north of L'viv; the derelict Great Synagogue on Zaporizhka has been earmarked for restoration and conversion into a museum of Galician Jewish history although the process is likely to take many years. The issues surrounding memorialisation in former Eastern Galicia are further explored in Omer Bartov's 2007 book *Erased*.

CHAPTER 16

CROATIA AND BOSNIA-HERZEGOVINA

Wartime Croatia – which encompassed most of modern Croatia and Bosnia-Herzegovina – was a unique case in the Holocaust, a state in which genocide of the Jews (and others) was principally carried out by the indigenous government rather than by the Nazis. Indeed, it is believed that no other regime earmarked a greater proportion of its *own* citizens for extermination.

Jews had lived along the Dalmatian coast since Roman times whilst Turkish control in the early modern period encouraged significant immigration from Spain and Portugal to Bosnia. However, most of Croatia was under Austrian rule from the sixteenth century which prevented widespread Jewish settlement until the 1780s. Thereafter, there was migration from other areas of the Austrian Empire, creating a heterogeneous community. The combined pre-war Jewish population of Croatia and Bosnia – both part of Yugoslavia – was close to 40,000.

Germany and its allies (Italy, Hungary and Bulgaria) invaded Yugoslavia in April 1941. The country was largely divided amongst the victorious powers but Hitler created the Independent State of Croatia (NDH) out of the territory of Croatia and Bosnia-Herzegovina (although Italy took the coastline) and installed Ante Pavelić's *Ustaše* movement in power. Pavelić and his followers shared the Nazis' obsessive hatred of Jews and Roma; both were rapidly stripped of civil rights in a series of decrees between April and June 1941. Pavelić even went so far as to redefine the clearly Slavic Croats as 'Aryans', a deviation from Nazi racial theories that Hitler was willing to indulge. The *Ustaše* extended their eliminationist racism to a third group, the Serbs, around 2 million of whom lived in the NDH. Indeed, the first great wave of *Ustaše* terror in the summer of 1941 was primarily directed at Serbs, with the judicial murder of the intelligentsia and chaotic rural massacres. The summer also saw the creation of a network of concentration camps, the largest and most notorious of which was the Jasenovac complex, to which tens of thousands of Jews, Roma and Serbs were sent in the following months. Supposedly labour camps, these institutions also served as places of mass extermination,

389

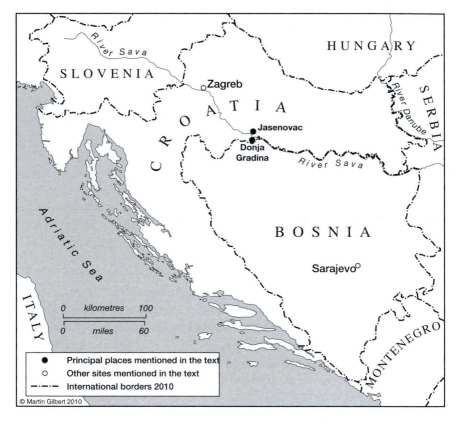

Croatia & Bosnia-Herzegovina

characterised by a level of brutality which shocked even the German military, itself engaged in the murder of Serbia's Jews at this time. Such misgivings were not shared by the SS; indeed, fear that the bloodshed might cease led the Germans to intervene in the spring of 1942 when it was agreed that remaining Jews would be deported to Auschwitz. Five transports in August 1942 and a further two in May 1943 were sent to Poland, carrying more than 6,500 Jews. It is believed that around 33,000 Croatian and Bosnian Jews were murdered by the Nazis and *Ustaše* along with most of the 30,000 or so Roma and at least 300,000 Serbs. Around 5,000 of the Jews who survived owed their lives to the protection of the Italians; following Italy's capitulation, the partisans stepped in. The terror only fully ended with the *Ustaše*'s final defeat in April 1945 when Pavelić and many other leaders escaped via the same channels as the Nazis to Argentina where the former dictator became an advisor to Juan Perón. Pavelić was shot by an unknown assailant in Buenos Aires in 1957 and, following Argentina's belated agreement to extradite him to Yugoslavia, fled to Spain where he finally died of his wounds in 1959.

The genocide in the NDH, and particularly at Jasenovac, was central to the Tito regime's sense of legitimacy. Memorialisation thus followed the dictates of Party doctrine – which exaggerated the death toll – and Tito prevented further research into the issue. This created a sense of grievance amongst many Croatian nationalists who believed that the record of the *Ustaše* was being used to discredit their aspirations: acrimonious debates about what happened in the war played a prominent role in the prelude to Yugoslavia's fragmentation. The Holocaust remains a source of embarrassment in Croatia and public memorialisation has been limited and often contentious. This was most clearly revealed in discussion of what to do with the Jasenovac memorial, damaged in the 1991–95 war. President Tudjman suggested its transformation into a memorial to all victims of the Second World War and of the later conflicts, a proposal swiftly dropped in the face of universal international criticism.

JASENOVAC

Nowhere has the legacy of the Holocaust been more controversial than at Jasenovac, the 'Auschwitz of the Balkans'. Like Auschwitz, Jasenovac was actually a group of camps, spread over a wide area around the Sava River on the modern border of Croatia and Bosnia. Two camps in neighbouring villages were established in the summer of 1941 but were soon superseded by the main camp (officially Jasenovac III) later that year. This was augmented by a number of other institutions, notably execution grounds at Donja Gradina across the river and a camp for women and children at Stara Gradiška almost 20 miles to the south-east (until June 1943, the population of Jasenovac III was exclusively male). What makes this history so contentious is the fact that the camp was created and administered not by the Nazis but by the *Ustaše*; it is thus intimately associated with the history of the only independent Croatian state before the 1990s and, therefore, central to the competing nationalist mythologies of the region. Certain facts are beyond question. Tens of thousands of prisoners were devoured by the Jasenovac system, primarily Serbs, Jews and Roma in line with the *Ustaše*'s demented racist philosophies. Very large numbers of these prisoners were murdered in horrific ways, mainly in Donja Gradina, whilst thousands of others died of disease (particularly typhus), starvation and sheer exhaustion.

The unanswerable question, and the source of much of the heated disagreement which continues to this day, is that of how many victims there were. The Communist position, still widely believed in Serbia, was that at least 700,000 people were murdered. If true, this would make Jasenovac the third deadliest camp in Europe, ranked only behind Birkenau and Treblinka. However, it is generally believed that the figure was exaggerated, perhaps deliberately: as with the long-claimed 4 million dead at Auschwitz, the higher the number of victims, the greater the moral legitimacy of Communism for having defeated such evil. There is evidence that a desire to maximise Yugoslavia's war reparations was also significant. In later years, Serb nationalists could equally use the 700,000 to justify resisting Croatian claims to statehood. The inflated figure rather inevitably provoked a reaction from Croatian historians, including the future president Franjo Tudjman, who went to opposite extremes: in their revisionist version, Jasenovac was merely a labour camp in which perhaps only 20,000 people died. The exact truth will never be known, given the lack of proper record-keeping by the *Ustaše* and their later destruction of what written evidence there was. However, historians have been able to establish at least minimum figures: the Jasenovac museum has identified 69,842 victims of whom 18,812 were children. Serbs account for almost 40,000 of this number, Roma close to 15,000 and Jews more than 10,000. It is reasonable to assume that the

Jasenovac (Photograph by the author)

actual numbers are rather higher. Ultimately, it cannot be denied that Jasenovac was a place of unspeakable horror and the deadliest non-Nazi concentration camp in the Axis.

The camp was destroyed by the *Ustaše* as the partisans approached in April 1945 and the large site was converted in 1968 into a memorial park dominated by a huge concrete memorial sculpture described by its creator Bogdan Bogdanović as a 'melancholy lotus'. It is surrounded by mounds which represent different buildings within the camp. Railway tracks run alongside the park's southern path, carrying a train of the type used to bring prisoners. At the western edge of the park, a nondescript Communist building houses the museum. This was badly damaged in the war of the 1990s – Jasenovac village has very visible scars from the conflict – and again revealed the ability of Jasenovac to divide: the Croats accused the Serbs of looting the museum, the Serbs alleged that objects were removed because of desecration by Croat forces. In any event, the

Bosnian Serbs eventually handed over the collection to the United States Holocaust Memorial Museum which has played a prominent role in the creation of the new exhibition, opened in 2006 (Tue–Fri, 9.00–5.00, Sat–Sun, 10.00–4.00; free; www.jusp-jasenovac.hr). This is evident in the even-handed approach, not least to the vexed question of numbers, and the extensive use of multi-media (including video interviews with survivors) although the dark interior and low positioning of the information panels are more reminiscent of Communist museums. Perhaps the most touching artefacts are the notebooks and drawing book of six-year-old Tedi Drausnik who was held in the Jasenovac complex with his mother and brother. All were eventually able to leave but Tedi's teacher, 17-year-old Vidoka Vuković, was murdered in 1944. By the entrance is a book listing the known victims of Jasenovac; it has 1,888 pages.

Jasenovac is by the A47 south of Novska: the road passes the site, the lotus clearly visible, before a turning a kilometre west of the museum

Donja Gradina (Photograph by the author)

leads back to the complex. There is an easily missed small memorial in the centre of Bročice, between Novska and Jasenovac off the A47: this was the site of the short-lived Jasenovac II camp in 1941. There are a small number of trains each day to Jasenovac from Novska which itself stands on the main Zagreb to Belgrade line.

DONJA GRADINA

Donja Gradina was the principal execution ground for Jasenovac, located just across the Sava River from the main camp. Prisoners were brought by barge and subjected to the full range of *Ustaše* savagery: hanging, throat-cutting, burning, beating with hammers. In Yugoslav times, it formed a part of the Jasenovac memorial complex but is now separated from the main area by an international border, being part of the Republika Srpska, the Serbian zone of Bosnia-Herzegovina. As a result, most of those who visit the site are Serbs; indeed, many visitors to Jasenovac are unaware of the existence of Donja Gradina. It is easy to reach, however, and helps to bring home the reality of the camp as well as to highlight the very different historical perspectives of Serbs and Croats.

The start of the memorial area is marked by the 'Poplar of Horror', the tree from which thousands of Jasenovac prisoners were hanged, now resting on stilts by the roadside. The road curves around the north of the site, following the course of the Sava; the large field and forest to the south contain most of Donja Gradina's mass graves, marked by raised banks of earth: 125 have been identified but there are probably more. As the road enters the forested area to the east, an Orthodox cross, a Star of David and a chakra wheel (for the Roma) represent the main victims. Large signs in the forest set out the widely held Serb view of Jasenovac which few historians would now accept: 700,000 victims of whom 500,000 were Serbs. Nearby are large canisters and vats which, according to the official version, were used to manufacture soap from the bodies of prisoners. The story that the Nazis made soap from the fat of Jewish victims is one of the great myths of the Holocaust which was widely believed even at the time. It may be that a similar process is at work here but during the 1999 trial of former commander Dinko Šakić, ex-prisoners testified that there were indeed failed attempts in Donja Gradina to make soap.

The site can be accessed from Jasenovac by crossing the Gradina border point across the river, accessed by a modern bridge a mile or so west of the museum. In theory, permission from the border guards is required to visit the memorial but this should be a formality. Although most people cross the border by car, it is eminently possible to do so on foot.

OTHER SITES

Zagreb was home to the largest Jewish population in Croatia, almost 12,000 strong in 1941. Most were murdered at Jasenovac or Auschwitz. There is a memorial to the victims, marked by a statue of Moses, in the south of the city's magnificent Mirogoj cemetery on Hermanna Bollea, north of the centre (www.gradskagroblja.hr). A car park at Praška 7, close to central Ban Jelačić square, stands on the site of Zagreb's synagogue, blown up by the *Ustaše* in 1941. It is marked by a memorial plaque but the Jewish community, currently located a couple of blocks east at Palmotićeva 16, hopes to build a new community centre and synagogue on the site.

Around 12,000 of Bosnia's pre-war Jewish community of 14,000 lived in Sarajevo. The former Sephardic synagogue on Mula Mustafe Bašeskije houses the city's Jewish museum, reopened in 2004 following closure during the siege of the 1990s. In the hills above the city, the Vraca memorial complex honours over 7,000 Jews along with other citizens and partisans who were killed in the war; however, the site was badly damaged during the siege.

S E R B I A

T he history of the Holocaust in Serbia is comparatively little known yet is of great significance, coinciding with and paralleling that in Poland and the Soviet Union. By the time the mass deportations began in much of the rest of Europe in 1942, Serbia's Jews, aside from a small number in hiding or fighting with the partisans, had already been murdered.

A small Jewish community had existed since the Roman period but only became a significant element once most of Serbia was incorporated into the Ottoman Empire (a process completed in the 1520s), facilitating the settlement of Sephardic immigrants from Spain and Portugal. Ashkenazi communities also developed in the northern provinces, taken over by Austria in the eighteenth century, which now border Hungary. Given the close association between Jewish prosperity and Ottoman rule, it is hardly surprising that Serbian independence in the nineteenth century caused unease. Although many Jews supported the independence movement, the fears of pessimists seemed justified when a series of restrictive laws were introduced from the 1830s onwards; full civil equality was only granted in 1889. The situation improved in inter-war Yugoslavia with prominent Jews playing a leading role in the country's economy and anti-Semitism largely absent from the political arena.

All was to change, of course, with the German invasion of April 1941. Although part of the northern Vojvodina region was given to Hungary, most of Serbia was under direct German military occupation alongside the quisling government of Milan Nedić. Initial policy followed that in other occupied nations with the familiar catalogue of legal separation, exclusion from professions, economic expropriation and forced labour. However, from the summer of 1941 this escalated into a policy of genocide with a speed matched only by the simultaneous killings in the USSR. It thus marked a key stage in the development of the Holocaust. The official justification for mass murder was the rapid emergence of partisan resistance which led the Germans to adopt a retaliation strategy of killing 100 Serbs for every soldier killed and 50 for every one wounded. This was expressed in a relentless campaign of terror against the civilian population, especially in the countryside, which paralleled

the *Ustaše* atrocities in Croatia. Thousands of Serbs were murdered but increasingly Jews were the target of the German violence. From August 1941, Jewish men were imprisoned in a handful of camps with wholesale slaughter beginning in the following month; by December, almost all were dead. Some historians have suggested that the murders in Serbia were a local affair, a way of filling the increasingly unachievable retaliation quotas the Germans had set themselves. However, Harold Turner, the SS chief in Serbia, perhaps let slip the truth when he noted that 'they had to be got rid of, anyway'. The anti-partisan campaign was a convenient cover in another sense in that the Wehrmacht could be left to carry out the killings, seeing the process as a military necessity. However, the army's sense of honour, which had had little difficulty in accepting the shooting of unarmed Jewish men or Serbian peasants, did balk at killing women and children. It was, therefore, decided to concentrate all remaining Serbian Jews in a single camp, Sajmište. When their planned deportation was delayed (the newly created Polish camps had many other victims waiting), it was decided to kill the women and children in situ: virtually the entire Jewish population was murdered by mid-May 1942, giving rise to Turner's famous boast that Serbia was the only country where the 'Jewish problem' had been solved. The most commonly quoted figure is that 14,500 out of 16,000 Serbian Jews died in the Holocaust. However, this excludes the Hungarian-controlled Vojvodina where several thousand more Jews lived: most also perished, through massacres in early 1942, use as forced labour, and deportation to Birkenau along with the Hungarian Jews in 1944.

Post-war Yugoslav memorialisation in Serbia was naturally the same as in Croatia, with a focus primarily on Serb suffering so that sites largely associated with the murder of Jews were overlooked. This began to change after the break-up of Yugoslavia although the wars and economic problems of the 1990s limited progress. Rather surprisingly, given their centrality to the nation's modern sense of identity, even locations where Serbs formed the majority of victims, such as Banjica and Jajinci, remain rather run-down.

BELGRADE

Belgrade was home to more than two-thirds of the Jews of German-occupied Serbia, with a 1941 population of 11,870. A Jewish presence in the city was recorded in Roman times and it had been an Ashkenazic centre of some note in the Middle Ages. However, it was Ottoman conquest in the sixteenth century and the consequent influx of Iberian refugees that gave Jewish Belgrade its identity, this latter group forming more than 80 per cent of the community. The city's rapid growth following Serbian independence was accompanied by further Jewish settlement.

Belgrade fell within a week of the invasion of Yugoslavia, occupied by the Germans on 13 April 1941. Loss of rights in the early months served as a prelude to the escalation of policy in late summer when all Jewish men were arrested; they were executed between October and December. The women and children were sent to Sajmište in December. Around 10,500 Belgrade Jews were murdered – the only survivors were those who had managed to hide in the city or flee to the partisans.

The traditional area of Jewish settlement was the Dorćol district which runs from the Old Town north to the Danube. The community is commemorated by a Holocaust memorial next to the river created by Nandor Glid, a Serbian Jewish Holocaust survivor who has designed memorials across Europe, including at Dachau. His trademark style of sculpted entwined bodies is used in this case to suggest the shape not only of a menorah but also of flames. The memorial is located next to a children's playground on the Danube embankment just to the east of Tadeuša Košćuška and the 25 May sports centre.

A few blocks further south, Tadeuša Košćuška intersects with Visokog Stevana. The grey corner building (number 2 on the latter street) was the former headquarters of the Jewish Women's Society which was converted into a Jewish hospital following the exclusion of Jews from the 'Aryan' healthcare system in 1941. On 19 March 1942, the patients were taken to Sajmište to become the first victims of the gassing; the doctors followed their charges a week later. Jevrejska runs parallel to Tadeuša Košćuška and, as its name suggests, was the heart of Jewish life, particularly around the intersection with Solunska. A handful of buildings preserve some traces of this past notably the magnificent Moorish-style edifice at Jevrejska 16 which housed the *Oneg Shabat* and *Gemilut Hasadim* charities; today it serves as a cultural centre.

Growing Jewish prosperity and integration in the late nineteenth century encouraged the wealthy to settle closer to the centre, attested to by the former merchants' mansions which punctuate the Communist architecture of Cara Dušana. The community's offices are located in a

large nineteenth-century building at Kralja Petra 71a which also houses
Belgrade's Jewish History Museum (Mon–Fri, 10.00–2.00 (despite the
entry plaque saying otherwise); free; www.jimbeograd.org). The displays
are somewhat dated, most obviously the final section on 'free socialist
Yugoslavia'. Nevertheless, the collection of old photographs and relics of
a now almost vanished life is affecting. A substantial section is devoted to
the Holocaust with items retrieved from Sajmište, Banjica and Jasenovac
displayed. The Moorish Beth Israel Sephardic temple – Belgrade's main
synagogue – stood around the corner until it was burned down by the
Nazis. The spot is now occupied by the National Museum's Gallery of
Frescoes at Casa Uroša 20; there is a memorial plaque by the entrance.
The only remaining synagogue (a large Ashkenazi structure guarded
behind high walls) is further south at Maršala Birjuzova 19. The synagogue
was apparently requisitioned for use as a brothel for the German military,
hence its survival.

East of the centre, the Sephardic Jewish cemetery at Mije Kovačevića
1 (Sun–Fri, 8.00–7.00 (until 5.00, Oct–Mar)) is opposite its small and
often closed Ashkenazi equivalent which adjoins Belgrade's principal
municipal cemetery. The complex of necropolises is completed by a
memorial site containing the graves of 2,000 partisans and Soviet soldiers
who died in the liberation of Belgrade in 1944. All can be reached by
taking tram 12 or buses 23, 27, 27L or 32 to the Novo Groblje stop.
At the rear of the Sephardic cemetery is a large Holocaust memorial
including a grave for the remains of 197 Belgrade Jews and plaques to
individual victims and families. To the right of the central path, a mass
grave holds the remains of 800 Jews who formed part of the Kladovo
transport by a memorial erected by the Vienna Jewish community. In
late 1939, a group of over 1,000 mostly Austrian Jews left Bratislava by
boat intent on reaching Palestine. After several false starts, they were
able to get as far as Yugoslavia before being stopped by a combination of
harsh weather which froze the Danube and the refusal of the Romanian
authorities, under British pressure, to allow passage. They were forced to
spend the winter in the small Danubian town of Kladovo initially on the
overcrowded boats and then in a tent camp. When they finally departed
in September 1940, it was not to the Black Sea but back northwards to
the town of Šabac where they remained through another winter, around
1,100 falling into the hands of the Germans in April 1941 – 200 or so
mainly younger refugees had managed to obtain certificates for Palestine

and had left days before the invasion. The men, together with Roma also held at Šabac, were murdered. The women of the Kladovo transport were sent to Sajmište in January 1942, sharing the fate of all of its Jewish inmates.

TOPOVSKE ŠUPE

Tupovske Šupe was a short-lived but deadly camp, its history marking the beginning of the German campaign of systematic genocide in Serbia. It was established in August 1941, officially as a transit camp for Jews, on the site of pre-war artillery barracks (the meaning of its name in Serbian) on the then southern edge of Belgrade. The first inmates were Jews from the north-eastern Banat region and by mid-October it had become clear what 'transit' meant in this context: all the men were taken away in groups – sometimes hundreds at a time – to be murdered, primarily at the Jajinci execution grounds south of the city. They were replaced by the Jewish men of Belgrade who in turn suffered the same fate as did Roma men also interned in the camp. In total, there were around 5,000 victims. In December 1941, the 300 or so remaining Jewish men were transferred across the Sava to prepare the new Sajmište camp; on completion of their work, they too were shot.

The grounds of the camp stand at the intersection of Bulevar Oslobođenja and Tabanovačka, just south of the busy Autokomanda road junction. Following post-war use as workshops, a number of buildings survive in a rather derelict state, enclosed behind fences. However, a small memorial park was created in 2006 on the edge of the complex, off Tabanovačka. A path leads across the grass to the surviving wall of an otherwise destroyed barrack on which has been placed a memorial plaque in the form of a Torah scroll with a short text.

The memorial park can be reached by taking trams 9, 10 or 14 or bus 33 from the centre of Belgrade to the Trg Oslobođenja stop. Tabanovačka is the eastern turning at the roundabout a few metres back; the park is around 200 metres along this street.

BANJICA

Banjica is the best-known camp amongst Serbs, a reflection of the fact that most of those who passed through it were partisans and other political prisoners rather than Jews. It was created in July 1941 in army barracks; unlike in Tupovske Šupe and Sajmište, the Germans shared the administration of the camp with officials of the Nedić regime. According to the preserved records, 23,697 people passed through it until its closure in October 1944 of whom 3,489 were executed. However, it appears that a large number of execution orders were destroyed whilst prisoners who were shot on arrival were not recorded, meaning that the total number killed was probably much higher. This is perhaps one reason why only 300 Jews are listed amongst Banjica's victims although a sadder explanation is that most were already dead by the time Jews started to be sent to the camp in 1942. Inmates were largely taken to Jajinci to be murdered although others were killed in Banjica itself and in the Belgrade cemeteries. Prisoners were also dispatched to camps further north including Auschwitz and Mauthausen.

After the war the camp reverted to military use, a role it still performs today. Unsurprisingly, the mostly modern complex is, therefore, not open to visitors. However, an annex of one of the few surviving wartime buildings houses a museum dedicated to the camp, albeit one which is frustratingly difficult to access. It did once keep regular opening hours but it is now necessary to ring 3674 877 or 2630 462 in advance to visit. Unfortunately, there is no guarantee that anyone will answer. Hopefully, the Belgrade City Museum (www.mgb.org.yu) which oversees the site will eventually restore easier entry. The exhibition itself was created under Communism and is thus rather old-fashioned in its approach although there are some interesting examples of prisoner artwork. A memorial room lists Banjica's victims.

Banjica was originally a village outside Belgrade but it has been swallowed up by the city's suburbs since the war. The army base stands on Pavla Jurišića Šturma, around a mile south of the Red Star football stadium. The entrance to the museum is a few yards north of the main gate. It can be reached by taking buses 40, 41, 59, 78 or 94 to the Banjica stop: Pavla Jurišića Šturma is the road opposite.

SAJMIŠTE

Sajmište (literally 'fairground') is deservedly the most notorious of the concentration camps in Serbia although it was technically within the territory of independent Croatia during the occupation. In October

1941, the Germans decided to intern all Serbian Jews in a single camp prior to their deportation; the NDH granted the use of pre-war exhibition grounds facing Belgrade on the west bank of the Sava. As Jewish men were already being murdered across Serbia, the camp was essentially designated for women and children. The surviving Jews of Belgrade were ordered to report to police in December 1941 and immediately sent to Sajmište (sometimes referred to as Semlin or Zemun) where they were soon joined by Jews from other parts of the country as well as Roma women and children. The large trade fair pavilions had naturally never been intended to serve as living quarters and conditions were consequently appalling. 'Floors' were created inside the pavilions by installing wooden scaffolding through which prisoners had to crawl whilst there was no heating, few toilets and just one shower room for the whole camp. When it became clear that deportations to Poland would take longer than intended, German officials complained to Berlin with the result that a gas van of the type used at Chełmno was sent to Sajmište in March. In the space of just nine weeks, at least 6,000 women, children and the small number of men who had thus far survived were murdered in this van whilst being driven through the streets of Belgrade. Each group was told that they were being relocated to a new, more comfortable camp – 100 people volunteered for the first journey – and driven across the river on a pontoon bridge and through the city to the execution grounds at Jajinci, by which time all were dead. Close to 8,000 Jewish inmates of Sajmište died, the remainder from disease and lack of food in the camp; the only survivors were a few women with foreign citizenship who had married Serbian Jews and the Roma women and children who survived the winter (the latter were released before the murder of the Jews began). Sajmište was then converted into a camp for political prisoners and remained in use until mid-1944: around 10,000 of the approximately 30,000 Serbs held in this period lost their lives. It was progressively abandoned after being hit in an American bombing raid in April 1944 (the target was actually the railway station across the river) and handed back to the NDH in May although Jews en route to other German camps were held there as late as September 1944; Jews thus formed the last as well as first inmates.

Although most of the camp was destroyed by the 1944 bombing, a few pavilions still exist. A large monument stands by the river but a memorial plaque, by the steps to the path leading to it, was stolen in 2006, meaning there is now no explanation of what is being memorialised. The post-war

Sajmište (Photograph by the author)

blocks between the monument and the Art Deco tower (the centre of the camp) stand on the site of two of the large pavilions which housed Jews and Roma. The largest pavilion of all, which held 5,000 Jewish women and children, was to the south of the tower. The surviving buildings are on the stretch of Staro Sajmište (a street which branches off in a number of directions) closest to the highway to the north. The former camp hospital – now the *Poseydon* nightclub at Staro Sajmište 20 – gained worldwide attention in 2007 when it booked the British band Kosheen; the band withdrew when they discovered the venue's history. The rather run-down Art Deco building on the opposite side of the road held both the shower room and the morgue. The two-storey building to the east of the *Poseydon* (by a small roundabout) was the 'pavilion of death' where often fatal beatings of prisoners took place when the camp held Serbs.

Sajmište lies on the west bank of the Sava, now part of New Belgrade. The memorial is hard to miss, by the embankment between the Brankov and Stari Savski bridges (the two northernmost on the Sava). The central tower can be clearly seen from the monument; the other surviving buildings are a block to its north.

JAJINCI

Jajinci was the largest killing centre in Serbia, the final resting place of thousands of Jews, Roma, partisans and political prisoners. It had served as an army shooting range before the war so it was no surprise that the Germans should turn it into an execution site. Amongst the earliest victims were the Jewish and Roma men of Tupovske Šupe along with others killed in the anti-partisan 'reprisals' from the summer of 1941. Prisoners from Banjica and Sajmište (after its conversion into a 'political' camp in summer 1942) were also shot there as were partisans captured in the countryside. The most appalling period was the spring of 1942 when the mass shootings were supplemented by the daily arrival of the Sajmište gas van and its terrible cargo. A team of seven Serb prisoners had to unload the van; once the deliveries ceased, they too were murdered. At least 80 trenches were dug just for bodies of the women and children of Sajmište. As in Poland and the USSR, the turn in the war led the Germans to attempt to destroy the evidence: from November 1943, a group of 100 Jewish and Serb prisoners, overseen by German policemen, were required to dig up bodies and burn them. This is one reason why there is no clear way of knowing how many people were killed at Jajinci although the fact that bodies were still being burnt almost up to the liberation in October 1944 suggests that the figure must have been large. The number most commonly quoted in Serbia is 80,000 although the Serbian Orthodox Church, rarely known for its restraint in such matters, has suggested 127,000. The figures were certainly in the tens of thousands, with evidence that an astonishing 68,000 bodies were disinterred by the disposal team in 1943–44.

The site was turned into a memorial park in 1964 (the twentieth anniversary of Belgrade's liberation) but is now rather neglected. There is little indication of its history beyond a small memorial wall at the park's entrance marked with a typically Communist relief of victims and heroic partisans. Aside from a quotation from the poet Desanka Maksimović closer to the main memorial area, this is the only text given. The landscaped park itself is dominated by a large abstract metal sculpture, vaguely suggestive of a dove of peace, atop a tall plinth, behind which are preserved a few posts from the shooting range. This is the central focus for annual memorial services but at other times the meaning would be opaque without any foreknowledge of Jajinci's history.

Jajinci village is just south of Belgrade, shortly after the lengthy Bulevar Oslobođenja turns into Ulica Umetnička. It can be reached by taking buses 401 to 407 from the Voždovac interchange (itself served by trams 9, 10 and 14 from central Belgrade) to the Maxima stop. The memorial park entrance is further along the road on the left.

OTHER SITES

The main internment centre in southern Serbia was the Crveni Krst (Red Cross) concentration camp in Niš; it is now a memorial museum (Mon–Fri, 9.00–4.00; Sat; 10.00–3.00; 50 RSD) located on Bulevar 12 Februar, north-west of the city centre. Around 30,000 people went through Crveni Krst, the majority Serb political prisoners. Over a third were murdered at an execution site on Bubanj hill overlooking Niš to the south-west; they included more than 1,000 local Jewish men shot in late 1941 (the women were sent to Sajmište). The site is now marked by a memorial complex centred around three large sculpted fists. In the city itself, the former synagogue, now used as an art gallery, stands on Ruđera Boškovića close to central Kralja Milana square. The Jewish cemetery was neglected for decades and part of the site was occupied by

Roma families. Since 2004 a cooperative effort of the local Jewish and Roma communities together with the city authorities and the American Joint Distribution Committee has seen much of it restored. For more information, contact the Niš Jewish Community at Čairska 28/2, south of the centre.

A particularly infamous massacre took place at Kragujevac, between Belgrade and Niš, in October 1941 following a partisan ambush of German troops in nearby Gornji Milanovac. After killing all male Jews and suspected Communists, the German military proceeded to arrest all adult men, even dragging entire classes of teenagers from the local school. Hundreds were shot in a period of seven hours. According to the army's figures, 2,324 men were killed in Kragujevac; this was in retaliation for 10 German soldiers killed and 26 wounded. The killing site in Šumarice, just west of the town, became a large memorial park in 1976 although it was damaged by NATO bombing in 1999.

Novi Sad, as capital of Vojvodina, was occupied by Hungary. During three days in January 1942, Hungarian troops massacred around 1,300 people, more than 800 of them Jewish, the remainder mainly Serbs. Although murders took place all over the city, the largest number were shot by the banks of the frozen Danube and their bodies thrown into holes in the ice. There is a memorial on the embankment by Kej Žrtava Racije, just south of Trg Neznanog Junaka. The city's synagogue was later used as a holding centre for deportees; the restored building at Jevrejska 11 on the western edge of the Old Town is now a cultural centre. There is a Holocaust memorial in the Jewish cemetery at the end of Doža Đerđa to the south-west.

CHAPTER 18

GREECE

G reece was home to Europe's oldest Jewish community, a community largely wiped out by the Holocaust. Although the level of the destruction varied by region, around 80 per cent of Jews were murdered.

Jews had lived in Greece from classical times with communities spread across the mainland and the islands, surviving the vicissitudes of Greek, Roman and Byzantine rule. It was the Turkish conquests in the fifteenth century which transformed the Jewish presence. Ottoman policy offered toleration and autonomy, and the Sultan issued an open invitation to settle in Greece when the Jews were expelled from Spain in 1492; in the ensuing decades, tens of thousands of Jews from Spain, Portugal and Italy migrated. This changed the character of Greek Jewry in two respects. Firstly, the majority were now Sephardic (i.e., Iberian) Jews, characterised by their use of the Judeo-Spanish or Ladino tongue. The Romaniot (i.e., Byzantine) Jews who had previously been the principal population increasingly followed the language and liturgy of the newcomers although Romaniot communities survived into the twentieth century in some communities such as Volos. Secondly, Jewish life was increasingly dominated by one city, Thessaloniki (Salonica), in which most Sephardim had settled. When Greece gained independence in the 1820s, Salonica remained under Turkish rule; the conquest of the city and its hinterland in 1912 dramatically increased the number of Jews living in Greece from 10,000 to more than 80,000. Despite emigration in the ensuing decades, there were still 77,000 Jews at the beginning of the war.

It was Mussolini's military misadventures which brought the Nazis to Greece, a failed Italian attack in 1940 prompting German invasion in April 1941. The country was divided into three zones of occupation (German, Italian and Bulgarian), an arrangement which meant that Greek Jews were not immediately subject to the level of persecution which had followed German advances elsewhere despite some early harassment. A key factor was the attitude of the Italians who controlled much of the mainland and who refused to implement anti-Jewish measures. As a result, systematic destruction did not begin until 1943. Unsurprisingly, Jews living in the

BULGARIA
Black Sea
ALBANIA
MACEDONIA
Thessaloniki (Salonika)
Sea of Marmara
GREECE
Larissa
Volos
Aegean Sea
TURKEY
Athens
Ionian Sea
KOS
Rhodes
RHODES
Principal places mentioned in the text
Other sites mentioned in the text
International borders 2010
Sea of Crete
0 kilometres 150
0 miles 100
CRETE
© Martin Gilbert 2010

Greece

German zone were the first victims: in 1942, they had been increasingly subjected to forced labour and expropriation of property; in February 1943, the yellow star and a degree of ghettoisation were introduced as a prelude to deportation. This zone included Thessaloniki with the result that the majority of Greece's Jews were rapidly transported to Auschwitz from March to June; few survived. Once this process was underway, the Germans turned to the Bulgarian zone (Thrace and eastern Macedonia). Despite their later refusal to hand over their own Jewish citizens, the Bulgarian authorities willingly rounded up the 5,000 or so Jews in their zone who were deported to Treblinka in March 1943. However, the Italians consistently refused to deport the Jews in their territories, even issuing false identity documents to help hundreds escape. The situation only changed in September 1943 when Italy surrendered to the Allies and Germany occupied the whole Italian zone. The previous pattern of registration, appropriation and deportation was repeated but with crucial differences. Forewarned by the experience of Thessaloniki, large numbers went into hiding whilst the Athens community records were destroyed to prevent the Germans acquiring them. When round-ups took place in March 1944, many Jews were thus able to evade them: it is estimated that approximately 50 per cent of Athenian Jews were not deported whilst in some cities such as Volos over 80 per cent of the inhabitants were saved. The attitude of many Greeks was crucial, particularly of prominent figures such as the Athens police chief Angelos Evert, who issued Christian identity papers, and, especially, Archbishop Damaskinos, the head of the Orthodox Church. The latter was the only senior churchman in occupied Europe to publicly condemn the Holocaust whilst privately he ordered churches and monasteries to give shelter to fleeing Jews. Even so, many still fell victim, especially in the islands. In total, around 55,000 Greek Jews were sent to Auschwitz in 1943 and 1944, enduring horrendous journeys, in some cases over a week long. Most perished on arrival. Adding those who died at Treblinka or from forced labour, it is estimated that between 60,000 and 65,000 died during the Holocaust.

Greece was slow to begin to properly memorialise the Holocaust. Suggested explanations have included a desire not to revisit the especially traumatic history of Greece in the 1940s, a sense that anti-Semitism was not an issue, and, more cynically, embarrassment at the wartime role of the local authorities in Thessaloniki. However, most communities have been memorialised since the late 1990s.

THESSALONIKI

The world's greatest Sephardic metropolis for almost five centuries, Greece's second city was home to the overwhelming majority of the country's Jews. Jewish settlement was recorded as early as the second century BCE but it was from the fifteenth century that Thessaloniki, or Salonica to its then inhabitants, became a Jewish city rather than a city in which Jews lived. After their expulsion from Spain, Jews were invited to settle by the Ottoman Sultans; they were seen as the key to reviving its population and economy both of which were declining long before the Turks wrested it from Byzantine control in 1430. Under this relatively benign Ottoman sovereignty, Salonica became the pre-eminent Jewish city in the northern Mediterranean. Jews formed the largest ethnic group, concentrated in the lower city (today's centre) whilst the Turkish elites occupied the hills by the northern walls. However, three developments in the early twentieth century dramatically altered Salonica and the position of the Jews within it. The Balkan War of 1912 brought an end to Turkish rule when the Greeks captured the city whilst a disastrous fire in 1917 swept through its historic Jewish heart, destroying most of the 37 synagogues and countless homes and businesses. The First World War was followed by a population exchange in 1922 in which most Turks were forced to leave, to be replaced by tens of thousands of Greeks who had been similarly expelled from Asia Minor. For the first time since 1492, Jews thus found themselves a minority in a Greek-dominated city. Given their relative peace and prosperity under the Ottomans, they were viewed as Turkish fifth columnists (and Communist sympathisers) by right-wing nationalists; these tensions erupted in the anti-Semitic Campbell riots in the summer of 1931. That said, anti-Semitism was less of a problem than anti-Turkish prejudice and in the 1930s Yom Kippur was made a public holiday. Although the Jewish population had fallen from a peak of 62,000 at the beginning of the century, it still exceeded 50,000 when the war began.

The Germans occupied Thessaloniki on 9 April 1941 and within a week had arrested community leaders. Representatives of Alfred Rosenberg's Frankfurt institute for the study of Jewry then systematically plundered the city's libraries and synagogues. However, although more than 600 Jews died of disease and starvation in the harsh winter of 1941–42, there were no more specifically anti-Jewish measures until the

Thessaloniki: Holocaust memorial (Photograph by the author)

summer of 1942, creating a false sense of security which was enhanced when Chief Rabbi Zvi Koretz (who had been sent to prison in Vienna in 1941) was allowed to return in January 1942. The community was thus completely unprepared in July 1942 when adult males were required to assemble in the city centre, humiliated and registered for forced labour. Even then, however, prolonged negotiations with the Germans led to their exemption after a massive ransom had been raised. This only served to convince optimists that the community could be saved, despite growing expropriation of Jewish property which culminated in the local council's seizure of the Jewish cemetery in December 1942. In fact, the delays caused growing frustration in Berlin, prompting Eichmann to dispatch his representatives Dieter Wisliceny and Aloïs Brunner in February 1943 with orders to rid the city of its Jews within two months. They immediately introduced the yellow star, followed by a series of decrees based on the Nuremberg Laws, as a prelude to creating a ghetto. However, this proved impossible to implement in the conventional sense of a single enclosed area. Instead, districts with predominantly Jewish populations in the suburbs remained as they were whilst all other Jews were forced to move to two designated zones by 25 February. Initially, Jewish homes were marked as such (Christians had not been evicted, rendering the quarters highly overcrowded) but their occupants could still come and go. However, on 6 March all of these areas were cordoned off and Jews forbidden to leave. In the meantime, a genuine ghetto had been created in the Baron Hirsch quarter by the railway station to serve as a transit camp for the deportations. The first transport, containing the quarter's inhabitants, was sent to Auschwitz on 15 March 1943. In the ensuing days, each district was cleared of its Jews, who were marched to the Baron Hirsch camp before being sent to Poland. By the end of May, most had been deported; the majority met their deaths in Birkenau immediately. Throughout this process, the Germans used Rabbi Koretz, who they had appointed head of the Jewish Council in December 1942, as their intermediary. Koretz is one of the most controversial Jewish leaders of the Holocaust, seen by his detractors as, at best, astonishingly naive in his faith in the Germans' word and consequent compliance with their orders. However, his reassurances were increasingly disbelieved and several hundred Jews fled to other parts of Greece, whilst the Italians were able to transfer a train of 320 to Athens in July. Nonetheless, 43,850 Salonican Jews were sent to Poland on 19 transports along with a further 2,000 from the neighbouring region; the final train, carrying 1,200 emaciated survivors of forced labour, left on 7 August 1943. An additional transport took Rabbi Koretz and other privileged Jews to Bergen-Belsen. It is believed that 96 per cent of Salonica's Jews were murdered.

The contemporary community numbers around 1,000 and it was not until 1997, when Thessaloniki was European City of Culture, that a Jewish Museum and a public Holocaust memorial were established to remind modern inhabitants of their city's past as the most glorious outpost of Spanish Jewry.

Central Thessaloniki

The old town was the heart of Jewish life for more than four centuries. However, it is hard today to discover traces of the Salonica of Jewish legend due to the 1917 fire. The Greeks saw in the disaster an opportunity to create a new, Hellenised urban fabric. Their principal aim was perhaps to eliminate remnants of Turkish Salonica but, equally, there was no attempt to preserve the Jewish character which had dominated the old city. Indeed, Jews who had lost their homes generally found themselves pushed to the new suburbs.

However, the centre is home to the Jewish Museum of Thessaloniki (Tue, Fri & Sun, 11.00–2.00; Wed & Thu, 11.00–2.00, 5.00–8.00; €3; www.jmth.gr), housed in one of the few Jewish buildings to survive the fire, at Agiou Mina 13. A couple of small rooms in the well-presented exhibition address the Holocaust. A cabinet displays objects from the camps, including personal items found in the debris of 'Canada' in Birkenau in 1945. There is also a focus on Jewish resistance, including the role of Greek Jews in the camp's 1944 *Sonderkommando* rebellion.

Plateia Eleftherias (Liberty Square), two blocks south-west, was the site of 'Black Sabbath' on Saturday 11 July 1942 when all Jewish men aged between 18 and 45 were required to assemble at 8 o'clock in the morning and kept in the square until late afternoon. Denied refreshments, the 9,000 men were forced to perform gymnastic exercises, doused with water and whipped in front of large crowds of spectators. They were also required to stare at the sun for minutes at a time; in the ensuing days several died of meningitis or brain haemorrhages. Two days later, they were ordered to reassemble, registered for forced labour and about 2,000 sent to projects across northern Greece, often in malaria-infested areas.

The labour conscription only ceased with the community's payment of a 2.5 billion drachmae ransom in late 1942, by which time 250 of the men had died. The square is now a car park but in its southern corner, by seafront Nikis, stands Thessaloniki's Holocaust memorial, relocated here in 2006 from the suburbs. The 1997 sculpture was the last work of the prolific Serbian architect and Holocaust survivor Nandor Glid, whose memorials can also be seen at Dachau and Belgrade. Like the latter, the Thessaloniki monument takes the form of a menorah in flames, its parts made up of contorted bodies.

South-east of the Jewish Museum, between Ermou and Irakliou, one of the few surviving relics of pre-war Jewish life is the Modiano Market, built in 1922 by Jewish merchant Eli Modiano. Bland Irakliou 26 opposite houses the modern community headquarters and the Yad Lazikaron Synagogue, the main house of worship for the small modern congregation. The only surviving pre-war religious building is the Monastirioton Synagogue, built in 1927, at Sygrou 35. It lies at the heart of the area between Egnatia and Agiou Dimitriou which was one of the two to which Jewish settlement was largely restricted in 1943. On 17 March 1943, Rabbi Koretz addressed an angry crowd in the synagogue, informing them that they had no alternative but to accept the deportations to Poland. On the way to the synagogue from the Jewish Museum or the market, one passes the former Hamza Bey mosque on Egnatia, a rare remaining Turkish structure. After the 1922 population exchange, the building was a telephone exchange and then the Jewish-owned *Attikon* cinema. In September 1942, the proprietor was interned in the Pavlos Melas camp until he agreed to cede management of the property to Greeks.

West and north

Thessaloniki's old train station, the point of departure for the transports, carries a memorial plaque. The small cream-coloured building, now a freight depot, is on Stathmou (north-west of the centre and south-west of the modern station), facing Stavrou Voutira which marks the entry to the former Baron Hirsch camp. The small houses of this area were originally constructed by the Austrian Jewish philanthropist and railway entrepreneur in the 1890s to accommodate refugees from the Russian Empire. It was suddenly transformed in March 1943 when wooden fences were erected around the quarter; the isolated inhabitants went for two days without food before the community was able to organise supplies. On 14 March, Rabbi Koretz addressed them in the local synagogue, announcing that they were to be deported to Kraków where they would find employment and a warm welcome from Polish Jewry. Fake Polish money was even handed out. Whether Koretz genuinely believed the lies is unclear, but his audience was less gullible, his reassurances being met with boos and cries. Once the 2,800 inhabitants of the Hirsch quarter had been sent on the five-day journey to Auschwitz the next morning, the area became the transit camp through which virtually all Salonican Jews passed over the next five months. Many of the original buildings survive around Stavrou Voutira, Sapfous and Patriarchou Kirillou although in very poor condition. Bus 12 to Anagenniseos or Ktiniatreio stops close by; it returns from the Terma stop by the old station.

Thessaloniki's post-war Jewish cemetery (Sun–Fri, 9.00–2.00; ring bell to enter) is some distance north of the centre on Dimitriou Karaoli (take bus 32 or 34 to AGNO and then a short walk westwards). Its 1962 Holocaust memorial was the only one in Thessaloniki for over 30 years; it is next to a memorial to the former Jewish cemetery. Towards the rear, a 2003 memorial commemorates the 12,898 Greek Jews who fought in the 1940–41 war against Italy and Germany; 513 died and 3,743 were injured. Amongst their number is Colonel Mordechai Frizis, the first senior officer to die in the campaign; his body was buried here in 2004 after transfer from Albania. At its eastern end, Dimitriou Karaoli meets Konstantinoupoleos: the Pavlos Melas army base which was used by the Germans as a camp for political prisoners, including Christians who hid Jews, is on the eastern side of the latter. There is also a graffiti-covered memorial to the Greek resistance on the corner of Dimitriou Karaoli and Konstantinoupoleos; close to here, buses 27, 38 and 56 run back to the centre.

East and south

The enormous campus of Thessaloniki's Aristotle University lies south-east of the centre, between Egnatia and Agiou Dimitriou. From 1495 to 1942, this was the site of Salonica's Jewish cemetery, which covered more than 350,000 square metres and held at least 400,000 graves. The cemetery lay just east of the old city walls, an area coveted by the council in its ambitious post-fire redevelopment plan. A 1937 agreement

417

(whereby the university would be given around 10 per cent of the land in return for relocating graves to new cemeteries outside the city) was never implemented by either side. However, the Jewish community's agony led the municipality to entreat the German envoy Max Merten to make transfer of the cemetery part of the ransom for the release of the Jewish forced labourers in 1942. The Jews refused and the agreement with the Germans seemed to preserve the cemetery. Undeterred, the Greek authorities seized it anyway, beginning demolition in December 1942. Although the Germans used some of the stone for themselves, the initiative came from the council and gravestones continued to be used in local building projects for decades afterwards. A 1946 law of restitution in theory allowed survivors to reclaim any remaining graves but the land was taken to belong to the state on the grounds that it had been deserted by its owners! The site is currently occupied by mostly unsightly 1960s blocks and there is nothing to indicate its past although fragments of the cemetery have clearly been used in the park around the observatory in the west of the campus. Remnants were unearthed during excavations for a new metro system in 2008 and the construction company has promised to display some of its finds in the stations. At present, the only properly preserved elements are found in the Jewish Museum; even there, the destruction is blamed on the Germans.

From the university, Egnatia curves to the right and becomes straight, south-running, Karamanli, also known as Nea Egnatia. Standing by the intersection with Papanastasiou, the Ippokratio hospital was formerly the Baron Hirsch hospital (buses 2, 10, 11 and 58, Ippokratio) which was requisitioned by the Germans in 1942. It is now a large complex but the original main building stands in the centre; its elegant front is accessed from the other side on Konstantinoupoleos. The small park outside the hospital between Karamanli and Papanastasiou was the original location of the Holocaust memorial and now contains a bust of Colonel Frizis, erected in 2007. A few streets further along Papanastasiou, between Priamou and Mitsaki, Plateia Evreion Martiron (Jewish Martyrs' Square) is a tiny park whose dedication to victims of the Holocaust is marked by a simple street sign. These locations were within the 151 district which was the centre of the second designated Jewish quarter in 1943.

Several blocks to the west, running largely parallel to Karamanli, lengthy Olgas preserves a few traces of the Jewish industrial and commercial elites of the late nineteenth and early twentieth centuries, notably surviving villas at 68, 162, 180 and 198, although the latter three are a long way south (take bus 5, 6, 8, 33 or 78 to the 25 Martirou stop on Papandreou and walk a couple of blocks east). Back towards the centre, the beautiful former home of the Archaeological Museum on Archeologiku Mousiou was built in 1902 as a Donmeh prayer house, a relic of one of the more curious aspects of Jewish Salonica's story. The false messiah Shabbetai Zvi gained a large following in the city before converting to Islam in 1666; Donmehs were those who continued to follow him, outwardly practising Islam whilst maintaining many Jewish beliefs and rituals. Around the corner, at Paraskevopoulou 13, is the former Allatini Jewish orphanage, now in a very poor state.

OTHER SITES

Curiously, the one former Jewish centre not to have a proper Holocaust memorial is Athens, something which Mayor Nikitas Kaklamanis has pledged to correct. There is, though, a monument in the Jewish cemetery on Agiou Georgiou in the suburb of Nikea. In addition, a square opposite Thissio metro station, north-west of the Agora, was renamed Plateia Ellinon Evreion Martiron in 1999. Nearby, on Melidoni, are two synagogues and the headquarters of what is now the largest Jewish community in Greece. In 2007, a plaque was added to the statue of Archbishop Damaskinos outside the Mitropolis cathedral, north of the Parthenon, honouring his role in the rescue of Jews, whilst a little further east is the Jewish Museum of Greece (Mon–Fri, 9.00–2.30; Sun, 10.00–2.00; €5; www.jewishmuseum.gr) at Nikis 39.

The first prominent Holocaust memorial was a sculptural ensemble incorporating a weeping woman erected in 1987 in Larissa. It commemorates both the 235 Jews from the city who were murdered in Birkenau in March 1944 and all Jewish victims of the Holocaust. The memorial is located on Plateia Evreion Martiron Katohis at the junction of Kyprou and Kentavron by the city's synagogue. North-east, on Erythrou Stavrou, is a square named after Anne Frank, marked by a memorial stone. Volos, south-east of Larissa, has a striking 1998 memorial to 155 victims (who formed part of the same transport) on Plateia Riga Fereou by the harbour, a short walk from the modern synagogue at the junction of Xenophontos, Moisseos and Platonos. In both cities, the majority of

Jews (more than 700 in each case) were saved through the efforts of the local inhabitants, the church and the Resistance.

One of the best-preserved Jewish quarters in Greece is La Juderia in the old city of Rhodes from where at least 1,700 Jews were deported on 23 July 1944 in one of the last transports to Auschwitz; the current community consists of around 40 people. There is a memorial on Plateia Evreion Martiron, in the north of the city near the port. Around the corner on Dossiadou, the Kahal Shalom Synagogue (Apr–Nov: daily, 10.00–4.00, free; www.rhodesjewishmuseum.org) houses the Rhodes Jewish Museum whose founder Aron Hasson, an indefatigable Californian scion of Rhodes Jewry, has also written an extensive guide to the island's Jewish heritage. For more on this and excursions to the large cemetery outside the town, see the museum's website.

CHAPTER 19

OTHER COUNTRIES

BULGARIA

Although Bulgaria's dictatorship handed the Jews of occupied Thrace and Macedonia (territories annexed from Greece and Yugoslavia) over to the Germans for deportation to Treblinka in 1943, it ultimately spared its own Jews. This was not entirely by choice, the regime having introduced its own programme of escalating anti-Semitism including the yellow star, forced labour and the expulsion of Jews from Sofia to the provinces. In the spring of 1943, the government indeed began to make preparations for their deportation as requested by the Nazis. However, widespread protests by political, religious and professional leaders, along with mass public demonstrations, persuaded King Boris III to intercede and stop the process, a decision doubtless made easier by the reversal of Germany's military fortunes. The result was that Bulgaria's Jewish population, some 50,000 people, was the largest in Axis-controlled Europe to be spared the Holocaust. This story is told in the museum contained in Sofia's Great Synagogue at central Ekzarh Yosif 16 (www.sofiasynagogue.com). The resistance was orchestrated by Deputy Speaker of Parliament Dimitar Peshev. His birthplace at Tsar Simeon I 11 in Kyustendil, near the Macedonian border, is now a memorial museum (daily, 9.00–5.00; 1 lv; www.kyustendilmuseum. primasoft.bg).

DENMARK

The rescue of the Danish Jews was one of the few consoling tales to emerge from the Holocaust. Although the operation was perhaps more feasible in Denmark than elsewhere – various German sources tipped off the Danes in advance of the proposed deportation and the Jewish community was relatively small – the transfer of 7,200 Jews along with 700 non-Jewish relatives to Sweden in October 1943 still represented an immense act of humanity and courage for which the entire Danish underground was awarded the title of Righteous by Yad Vashem. Not everyone escaped: 481 Jews were arrested and sent to Theresienstadt

Other countries

but they too – aside from 51 mainly elderly people who had since died – were allowed to depart for Sweden just before the end of the war. Israel Plads, a popular Copenhagen square near the Nørreport gate and Metro station, contains a boulder from Eilat donated in gratitude. The story of the rescue is told in the Jewish Museum (designed, like Berlin's, by Daniel Liebeskind) at Proviantpassagen 6 in the heart of the city (June–Aug: Tue–Sun, 10.00–5.00; Sept–May: Tue–Fri, 10.00–4.00; Sat–Sun, 12.00–5.00; 40 DKK; www.jewmus.dk) and in the Resistance Museum at Churchillparken (Tue–Sun, 10.00–3.00 (until 5.00, May–Sept); free; www.natmus.dk/sw23424.asp) which includes plaques and letters of thanks donated by Jewish communities from across the world.

LUXEMBOURG

Approximately 3,500 Jews lived in Luxembourg in 1940, most of them refugees. It is estimated that almost 2,000 lost their lives, the majority after fleeing to Vichy France and then being deported to Auschwitz. However, 674 were deported from the Duchy itself to Łódź, Auschwitz and Theresienstadt. A simple but dignified memorial at Hollerich station (from where the trains departed) on Rue de la Déportation commemorates them along with Luxembourgers conscripted into the Wehrmacht or forcibly resettled in Germany. There is also a museum at the site.

MACEDONIA

Macedonia, taken over by Bulgaria during the dismemberment of Yugoslavia in 1941, was home to around 7,800 Jews. All, with the exception of those who fled to the partisans or went into hiding, were deported to Treblinka in March 1943; only 200 Macedonian Jews are known to have survived the war. In a widely praised restitution deal, the government has transferred the assets of heirless murdered Jews to the community in order to construct the new Holocaust Memorial Centre in Skopje. This is located on the site of the former Jewish quarter (destroyed during a 1963 earthquake and then occupied by a ramshackle bus station) just off Bulevar Goce Delčev opposite the Kale fortress on the north-east bank of the Vardar. There is also a memorial within the Tutunski Kombinat tobacco factory complex at 11 Oktomvri 125 where Jews were held prior to deportation.

MOLDOVA

Most of modern Moldova fell within the former tsarist province of Bessarabia which was part of Romania from 1918 until occupied by the USSR in 1940. Following Romanian reconquest in Operation Barbarossa, tens of thousands of Jews were forced into Transnistria in late 1941; most of those who survived the initial death marches subsequently died in Transnistria's ghettos and camps. However, thousands were also murdered in Moldova itself by both Romanians and Germans in the summer of 1941. There is a memorial in Chişinău (Kishinev) to the more than 10,000 Jews held in a ghetto between the massacres and the Transnistrian deportations: this is in a small park on Str. Ierusalim (between Bulevardul Renaşterii and Str. Puşkin). A memorial in Parcul Alunelul, north-west of the centre, honours victims of the 1903 pogrom, the most notorious of the tsarist era. The Jewish cemetery is nearby on Str. Milano. The one still active synagogue is at central Habad-Liubavici 8. For other sites in the capital and elsewhere in Moldova, see www.jewishmemory.md.

NORWAY

Around 1,700 Jews lived in Norway of whom 763 were deported to Auschwitz in 1942–43 (900 were able to escape to Sweden with the assistance of the Resistance) despite public protests by the Protestant Church; 24 of the deportees survived. A memorial was erected in 1948 in the Jewish section of Oslo's eastern cemetery at Tvetenveien 7 in the Helsfyr suburb. There is an exhibition on the Holocaust in Norway in the Villa Grande, the former mansion of the collaborationist prime minister Quisling, at Huk Aveny 56 on the Bygdøy peninsula (daily, 11.00–4.00; kr. 50; www.hlsenteret.no). Its history is also related in the new Jewish Museum in a former synagogue at Calmeyers gate 15b near the centre (Tue, 10.00–3.00; Thu, 3.00–8.00; Sun, 11.00–4.00; kr. 50; www.jodiskmuseumoslo.no).

ROMANIA

The vile regime of Ion Antonescu participated fully in the Holocaust beyond its borders yet its legacy within Romania proper was more ambiguous. In Bessarabia (modern Moldova), Bukovina and Transnistria (both in modern Ukraine), the Romanians perpetrated genocide on a scale matched only by the Nazis and the Croat *Ustaše*, with a death toll of at least 250,000 Jews as well as more than 10,000 Roma. However, in the *Regat* or Old Kingdom (the territories of Romania at its independence in 1859) the outcome was rather different. The Jews of these regions were certainly subject to deprivation of civil rights and expropriation of property not to mention appalling pogroms. However, growing doubts over the likelihood of German victory prompted Antonescu to abandon plans to deport the *Regat* Jews to Bełżec in 1942 although they remained in a precarious position until he was overthrown in August 1944.

A Holocaust memorial is currently being constructed in Bucharest in a small park by the Dâmbovița river bordered by Lipscani, Ion Brezoianu, Mihai Voda and Anghel Saligny. There is also a memorial hall in the city's Jewish Museum which occupies a former synagogue at Mămulari 3.

The most horrific pogrom within the *Regat* took place in Iași in June 1941 when Romanian soldiers, police and townspeople murdered an estimated 8,000 Jews. Another 5,000 were crammed into cattle cars attached to two trains which spent a week travelling backwards and forwards across the countryside; most died of suffocation or thirst. This horror is recalled by a memorial outside the Great Synagogue at Sinagogilor 7 between Sărărie and Cucu.

However, the area of greatest Jewish suffering within Romania's modern borders was Transylvania which was acquired from Hungary in 1920 and lost again in 1939. Its Jews became victims of the Hungarian deportations of 1944: more than 200,000 were murdered. There is a memorial museum at Vladimirescu 1 in Sighetu Marmației in the house from where Elie Wiesel was taken to Auschwitz in 1944. The small town of Șimleu Silvaniei is home to the privately funded Holocaust Memorial Museum of Northern Transylvania in the former synagogue at Piata 1 Mai 1 (Mon–Fri, 10.00–5.00; Sat–Sun, 11.00–3.00; free; mmhtn.org).

RUSSIA

In no country is memorialisation of the Second World War more deeply embedded within national culture than in Russia. Memorialisation of the Holocaust, however, is a rather different matter. In part, this simply reflects the fact that most Soviet Jews lived in other republics whilst major centres of Russian Jewish life such as Moscow and Leningrad were never captured by the Germans. Nonetheless, the absence of Holocaust memorials clearly had more insidious roots, the same ideological dictates which long prevented proper memorialisation of sites such as Babi Yar and Ponar.

Russia does now have a central Holocaust memorial of sorts within Moscow's massive Victory Park complex, created in the 1990s in the city's west on Prospekt Marshala Grechko (Park Pobedy Metro), in the form of a memorial synagogue which also contains a small exhibition on the Holocaust. Victory Park also contains an astonishing monument, *People's Tragedy*, whose collapsing row of large sculpted emaciated and naked figures is clearly influenced by a number of Holocaust memorials; Jews are explicitly included within this commemoration of all Soviet victims of the war. The Holocaust will also be addressed by the Museum of Tolerance on Obraztsova in the north of the city which will be the largest Jewish museum in the world when it opens in 2011.

SLOVENIA

Compared to the rest of the former Yugoslavia, few Jews lived in Slovenia. The largest community (no more than a few hundred) was based in the north-eastern city of Murska Sobota, near the Austrian and Hungarian borders; most of its members were murdered at Birkenau in the 1944 Hungarian deportations. The site of the former Jewish cemetery on Panonska now contains a simple memorial using salvaged tombstones.

SWEDEN

Neutral Sweden is famed for taking in Jewish refugees from Norway and Denmark during the war and for the role of Raoul Wallenberg in saving Jewish lives in Budapest. In reality, Swedish policy was rather more complex, especially in the earlier stages of the war when the country found itself encircled by the Axis and, therefore, unable to avoid some collaboration: few people know, for example, that German soldiers and equipment were transported through Sweden to Finland during the invasion of the USSR. Nonetheless, it did prove to be a safe haven for Jews and continued to be after the war when it took in more than 10,000 survivors. A striking Holocaust memorial was created by the Great Synagogue at Wahrendorffsgatan 3 (Kungsträdgåden T-bana) in Stockholm in the 1990s: large granite slabs list the names of 8,500 murdered relatives of these survivors. Around the corner, in a small harbourside square, is a controversial abstract memorial to Wallenberg, consisting of scattered sculpted pieces.

UNITED KINGDOM

As the only European belligerent never to be allied to or invaded by Nazi Germany, Britain was spared the Holocaust (although three Jewish women on occupied Guernsey were deported to Auschwitz and other Jews in the Channel Islands sent to labour camps in France). However, London's Imperial War Museum on Lambeth Road (Lambeth North tube) inaugurated an impressive permanent exhibition on the Holocaust in 2000 (daily, 10.00–6.00; free; london.iwm.org.uk). Also in London, there is a memorial outside Liverpool Street station to the *Kindertransport*, the programme whereby the UK took in almost 10,000 Jewish children from the Reich between *Kristallnacht* and the outbreak of war; most of the children never saw their parents again.

The Beth Shalom Holocaust centre (Mon–Fri, 10.00–5.00; £7; www.holocaustcentre.net) is a privately run memorial, museum and educational facility located in Laxton, a village in Nottinghamshire. It is linked to the Aegis Trust, an organisation which works to prevent genocide in the world today.

FURTHER READING

A fully comprehensive guide to Holocaust reading would require a book in itself so the following list is impressionistic with an emphasis on books which should appeal to the general reader. Where there are different publishers, the British is given first, the American second.

Two readable classic histories are Martin Gilbert, *The Holocaust: the Jewish Tragedy* (HarperCollins/Holt) and Lucy Dawidowicz, *The War Against the Jews 1933–45* (Penguin/Bantam). Saul Friedländer's monumental *Nazi Germany and the Jews. Volume 1: The Years of Persecution 1933–39* and *Volume 2: The Years of Extermination 1939–1945* (Phoenix/ Harper Perennial) is an astonishingly wide-ranging account, integrating analysis of the perpetrators with a clear focus on the victims. Christopher R. Browning, *The Origins of the Final Solution* (Arrow/ Bison) explores the evolution of Nazi policy from the outbreak of war to 1942 in forensic detail. An essential work of reference is Martin Gilbert, *The Routledge Atlas of the Holocaust* (Routledge). Lyn Smith, *Forgotten Voices of the Holocaust* (Ebury Press; published in the USA as *Remembering: Voices of the Holocaust*, Basic) tells the story through the words of the survivors whilst Primo Levi, *The Drowned and the Saved* (Abacus/Vintage) is a series of often uncomfortable meditations by the best-known survivor of all. Nicholas Stargardt, *Witnesses of War* (Pimlico/Vintage) examines the experiences of Jewish, Polish and German children. Martin Gilbert, *The Righteous* (Black Swan/Holt) salutes the courageous few who saved Jewish lives. The same author's *Holocaust Journey* (Phoenix/Columbia University Press) is a moving account of a tour through the Holocaust sites of central Europe.

The story of the Holocaust in France is told by Susan Zuccotti, *The Holocaust, the French and the Jews* (University of Nebraska Press) and Renée Poznanski, *Jews in France during World War II* (Brandeis University Press). Michael R. Marrus and Robert O. Paxton, *Vichy France and the Jews* (Stanford University Press) is a devastating study of the Pétain regime. Serge Klarsfeld, *French Children of the Holocaust* (New York University Press) serves as a haunting memorial. Far less has been written about Belgium but Marion Schreiber, *The Twentieth*

Train (Atlantic/Grove Press) uses the 1943 attack on the Auschwitz-bound transport to also say much about the Holocaust in the country. The classic account for the Netherlands is Jacob Presser, *Ashes in the Wind* (Souvenir Press/Wayne State University Press), now supplemented by Bob Moore, *Victims and Survivors* (Hodder Arnold). Anne Frank, *Diary of a Young Girl* (Penguin/Bantam) needs no introduction; the thoughts and experiences of another remarkable young woman are most accessibly recorded in Etty Hillesum, *Letters from Westerbork* (HarperCollins). Susan Zuccotti, *The Italians and the Holocaust* (University of Nebraska Press) is an excellent overview whilst Alexander Stille, *Benevolence and Betrayal* (Picador) explores the Holocaust through the stories of five Italian Jewish families. Robert Katz, *Fatal Silence* (Phoenix; published in the USA as *The Battle for Rome*, Simon & Schuster) is a gripping account of the German occupation which covers the Roman Holocaust, the Ardeatine Caves massacre, the role of the Papacy and much else.

The persecution of Jews in Germany and Austria is thoroughly covered in the general histories mentioned above as well as by accounts of the Nazi regime such as Richard J. Evans, *The Third Reich in Power* and *The Third Reich at War* (Penguin) and Michael Burleigh, *The Third Reich: a New History* (Pan/Hill and Wang). Marion A. Kaplan, *Between Dignity and Despair* (Oxford University Press) examines Jewish responses. Martin Gilbert, *Kristallnacht* (HarperCollins) sets out the scale of the November pogrom. Victor Klemperer, *I Shall Bear Witness* and *To the Bitter End* (Phoenix; published in the USA as *I Will Bear Witness 1933–41* and *1942–45*, Modern Library), a publishing sensation in Germany in the 1990s, are the revealing diaries of a convert who survived thanks to his mixed marriage but who nonetheless found himself caught in the maelstrom. Gertrude Schneider, *Exile and Destruction* (Greeenwood Press/Praeger) mixes personal experience with a clear history of the Holocaust in Austria whilst Gordon J. Horwitz, *In the Shadow of Death* (I.B.Tauris) is an exemplary study of Mauthausen and its relationship with the local community. Henry Friedlander, *The Origins of Nazi Genocide* (University of North Carolina Press) and Michael Burleigh, *Death and Deliverance* (Cambridge University Press/Pan) address 'euthanasia' and its connection with the Holocaust.

Callum MacDonald and Jan Kaplan, *Prague in the Shadow of the Swastika* (Melantrich) is a well-illustrated overview of the Czech capital whilst Heda Margolius Kovály, *Under a Cruel Star* (Holmes & Meier) is an infinitely wise memoir of Jewish life under two dictatorships. Gonda Redlich, *The Terezin Diary* (ed. Saul S. Friedman, University Press of Kentucky) records the often tormented thoughts of one of the ghetto's youth leaders. There is much less material for Slovakia although Livia Bitton-Jackson, *I Have Lived a Thousand Years* (Simon & Schuster) is a classic survivor's account. Eastern Slovak Jewish communities such as Bitton-Jackson's are covered in histories of the Holocaust in Hungary. The most comprehensive of these latter is Randolph L. Braham, *The Politics of Genocide* (Wayne State University Press) whilst Krisztián Ungváry, *Battle for Budapest* (I.B. Tauris; published in the USA as *The Siege of Budapest*, Yale University Press) recalls the chaotic last days of Nazi and Arrow Cross rule in the city. Béla Zsolt, *Nine Suitcases* (Pimlico/Random House) is an unflinching survivor's memoir.

There is naturally a vast literature on Poland. A beautiful introduction is Jack Kugelmass & Jonathan Boyarin (eds.), *From a Ruined Garden* (Indiana University Press), a compilation of extracts from the memorial books to lost communities written by survivors. Israel Gutman, *The Jews of Warsaw* (Indiana University Press) relates the history of the ghetto. Several of its leading figures left records, including Adam Czerniaków, *The Warsaw Diary* (ed. Hilberg, Staron & Kermisz, Ivan R. Dee), Emmanuel Ringelblum, *Notes from the Warsaw Ghetto* (ibooks), and Janusz Korczak, *Ghetto Diary* (Yale University Press). Another classic diary is Chaim A. Kaplan, *Scroll of Agony* (ed. Abraham I. Katsh, Indiana University Press) whilst two accounts by survivors are Yitzhak Zuckerman, *A Surplus of Memory* (University of California Press) and Wladsylaw Szpilman, *The Pianist* (Phoenix/Picador). Gordon J. Horwitz, *Ghettostadt* (Belknap Press) is the first major English history of wartime Łódź whilst a unique contemporary record is *The Chronicle of the Łódź Ghetto* (ed. Lucjan Dobroszycki, Yale University Press). The remarkable pictures of ghetto life produced by two photographers are compiled in Mendel Grossman, *My Secret Camera* (text by Frank Dabba Smith, Frances Lincoln) and Henryk Ross, *Łódź Ghetto Album* (text by Thomas Weber, Chris Boot). David Sierakowiak, *The Diary* (ed. Alan Adelson, Oxford University Press) gives an intelligent teenager's perspective on life in Łódź. *Aktion Reinhard* is addressed in Yitzhak Arad, *Belzec, Sobibor, Treblinka* (Indiana University Press); Thomas Toivi Blatt, *From the Ashes of Sobibor* (Northwestern University Press) and Jules Schelvis, *Sobibor* (Berg) are histories by survivors of the death camp. The classic survivor accounts of Auschwitz are, of course, Primo Levi, *If*

This Is a Man (Abacus; also published as *Survival in Auschwitz* by various publishers) and Elie Wiesel, *Night* (Penguin/Hill and Wang). One of the earliest examples of the genre is Olga Lengyel, *Five Chimneys* (Academy Chicago), remarkable for its dispassionate prose. Debórah Dwork & Robert Jan van Pelt, *Auschwitz: 1270 to the Present* (W. W. Norton) is a highly informative study. Jan T. Gross, *Neighbours* (Arrow) examines the Jedwabne massacre to raise difficult questions about Polish-Jewish relations.

Ilya Ehrenburg & Vassily Grossman, *The Complete Black Book of Russian Jewry* (ed. David Patterson, Transaction) is the classic compilation, banned by Stalin, of accounts by survivors and eyewitnesses of the Holocaust in the USSR. Yitzhak Arad, *Ghetto in Flames* (Yad Vashem) is a clear history of the Vilna ghetto whilst Herman Kruk, *The Last Days of the Jerusalem of Lithuania* (ed. Benjamin Harshav, Yale University Press) is the diary of a well-informed observer. Chaim Grade, *My Mother's Sabbath Days* (Knopf) is the memoir of a Yiddish poet who fled to central Asia; its beautiful vignettes of pre-war life make the account of his return to the ruined Jewish city all the more poignant. Avraham Tory, *Surviving the Holocaust* (ed. Martin Gilbert, Pimlico/Harvard University Press) is an important record of the Kovno ghetto. Gertrude Schneider, *Journey into Terror* (Praeger) addresses the Riga ghetto, mainly focussing on the Reich Jews sent there, the author among them. There is material on the Estonian camps in the *Black Book* and the Arad and Kruk books on Vilna. For Belarus, a recent history is Barbara Epstein, *The Minsk Ghetto 1941–1943* (University of California Press) whilst Hersh Smolar, *The Minsk Ghetto* (Holocaust Library) is an account by one of the underground leaders. Nechama Tec, *Defiance* (Oxford University Press) and Peter Duffy, *Brothers in Arms* (Arrow; published in the USA as *The Bielski Brothers*, HarperCollins) deal with the most remarkable partisans of all. Less has been written about Ukraine than might be imagined although Boris Zabarko (ed.), *Holocaust in the Ukraine* (Vallentine Mitchell) is a compilation of survivor testimony whilst Karel C. Berkhoff, *Harvest of Despair* (Belknap Press) addresses the Holocaust within Ukraine's wider wartime experience. Anatoly Kuzentsov, *Babi Yar* (Penguin) is presented as a novel but is nonetheless a factual account. Two survivors of L'viv and Janowska tell their stories in Leon Weliczker Wells, *The Janowska Road* (Halo Press) and Samuel Drix, *Witness to Annihilation* (Brassey's). Eliyahu Yones, *Smoke in the Sand* (Gefen) is a recent history of the ghetto.

Omer Bartov, *Erased* (Princeton University Press) is a critical study of the amnesia which afflicts modern western Ukraine. For an exploration of the same region with an ultimately happier ending of sorts, read Daniel Mendelsohn's brilliant *The Lost* (Harper Perennial).

Very little has been written in English about the Holocaust in Yugoslavia although the murders in Serbia are addressed in Browning's *Origins of the Final Solution* (see above) whilst Misha Glenny, *The Balkans* (Granta/Penguin) provides an overview. The latter also includes the Holocaust in Greece, as does Mark Mazower, *Inside Hitler's Greece* (Yale University Press). Mazower's *Salonica, City of Ghosts* (HarperCollins/Vintage) is a history of the Sephardic metropolis and its destruction.

INDEX OF SITES

Bold type indicates principal entries